# DIMINUTIVE, AUGMENTATIVE AND PEJORATIVE SUFFIXES IN MODERN SPANISH

(*A Guide to their Use and Meaning*)

# DIMINUTIVE, AUGMENTATIVE AND PEJORATIVE SUFFIXES IN MODERN SPANISH

*(A Guide to their Use and Meaning)*

## 2nd EDITION

*by*

## ANTHONY GOOCH, M.A.

LECTURER IN SPANISH
LONDON SCHOOL OF ECONOMICS AND POLITICAL SCIENCE
UNIVERSITY OF LONDON

## PERGAMON PRESS

*Oxford · New York · Toronto · Sydney · Braunschweig*

Pergamon Press Ltd., Headington Hill Hall, Oxford

Pergamon Press Inc., Maxwell House, Fairview Park, Elmsford, New York 10523

Pergamon of Canada Ltd., 207 Queen's Quay West, Toronto 1

Pergamon Press (Aust.) Pty. Ltd., 19a Boundary Street, Rushcutters Bay, N.S.W. 2011, Australia

Vieweg & Sohn GmbH, Burgplatz 1, Braunschweig

First edition 1967

Second edition 1970

Library of Congress Catalog Card No. 75-111075

*Printed in Great Britain by A. Wheaton & Co., Exeter*

08 015808 0 (hard cover)

*To Adela*

No hay lenguaje, ni lo ha habido, que al nuestro haya hecho ventaja en abundancia de términos, en dulzura de estilo, y en ser blando, suave, regalado y tierno y muy acomodado para decir lo que queremos.

(MALÓN DE CHAIDE (1530—89), *La Conversión de la Magdalena*)

Sepa, pues, todo buen español, y todo el mundo, que tenemos una lengua abundantísima y suave, y que podemos usar de ella con la mayor propiedad y energía, con brevedad, sublimidad, elegancia, armonía, y por decirlo en una palabra, con elocuencia.

(MAYÁNS Y SISCAR (1699—1781), *Orígenes de la Lengua Española*)

P. — ¿Qué pasa? Alejandra ... ¿es mujer de historia?
A. — De historia, así, en singular, no creo; ahora, de historias, sí.
P. — Vaya ... ¿Y el canciller?
A. — De historietas.
P. — *(Con orgullo de hispanohablante)* ¡Qué lengua más expresiva la nuestra! ¿verdad, Angel? ¡Cuántos matices caben en una misma palabra, según se use en singular o en plural o en diminutivo ...!

(J. CALVO-SOTELO (b. 1905), *Una Muchachita de Valladolid*)

# Contents

# *Preface*

It has been said that Spanish is an easy language to learn badly, and it is certainly true that the linguistically unambitious can get by in it on a very mediocre level of achievement. They pay, however, for their lack of zeal by being condemned to live in a shadowy world in which ideas are only half apprehended and meanings only half expressed. It has also been said that Spanish is a difficult language to learn really well, and this too is true. However, there are some who maintain that to seek perfection in a foreign tongue is a vain endeavour not worth the admittedly great effort involved. They contend that language is but a means to an end and that the end can be achieved without paying too much attention to the finer points of the means. There is little doubt that they are wrong. What end do we have in view when we study Spanish? To comprehend the ideas and feelings which Spaniards express in their language, both in written and spoken forms, and to convey in that language our own ideas and feelings. And our degree of success will be in direct proportion to the degree of perfection we have attained in the use of our instrument, either passively or actively or in both ways. The subtle shades of meaning expressed or required to be expressed in a rapid idiomatic conversation, the involved concepts and deep emotions conveyed or required to be conveyed in a subtle novel or poem — these things are only within the full grasp of those who have a real command of the language.

It is hoped that this book will, in some small measure, help those who desire such a command of Spanish, who wish to learn to *hilar fino*, who have decided to *aspirar a mucho* even though they know that they may well have to *quedarse en menos*. And they may have to be content with less because there lie between them and their goal considerable obstacles — to mention a few, the pronunciation, the main difficulty of which lies precisely in its deceptive simplicity, the subtleties of *ser* and *estar* and of the reflexive, the pitfalls of the subjunctive, the wealth of the vocabulary and the intricacies of the suffixes, of which there are in all some two hundred. And it is with a section of these latter — the most complex — that we are now concerned.

The fundamental aim of the present volume is to provide the English-speaking student with a really full guide to the semantic labyrinth of the principal Spanish diminutive, augmentative and pejorative suffixes. This can probably best be achieved by the systematic presentation of numerous examples, and so a wide selection has been made of what are, semantically and from the point of view of contemporary usage, the most important and interesting words formed with each suffix. These words have been arranged in alphabetical lists, and in all cases in which a suffix has several different uses a separate list has been provided for each of them, in most instances followed by a series of illustrative quotations from standard authors.[1]

Only where forms with suffixes have a changed or specialized meaning in relation to that of the root-words are these latter listed, since, with this exception, it is, in general, abundantly clear what the root-word and its sense are.

An attempt has been made in all cases to find a translation which not only renders faithfully the exact sense but also conveys the right undertones, a translation which will conjure up in the mind of the English reader ideas and associations as closely equivalent as possible to those produced in a Spaniard by the original. Equivalents are, however, by no means always easy to find, and in a limited number of cases, recourse has been had to regional terms and to expressions associated with particular periods and social classes. It is hoped that the reader will be benevolent with such shortcomings.

The wealth of meaning contained in many of the suffixes will be seen from the plurality of English words often required in translation.

It is certainly not claimed that all possible forms and meanings are given for every suffix listed, since this would represent a well-nigh

---

[1] Forms so illustrated are indicated by the symbol † in front of them.

endless task. Again, attention has been given to comparative study, in order, especially, to highlight similarities between apparently opposed terms and contrasts between terms which at first sight appear synonymous; but here, too, the possible ramifications are almost limitless.[1]

The raw material for the book has been culled from diverse sources — from modern Spanish literature, from newspapers and magazines of standing and from live conversation. For the literary examples a detailed linguistic study has been made of a series of representative texts by standard authors, and in the case of the other sources mentioned care has been taken to check and cross-check all evidence in authoritative reference books and by putting countless questions to a large number of well-educated and linguistically-conscious native speakers.

The attention given in most dictionaries and grammars to the suffixes is scant, with the result that the importance of the role they play — frequently quite a fundamental one — is not generally realized. It is hoped that this book will help the student to comprehend that role more exactly and that it will also, as a consequence, enable him to see in truer perspective wider aspects of the language, that it will guide him towards a fuller understanding of the nature of popular speech — to which these suffixes in large part belong — and so put him in a position to appreciate better the world of literature and to acquire a genuinely balanced view of Spanish as a whole.

My sincere and deep thanks for assistance in the long preparation of this study are due to many: to the late Mr. L. B. Walton, Miss M. Crosland and all my former colleagues in the Spanish Department of the University of Edinburgh, and especially to Professor A. A. Parker, without whose conscientious and scholarly guidance the work might never have been published; to the Editors of the Pergamon Oxford Spanish Series, Mr. H. Lester, Professor G. Ribbans and Professor R. B. Tate, from all of whom I have received encouragement and advice, Professor Tate having carried

---

[1] In order to keep this volume within bounds the question of multiple suffixes has not been specifically treated. Nevertheless, many of the most important examples of words showing multiple suffixation are included.

out for me a particularly painstaking check of the manuscript; and to a host of patient and intellectually generous Spaniards whose number is so great that it would scarcely be possible for me to mention them all but not one of whom is forgotten by me. However, I must make specific mention of Don Carlos Clavería, Don Salvador Fernández Ramírez, Don Rafael Lapesa and especially Don Dámaso Alonso, whose jovial erudition and friendship have meant a great deal to me. I am also indebted to Professor W. C. Atkinson of the University of Glasgow; to Professor D. McMillan of the University of Edinburgh and to Professor Yakov Malkiel of the University of California for valuable information. And finally I must declare my gratitude to my Alma Mater, Edinburgh University, and to the Carnegie Trust for their generous financial support.

A. G.

# *Introduction*

## 1. GENERAL

To isolate one aspect of a language for detailed research is dangerous; it can lead to what has been called "linguistic nihilism", that is, the turning of language phenomena into ends in themselves, and this most certainly constitutes a sterile aberration. On the other hand, it sometimes happens that a particular aspect of a language is so far-reaching in its effects or so significant in its implications that it merits special attention precisely because, being in itself a limited field, it nevertheless automatically leads on to and links up with numerous others.

In a work of monumental erudition the Swedish scholar Bengt Hasselrot describes the diminutive suffixes in the Romance languages as "sujet le moins rébarbatif peut-être qu'on puisse trouver à l'intérieur de notre linguistique si souvent aride".[1] It can certainly be said that in Spanish the diminutive, augmentative and pejorative suffixes represent a deeply rewarding study, for they not only give contact with a very wide range of many of the most fundamental words in the language, but, in addition, they reveal speakers' and writers' attitudes, in varying circumstances, to the concepts expressed by those words.

## 2. EXPRESSION OF EMOTION; INFLUENCE OF CHILDHOOD; THE POET

By means of diminutive, augmentative and pejorative suffixes it is possible for the Spaniard to convey in a highly graphic way extremes of feeling which overflow the banks of ordinary, factual,

[1] *Études sur la formation diminutive dans les langues romanes* (Uppsala, 1957), p. 3.

I

detached expression — to convey those things which belong more to the warmth of the heart than to the coolness of the head.

And so it is that the so-called diminutive suffixes are often not used primarily to convey an idea of smallness, but to express affection or to produce a favourable reaction in the person addressed; the so-called augmentatives not to indicate bigness so much as to convey abuse. Thus in a popular ballad[1] a mother who wishes Saint Christopher to find a husband for her daughter prays to him as follows:

> San Cristobalito,
> manitas, patitas,
> carita de rosa,
> dame un novio pa mi niña que la tengo mosa.[2]

But when her son-in-law turns out to be little to her liking her tone changes:

> San Cristobalón,
> manazas, patazas,
> cara de cuerno,
> como tienes la cara me diste el yerno.[3]

One or two further examples will show how gentle persuasion can be brought to bear through the use of a suffix:

> — Vamos, joven, ¡valor! Este aloncito nada más. Me ha dicho Fernanda que le desagrada muchísimo que usted no coma.[4]
> (PALACIO VALDÉS, *La Hermana San Sulpicio*, p. 121[5])

Toma un poco de esta agüita[6] (e.g. talking to a child).

Sentadito. No seas pesadito[7] (e.g. talking to a child or a dog).

Such language naturally has a special place in the speech of children and of those who deal most with them — women. Hence the standard diminutive -*ito* occurs in many well-known names of the child's

---

[1]RODRÍGUEZ MARÍN (*Cantos populares españoles*, quoted by A. ALONSO in *Estudios lingüísticos*, p. 209. See Bibliography.)

[2]"Darling (little) St. Christopher, nice (little) hands, sweet (little) feet, cute (little) pink face. . ."

[3]"St. Christopher, you (great) oaf, clumsy (great) fists, ugly (great) feet . . ."

[4]". . . Just this one nice (little) wing of chicken. . ."

[5]For edition in this and all subsequent cases see list at end of book.

[6]"Have a little of this nice water."

[7]"Just sit there nicely. Don't be a nuisance, there's a good (little) chap."

world: *Pulgarcito, Caperucita Roja, Blancanieves y los siete enanitos.*[1]
Similarly *misito* (also *michito*) equals "pussy cat", and so on.

Spanish children automatically apply diminutive suffixes to small
and attractive persons and things, but by extension they, and indeed
their elders too, often apply them also in cases where there is no
question of smallness and perhaps not even any great idea of attrac-
tiveness either, in cases where they wish to reduce something to proportions which are for them *emotionally* manageable. Here the diminutive suffix gives an insight into what is a deep-rooted human
characteristic: fear of things that are big and a concomitant desire
to reduce them to friendly proportions. This can perhaps be best
expressed by the poet, for he, even when he is a grown man, has a
heightened sensitivity which makes him aware of the presence of the
child within him, and enables him to appreciate the influence of
childhood on his years of maturity. García Lorca has this to say:

> . . . Diminutivo asustado como un pájaro, que abre secretas cámaras de
> sentimiento . . .
>
> El diminutivo no tiene más misión que la de limitar, ceñir, traer a la
> habitación y poner en nuestra mano los objetos o ideas de gran perspectiva.
>
> Se limita el tiempo, el espacio, el mar, la luna, las distancias, y hasta
> lo prodigioso: la acción.
>
> No queremos que el mundo sea tan grande ni el mar tan hondo. Hay
> necesidad de limitar, de domesticar los términos inmensos.[2]

Amado Alonso, in an essay of fundamental importance entitled
*Noción, emoción, acción y fantasía en los diminutivos,*[3] shows how, in
the work of Jorge Luis Borges, the same phenomenon occurs, how
the diminutive suffix is used to bring aspects of the outside world
within the sphere of the poet's own inner life and to express the
personal emotional relationship thus established:

> "Quiero la calle mansa
> con las balaustraditas repartiéndose el cielo",
> dice el poeta argentino J. L. Borges, muy dado a estos diminutivos. Se

---

[1] Little Tom Thumb (Fr. *Le Petit Poucet*); Little Red Ridinghood (Fr.
*Le Petit Chaperon Rouge*); Snow-white and the Seven Dwarfs (Fr. *Blancheneige
et les sept nains*). Notice in particular the much less colourful English and
French equivalents in the last case.

[2] *Impresiones (Granada)* in *Obras Completas*, Aguilar, tercera edición (Madrid,
1957), p. 3.

[3] In *Estudios lingüísticos*. See Bibliography.

denuncia la emoción que las balaustradas provocan al poeta ("el diminutivo es el signo de un afecto"); pero también reconocemos aquí una detención imaginativa. Diminutivos que se paran sobre lo valioso de las cosas, sobre lo que nos afectan. La expresión de vida de las balaustradas y el sentirlas dentro de su misma esfera vital (lo que de sentido localista tiene la poesía de Borges) es lo que al poeta le afecta y lo que poetiza con el diminutivo (p. 219).

And so the emotional language of the child influences and colours the life of the poet and indeed the lives of all human beings throughout their existence, since childhood, in one form or another, is always with us:

¿ Y por qué le llamaba todo el mundo y le llama todavía casi unánimemente *Juanito* Santa Cruz? Esto sí que no lo sé. Hay en Madrid muchos casos de esta aplicación del diminutivo o de la fórmula familiar del nombre, aun tratándose de personas que han entrado en la madurez de la vida. Hasta hace pocos años, al autor cien veces ilustre de *Pepita Jiménez*, le llamaban sus amigos y los que no lo eran, *Juanito* Valera. En la sociedad madrileña, la más amena del mundo porque ha sabido combinar la cortesía con la confianza, hay algunos *Pepes*, *Manolitos* y *Pacos* que, aun después de haber conquistado la celebridad por diferentes conceptos, continúan nombrados con esta familiaridad democrática que demuestra la llaneza castiza del carácter español. El origen de esto habrá que buscarlo quizá en ternuras domésticas o en hábitos de servidumbre que trascienden sin saber cómo a la vida social. En algunas personas, puede relacionarse el diminutivo con el sino. Hay efectivamente Manueles que nacieron predestinados para ser *Manolos* toda su vida.

(PÉREZ GALDÓS, *Fortunata y Jacinta*, I, p. 12)

### 3. STRESS, AMBIVALENCE AND INDIVIDUALITY

Continuing for the moment to consider the diminutives, we find very often that their purpose is to pin-point an image, to focus attention on a particular word, and that the precise interpretation to be given to the suffix — whether a favourable or unfavourable one, for example — depends upon the context and upon accompanying words. Amado Alonso expresses this idea as follows:

Parece como si la constante en el diminutivo fuera ese destacar la representación del objeto, como si realmente fuera signo de eso; modos de pensar que suponen representación y no sólo concepto; fantasía y no mera razón o referencia lógica; pensar en la cosa y no sólo apoyarse en la palabra. Luego, la situación, los consabidos y el contexto dan los indicios de cuál es el motivo de esa atención privilegiada, si la ternura o el desamor por el objeto, si el acercamiento o el apartam iento de él, si la complacencia o la displicencia, si el saboreo o el disgusto, si la insistencia enfática en el objeto o la detención en el interés con que lo vemos (*op. cit.*, p. 225).

And he goes on to say this:

> ... mi clasificación no pretende constituir un rígido casillero en cuyos compartimientos estancos vayamos encajando unos u otros diminutivos, seguros de que no tienen nada que ver con las otras casillas. Para ajustarnos a la verdad, más bien nos conviene imaginarnos cada diminutivo como un torzal de diversas fuerzas espirituales, en cuya forma y colorido ha predominado una de las vetas (*op. cit.*, pp. 227, 228).

Thus -*ito*, basically a diminutive suffix, is more often than not used to express affection rather than diminution, is sometimes used to stress or underline a word in such a way as to imply almost augmentative force, and can even be used ironically with strong pejorative implications. -*illo*, again fundamentally a diminutive, has a definite pejorative bias, which does not, however, prevent its being used on occasion with affectionate intention. -*ón*, despite its pejorative tendency, is often used to augment meanings that are favourable, and can also attenuate and even have diminutive force. And -*azo* can stress equally what is favourable and what is not.

An outstanding feature, then, of the most important of the so-called diminutive and augmentative suffixes is this element of ambivalence, which means that to attempt to pigeon-hole them in any rigid and exclusive fashion leads inevitably to over-simplification and to the danger of error. Despite the fact that the arranging of suffixes in categories and the formulation of general guiding principles in relation to them is the main object of this book, it is essential to bear in mind constantly that the context and particular circumstances of each case must be the final arbiter.[1]

[1] Examples of arbitrary usage are not hard to find and sometimes occur in decidedly unlikely contexts. An example in point is the use of three different and rather colloquial suffixes by Doña Emilia Pardo Bazán in the following passage, in which the aristocratic milieu would seem to require the use of the more literary *pequeño* or at least of the standard -*ito* in all three instances:

> El tocador ... lucía un complicado surtido de peines de pelo y barba, toallicas, frasquetes, brochas y espejillos de formas raras ...
>
> (*Mujer* in *Obras Completas*, II, Aguilar (Madrid, 1947), p. 1330)

## 4. OUTSTANDING FEATURES OF THE THREE GROUPS
## OF SUFFIXES

Thus far just sufficient has been said to show that we are dealing with suffixes which are, to use the Spanish term, *polifacéticos*, that is to say "having many facets", "versatile", and now some of the most important of these facets will be considered in a more systematic form.

### (i) *The Diminutives*

(a) *-ito* and *-illo*. We shall begin by looking at what may be considered the two most basic Spanish diminutive suffixes: *-ito* and *-illo*.

These endings are frequently used purely with the idea of smallness: *banquito* and *banquillo*, *arenitas* and *arenillas* can, and generally do, mean simply "small bench" and "small or fine grains of sand".

However, as has been indicated above, in the case of *-ito*, it is essential to grasp the idea of the fundamentally favourable and often affectionate implication which is so commonly contained in this ending: *un pueblecito* = "a nice little village", *una niñita* = "an attractive little child". And with this must be contrasted the pejorative impression so frequently conveyed by *-illo* : *un regalillo* = "a modest or wretched little gift", *gentecilla* = "petty riff-raff".[1] Thus the word *animalito*, for example, immediately indicates a favourable attitude on the part of the user: *es un animalito precioso* = "he's a lovely (attractive) little creature". (Here the propitious idea adumbrated in *animalito* is made explicit by *precioso*.) Conversely, *animalillo*, while it can be used in a similar way, is far more likely to appear in an expression such as *¡qué animalillo más repugnante!* = "what a revolting (wretched) little creature", and so to approach to the more specifically pejorative *animalejo* or *animalucho*. Thus, *unos pepinitos estupendos* = "some excellent (attractive) little cucumbers", may be contrasted with *unos pepinillos malísimos* = "some really atrocious

[1] It would not be easy to find a clearer example than this one, taken from Pío Baroja (*Paradox, Rey*, p. 180):

¿Hay nada más repulsivo, más mezquino, más necio, más francamente abominable que un hombrecillo de ésos con los nervios descompuestos que se pasa la vida rimando palabras o tocando el violín?

(miserable) little cucumbers"; *aquí fuera hace fresquito* = "out here it's nice and cool" (said, for example, by someone emerging from a hot atmosphere), with *hace fresquillo* = "it's (unpleasantly) chilly", "it's chillyish".

This does not, however, mean that no Spaniard would ever use *fresquito* in the unfavourable sense of *fresquillo*. The reader must always bear in mind Amado Alonso's *veta que predomina — que predomina pero que no excluye*.

Often we find expressions in which favourable and unfavourable strands of meaning are so intimately interwoven as to be inextricable one from the other: *es un granujilla simpático* = "he's a likeable little rogue". *Granuja* is a pejorative word; hence *granujilla*. Notwithstanding, the *granuja* or *granujilla* can be *simpático*.

And we find that *-ito* has a common colloquial use in which, anomalously, there are not only pejorative but often even augmentative implications: *¡qué añito!* = "what a year!" (i.e. what a really terrible year!); *¡qué asquito!* = "what an utterly revolting business!"; *¡mucho cuidadito!* = "you just go jolly carefully!"; *¡dinerito le habrá costado!* = "it must have cost him a pretty penny!"; *¡vaya tiempecito!* = "this is quite some weather!" (here the sense of *tiempecito* is basically that of *tiempazo espantoso*); *también él tiene sus titulitos* = "he has quite a few titles (or degrees) himself!"

It has also been seen how a suffix may be used for the purpose of persuasion, and we find that the allied attitudes of deference and courtesy can be indicated in the same way: *un momentito (momentillo, momentín), por favor* = "just a moment, please"; *¿alguna cosita (cosilla) más, señora?* = "anything else at all, madam?"[1]

---

[1] The author once overheard the following conversation in which it was the customer who, in a similar manner, used what might be called an "apologetic" diminutive:

Assistant — *¿Qué desea?*
Customer — *Crema Nivea, por favor.*
A. — *¿En caja o en tubo?*
C. — *Deme un tubito.*
A. — *¿Grande o pequeño?*

The purely "apologetic" sense of *tubito* ("just a tube") was instinctively grasped by the assistant, as can be seen from her final question.

Again, it has been seen how Spanish, by means of a suffix, manages to give colour to an expression. The example already quoted — *Blancanieves y los siete enanitos* (i.e. *"dear little* dwarfs") — is but one. Another is *el mundillo del cine* = "the world of cinema" (i.e. the *narrow little* world of the cinema).

An extremely important function of these suffixes is to express what is, in relation to the root word, a specialized or completely changed sense, e.g.

-*ito* : *manguito* = muff (< *manga* = sleeve)
-*ita* : *tortita* = waffle (< *torta* = type of cake)
-*illo* : *platillo* = saucer (< *plato* = plate)
-*illa* : *calderilla* = small change (< *caldera* = boiler)

Here again, however, there exists a marked difference between the two, in so far as -*ito* is comparatively little used in this way, whereas it is an outstanding feature of -*illo*.

Sometimes the semantic connection is easy to follow: *ajillo* = "chopped garlic" (i.e. *small* pieces of garlic); *carbonilla* = "coal-smuts" (i.e. *small* particles of coal dust). But in many cases the change is a much more violent one: *barquillo* = "wafer" (< *barco* = "ship" — because Spanish wafers were originally boat-shaped); *parrilla* = "grill" (< *parra* = "vine" — because of the resemblance between the criss-crossing vine shoots on a trellis and the criss-cross iron-work of a grid).

Comparison shows how often -*illo* is used to indicate such specialized or changed meaning, as opposed to what is frequently straightforward diminutive sense in -*ito* : *bolsillo* = "pocket" / *bolsito* = "small handbag" (< *bolso* = "handbag"); *gatillo* = "trigger" / *gatito* = "small cat, kitten" (< *gato* = "cat"); *cabecilla* (m.) = "ring-leader, partisan leader" / *cabecita* = "small head" (< *cabeza* = "head"); *patilla(s)* = "side-whisker(s), side-board(s)" / *patita(s)* = "little leg(s) or paw(s)" (< *pata* = "leg, foot, paw").

Nevertheless, we do find a group of words in which -*ito* is used to convey a combined diminutive and semi-specialized sense — words denoting the young of animals (cf. English -let and -ling): *cabrito* = = "small or young goat, kid"; *cisnecito* = "small or young swan, cygnet"; *patito* = "small or young duck, duckling"; *perrito* = "small or young dog, puppy" (*-illo* is also so used on occasion, e.g. *leoncillo* = "small or young lion, lion cub").

Something has already been seen of the very special place which -ito has in the language of children, and it may now be added that this is particularly evident in words of the type just considered. Thus *cerdito* = "small or young pig, piglet", when used by a Spanish child tends to have the sort of tone associated in English with expressions such as "baby pig", "piggy". An extreme case of this tendency is *osito*, which is almost universally reserved for "toy or teddy bear", the basic literal sense of "bear cub" being generally rendered by *osezno*. Another similar instance is that of *lobito*, which may be used, somewhat contradictorily, to mean "big bad wolf",[1] "wolf cub" being *lobato*.

-ito is indeed so widely used in hypochoristic expressions that it is often deliberately avoided in normal speech. Hence a Spaniard wishing to express the concept "small wood" may well prefer to say *bosque pequeño* or perhaps *bosquecillo*, rather than use *bosquecito*, which has about it the ring of "cute or ducky little wood".[2]

(b) *Other diminutives.* The other main diminutive suffixes may conveniently be divided into three sections:

---

[1] As in this passage from Carmen Laforet (*Nada*, p. 121):
  — ¿No te da miedo andar tan solita por las calles? ¿Y si viene el lobito y te come?

It is interesting to compare this other passage from Emilia Pardo Bazán (*Los Pazos de Ulloa*, p. 47):
  — ¡ Si no callas, viene el cocón y te come! (big bad bogeyman)
  *Lobito* and *cocón* — *les extrêmes se touchent.*

[2] Conversely, -ito may be used just for this very reason, in cases where a contemptuous effect is desired, e.g.

Y debo confesar que a mí me produce una más honda y más fuerte impresión estética la contemplación del páramo, sobre todo a la hora de la puesta del sol, cuando lo enciende el ocaso, que uno de esos vallecitos verdes que parecen de Nacimiento de cartón. Pero en el paisaje ocurre lo que en la arquitectura: el desnudo es lo último que se llega a gozar. Hay quien prefiere una colinita verde, llena de arbolitos de jardín, a la imponente masa de uno de los grandes gigantes rocosos de la tierra.

    (UNAMUNO, *Andanzas y Visiones Españolas*, pp. 51, 52)
[i. e. "sweet" little valleys, "nice" little hill, "cute" little trees.]

1. Those which have a marked tendency to favourable and affectionate implication and are thus satellites of *-ito* *(-ico, -ín)*.

2. Those which have a strong tendency to unfavourable and contemptuous implication and can thus be regarded as more specifically pejorative-biased companions of *-illo* *(-ejo, -uelo)*.

3. One with a decidedly jocular bias *(-ete)*.

### (ii) *The Augmentatives*

(a) *-ón.* Since *-ón* is undoubtedly the most versatile of the augmentative group it is natural that it should occupy first place.

When used to form nouns and adjectives describing types of person — incidentally often more with an implied than an explicit augmentative idea — it has a marked tendency to be used in words of a pejorative nature: *matón* = "bully"; *respondón* = "(much) given to answering back". It will be observed that many of these terms belong especially to what may be called schoolboy language, and that they are, in a number of cases, paralleled by somewhat exceptional and anomalous forms in *-ica* (m.):[1] *acusón, acusica* = "telltale"; *llorón, llorica* = "cry-baby".

Nevertheless, *-ón* can be used to reinforce favourable words, e.g. *simpaticón* = "extremely likeable or easy to get on with", although even in such a case as this there is a shade of pejorative meaning, the implication being almost that of "perhaps a bit *too* easy to get on with". This latent criticism becomes rather more explicit in *bonachón* = "thoroughly easy-going", "good-natured to a fault", the balance being tipped by the pejorative force of the preceding suffix *-acho*.

It is important to notice a subtle and contradictory attenuative case of *-ón*, when used with certain words and in certain circumstances. An outstanding example of this is *sinvergonzón (sinvergüenzón)*, which tends to be used rather like "*proper* or *regular* rogue or devil" in English, i.e. the addition of a stressing element (in Spanish a suffix, in English an adjective) suggests a certain familiarity or intimacy of speech which acts as an attenuant, the bald basic form thus resulting more severe than the so-called augmentative: *sinvergüenza* =

---

[1] Exceptional and anomalous in so far as *-ico* is a suffix with a strongly favourable bias.

"rogue", "rotter". Other words in which this tendency is marked are: *egoistón, gandulón, hipocritón, ignorantón, inocentón* and *simplón* (also *simplote*), *perezosón, viciosón*. However, the fact that *-ón* is often used affectively in such words by no means precludes the possibility of the augmentative function. Once again circumstances, context or tone of voice are our guide: *eres un egoistón, pero te quiero* = "you're a (properly) selfish devil, but I love you"; *es un egoistón de marca* = "he's a completely selfish individual".

The following are words in which the function of *-ón*, if not exclusively attenuative, is certainly predominantly so: *coquetón, malón* (also *malote*), *tontón, torpón, tristón : ¡qué malón eres!* = "how (very) *naughty* you are!" [not "bad" or "wicked"];[1] *¡claro que vas a ir, tontón!* = "of course you're going to go, you big *silly!*" [not "you utter fool"]; *estaba tristón* = "he was in a (properly) *mournful* mood" [not "in an utterly dejected mood"].[2]

In nouns denoting things *-ón* is used to stress neutrally, favourably or unfavourably, according to the meaning of the root word and to circumstances: *gotón* = " huge or heavy drop"; *memorión* = "phenomenal memory"; *novelón* = "tediously long novel" (an exceptionally big memory is, of course, considered a desirable thing, while an exceptionally long novel is, as a rule, not). Finally in this group there may occur cases of complete ambivalence in one word: *un programón imponente* = "a magnificent (big) programme"; *un programón pesadísimo* = "an insufferably tedious (long) programme".

*-ón* is also used to denote action or result of action, often with augmentative-pejorative implication: *empujón* = "push", "shove"; *darse un atracón de algo* = "to have a blow-out of something".

Specialization or change of sense, found in so many suffixes, gives another group: *toallón* = "bath or beach towel" (< *toalla* = "towel"); *cinturón* = "belt" (< *cintura* = "waist").

Finally, we come to a use in which a diminutive sense is conveyed, although here once more the pejorative strain may be clearly discerned.

---

[1] Another example: *deben de ser muy malones* = "they must be very poorish or middling", in which *malón* is equal to the diminutive-pejorative *malejo*.

[2] *El "tristón" está menos afligido que el simplemente "triste"* (Julio Casares, *Introducción a la lexicografía* (Madrid, 1950), p. 116). Hence *tristoncete* = "on the mournful side", "rather under the weather".

Examples are: *montón* = "heap" (< *monte* = "hill"; *ratón* = "mouse" (< *rata* = "rat"); *terrón* = "clod of soil" (< *tierra* = "land"); *pelón* = "having very little hair or bald" (< *pelo* = "hair"). (Cf. Fr. *aiglon* = "eaglet"; *chaton* = "kitten"; *raton* = "young rat"; *Marion* = "young Mary".)[1]

(b) *-azo*. There are two outstanding uses of this suffix, corresponding to uses we have just seen in *-ón*.

However, *-azo* is more fully ambivalent than *-ón*, being used to emphasize *equally* concepts of a pejorative or favourable nature: *latazo* = "hell of a bore"; *exitazo* = "colossal success". This total ambivalence of *-azo* can be seen very clearly in the following instances:

> *un filosofazo magnífico* = "a superb philosopher"
> *un filosofazo de tres al cuarto* = "a tin-pot philosopher"
> *una barbaza imponente* = "a magnificent big beard"
> *una barbaza feísima* = "a hideous great beard"

In its second main use *-azo* indicates action or result of action and, in particular, the idea of a blow, both in a literal and a figurative sense: *le mató de un hachazo* = "he killed him with a blow from an axe"; *te pegaré un telefonazo* = "I'll give you a ring" (cf. Fr. *coup de hache, coup de téléphone*). Often a certain augmentative force is combined with this use: *dio un frenazo* = "he braked *hard*", "he *jammed on* the brakes".

(c) *-ote*. Similar in many ways to *-ón*, *-ote* has a strongly pejorative bias and yet at the same time can also be used attenuatively, so that *herejote*, for example, said with a jocular tone of voice, may well produce a milder effect than the bald *hereje*.

(d) *-udo*. This exclusively adjectival suffix is also found particularly in pejorative words.


(iii) *The Pejoratives*

This group, while of great interest, offers a much more simple picture than the other two and can be left to speak almost entirely for itself. Categories can be drawn up on the following lines: (a)

[1] See Spitzer, *Das Suffix -one im Romanischen*. Geneva, 1921.

straightforward pejoratives (the majority); (b) pejoratives with diminutive bias (e.g. -*ucho*); (c) pejoratives with augmentative bias (e.g. -*acho*). These differences, however, are not great, and moreover only in a very few cases do we find the complication of the "specialized or changed sense" section. No alteration in rigorous alphabetical order has therefore been made in the case of the pejoratives.

It will be noticed that the diminutives have been given rather specially detailed treatment in this introduction. This is due to the complexity of the group and also to the fact that many of the points covered in connection with the diminutives are related to or apply indirectly to the augmentatives, which have thus been felt to need slightly less full treatment. And the pejoratives, for the reasons stated, have been despatched summarily. All of them convey their message unaided in the body of the book. The aim here has been no more than to indicate a few highlights, to essay a number of guiding principles and to whet the reader's appetite sufficiently to lead him on to a close study of the individual sections, in which he will find the detail necessary to gain a true understanding of and feeling for the subject.

## 5. CROSS CURRENTS AND EXTREMES WHICH MEET

Cross currents between one section and another within a group, involving whole series of synonymous or nearly synonymous expressions, are very common. Here three instances will suffice as an introduction to the numerous examples contained in the body of the book: *besito — besico — besín; cabezón — cabezota — cabezudo; aldehuela — aldeúcha — aldeorrio*.[1]

However, such cross currents are also found between the three main groups, and this, particularly in the case of diminutive-augmen-

---

[1] In the following passage from Pereda (*Peñas Arriba*, p. 54) two augmentative forms of *hombre* are used within a few lines of each other:

— Vaya, añadió, mirando alternativamente al cura y al hombrón del otro banco... Después, dijo mi tío, refiriéndose al hombrazo del banco frontero...

And, had he wished, the author could have had recourse also to *hombrote* and *hombretón*.

tative correspondences, is, on first contact, surprising and indeed an apparent contradiction in terms.

Thus, as has already been seen, *¡vaya tiempecito!* (iron.) more or less equates with *¡qué tiempazo más espantoso!*, just as in English "this is quite some weather" (iron.) more or less equates with "this is really atrocious weather". Similarly *es un problemita, ¿verdad?* (iron.) (= "it's quite a little problem, isn't it?") has fundamentally the same sense as *es un problemón, ¿verdad?* (= "it's a hell of a problem, isn't it?"), and in like manner *facilito* (= "nice and easy") is really very close to *facilón* (= "it's contemptibly easy, it's simplicity itself"). And again it transpires that *ser muy honradito* (= "to be a regular little model of honesty") is not very far in basic meaning from *ser muy honradote* (= "to be honest as the day, to be honest to a fault"),[1] and that *ya eres mayorcito* (= "you're a big little laddie now") conveys substantially the same meaning as *ya eres mayorzote* (= "you're a great big lad now").

Thus we discover that, since *-ito* is used in these cases not to diminish but to stress, we are not dealing with what appear at first sight to be diametrically opposed senses, but in fact with two aspects of one single sense.

6. POPULAR AND FORMAL LANGUAGE; REINFORCEMENT AND TAUTOLOGY; TRANSFERENCE, WIT AND VARIETY; DANGERS

It is now clear that the suffixes we are dealing with belong to the realm of popular, personal, colloquial language rather than to formal, impersonal or literary style. That is why the most fertile sources of written examples are to be found in those novelists and

---

[1] In this example we see with particular clarity that, although the basic meaning — that of complete honesty — is the same, there nevertheless exists a subtle difference between the two words — a difference in psychological stress. *Honradito* can itself be used to imply two quite different things: (i) that the person in question is regarded affectionately as being utterly honest, or (ii) that the person's honesty is unquestionable but of a timid, niggardly kind. *Honradote* also suggests a certain affection but, above all, implies that the person described carries his honesty with heartiness and generosity.

playwrights who depict scenes and describe situations of ordinary Spanish life, e.g. Benito Pérez Galdós, Vicente Blasco Ibáñez, Pío Baroja, Camilo José Cela, Joaquín y Serafín Alvarez Quintero, Antonio Buero Vallejo, to mention a few. Conversely, in the work of a philosophical author such as Ortega y Gasset little suffix material is to be found.[1]

Not surprisingly, we find that the function fulfilled in popular language by diminutives is covered in formal style by adjectives and adverbs: *pequeño, reducido, diminuto, minúsculo*; *un poco, un tanto, algo*. Similarly, the augmentatives are parallelled by such terms as: *grande, inmenso, gigantesco, ingente, descomunal, desmedido, desmesurado, desorbitado, extremado*; *muy, completamente, sumamente, totalmente*; and by the superlative *-ísimo*.[2] And the pejoratives have their equivalents in *malo, miserable, atroz, espantoso, horrible, horrendo, infame, nefando*; *desagradablemente, despreciablemente, miserablemente*.

Nevertheless, it is not uncommon to find a combination of the two elements — a more or less literary adjective is often used to reinforce or boost a word already given the popular stress of a suffix, e.g. *un talentazo*[3] *descomunal*.

Many originally literary adjectives are indeed today widely used in colloquial language and have as a result become somewhat debased,

---

[1] Nevertheless, even in the most academic prose the odd case does occur from time to time, e.g.

El estruendoso instrumento militar ... sobresaltó al vecindario: a unos de temor y a otros de esperanza; luego corrió por toda la ciudad el *notición* de que 500 jinetes almorávides se hallaban al pie de los muros; ...

(MENÉNDEZ PIDAL, *El Cid Campeador*, p. 190)

The clamorous military instrument ... startled the populace, filling some with terror and others with hope; then there spread swiftly throughout the entire city the stupendous news that 500 Almoravide horsemen were at the foot of the walls.

[2] Notwithstanding, *-ísimo* often appears in expressions of a decidedly popular type: *grandísimo sinvergüenza*. It can even be added, sometimes rather contradictorily, to a word bearing a diminutive suffix: *chiquitísimo; — es malejo, ¿verdad? — malejo no, malejísimo*. Examples of still further popular uses are: *hace friísimo; lo ha intentado no sé cuantísimas veces; sabe tantísimo, que tiene forzosamente que aprobar*.

[3] Note how the popular *ser un talentazo* is parallelled by the more academic *ser un superdotado* (popular suffix = learned prefix). See under *-azo* (A).

e.g. *estupendo, imponente, impresionante, soberbio* (= "great", "smashing", "terrific", etc.).

A particularly curious tendency in this regard is the use, with a similar sense, of such expressions as *bárbaro, bestial* and *brutal*.

So we find that phrases of the type *un sueldazo bestial, una casaza imponente*, abound in every-day speech, and are accompanied by a whole host of others: *un broncazo de padre y muy señor mío (de no te menees), un tormentón de miedo (de mil pares de demonios), un tacañote de tomo y lomo, empleíllo de mala muerte, artistucho de tres al cuarto.*

Of course, such expressions bolster the force of the suffix, but they are, in fact, to a large extent tautological, in so far as basically they represent a repetition of the function already fulfilled by that suffix.

In the following passage from Carlos Arniches (*Es mi hombre*, p. 44) we find another similar type of repetitive stressing:

SOLE — A ése le veis, antes de "naa", de rodillas y a mis pies.
PURA — Me parece que te falla.
SOLE — De rodillitas y a mis pies. Está dicho.

Here the idea contained in *de rodillitas* (= "at my *very* feet", "*positively* at my feet") is reinforced, somewhat unnecessarily from a strict point of view, by *está dicho* ("I've said it and I stick to it", "mark my words").[1]

Finally, note must be taken of one other case of popular tautology, involving the use of *algo* with a diminutive ending, as, for example, in *está algo deprimidillo*, where *algo* simply foreshadows the attenuative force of *-illo*, but does not really modify the meaning ("he's just a bit under the weather").

This is now a suitable moment to consider another suffix phenomenon of a definitely popular nature — transference. In the examples which follow it will be seen how suffixes expressing affection or tenderness for a child are unconsciously switched from the word *niño* or *niña* or *pobre* to a qualifying adjective or, more surprisingly, to a more or less directly connected noun. Thus *el pobre está muy cansadito* is simply a popular, unconscious transference of *el pobrecito está cansado*. Similarly, in *el niño es un tragoncillo*, although the idea may indeed be to attenuate the force of *tragón*, nevertheless, again, the

---

[1] See Alonso, *Estudios lingüísticos*, p. 216.

phrase may merely represent a switching round of *el niñillo es un tragón*; *el niño tiene tres añitos* does not mean, as might possibly be deduced, *el niño tiene tres años nada más* or *el niño apenas tiene tres años*, but is merely another way of saying *el niñito tiene tres años*; and, again, *la niña tiene sangrecilla en la cara*, although it could mean *la niña tiene un poco de sangre en la cara*, will probably signify rather *la niñilla tiene sangre en la cara*. An especially surprising example is *la niña me coge la manica* (= *la niñica me coge la mano*), in which the affection felt by the speaker is transferred linguistically to the speaker's hand because it represents the point of physical contact with the child. (Cf. *dame la manita*, which can certainly mean "give me your little hand", but is just as likely to mean "give me your hand, *dear*", in which case the idea conveyed by the suffix goes not, in fact, with *mano* but with its possessor, the person addressed.) Nor is suffix transference confined to personal cases or to particular endings: *un sendero estrechuelo* = *un senderuelo estrecho*, *un vestido estampaducho* = *un vestiducho estampado*.

We come now to yet another popular aspect of the diminutive, augmentative and pejorative suffixes, to what Leo Spitzer calls their *playful* element.[1] Something of this has already been seen in such expressions as *dinerito le habrá costado* (= "it must have cost him a pretty penny"), in which a strain of humour runs through the basic irony.

Certain suffixes are particularly known for their jocular implications, notable among these being *-ete*. Thus the following sentence, in which *dinerito* could also be used, as in the example above, is given an especially playful tone by the use of the form *dinerete*: *¡a ver si aflojáis el dinerete!* = "how about you people coming across with the jolly old cash?" And, similarly, *caballerete* is just right in an exclamation such as this: *pues, ¡caramba con el caballerete este!* = "well, well, a fine gentleman this is turning out to be!", "well, well, what do you think of our fine gentleman here?"

Another suffix frequently used in a jocular manner is *-orio*, as in the words *jolgorio*[2] (= "jollification", "high-jinks", "living-it-up") and *vejestorio* (= "old crock", "old wreck").

---

[1] See *Beiträge zur romanischen Wortbildungslehre*, Geneva, 1921.

[2] The variant *jolgación*, overheard by the writer in the phrase *¡viva la jolgación!*, is an interesting example of how people will actually invent new expressions

However, it should be borne in mind that any suffix can be used to produce a comic effect, according to circumstances, and that the suffixes we are describing naturally lend themselves to punning of all kinds. Thus, Camilo José Cela, tongue in cheek, reports that in the village of Guisando *a los protestantes les llaman protestones*[1] (*Judíos, Moros y Cristianos*, p. 274); and Miguel Pérez Ferrero tells us how at a school attended by Pío Baroja one of the masters *a los chicos acusones*[1] *les llamaba acusativos* (*Vida de Pío Baroja*, p. 43).[2]

Is it then any wonder that on a certain occasion a Spaniard, in conversation with the author, said to him: *Los sufijos son la sal y la gracia del español; sin ellos, nuestra lengua sería como una comida buena, de excelente calidad, pero sosa?*

As a foretaste of what is to come in the main part of the book a little of this *gracia* or *ajilimójili*, a little of the immense variety contained in the Spanish suffixes is now presented to the reader in the form of a few particularly interesting quotations:

> Don J. — ¡Qué *borriquito* es el pobre; qué *borriquito*!
>
> J. — Pues mire usted: si se ha llegado a creer ese *borriquito*, como usted le llama, o ese *borricazo*, como le llamo yo, que porque tuvimos unas tonterías de chiquillos ya no me va a gustar a mí ningún [otro] hombre, se equivoca en más de la mitad.
>
> (Álvarez Quintero, Puebla de las Mujeres, p. 33)

> Don J. — What a silly ass the poor chap is; what a silly ass!
>
> J. — Well, look here; if that silly ass, as *you* call him, or that thundering ass, as *I* call him, has got the idea into his head that [just] because there

---

in order to produce a comic effect. Thus, the speaker in question, finding the normal *juerga* tame and the humorous *jolgorio* unoriginal, went a step further and coined his own word. Other terms similarly coined on the spur of the moment, to the writer's knowledge, are *verdez* and *buenudo*. *Verdez* came into being as a result of a speaker's desire for a jocular noun to correspond to *verde* in its idiomatic sense of "blue", "risqué", "vulgar". (Cf. the normal *verdor* = "greenness" and *verdura(s)* = "green vegetable(s)".) *Buenudo* was created to replace *buenazo* in order to produce a humorous reiterative effect in the phrase *es un chico cachazudo y buenudo*.

[1] See under *-ón* (A).

[2] Somewhat similarly, the more scanty a bikini bathing-costume, the more likely it is to elicit the humorously contradictory augmentative form in such an exclamation as *¡Qué bikinón!*

was a little childish flirting between us I'm not going to be interested any more in any other man, he's got another idea coming.

Lo difícil ... es el elogio de las cosas detestables, de las ... insoportables cosas de Madrid; ...¡El polvo y la suciedad de Madrid! ¡Las *callejuelas* y los *callejones* ... de Madrid! ¡Los desérticos alrededores de Madrid! ... esas *cosillas, cosas* y *cosazas* de Madrid.

(SAINZ DE RODLES, *Cuerpo y Alma de Madrid*, p. 1274)

What is [really] difficult ... is [to find a way] to praise the hateful ... the insufferable things about Madrid; ... Madrid's dust and dirt! Madrid's mean little lanes and narrow alleys! Madrid's desert-like outskirts! ... those wretched little things, ordinary things and hideous great things about Madrid.

... *Clarín*, el más ilustre y temido crítico de su tiempo, aunque no siempre el más justo ni amable. Hombre apasionado y atrabiliario, pone tal pasión en sus *clarinazos* críticos, que a veces se confunde con la grosería y el favoritismo.

(BRAVO-VILLASANTE, *Vida y Obra de Emilia Pardo Bazán*, p. 85)

... Clarion, the most celebrated and feared critic of his time, although not always the fairest or most kind. A vehement and acrimonious man, he put such ardour into his clarion blasts of criticism that his attitude was sometimes indistinguishable from scurrility and favouritism.

... al decir de Ramoncita, el deseo de hallar marido en una mujer podía dividirse en tres etapas. Desde los quince a los veinte debía llamarse el período de las *ganitas*, de los veinte a los veinticinco, el de las *ganas*, y de los veinticinco a los treinta, el de las *ganazas*.

(PALACIO VALDÉS, *La Hermana San Sulpicio*, p. 172)

... according to Ramoncita, a woman's desire to find a husband could be divided into three stages. From fifteen to twenty should be called the period of "getting eager", from twenty to twenty-five the period of "being definitely eager", and from twenty-five to thirty the period of "being madly eager".

La niña chica era la gloria de Platero. En cuanto la veía venir hacia él ..., llamándolo mimosa: — ¡Platero, *Platerillo!*, el *asnucho* quería partir la cuerda... Ella le pegaba *pataditas*, y le dejaba la mano... en aquella *bocaza* rosa, ... lo llamaba con todas las variaciones mimosas de su nombre: — ¡Platero! ¡Platerón! ¡Platerillo! ¡Platerete!

(JIMÉNEZ, *Platero y yo*, pp. 74, 75)

The little girl was Platero's joy. As soon as [the donkey] saw her coming towards him..., calling to him wheedlingly: — "Platero, darling little Platero!" — the wretched creature used to try to break the rope... She would give him gentle little kicks and put her hand ... in that great pink mouth [of his] ... she would call him by all the wheedlingly affectionate variations of his name: — "Platero! Platero, you great goof! Darling little Platero! Cute old Platero"!

A. — Tanto mejor. Le aseguro a usted que uno de mis tormentos en este *poblacho* ..., usted perdone ...

Don J. — No, *hijito*, no; si yo pienso lo mismo que tú; esto es un *poblachito*, un *poblachito*.

(ALVAREZ QUINTERO, *Puebla de las Mujeres*, p. 50)

A. — So much the better. I assure you that one of the things that torment me in this dump of a village ..., I beg your pardon ...

Don J. — No, my dear boy, no; why I'm of the same opinion as yourself; this is a poor little, dump, a poor little dump.

Ascaso daba por cierto que los nacionales habían desenterrado a Galán y García Hernández y los habían vuelto a fusilar .... Un compañero de Teo, voluntario catalán, comentó: Bueno, ellos habrán refusilado, pero yo a la palabra *sacerdote* le he quitado el *sa*.[1]

(GIRONELLA, *Un Millón de Muertos*, p. 235)

Ascaso accepted as sure fact that the Nationalists had dug up the bodies of Galán and García Hernández and had shot them for a second time. ...One of Teo's comrades, a Catalan volunteer, remarked: "Well, *they* may have done some double executing, but *I've* substituted for *priest* the word *beast*".

Precisely because of the popular and intimate nature of the diminutive, augmentative and pejorative suffixes, words can be created which, perhaps more than any others, have to be used by the right person, in the right place, at the right time. It must be remembered that, in a foreign tongue, familiar speech is, in some ways, considerably harder to master than learned or literary expression, for this latter, although in every language it has its special characteristics, is intrinsically much more international.

As has been seen, the suffixes dealt with belong particularly to those linguistic areas which express basic human feelings, and often express them with great force. As a result, in a foreigner the use of many of these terms may well appear either ridiculous or presumptuous, jarring on the hearer and striking him as a violation of things which are really only for the lips of a native. Thus the foreigner who presumed, for example, to talk about *estos curánganos* might easily

---

[1] Play on words *sacerdote* (< L. *sacerdos*, *-otis*) and *cerdote* (< *cerdo+ote*).

offend even the most anti-clerical Spaniard. Let the reader therefore beware and bear in mind that in the case of many of the words in this book it is important to understand them but dangerous to use them. The *metedura de pata*, so easy at all times, is here especially so.

We have an outstanding example in the numerous *palabrotas y tacos* (vulgar expressions and swear words) which have been formed in Spanish by means of suffixes, and which are in extremely frequent use by male Spaniards *of all classes*.[1] However, they are almost always uttered with such naturalness that they somehow seem to possess a certain wittiness, a saving grace often absent in equivalent English expressions. Words of this type appear, moreover, in standard authors, and hence to ignore them totally would be as great an error as to harp excessively upon them. For these reasons it has been considered justified to include one or two of the most common, e.g. *cabrón*, *puñeta*.

## 7. MIRAGE SUFFIXES; HISTORICAL CONSIDERATIONS; REGIONAL USAGE; LATEST ADMISSIONS TO THE ACADEMY DICTIONARY

### (i) *Mirage Suffixes*

Etymology[2] is not a direct concern of this book, but a few observations on the subject will, nevertheless, perhaps be of interest and assistance to the reader, in so far as it may well be disconcerting to realize that there are a great many words which end in what is apparently a Spanish suffix, but which, in fact, do not represent a Spanish root plus a Spanish suffix at all. An outstanding case is that of a whole series of terms in *-illo*, *-illa*, which are the result of direct

---

[1] As might be expected, the incidence among women is far less, although here a distinction should be made between upper and lower social strata. In the latter there are many who might say, with Galdós's Fortunata, *pueblo nací y pueblo soy; quiero decir ordinariota y salvaje,* and of whom we might add that so is their language. (Quotation from *Fortunata y Jacinta*, III, p. 110.)

[2] Those wishing for further information on etymology should consult the bibliography.

development from an original Vulgar or Popular Latin diminutive word, the diminutive sense, however, having become lost:

| | | |
|---|---|---|
| *castillo* | = | castle *(< castellu(m) < castrum)* |
| *caudillo*[1] | = | leader *(< capitellu(m) < caput)* |
| *colmillo* | = | eye-tooth, fang, tusk *(< columellu(m) < columella)* |
| *cuchillo* | = | knife *(< cultellu(m) < culter)* |
| *martillo* | = | hammer *(< martellu(m) < martulus)* |
| *tobillo* | = | ankle *(< tubellu(m) < tuber)* |
| *astilla* | = | stick *(< astella(m) < astula)* |
| *hebilla* | = | buckle *(< fibella(m) < fibula)* |
| *postilla* | = | scab *(< pustella(m) < pustula)* |
| *rodilla* | = | knee *(< rotella(m)[2] < rotula)* |

But the diminutive idea sometimes survives:

*monaguillo* = acolyte, altar boy *(< monachellu(m) < monachus)*

Again, in some words the coinciding of the ending with the diminutive *-illo* is purely a product of chance:

| | | |
|---|---|---|
| *membrillo* | = | quince *(< L. melimelum)* |
| *quisquilla* | = | shrimp *(< L. quisquiliae)* |
| *chinchilla* | = | chinchilla (< a Quechua Indian word) |

And in yet other instances the ending occurs in words the origin of which has not been conclusively explained, and thus remains itself unexplained:

| | | |
|---|---|---|
| *escotilla* | = | hatchway (connected with Fr. *écoutille* and Eng. *scuttle*) |
| *gavilla* | = | sheaf, stook (possibly of Celtic origin or from L. *cavu(m)*) |
| *polilla* | = | moth (possibly connected with L. *papilio*)[3] |

---

[1] It is interesting to compare with this word the term *cabecilla* = "ring-leader", "partisan leader" *(< cabeza (< caput) + illa)*.

[2] Hypothetical form.

[3] *-illo, -illa* is a particularly complex ending, both from the etymological point of view, of which we see just a little here, and from the standpoint of semantics, which is our main concern (see section *-illo* in body of book), and

Another case is that of -*eja*, which also often represents direct development from an original Latin diminutive form, with total loss of diminutive meaning:

*abeja* = bee (< *apicula(m)* < *apis*)
*oreja* = ear (< *auricula(m)* < *auris*)[1]

Again, many words in -*ete*, -*eta* have come into Spanish from French and Italian:

*billete* = ticket (< *billette* O. Fr. [mod. *billet*])
*bufete* = buffet lunch, etc. (< *bufet* O. Fr. [mod. *buffet*])
*bayeta* = duster (< *baiette* O. Fr.)
*maleta* = suitcase (< *malete* < *male* O. Fr. [mod. *malle*])
*tarjeta* = card (< *targette* O. Fr.)
*cuneta* = ditch (< [*la*]*cunetta* It.)
*espoleta* = fuse (< *spoletta* It.)
*estafeta* = sub post-office (< *staffetta* It.)

Exceptionally, a few of these words have been included in the body of the book, because Spanish forms of the root-words exist, to which they can be related, and because there is in them a diminutive sense, e.g. *furgoneta* = "van"; "shooting brake type of car" (< Fr. *fourgonnette*); *glorieta* = "small square or circus" (< Fr. *gloriette*); *metralleta* = "sub-machine-gun" (< Fr. *mitraillette*). (The Spanish root-words to which they can be related are *furgón*, *gloria*, *metralla*.)[2]

Similarly, words in -*alla* have been included because, although they are of Italian origin, they retain a pejorative or augmentative sense in Spanish:

---

it is of incidental interest to note that it is proliferating in Spanish America, where it appears in many expressions not used in Spain: *altillo* = "attic" (Sp. *desván*); *conventillo* = "tenement" (Sp. *casa de vecindad*); *canilla* = "tap" (Sp. *grifo*); *estampilla* = "postage-stamp" (Sp. *sello postal*); *frutilla* = "strawberry" (Sp. *fresa, fresón*); *tropilla* = "flock", "herd" (Sp. *rebaño, manada*).

[1] Cf. *canijo* = "feeble, weakish, weakling", which similarly does not represent *can* + *ijo*, but derives from *caniculu(m)* < *canis*, in this instance, however, with retention of diminutive sense.

[2] Often such words are used despite the existence of good *castizo* terms, e.g. *marioneta* (< *marionnette*) for *títere*.

*antigualla* < *anticaglia*
*canalla* < *canaglia*
*gentualla* < *gentaglia*
*muralla* <*muraglia*
(See under section -*alla*)

Sometimes the endings of words of Arabic origin coincide fortuitously with Spanish suffix forms. A particularly interesting example is *mamarracho* = "grotesque object" (< *muharráğ*), in which both because of form and sense the ending of the word immediately suggests the Spanish -*acho* (< L. *aceu(m)*). We see similar coincidences in *machucho* = "of mature years" (< *ma'ğuğ*), where the first reaction is to think of *macho* + *ucho*, and in *zoquete* = "cloddish fellow", "country bumpkin" (< *suqáṭ*), where the Spanish suffix -*ete* not unnaturally suggests itself. *Azulejo* = "coloured tile", and *tabuco* = "hovel", "wretched room" (cf. *cuartucho*, *cuchitril*), are two other words in whose form Arabic is probably the determining factor, although their endings may also have been influenced by the Spanish suffixes -*ejo* and -*uco*.

## (ii) *Historical Considerations*

Naturally, much modern suffix usage has its roots firmly in the history of the language, as can be seen in the following quotation, again from Amado Alonso, whose words link up examples from the past with points which have been made in a previous section of this book concerning ironic use of -*ito* and pejorative use of -*illo* in the Spanish of today:

> El sufijo -ito, por lo común cariñoso, es despectivo y rebajador aplicado al enemigo: — A lo que dijo Don Quijote, sonriéndose un poco: — ¿Leoncitos a mí? ¿A mí leoncitos, y a tales horas? (II, 117). Este esquema idiomático es hoy todavía productivo: ¡capitancitos a mí!, ¡alcalditos a mí!, ¡toritos a mí!, ¡sermoncitos a mí! Encierra un contrarreto. El diminutivo pretende un rebajamiento del contrario o del obstáculo... "leoncitos" es pseudodesvalorativo, pero en verdad emocional, ya que ni siquiera ha visto Don Quijote los leones. El diminutivo rebajador era frecuente en la época clásica con nombres propios: Góngora llamó a Lope Lopillo, Quevedo a Góngora Gongorilla.

Este poder injuriante debe venir del uso del diminutivo con nombres propios de servidores y gentes de menor estado. No me parece haya sido la base la idea de tamaño reducido. Expresa familiaridad impertinente. El llamar con diminutivo a los sirvientes y gente menor en general, tenía tradición secular. Ahí el diminutivo, pretendiendo expresar afección, denunciaba condescendiente superioridad. Recojo del Arcipreste de Talavera, Corbacho, Madrid, 1901, p. 166, este pasaje instructivo: — "E lo peor que algunas non tienen arreos con que salgan, ni mujeres nin moças con que vayan, e dizen: — Juanilla, veme a casa de mi hermana que me preste su aljuba, la verde, la de Florencia. Inesica, veme a casa de mi comadre que me preste su crespina e aun el almanaca. Catalinilla, ve a casa de mi vecina que me preste su cinta y sus arracadas de oro. Francisquilla, ve a casa de mi señora la de Fulano, que me preste sus paternostres de oro. Teresuela, ve en un punto a mi sobrina que me preste su pordemás el de martas forrado. Mencigüela, corre en un salto a los alatares o a los mercaderes, traeme solimán e dos oncillas de cinamono, o clavo de girofre para levar en la boca . . ." *(op. cit.*, p. 203).

On the other hand historical study, not surprisingly, often brings to light contrasts with modern practice. Thus we find that in the past some suffixes enjoyed a much greater vogue than they do now. Outstanding cases are -*ico* and -*uelo*, which we have just seen used in a passage from the fifteenth century *Corbacho* (the form *Teresuela*, for example, is, in modern Spanish, rare in the extreme), and which we see again in this quotation from the celebrated *Celestina* (published 1499):

— ¿Qué dirás a esto, Pármeno? ¡Neciuelo, loquito, angelico, perlica, simplecico! ¿Lobitos en tal gestico? Llégate acá, putico . . .[1]

-*ico* and -*uelo* are certainly still used in standard Spanish, but the position they occupy today is very much less prominent than it was of old.

Differences in usage are, however, to be found even in comparison with so recent a period as the nineteenth century. Thus, in *El Sombrero de Tres Picos*, Alarcón uses the form *narigón*, which has since fallen out of fashion and been replaced by *narigudo*: *Lucas era . . . muy moreno, barbilampiño, narigón, orejudo y picado de viruelas (op. cit.*, pp. 48, 49) (See under -*udo* ) Again, in Pereda we find *salona* and *sillona*, which are logical feminine forms built on *sala* and *silla*, but which have, nevertheless, been almost entirely superseded by *salón* and *sillón*.

[1] *Clásicos Castellanos* edition, Espasa-Calpe (Madrid, 1955), I, p. 95.

It is also possible to trace semantic differences between nineteenth- and twentieth-century usage. Thus, *confianzudo*, which appears formerly to have been used on occasion with the meaning "trusting", "over-trusting",[1] is today found only in the sense "familiar", "over-familiar", "given to taking liberties" (see under *-udo*). Another similar case is that of *fortunón* used, as in the following quotation from Pardo Bazán, in the sense "immense good fortune": *Y de este rencor temo que no le ha curado ni medio aliviado el fortunón — para él tiene que serlo — de entrar en mi casa* (*La Sirena Negra*, p. 1044). In the Spanish of today this idea is expressed by *suertaza*, the word *fortunón* being used only with the meaning "immense amount of money".

However, it is important to realize that in such cases as the last two the change in meaning is in the root-word just as much as, if not a great deal more than, in the suffix.[2]

## (iii) *Regional Usage*

Certain suffixes, almost always affective diminutives, are considered typical of certain areas, and although a detailed consideration of regional usage falls outside the scope of this book, nevertheless, in so far as there are many points of contact between what is regional and what is standard, it is felt that some mention of this aspect of the subject is desirable.

The suffix *-ico, -ica* is associated especially with Aragon and Navarre. Thus, the famous Patron Saint of Saragossa, *La Virgen del Pilar*, is known affectionately in the locality as *La Pilarica*, while the names given locally to the inhabitants of Navarre and of the provincial capital Pamplona are, respectively, *navarricas* and *pamplonicas*[3]

[1] For example, in this passage from Galdós:
La chica era confianzuda, inocentona, de éstas que dicen todo lo que sienten así lo bueno como lo malo (*Fortunata y Jacinta*, I, p. 110).

[2] In this connexion it is interesting to observe that a great deal of the variety in meaning of suffix terms derives, as might be expected, from diversity of origin in root-words. Thus, *carrillo* from *carro* = "small cart", while *carrillo* from *cara* = "cheek", "jowl"; and *chuleta* from an original Valencian *xulla* = "chop", "cutlet", while *chuleta* connected with *chulo* = "bellicose or pugnacious type of individual". [In student circles *chuleta* has yet another sense: "crib".]

[3] *-ica* is, in certain cases, as here, used with masculine or common gender.

(Castilian *navarros, pamploneses*). -ico is typical, too, of Granada,
where *bonico* and *pobretico* rival and alternate with *bonito* and *pobrecito*,
and where the Punch and Judy Show, known generally in Spain as
*el guiñol* (Fr. *guignol*), is called popularly *los cristobicas* (after *Cristóbal*,
the central figure).[1] This ending also occurs exceptionally in Asturias
in the word *andarica*, which denotes a type of crab akin to that called
in the Basque Provinces *changurro* and elsewhere in Spain given the
curious name *buey de Francia*.[2]

-*ín*, -*ina* is the typical suffix of Asturias[3], a very well-known
expression being *culín de sidra*, which denotes a small quantity of
cider filling only the bottom part of the glass, while *andarina* is the
regional term for *golondrina*. However, -*ín*, is also used in Granada in a
series of exceptional words in which it is often combined with -*ar*
and usually has augmentative sense:

*achuchín* = tight squeeze or crush, e.g. in a crowd  (< *achu-
              char* = to squeeze or crush)
*calorín*  = fierce heat (< *calor.* cf. *calorazo*)
*fogarín*  = fierce heat or blast of very hot air  (< *fuego* + *ar* +
              *in*)
*humarín* = dense smoke (< *humo* + *ar* + *ín.* cf. *humazo*)
*lapachín* = very muddy spot (< *lapachar* = marshy area)
*polvarín* = thick cloud of dust (< *polvo* + *ar* + *ín.* cf. *polva-
              reda*)

[1] Another Granadine expression is *ser una habica  (< haba + ica) partida
con* = "to be exactly the same as", "to be the spitting image of".

[2] This *andarica, changurro* or *buey de Francia* is more or less the same creature
as the usual British crab. It should not be confused with the *centollo* (also
*centolla*) = "spider crab", or with the *nécora* = "small or baby crab". The
term *cangrejo* is vague and requires qualifying words to specify its meaning,
as in the expression *cangrejo de río* = "fresh-water crab or crayfish" [cf. *cigala* =
"sea-water crayfish"].

[3] A *madrileño* who had been living for some months in Asturias is reported
to have said on a certain occasion:

Aborrezco hasta tal punto este diminutivo -ina, que ahora ya digo "voy
a tomar una aspirita" y "voy a ponerme la gabardita".

The joke is not very good, but it is interesting as yet another example
of how the suffixes lend themselves to word-play, and also as showing
how repeated use of a suffix can cause annoyance.

The feminine *-ina* is also used in Andalusia, e.g. *hambrina* = "ravenous hunger" (cf. the provincial augmentative *-era* : *hambrera*, *cansera*, *hartera* = "ravenous hunger", "complete weariness", "utter sickness" (fig.)).

*-iño* is the typical suffix of Galicia,[1] where *dinerito* and *temporadita*, for example, thus become *dineriño* and *temporadiña*. And it is interesting to observe that, because homesickness is an ill to which *gallegos* are especially prone, the Galician word *morriña* has come to be of general use in Spanish, even ousting to a certain degree, in this specific sense, the more standard words *nostalgia* and *añoranza*.

Again, *-ino* is associated with Extremadura, and *-uco* with Santander, a province known indeed to her sons as *la tierruca*.

*-illo*, too, is a regional suffix in so far as it is associated especially with Seville,[2] but, on the other hand, its use is so widespread that it can be considered almost as standard as the pure Castilian *-ito*, and, indeed, with the exception of *-iño*, all the endings we have just mentioned, apart from their regional function, also constitute important secondary suffixes of the standard language.

Finally, it seems appropriate to observe that, as might be expected, completely standard suffixes are liable to be used in any region to form words not normally used anywhere else, a good example being the expression *sombrón*, rarely heard outside Andalusia and derived from *sombra* + *ón*, with the meaning "dull, graceless or unwitty person" (cf. the phrase *tener mala sombra*).

## (iv) *Latest Admissions to the Academy Dictionary*

Until a short time ago the Real Academia Española followed a somewhat strict and narrow criterion which denied recognition to a large number of extremely common suffix-formed words of a popular type. However, this policy has now changed and many new admissions to the official dictionary have recently been made. Don Julio Casares, the former secretary of the Docta Corporación, wrote,

[1] Also used to some extent in Galicia is the suffix *-olo*, as in *amigolo* = *amigote* and in *querindolo* = *querindango* (see under *-ote* and *(ind)ango*).

[2] *Agüilla*, for example, is used in Seville (and in other parts of Andalusia) to mean "drizzle", whereas in Castilian the term is *llovizna* (popular *calabobos*) (cf. *orvallo* in Asturias and Galicia, and *chirimiri* in the Basque country).

not long before his recent death, a series of articles[1] giving details of these admissions, a few of which, along with Don Julio's remarks, are listed below:

| | |
|---|---|
| *amigacho* | — despectivo, sobre todo en boca de la esposa refiriéndose a los compinches del marido. |
| *blanduzco* | — se aplica, con intención levemente despectiva, a lo que está algo blando cuando sería de desear que no lo estuviese. |
| *bromazo* | — aumentativo de broma, que se aplica cuando ésta pasa de la raya y resulta particularmente molesta o desagradable. |
| *lechazo* | — equivale en buena parte de España a cordero lechal. |
| *mariposón* | — galanteador versátil. |

And not only does the Academy now admit such words much more readily than was previously the case but is even itself responsible for certain innovations in usage:

> Contestando a la consulta de una entidad oficial, que preguntaba... cómo podría nombrarse en castellano lo que los ingleses llaman "grill-room" la Academia propuso que se dijera "parrilla", traduciendo así la primera parte, "grill", del vocablo compuesto inglés. La propuesta tuvo fortuna y hoy es de uso general.

As a final example of the way popular suffix words, and indeed popular expressions of all kinds are now being officially recognized as never before, we quote below a further passage by Julio Casares in which he ingeniously brings together a whole medley of recent admissions:

> Érase que se era — y va de cuento — una borrachería, donde un militar de los de cuchara, jactancioso y pinturero, se las daba de machote refiriendo imaginarias proezas ante un improvisado auditorio, sin que nadie le parase los pies ni se atreviese a decir ni pío. Allá se iba con él otro pollastre

---

[1] Collected and published in *Novedades en el diccionario académico (La Academia Española trabaja)*, Aguilar (Madrid, 1963).

que presumía de jabato. Era simplemente un caso perdido, sinvergonzón, golfante y tan cagueta y temerón que ni a la de tres hubiera osado enfrentarse con el militar. En el abigarrado grupo allí reunido figuraba una taquimeca chatunga que estaba algo ida o barrenada, por no decir francamente locatis o mochales, juntamente con algunos jóvenes de muy diversa condición: los había retorcidos, malpensados y con las de Caín y, en contraste con éstos, se hallaba un muchacho formalote, comprensivo, aunque un tanto finolis y suficiente, es decir, propenso a la pedantería. No faltaba el conocido tipo del primavera, pasmado, despistado o que se hace el longui, ni el del pelmazo, cataplasma y sangregorda. Se completaba la reunión con algún que otro malasombra, malapata, patoso y gafe, y con varios aficionados al trago, que ya traían su correspondiente tablón, trompa o mordaga. Sucedió al fin que el acompañante de una furcia, que, por cierto, era una real moza, creyó advertir que un vivales se estaba timando con ella. Se le ahumó el pescado y, tras un intercambio de palabras gruesas, sacó a relucir la herramienta, con lo que todos salieron por pies y . . . colorín colorado.

(Julio Casares)

Once upon a time — and this is a story mind you — there was a binge, at which a regular soldier, one of those who have come up from the ranks, a boastful and affectedly conceited type, was making himself out to be a real he-man by recounting imaginary feats before an improvised audience, without anyone pulling him up or daring to say a word. Very much of a muchness was another young chappie who fancied himself as a lion of bravery. He was nothing but a hopeless case, a completely shameless rogue, a wastrel and such a scaredy cat and out-and-out funker that wild horses would not have made him dare to stand up to the soldier. In the motley crowd there gathered together was to be seen an attractively snub-nosed short-hand typist who was somewhat gone or addle-headed, not to say quite definitely crazy or cracked, along with a number of young men of differing sorts: tortuous ones, suspicious-minded ones, ill-willed ones and, contrasting with these, a thoroughly well-behaved, understanding lad, although a little lah-de-dah and self-satisfied, in other words inclined to pedantry. There was not wanting the well-known sucker, dope, all-at-sea type or the kind who makes himself out to be a fool, nor was there any lack of prize bores, pains-in-the-neck or insufferably phlegmatic individuals. And the gathering was completed by the odd graceless type, and one or two bad luck merchants, clumsy oafs and jinxes and also by several drink-addicts who were already suitably pie-eyed, canned or sozzled. Finally what happened was that the escort of a lady of the town, who, incidentally, was a fine buxom wench, thought he saw a sharp practitioner making eyes at her. He flew into a temper and, after an exchange of strong language, whipped out a knife, with the result that they all left as fast as their legs would carry them and . . . so our tale ends.

# 8. FORMATION

The reader will find useful basic rules regarding formation with suffixes in most standard grammars, e.g. the *Gramática de la lengua española* of the Real Academia and *A Manual of Modern Spanish* by L. C. Harmer and F. J. Norton. Usage is, however, often arbitrary, and the only really practical and satisfactory guide is experience.

The following phenomena should be watched for with special attention:

(i) Intercalation, for the sake of euphony, of the *theta* sound ($\theta$) in the form of the letters *c* and *z*,[1] sometimes involving an increase in syllables:

| | |
|---|---|
| *cisnecito* | < *cisne* |
| *piececito* | < *pie* |
| *nubecita* | < *nube* |
| *lucecita* | < *luz* |
| | |
| *saborcillo* | < *sabor* |
| *fuentecilla* | < *fuente* |
| | |
| *reyezuelo* | < *rey* |
| *bestezuela* | < *bestia* |
| | |
| *avionzucho* | < *avión* |
| *clasezucha* | < *clase* |

Arbitrariness is illustrated here by the existence of such pairs as *manita, manecita* and *manilla, manecilla*.[2] And, again, we find that in Spanish America *pueblito* and *tiempito*, for example, are in general use, whereas in Spain only *pueblecito* and *tiempecito* are normally found.

---

[1] Sometimes the letter *t* is so used, as in *cafetito (café + t + ito)*, and, in Andalusia, the letter *l*, as in *cafelito (café + l + ito)*, *bistelito (bisté + l + ito)*, *Joselito (José + l + ito)*.

Thus the manufacturers of a brand of coffee called *LAZO* are able to publicize their product by means of this play on suffixes:

No pida usted un *cafelito*;
pida usted un *CAFELAZO*.

[2] For difference in sense see under appropriate section.

**(ii)** Change of diphthong to simple vowel as a result of shifted stress:

| | |
|---|---|
| corpachón }<br>corpezuelo } | < cuerpo |
| calentito }<br>calentucho } | < caliente |
| dentudo | < diente |
| forzudo | < fuerza |
| membrudo | < miembro |

However, double forms often exist:

| | |
|---|---|
| sinvergonzón }<br>sinvergüenzón } | < sinvergüenza |
| poblacho }<br>·pueblucho }<br>pueblón } | < pueblo |
| ceguezuelo }<br>cieguezuelo } | < ciego |

In other cases, again, no change takes place:

| | |
|---|---|
| fiestón | < fiesta |
| buenazo | < bueno |
| nietezuelo | < nieto |

**(iii)** Change of gender:

| | |
|---|---|
| alegrón | < alegría |
| manchón | < mancha |
| bromazo | < broma |
| tortazo | < torta |
| carbonilla | < carbón |
| zapatilla | < zapato |

Nevertheless, double forms are found here also:

$$
\left.
\begin{array}{l}
nieblazo \\
nieblaza \\
(cf.\ neblina)
\end{array}
\right\} \quad < \ niebla
$$

$$
\left.
\begin{array}{l}
memorión \\
memoriona
\end{array}
\right\} \quad < \ memoria
$$

$$
\left.
\begin{array}{l}
tenducho \\
tenducha
\end{array}
\right\} \quad < \ tienda
$$

(iv) Endings of masculine words the basic form of which terminates in –a:

$$
\left.
\begin{array}{l}
carlistilla \\
\text{but}\ carlistón
\end{array}
\right\} \quad < \ carlista
$$

$$
\left.
\begin{array}{l}
comunistilla \\
\text{but}\ comunistón
\end{array}
\right\} \quad < \ comunista
$$

$$
\left.
\begin{array}{l}
curilla \\
curita \\
\text{but}\ curete \\
curazo \\
curángano
\end{array}
\right\} \quad < \ cura
$$

Cf. the exceptional

    *chuleta*          < *chulo*

Cf. the retention of –a and –s in adverbial expressions:

| | |
|---|---|
| *arribota* | < *arriba* |
| *cerquita* | < *cerca* |
| *lejotes* | < *lejos* |

Finally, it will be observed that, as a rule, suffix-formed nouns derive from nouns, suffix-formed adjectives from adjectives and suffix-formed nouns denoting types of person from nouns denoting, likewise, types of person. This is not, however, always the case, as can be seen in these few examples in *-ón*, and *-udo* :

| | |
|---|---|
| *acusón* | < *acusar* |
| *mirón* | < *mirar* |
| *respondón* | < *responder* |
| | |
| *barbudo* | < *barba* |
| *cabezudo* | < *cabeza* |
| *talludo* | < *tallo* |
| | |
| *hambrón* | < *hambre* |
| *hampón* | < *hampa* |

# Chapter I. Diminutives

## -ito(A) NOUN — MASCULINE

*(Diminutive — often affectionate, but also used ironically with augmentative-pejorative force)*

| | |
|---|---|
| †abogadito | = little lawyer, budding young lawyer. |
| agujerito | = little or small hole. |
| †alzacuellito | = small, nice little or lah-de-dah dog-collar. |
| †amiguito | = little friend; fine friend. |
| †animalito[1] | = small creature, (delightful) little creature. |
| †añito[2] | = little year; delightful year; terrible year. |
| asquito[3] | = really rotten business, utterly revolting affair. |
| †barnicito[4] | = slight varnish; slight (but pleasant) veneer (fig.). |
| besito | = small kiss, (delightful) little kiss. |
| bolsito[5] | = small handbag, (ducky) little handbag. |
| borreguito[6] | = small lamb, (delightful) little lamb, baby lamb, lambkin. |
| bracito | = small arm, (charming) little arm. |
| burrito | = small donkey, (nice) little donkey, neddy. |

[1] Cf. *animalillo* = (modest or wretched) little creature.

Cf. *animalejo*. See under *-ejo*.

Cf. *criaturita*. See under *-ita*.

[2] E.g. *el niño tiene dos añitos nada más* = the little chap is only a bare two years old; *¡qué añito!* = what a (terrible) year (this has been, that was)!

[3] E.g. *¡qué asquito!* = what a thoroughly revolting business!

[4] See under Examples from Literature.

Cf. the usually pejorative tone attached to *barnicillo*, e.g. *tiene un barnicillo de cultura, pero nada más* = he has a thin (mere) veneer of culture, but nothing more. See under *-illo*.

Cf. *culturilla*. See under *-illa*.

[5] Cf. *bolsillo* = pocket. See under *-illo*.

[6] Has a special use in the phrase *borreguitos blancos* = white horses (waves). Cf. *corderito*. See below.

| | |
|---|---|
| *caballito*[1] | = small horse, (cute) little horse, baby horse, pony. |
| *cabrito* | = little goat, kid. |
| *cafetito* | = small coffee or café, (delightful) little (cup of) coffee or (charming) little café. |
| †*calorcito*[2] | = slight sensation of warmth, (delightful) sensation of warmth. |
| *caminito*[3] | = small roadway, (delightful) little roadway or path. |
| *cartoncito* | = small piece of cardboard. |
| *cerdito*[4] | = little pig, piglet. |
| †*cielito*[5] | = delightful sky; little dear, darling. |
| *cisnecito*[6] | = little swan, cygnet. |
| *clarito* | = small clearing or glade, (delightful) little glade. |
| *clavito*[7] | = small nail, (cute) little nail; small clove. |
| *cochecito*[8] | = small car, (cute) little car; child's pram; wheel chair. |
| *conejito*[9] | = little rabbit, bunny. |
| *copito*[10] | = little flock, fleck or flake. |
| *corazoncito* | = tiny heart, dear little heart. |

[1] This word is used in several popular expressions. The *tiovivo*, i.e. merry-go-round, roundabout, is often called by children *los caballitos* (in Spanish America *las calesitas*). Another name for the *libélula* (= dragon-fly) is *caballito del diablo*, and for the *hipocampo* (= sea-horse) *caballito de mar*. (Cf. *conejillo de Indias* = *cobayo*. See under *-illo*.)

[2] Cf. *calorcillo* — same sense.

[3] Cf. *caminillo* = (modest or miserable) little roadway or path.
Cf. *carreterita, carreterilla*. See under *-ita, -illa*.

[4] Cf. *cochinillo* = sucking pig. See under *-illo*.
Cf. *lechón* — similar sense. See under *-ón*.

[5] Cf. *cielín* — used especially in the second or figurative sense. See under *-ín*.

[6] Cf. *polluelo de cisne* — same sense, but more technical.

[7] Cf. *tachuela* = tack, tin-tack.

[8] Cf. *cochecillo* = (modest or miserable) little car.
E.g. *estamos muy contentos con el cochecito* = we're very pleased with our (cute) little car; *nuestros vecinos se han agenciado un cochecillo de esos muy pequeñajos* = our neighbours have got themselves one of those miserable, really fiddling little cars.

[9] Cf. *conejillo* — similar sense.
Cf. *conejillo de Indias*. See under *-illo*.

[10] E.g. *copitos de nieve* = tiny snow flakes.

| | |
|---|---|
| *corderito*[1] | = little lamb, lambkin. |
| *corralito* | = (nice) little yard; child's play-pen. |
| *cuidadito*[2] | = great care. |
| *dedito*[3] | = small finger or toe, (charming) little finger or toe, "fingy-wingy", "toesy-woesy". |
| *dientecito*[4] | = small tooth, (cute) little tooth, "toothy-peg", "toosy-peg". |
| *dinerito*[5] | = "pretty penny". |
| †*durito*[6] | = jolly old five-peseta piece. |
| *enanito*[7] | = small dwarf, dear little dwarf. |
| *escotito*[8] | = attractive or delightful neckline. |
| *gatito*[9] | = small cat, (sweet) little cat, kitten. |
| *globito* | = small balloon, (attractive) little balloon. |
| *golpecito* | = light blow or knock, tap. |
| †*guantecito* | = small glove, (delightful) little glove. |
| *hombrecito*[10] | = small man, (pleasant) little man. |
| *hotelito* | = small hotel, (nice little hotel); small private villa. |
| "*jaibolito*" | = small "high-ball", (nice) little "high-ball". |
| *jerseycito* | = small pull-over, (cute) little jumper. |

---

[1] Cf. *corderillo* — similar sense.
   Cf. *corderuelo* — similar sense.
   Cf. *cordero lechal, lechazo* = sucking lamb.
   Cf. *cordero recental* = new-born lamb, sucking lamb.
   Cf. *ternasco* (Aragonese) = sucking lamb.
   Cf. *lechón* = sucking-pig. See *borreguito* and *cerdito,* above.
[2] E.g. *¡mucho cuidadito!* = just you take jolly good care!
[3] Cf. *dedillo* — similar sense. For *saber(se) al dedillo* see under *-illo*.
   Cf. *dedín* — similar sense.
[4] Cf. *dientecillo* = (miserable) little tooth.
[5] Cf. *dinerillo* — similar sense. See under *-illo*.
   Cf. *dinerete* — similar sense. See under *-ete*.
   Cf. *piquito* — similar sense.
[6] Cf. *durete* — similar sense. See under *-ete*.
[7] *Blancanieves y los siete enanitos* = Snow-white and the Seven Dwarfs.
   Cf. *enanillo* = (miserable or wretched) little dwarf.
[8] Cf. *escotazo.* See under *-azo*.
[9] Cf. *gatillo.* See under *-illo*.
   Cf. *michito* = pussy [*misito* (Andalusia)].
[10] Cf. *hombrecillo* = (insignificant) little man.

| | |
|---|---|
| *jovencito* | = young chap or fellow, youngster; fine, bright or smart young laddie. |
| *ladroncito*[1] | = small thief, (engaging) little thief. |
| *librito*[2] | = small book, (delightful) little book. |
| *momentito*[3] | = brief moment, just a moment. |
| *montoncito* | = small pile, (nice) little pile. |
| †*muchito* | = quite a lot, quite a tidy amount. |
| *negrito*[4] | = little negro child, piccaninny. |
| *niñito*[5] | = small child, (engaging) little boy, tiny tot. |
| *ojito*[6] | = small eye, (dear or sweet) little eye, "eygy-pygy" |
| *osito*[7] | = small bear, (delightful) little bear, baby bear; toy bear, teddy. |
| *pajarito*[8] | = small bird, (sweet) little bird, "dicky" bird. |
| *pañuelito* | = small handkerchief, (cute) little "hanky". |
| *papaíto* | = daddy, daddykins. |
| *pasito*[9] | = small or short step, (light or dainty) little step. |
| *patito* | = small duck, (charming) little duck, duckling. |
| *perrito*[10] | = small dog, (sweet) little dog, puppy. |
| *pichoncito*[11] | = (delightful) young pigeon. |

[1] Cf. *ladronzuelo*. See under *-uelo*.

[2] Cf. *librillo* = (modest or miserable) little book.

Cf. *librete*. See under *-ete*.

[3] Cf. *momentillo, momentín* — similar sense. See under *-illo, -ín*.

[4] It is curious to note that "piccaninny" derives from the Portuguese diminutive *pequenino*.

[5] Cf. *niñillo* — similar sense or slightly pejorative, e.g. *un niñillo harapiento* = a ragged little child or fellow.

[6] Cf. *ojillo, ojuelo* = (beady, cunning) little eye. See under *-illo, -uelo*.

[7] Cf. *osezno* = bear-cub (more technical).

[8] Cf. *pajarillo* — similar sense or slightly pejorative, e.g. *un pajarillo feo* = an ugly little bird.

[9] Cf. *pasillo* = passage, corridor. See under *-illo*.

[10] Cf. *perrillo* — similar sense or pejorative, e.g. *un perrillo sucio* = a dirty, miserable little dog.

Cf. *cachorro* = puppy (more technical).

Cf. *cachorrito* = (engaging) little puppy.

Cf. *cachorrillo* = (miserable) little pup.

[11] Much used as a term of endearment equivalent to such expressions as "lovey-dovey".

| | |
|---|---|
| *piececito* | = small or tiny foot, (dainty) little foot, "footsy-wootsy". |
| *piquito*[1] | = small beak or peak; tidy little sum. |
| *platito*[2] | = small plate, (sweet) little plate; (nice or fine) little dish. |
| *pollito*[3] | = small chicken, (cute) little chicken, chick; (dapper) young man. |
| *pucherito(s)*[4] | = attractive pout(ing). |
| *pueblecito*[5] | = small village, (charming) little village, hamlet. |
| *puertecito*[6] | = small port or harbour, (attractive) little port or harbour; (attractive) little mountain pass. |
| *ratito* | = short while. |
| *santito* | = small saint, (charming) little saint (e.g. statue); proper or regular little saint (fig.). |
| *señorito* | = young gentleman, young man of the privileged classes; lordling, young upper-class parasite; young man-about-town, young gad-about. |
| *solterito* | = young bachelor, dapper, eligible or nice young bachelor. |
| †*sueñecito*[7] | = short sleep, nice little sleep, nap. |
| †*tallecito*[8] | = small waist, nice slender waist, wasp waist. |
| *taquito(s)* | = nice little brick(s) (children's toy). |
| †*tenientito*[9] | = young lieutenant, dapper, dashing, sprightly or spruce young lieutenant; officious young lieutenant (iron.). |

---

[1] Cf. *dinerito*, above.
[2] Cf. *platillo* = saucer. See under *-illo*.
[3] Cf. *polluelo* = chick.
[4] *Hacer pucheritos* = to pout attractively.
[5] Cf. *pueblito* — form used mainly in Spanish America.
   Cf. *pueblecillo* = (miserable) little village. See under *-illo*.
[6] Cf. *puertito* — form used mainly in Spanish America.
   Cf. *puertecillo* = (modest) little harbour. See under *-illo*.
[7] Cf. *sueñecillo* — similar sense. See under *-illo*.
[8] Cf. *cinturita* — same sense. See under *-ita*.
[9] Cf. *oficialete* — similar sense. See under *-ete*.

| | |
|---|---|
| *tiempecito*[1] | = short time; nice, pleasant weather; foul weather (iron). |
| *titulito*[2] | = (nice) little title or degree. |
| *toquecito* | = small touch, light touch, (nice) gentle touch. |
| †*tortolito* | = (delightful) little turtle-dove; (charming) young love-bird (fig.). |
| *trajecito*[3] | = small suit, (nice) little suit. |
| *viajecito*[4] | = short journey, voyage or trip; (pleasant) little journey; terrible journey (iron.). |
| *zapatito*[5] | = small shoe, (charming) little shoe. |

## -ito EXAMPLES FROM LITERATURE
## (GROUP A)

— ¿Y qué le parece del rapaz . . .? ¿Verdad que no mete respeto?
— ¡Bah! . . . Ahora se estila ordenar mequetrefes . . . Y luego mucho de *alzacuellitos, guantecitos* . . ..

(PARDO BAZÁN, *Los Pazos de Ulloa*, p. 32)[6]

"And what do you think of the lad . . .? He doesn't inspire much respect, does he?"

"Bah . . .! It's the fashion nowadays to ordain whipper-snappers . . ..
And then plenty of lah-de-dah dog-collars, plenty of lah-de-dah [white] gloves. . . ."

---

[1] E.g. *¡qué tiempecito más agradable!* = what very pleasant weather!; *¡vaya tiempecito!* = some weather!, talk about weather!
Cf. *tiempazo* = glorious or foul weather. See under *-azo*.
Cf. *tiempito* — form used mainly in Spanish America.
Cf. *ratito* = short while. See above.
Cf. *temporadita* = short spell. See under *-ita*.

[2] Cf. *titulillo* = (modest or miserable) little title or degree.

[3] Cf. *trajecillo* = (modest or wretched) little suit.

[4] E.g. *fue un viajecito precioso* = it was a delightful (little) trip; *¡caramba con el viajecito!* = what a trip!, talk about a (shocking) journey!

[5] Cf. *zapatico, zapatín* — similar sense. See under *-ico, -ín*.

[6] For edition in this and all subsequent cases see list at end of book.

— ... me sé de memoria a muchos de nuestros *amiguitos*...
¿De dónde habrá sacado éste, y el otro y el de más allá los veinte
mil *duritos* que le ha costado la fiesta y los dos millones del piso...?
(CALVO-SOTELO, *La Muralla*, p. 90)

"... I know many of our fine friends only too well.... Where
can Tom, and Dick and Harry have got the tidy little sum of six-
hundred quid, which is what the [wedding] party cost, and the
twelve thousand to buy a flat...?"

— Ese indio salvaje, después de costarme doce mil francos y la
comida de los animales, ..... ¡Y no comen los *animalitos*![1] Y el
público no se divierte.... ¡Un buen negocio!
(BENAVENTE, *La Noche del Sábado*, p. 103)

"That uncivilized Indian, after costing me twelve thousand
francs and the animals' food, .... And you should just see the brutes[1]
eat! And the audience isn't entertained. ... A fine deal [this has
turned out to be]!"

¡Qué *añitos* de zozobras, revoluciones, batallas por el Poder,
levantamientos carlistas, conspiraciones, barricadas, pronunciamien-
tos, ... motines... confusión...!
(SAINZ DE ROBLES, *El Madrid de 1761 a 1861*, p. 142)

What frightful years of anxiety, revolution, battling for Power,
Carlist risings, plotting, barricades, military insurrection, ...
mutinying... disorder...!

... ese pasatiempo de gentes sin mucho que decir pero con un
amable *barnicito* de cultura, que se llama "el placer de la con-
versación".
(CELA, *Judíos, Moros y Cristianos*, p. 22)

... that pastime of people without a great deal to say but with
an agreeable even if only slight veneer of culture, that pastime
called "the pleasure of conversation".

---

[1] The *animalitos* in question are elephants.

43

Con una mano sostenía la pipa, . . . Le agradaba sentir el *calorcito* de la *cazoleta*★[1]. . ..

(POMBO ANGULO, *Hospital General*, p. 72)

In one hand he held his pipe,... He liked to feel the gentle warmth of the bowl . . .

. . . el primer día en que una sonrisa borró la grave y cómica seriedad de la diminuta cara . . . la madre pensó chochear de alegría.
— ¡Otra vez, otra vez! — exclamaba — ¡ Encanto, *cielito*, *cielito*, *monadita*★[1] mía, ríete, ríete!

(PARDO BAZÁN, *Los Pazos de Ulloa*, p. 263)

. . . the first day a smile wiped away the solemn and comic seriousness from the tiny face . . . the mother thought she was going to lose her wits with delight.
"Again, again!" — she cried — "My delight, my little darling, my little darling, my pretty little thing, laugh, laugh!"

— Y cuando un señorito se gasta cien *duretes*★ con una mujer, dicen que ha arruinado a la familia. Pues no quiero hablar de los que viven de gorra, como *muchitos* a quienes yo conozco. . ..

(PÉREZ GALDÓS, *La de Bringas*, p. 253)

"And when a young gentleman splashes out a jolly old twenty[2] quid on a woman, people say he's ruined the family. Well, I wouldn't like to talk about those who sponge for a living, like quite a few I know . . .."

— ¿Qué, *Rociíto*? ¿A la calle? . . . Llevo media hora dándole vueltas a la idea. Y, ¿qué quiere, *Medardito*? Estoy resuelto.

(PASO, *Los Pobrecitos*, p. 193)

---

[1] Here and throughout the book an asterisk (★) is used to draw the reader's attention to a suffixed form other than that under immediate consideration.

[2] A nineteenth-century equivalent. Then, *cinco duros* were worth one pound sterling.

"What's this, Rocío, my dear? Going out? . . . I've been turning the idea over in my mind for the last half hour. And, dash it all, my dear Medardo, my mind's made up."

— . . . Esto de los *sueñecitos* no me hace tilín. Para mí, más que modorra, son verdaderos síncopes.

(PARDO BAZÁN, *Los Pazos de Ulloa*, p. 243)

" . . . I'm not at all happy about this business of the jolly old naps. In my view they are regular fainting fits rather than drowsiness."

— . . . Yo no me aprieto tanto. Eso se deja para las *gordonas*★ que quieren ponerse un *tallecito* de sílfide. . ..

(PÉREZ GALDÓS, *La de Bringas*, p. 258)

" . . . I don't do myself up as tight as that. That's for hefty great creatures who want to get the slender waist of a sylph . . .."

Para aquellas muchachas, todo lo que no fuera esperar en el balcón al *tenientito* o al *abogadito* socio del Ateneo, tomaba el carácter de una extravagancia.

(BAROJA, *La Dama Errante*, p. 31)

For those young women everything but waiting on the balcony for a dapper young lieutenant or a budding young lawyer who was a member of the Atheneum Club, took on the character of something that was utterly absurd.

CARLOS. — Ha sonado un beso . . ..
DON PABLO. — (Cordial) ¡Qué falta de formalidad! ¿Quiénes son los *tortolitos* que se arrullan aquí? ¡Tendré que amonestarlos!

(BUERO VALLEJO, *En la Ardiente Oscuridad*, p. 46)

CARLOS. — I heard a kiss . . ..
DON PABLO. — (Genially) What a lapse from proper behaviour! Who are our fine young love-birds billing and cooing here? I shall have to upbraid them!

*(Changed or specialized sense[1])*

| | |
|---|---|
| *carrito* | = trolley (e.g. for carrying food to table). |
| (< carro | = cart, waggon) |
| *eduardito[2]* | = teddy-boy. |
| (< Eduardo | = Edward) |
| †*gallito[3]* | = cock-of-the-walk, coxcomb. |
| (< gallo | = cock) |
| *hotelito[4]* | = (small) detached private residence. |
| (< hotel | = hotel) |
| *llanito* | = Gibraltarian, native of Gibraltar (popular expression). |
| (< llano | = flat; plain) |
| *manguito[5]* | = muff; tourniquet. |
| (< manga | = sleeve) |
| *mantelito* | = doyley. |
| (< mantel | = table-cloth) |
| *periquito[6]* | = budgerigar, budgie, love-bird. |
| (< perico | = parakeet) |
| †*pinito(s)[7]* | = first step(s), first attempt(s) at walking; first attempt(s) (at anything.) |
| (< pino | = standing up; steep) |

[1] Other words used with both basic and changed or specialized meanings are given in section A.

[2] Term specially coined to render the English and not in very common use.

[3] Not dissimilar in meaning is *chulito*.

[4] Although *hotel* also is sometimes used with the meaning "detached private residence", this sense tends to attach particularly to the diminutive form.

[5] Very little used in the second sense, which is generally rendered by *torniquete*.

[6] *Periquito entre ellas* = ladies' man. Love-birds (fig.) = *tórtolos*.

[7] *Hacer pinitos* = to toddle.

Así domeñó Ignacio a Enrique, el *gallito* de la calle, un *mandón*★,
un verdadero *mandón*★, a quien nadie de su igual había podido....
(UNAMUNO, *Paz en la Guerra*, p. 22)

In this way Ignacio mastered Enrique, the cock-of-the-walk in
that street, a domineering type, a properly domineering type,
whom no one of his age and build had bettered.....

... un *mamón*★ en brazos liado en trapos... el *pillín*★ de cinco
años, hablador y travieso, ... los que hacen sus primeros *pinitos*...
los *pilletes*★ que enredan en las calles... los *talluditos*★ que usan
ya bastón y ganan premios en los colegios....
(PÉREZ GALDÓS, *Fortunata y Jacinta*, I, p. 168)

... a babe in arms wrapped in rags... the talkative, mischievous
little rogue of five years old... the children making their first
attempts at walking... the young rascals who get up to tricks
in the streets... the budding young gentlemen who have got to
the stage of carrying a walking-stick and winning prizes at school....


*-ito (C) ADJECTIVE*
*(And past participle used adjectivally)*

†acabadito[1]  = nice and finished; just freshly or newly finished.
  ancianito[2]  = quite old, pretty old, getting on rather in years.
  aplicadito[3]  = really studious, nice and diligent.


[1] E.g. *ya está acabadito el trabajo* = now (at last) the work's nice and finished;
*un reloj acabadito de robar* = a just freshly stolen watch; *un reloj acabadito de
birlar* = a just freshly pinched watch. (These last two are phrases which might
well be spoken by a pick-pocket, for example.)
[2] E.g. *un señor ancianito* = a pretty elderly (little) gentleman.
[3] E.g. *¡qué niño más aplicadito!* = what a very studious little chap!, what a
delightfully studious little "manny"!

| | |
|---|---|
| *aprendidito*[1] | = carefully learned up. |
| *arregladito*[2] | = nicely fixed up; nice and neat and tidy. |
| *arrimadito*[3] | = very close, nice and close or snug. |
| †*bonito*[4] | = pretty, delightful, fine. |
| *calentito*[5] | = nice and warm, lovely and warm, pleasantly hot; a bit sexy, nice and sexy. |
| †*calladito*[6] | = nice and quiet, delightfully quiet. |
| *cansadito*[7] | = a bit tired, rather tired; very tired. |
| †*coladito* | = nicely slipped in or through; properly or quite gone (on someone). |
| *coloradito* | = a bit red, rather red; very red; nice and ruddy, delightfully red or ruddy. |
| *completito*[8] | = quite complete or full, very complete or full; nice and complete or full. |
| *crecidito*[9] | = quite tall, etc. |
| *cumplidito*[10] | = very courteous, delightfully polite; fully (of age). |
| *delgadito* | = rather thin or slender; nice and thin or slender. |
| *despejadito*[11] | = very clear, nice and clear. |
| †*dobladito* | = carefully or nicely folded. |
| *dormidito*[12] | = fast asleep, nicely asleep. |

[1] E.g. *tiene la lección bien aprendidita* = he's got the lesson really quite off pat, he's got the lesson really well mugged up.

[2] Cf. *ordenadito*, below.

[3] See *pegadito*, below.

[4] *Bonito* (dimin. of *bueno*) is widely used with the ironic sense of "fine", e.g. *¡bonita manera de contestarme!* = a fine way to answer me! Cf. such expressions as: *¡valiente manera de hablar!*, *¡vaya una manera de hablar!* = a fine way to talk!; *¡valiente sinvergüenza!*, *¡vaya un sinvergüenza!* = a fine rogue or specimen!

[5] Cf. *calentón, calentorro, calentucho*. See under *-ón, -orro, -ucho*.

[6] E.g. *¡a ver si te estás quieto y calladito!* = let's see if you don't fidget and keep nice and quiet!

[7] E.g. *el pobre está muy cansadito* = the poor boy (man) is really very tired.

[8] E.g. *tiene una colección bastante completita* = he has a really pretty complete collection.

[9] See *mayorcito, talludito*, below.

[10] E.g. *tiene los cincuenta años bien cumpliditos* = he's certainly a (jolly) good fifty, he's certainly (very) well over the fifty mark.

[11] E.g. *¡qué cielo tan despejadito!* = what a delightfully clear sky!

[12] E.g. *está completamente dormidito, angelito* = he's quite fast (sound) asleep, dear little chap.

48

| | | |
|---|---|---|
| *durito*[1] | = | good and hard, nice and firm. |
| *echadito*[2] | = | lying down nicely. |
| *empeñadito*[3] | = | really determined, properly set (on something); nicely pawned. |
| *enfermito*[4] | = | a little ill, rather ill, poorly. |
| *facilito*[5] | = | pretty easy, nice and easy. |
| *finito*[6] | = | quite refined, very refined; nice and thin. |
| †*formalito* | = | quite well-behaved, very well-behaved; pretty reliable. |
| *fresquito*[7] | = | quite cool or fresh, nice and cool or fresh, pleasantly cool or fresh. |
| †*fritito*[8] | = | nicely fried, nice and crispy; quite asleep. |
| *gordito* | = | quite fat, nice and plump, pleasantly chubby. |
| *guapito*[9] | = | quite handsome, handsomish; pretty handsome. |
| †*guardadito* | = | carefully or neatly put away. |
| *honradito*[10] | = | quite honest; pretty honest, very honest. |

[1] E.g. *unos tomates duritos* = some nice firm tomatoes.

[2] E.g. *¡echadito!* (to a dog) = lie down like a good boy, lie down, there's a good chap!

[3] E.g. *tú, empeñadita, ¿eh?* = you're properly set on it (on having your way), aren't you? (cf. *te has propuesto salirte con la tuya, ¿verdad?* = you're determined to have your own way, aren't you?).

[4] See *malito*, below.

   Cf. *enfermucho, malucho*. See under *-ucho*.

[5] Cf. *facilón*. See under *-ón*.

   Cf. *dificilillo*. See under *-illo*.

Note the use of *-ito* with *fácil* (i.e. with a word of favourable implications) as compared with the use of *-illo* in the case of *difícil* (i.e. in the case of a word of unfavourable implications). *Dificilito*, if not non-existent, is most certainly rare.

[6] E.g. *es una chica bastante finita* = she's a really quite refined girl, she's a really very refined girl; *unas lonchas finitas de fiambre* = some nice thin slices of cold meat.

   Cf. *finillo, finucho*. See under *-ucho*.

[7] Cf. *fresquillo, fresquete, frescazo*. See under *-illo*.

[8] Note the phrase *quedarse frito* = to fall asleep, doze off.

[9] Cf. *guapillo*. See under *-illo*.

This is a case in which there is practically no difference between *-ito* and *-illo*.

[10] Cf. *honradote*. See under *-ote*.

| | | |
|---|---|---|
| *igualito*[1] | = | just the same, exactly like, positively identical. |
| †*malito*[2] | = | a little ill, rather ill, poorly. |
| †*mayorcito*[3] | = | quite grown-up, pretty grown-up; getting on rather (in years); pretty tall. |
| *mejorcito*[4] | = | quite a bit better, a good deal better. |
| †*mimadito*[5] | = | quite spoiled, rather spoiled; pretty spoiled. |
| *morenito*[6] | = | nice and dark, pleasantly dark; small and dark. |
| *nuevecito*[7] | = | nice and new, beautifully new, brand spanking new. |
| †*ordenadito*[8] | = | nice and neat, delightfully tidy. |
| *pasadito*[9] | = | a little passed; really well done, nicely browned (of meat). |
| *pegadito*[10] | = | nicely stuck; very close, nice and close. |
| *peladito*[11] | = | a little or rather bare; quite or pretty close-cropped. |

[1] E.g. *¡son igualitos, igualitos!* = they're just absolutely alike, they're just the spitting image of each other.

[2] Cf. *malillo, malejo.* See under *-illo, -ejo.*

*Malito* is very rarely used with any other meaning than that of *enfermito.* (See, however, quotation from Baroja in Examples section.) See *enfermito,* above.

[3] E.g. *Juanito ya es mayorcito* = Johnny's quite grown-up now; *el señor Alvarez ya es mayorcito* = Señor Alvarez is getting on quite a bit now; *¡qué mayorcito está su hijo!* = how very tall your son has grown! The following use is also worthy of note: *ya vas siendo mayorcito para estos juegos* = you're getting a pretty big boy now for these games. Cf. *mayorzote.* See under *-ote.*

Cf. *crecidito, talludito.* See *talludito,* below.

[4] E.g. *ya está mejorcita, ¡gracias a Dios!* = she's quite a bit better now, thank Heaven! (adverbial use).

*Mejorcito* is also much used as a neuter noun, e.g. *esto es de lo mejorcito que ha escrito* = this is some of the very best stuff he's written. Similarly, *peorcito.*

[5] Cf. *mimadete* — similar sense.

[6] Cf. *morenazo, morenón, morenote.* See under *-ote.*

[7] E.g. *un duro nuevecito* = a bright new five-peseta piece.

[8] Cf. *arregladito,* above.

[9] E.g. *está muy pasadito de moda* = it's really quite out of fashion or out of date; *me gusta la carne bien pasadita* = I like my meat really nice and well done.

[10] Cf. *arrimadito,* above.

[11] E.g. *¡qué peladito estás!* = they've certainly given you a pretty close crop!, you look like a close-shorn lamb!

Cf. *peladete* — similar sense.

| | | |
|---|---|---|
| *pesadito*[1] | = | a little or rather heavy or tedious; quite or pretty tiresome. |
| *pobrecito*[2] | = | poor little (chap, fellow, etc.). |
| *poquito*[3] | = | just a little, quite a little, very little. |
| *queridito* | = | darling, dearest. |
| †*quietecito* | = | nice and still, lovely and still. |
| *rapidito* | = | nice and quick, delightfully quick; double quick. |
| *reservadito*[4] | = | carefully or nicely reserved. |
| *seguidito*[5] | = | following right on, right together. |
| *sencillito* | = | nice and simple or plain, delightfully straightforward or unassuming. |
| *sentadito*[6] | = | properly seated, sitting delicately or daintily. |
| †*solito* | = | quite alone, all by oneself, all on one's own. |
| *suavecito* | = | nice and soft or gentle, delightfully soft or gentle. |
| *sueltecito*[7] | = | nice and loose. |
| *talludito*[8] | = | quite or pretty tall, getting tallish; quite or pretty grown-up; getting a wee bit long in the tooth. |

[1] E.g. *¡no seas pesadito!* (e.g. to a child or dog) = don't be tiresome, there's a good (little) chap or fellow.
Cf. *pesadón, pesadote.* See under *-ote.*

[2] *pobrecito* is used very widely as a substantive, e.g. *el pobrecito está muy agotadito* = the poor little fellow is really quite played out.
Cf. *pobrecillo* — very similar sense. See under *-illo.*
Cf. *guapito, guapillo.*

[3] E.g. *muy poquito azúcar, por favor* = just a very little sugar, please.
Cf. *poquillo* — similar sense.

[4] E.g. *ya tengo las entradas reservaditas* = now I've got the tickets nicely reserved.

[5] E.g. *tres veces seguiditas* = three times, one right after the other, three times bang on top of one another; *¡en seguida, pero en seguidita, señor!* = right away, positively just right away, sir!

[6] E.g. *¡tú ahí, sentadito!* = you just sit there quietly or properly!; *la niña estaba sentadita en el suelo* = the little girl was sitting daintily on the floor.

[7] E.g. *el arroz ha salido sueltecito* = the rice has turned out nice and loose (i.e. the grains loose from one another). Cf. *este arroz está blanducho* = this rice is soggy (i.e. the grains stuck together). See *blanducho,* under *-ucho.*
Cf. *sueltecillo.* See under *-illo.*

[8] Cf. *crecidito* — similar sense. See above.
See also *mayorcito,* above.

| †*tamañito* | = quite small, made to look very small. |
| †*tiernecito* | = nice and tender, quite tender; nice and young, very young; sweetly affectionate. |
| †*todito* | = quite all or every, absolutely all or every. |
| *traducidito*[1] | = carefully or nicely translated. |

## -*ito EXAMPLES FROM LITERATURE*
## (GROUP C)

— Aquel día . . . , ¿sabes?, *acabadita* de marcharte tú, estuvo en casa de la Paca Juanito Santa Cruz.

(Pérez Galdós, *Fortunata y Jacinta*, II, p. 228)

"That day . . . , you know, when you had only just left, Johnny Santa Cruz paid a visit to the house of that Francisca woman."

— El pobre hombre ha salido de la cárcel, . . . y se va a dedicar a hacer moneda falsa.
— ¡Un *bonito* oficio!

(Baroja, *La Ciudad de la Niebla*, p. 224)

". . . The poor fellow has [just] come out of jail, . . . and he's going to take up forgery."
"A fine trade!"

El niño, que estaba *calladito* en el comedor, empezó a llorar también con grandes *lagrimones*★.

(Laforet, *Nada*, p. 207)

The little boy, who had been as quiet as a mouse in the dining-room, also began to cry with great big [welling] tears.

El muchacho se enamoró de la "Mañitas" como un loco o como un tonto. Estaba "*colaíto, colaíto*", según el dictamen de la señorita no sé cuántas de la derecha.

(Pérez Lugín, *La Casa de la Troya*, p. 14)

The chap fell madly or idiotically in love with "Mañitas". In the judgment of one young lady, who was one or other of the girls

---

[1] E.g. *una frase bien traducidita* = a sentence all nice and translated.

on the right wing of the chorus, he was "properly gone on her, properly gone on her".

— ... Han desaparecido mis ahorros. Ciento sesenta y cinco mil pesetas en billetes grandes y chicos. Todos *dobladitos* por mí misma .... En una cartera negra, grande, los tenía *guardaditos* ....

(Paso, Los pobrecitos, p. 247)

"... My savings have disappeared. A thousand pounds in large and small notes. All nicely folded by myself .... I had them carefully stored away in a large, black briefcase ...."

— A ver si eres *formalito* y no das jamás ningún disgusto serio a tu madre ....

(Zunzunegui, ¡Ay, Estos Hijos!, p. 8)

"Let's see if you are a really good little boy and you never give your mother any cause for serious anxiety ...."

Don Pablo. — Me quedé *fritito*, hijo, *fritito*. Muchas gracias.
Lorencito. — ¿Astá osté mejir, Dinablo?[1]
Don Pablo. — (A Medardo) ¿Qué dice?
Medardo. — Que si está usted mejor.
Don Pablo. — ¡Ah, sí, *guapito*\*! Mucho mejor. Se conoce que en la cama he entrado en reacción ....

(Paso, Los Pobrecitos, p. 213)

Don Pablo. — I dozed right off, my boy, dozed right off. Thank you very much.
Lorencito. — Are y' berrer, Dinablo?[1]
Don Pablo. — (To Medardo) What's he say?
Medardo. — He's asking if you're better.
Don Pablo. — Oh, yes, laddie! Much better. Evidently in bed my circulation has got going.

— ¿No te dormirás mañana, como la última vez?
— No, doctor. Tendrá el desayuno a su hora. Estaba muy *malito*, doctor.

(Pombo Angulo, Hospital General, p. 22)

[1] *Sic.* Defective speaker.

"You won't oversleep tomorrow, like on the last occasion?"
"No, doctor. You'll get your breakfast at the proper time. I was very poorly, doctor."

[Cf. this use of *malito*:

> — Parece mentira que por unos mulatos
> estemos pasando tan *malitos* ratos;
> a Cuba se llevan la flor de la España,
> y aquí no se queda más que la morralla.
> (Words of song quoted by Baroja in
> *El Arbol de la Ciencia*, p. 542)

It's unbelievable that because of a few mulattoes we should be having such a jolly thin time of it; the flower of Spanish manhood is being carried off to Cuba, and all that's left here is the dregs.]

...pero a los demás chicos..., algunos ya *mayorcitos*, no les agradó la presencia del sacerdote, y terminaron llamando a quienes acompañaba el cura: "los biberonarios".
(ZUNZUNEGUI, *¡Ay, Estos Hijos!*, p. 24)

...but the rest of the boys..., some of them now regular little young men, didn't care for the priest's presence, and they ended up by calling those who were accompanied by him "the baby-bottle brigade".

[Another example, interesting for its translation:

Tampoco lo de Salvadora es un retrato, sino un apunte, o, mejor, una serie de apuntes: de niña, de *mayorcita*, de mujer hecha y derecha.
(TORRENTE BALLESTER, in *Baroja y su mundo*, p. 133)

Neither does what the author tells of us of Salvadora constitute a portrait, but a sketch, or rather, a series of sketches: (Salvadora) as a little girl, (then) when she is in her teens, (and) as a fully-fledged woman.]

— ...esas cosas las hace usted por lo muy *mimadito* que está. Tía que le cuida, mujer guapa que le mima también.....
(PÉREZ GALDÓS, *Fortunata y Jaciuta*, IV, p. 27)

54

"... you do those things because you are just so thoroughly spoiled. An aunt to look after you, a beautiful wife to spoil you as well...."

— Hija, siempre llevas de todo. Cuidado que eres *ordenadita*, hay que ver.... Desde luego vas a hacer una esposa modelo.... Bueno; pues voy a ver si me arreglo, y me pongo un *poquito*★ decente. En lo que cabe, ¿eh?[1] Hasta *lueguito*.★

(MIHURA, *Maribel y la Extraña Familia*, p. 146)

"Darling, you always have everything that's needed with you. You really are a little marvel of orderliness, it's remarkable.... You're certainly going to make a model wife.... Well, I'm going to see about tidying myself up, then, and making myself a wee bit respectable. As far as that's possible, of course![1] See you in just a while."

— ¿No te da miedo andar tan *solita* por las calles? ¿Y si viene el *lobito*★ y te come?

(LAFORET, *Nada*, p. 121)

"Aren't you frightened to go about the streets so all by yourself? Supposing the big, bad wolf comes along and eats you up...?"

El idilio se acentuaba cada día, hasta el punto de que la madre de *Barbarita*★... decía a ésta: Pero, hija, vais a dejar *tamañitos* a los Amantes de Teruel.

(PÉREZ GALDÓS, *Fortunata y Jacinta*, I, p. 42)

Their love became more idyllic every day, reaching such extremes that young Barbara's mother... would say to her: "But, darling, you're going to put the 'Lovers of Teruel' quite in the shade."

— ... Esta sí que desde muy *tiernecita* decía lo que había de ser: ¡siempre tan *quietecita*! ... Cuando las demás estaban en el recreo, ella iba a la capilla *solita*....

(PALACIO VALDÉS, *La Hermana San Sulpicio*, p. 63)

"... But *this* was one who it was obvious from her very earliest years what she was going to be: always so nice and tranquil!

---

[1] The speaker is a prostitute.

... When the other girls were at play, she would go all by herself
to the chapel ...."

— ... en fin, habías de declarar todos, *toditos* los síntomas de
esa maldita enfermedad ....

(PÉREZ GALDÓS, *Fortunata y Jacinta*, IV, p. 47)

". . . in short, you would have to confess every, absolutely every
symptom of the accursed malady ...."

## *-ito*, *-ita* (D) ADVERB, CONJUNCTION

| | |
|---|---|
| *bajito* | = very softly, very quietly. |
| *cerquita* | = nice and near, very near, hard by. |
| †*(en) cuantito* | = just as soon as. |
| *despacito* | = very slowly, very gently, nice and slowly or gently, easy does it. |
| †*enfrentito* | = right opposite. |
| *(a) gustito* | = really comfortable, really at home. |
| *(hasta)lueguito* | = (see you) in just a while, (see you) very soon. |
| *(de) prisita* | = in a great hurry, double-quick. |
| †*prontito* | = very soon; very early; double-quick. |

## *-ito* EXAMPLES FROM LITERATURE
## (GROUP D)

En *cuantito* no sea pecado mortal los tendrás [besos] ... hasta
que te hartes.

(VALERA, *Juanita la Larga*, p. 267)

"Just as soon as it isn't a mortal sin you'll have them [kisses] ...
to your heart's delight."

— ... tuerza a la derecha, suba otra *escalerilla*,★ y allí *enfrentito*
tiene usted su despacho.

(PALACIO VALDÉS, *La Hermana San Sulpicio*, p. 321)

". . . turn [to the] right, go up another short flight of stairs, and there right opposite you'll see his office."

— ¡Esto ya no se puede sufrir! — vociferó el brigadier, montando en cólera . . . — Diga usted *prontito* lo que sabe, pues de otro modo vamos a estar mal . . . .

(PALACIO VALDÉS, *Marta y María*, p. 161 )

"This can be endured no further!" bellowed the brigadier-general, becoming furious . . . . "Say what you know double-quick, because otherwise we are going to fall out . . . ."

## -ita (A) NOUN — FEMININE

*(Diminutive — frequently with undertones of affection or irony)*

| | |
|---|---|
| *agüita* | = (nice or delightful) little drop of water. |
| *alfombrita*[1] | = small carpet, (charming) little carpet. |
| *boquita*[2] | = small mouth, (sweet) little mouth. |
| *bolsita*[3] | = small bag, (cute) little bag. |
| *braguita(s)* | = panty, panties. |
| *callecita*[4] | = small street, (delightful) little street. |
| *camita*[5] | = small bed, (delightful) little bed; jolly old bed. |
| *canita*[6] | = small white hair; jolly old white hair. |
| *carita*[7] | = small face, (sweet) little face. |
| *carreterita*[8] | = small road, (charming) little road. |
| *casita*[9] | = small house, (delightful) little house; cottage. |

[1] Cf. *alfombrilla*. See under -*illa*.
[2] Cf. *boquilla*. See under -*illa*.
[3] Cf. *bolsito, bolsillo*, etc. See under -*illo*.
[4] Cf. *calleja, callejuela*, etc. See under -*eja*.
[5] E.g. *hora de irse a la camita* = time to go to jolly old bed, time for jolly old bed.
Cf. *camilla*. See under -*illa*.
[6] *Echar una canita al aire* = to have a fling, go on a spree.
[7] E.g. *¡qué carita más diminuta!* = what a tiny, (sweet) little face!
[8] Cf. *carreterilla*. See under -*illa*.
Cf. *caminito*. See under -*ito*.
Cf. *caminillo*. See under -*illo*.
[9] Cf. *casilla*. See under -*illa*.
*Casita de campo* is the nearest one can approximate in Spanish to the English "country cottage". Cf. *casucha, choza* = hovel.

| | |
|---|---|
| *cigalita*[1] | = small crayfish, (nice) little crayfish. |
| *copita*[2] | = small wine-glass or glass of wine, (nice) little wine-glass or glass of wine. |
| *cosita*[3] | = small thing, (nice) little thing. |
| *criaturita*[4] | = small child or baby-in-arms, (delightful) little infant. |
| *cucharita*[5] | = small spoon, (delightful) little spoon. |
| *culpita* | = small amount of blame; jolly old blame or fault. |
| *cunita*[6] | = small cradle or cot, (delightful) little cradle or cot. |
| *escamita*[7] | = small flake or scale, (pretty) little flake or scale. |
| *estrellita* | = small star, (delightful) little star. |
| *faldita*[8] | = small skirt, (charming) little skirt. |
| *finquita* | = (nice) little estate or piece of property. |
| *florecita*[9] | = small flower, (charming) little flower. |
| *frasecita*[10] | = short sentence or phrase, (delightful) little sentence or phrase; quite a sentence or phrase (iron.). |

[1] Cf. *cigalilla* = (fiddling) little crayfish.

Cf. *gambita* = (delightful) little prawn.

Cf. *langostino* = Dublin Bay prawn, giant or king prawn.

[2] Widely used in the sense of "(little) drink", e.g. *¿vamos a tomar una copita?* = shall we go and have a (little) drink? *Copa* itself is used in just the same way, and in expressions such as that quoted there is very little difference between the basic word and its diminutive form. This applies also when the words are used to mean "glass of brandy" or "liqueur", as in *café y copita* (*copa*).

[3] A word very popular with shop assistants as a courtesy expression, e.g. *¿alguna cosita más, señora?* = (is there) any other little thing (you require), Madam?, (is there) anything else at all, Madam?

Cf. *cosilla* = (modest or miserable) little thing or object.

[4] For "little creature" see *animalito*, under *-ito*.

[5] Cf. *cucharilla*. See under *-illa*.

[6] Cf. *cunilla* = (modest) little cradle or cot.

[7] Cf. *escamilla* = (nasty) little flake or scale.

[8] Often used to refer to the Scottish kilt, e.g. *un escocés con su faldita* = a Scotsman with his jolly old kilt.

[9] Cf. *florecilla* = (modest or poor) little flower.

Cf. *florezucha* = rotten old flower, wretched flower. See under *-ucha*.

[10] Cf. *frasecilla* = (modest or despicable) little sentence or phrase.

Cf. *frasezucha* = miserable sentence. See under *-ucha*.

| | |
|---|---|
| *gambita*[1] | = small prawn, (nice) little prawn. |
| *hormiguita* | = small ant, (sweet) little ant; busy little bee (fig.). |
| †*lengüecita* | = small tongue, (cute) little tongue; terrible tongue (iron.). |
| *mamaíta* | = mummy, darling "mumsie". |
| *manita*[2] | = small hand, (delightful) little hand. |
| *mesita*[3] | = small table, (delightful) little table. |
| †*nochecita* | = short night; delightful night; terrible night (iron.). |
| †*nubecita*[4] | = delightful (little) cloud. |
| *palmadita* | = gentle pat or slap, little clap. |
| †*palomita*[5] | = (charming) little dove. |
| *patita*[6] | = small foot or leg (usually of animals and insects), (sweet) little foot or leg. |
| *perrita*[7] | = small bitch, (delightful) little dog, puppy. |
| †*personita* | = (nice) little person; fine person (iron.). |
| *petaquita* | = small tobacco-pouch, (charming) little tobacco pouch. |
| *princesita* | = small princess, (sweet) little princess. |
| *siestecita* | = short nap, nice little nap, jolly old nap. |
| *sirenita* | = little mermaid, (delightful) little mermaid. |
| *solterita* | = young unmarried woman, (sprightly) young spinster. |
| †*suertecita* | = (nice) bit of luck; fine or terrible luck (iron.). |
| *tacita*[8] | = small cup, (delightful) little cup. |

[1] Cf. *gambilla* = (fiddling) little prawn.

[2] Note special use in expressions such as *José "el manitas"* = light-fingered Joseph. For *manitas de cerdo, manitas de cordero* see section B. The form *manecita* is also common. Cf. *manilla, manecilla*. See under *-illa. hacer manitas* = to spoon.

[3] Cf. *mesilla*. See under *-illa*.

[4] Cf. *nubecica, nubecilla* — similar sense. See under *-ica, -illa*. See Examples from Literature.

[5] For *palomitas* see section B.

[6] Note the colour given by the diminutive in such phrases as: *ha metido la patita* = he's rather put his foot in it, he's put his jolly old foot in it; *le puso de patitas en la calle* = he gave him his jolly old marching orders, he jolly well sent him packing.

[7] Cf. *perrilla* = (miserable) little dog. Cf. *perrito, perrillo*. See under *-ito, -illo*.

[8] The city of Cadiz is sometimes called *La Tacita de Plata* because of the brilliant silvery sheen from its sun-bathed, cup-shaped bay.

| | | |
|---|---|---|
| †*tardecita* | = | (nice) little afternoon or evening; fine or terrible afternoon or evening (iron.). |
| *tijeritas* | = | small pair of scissors, (charming) little pair of scissors. |
| *ventanita*[1] | = | small window, (cute) little window. |
| †*viejecita*[2] | = | small old woman, (sweet) little old woman. |
| *vueltecita*[3] | = | short stroll, spin or run, (delightful) little stroll, spin or run. |

## -ita EXAMPLES FROM LITERATURE: (GROUP A)

— . . . Me najo de allí, güelvo a mi *Españita*,[1] [y] entro en Madriz mu callaíto, tan fresco . . . .[5]

(PÉREZ GALDÓS, *Fortunata y Jacinta*, I, p. 284)

". . . I do a scarper from there, I comes back to dear old Spain,[4] [and] I get into Madrid proper nice an' quiet, as cool as yer please . . . ."[5]

Pero la pillería había roto ya en espantoso e infamante vocerío. ¡Qué *lengüecitas*!

(BLASCO IBÁÑEZ, *Flor de Mayo*, p. 194)

But by now the crowd of urchins had broken into a fearful and abusive clamour. What a really foul-mouthed mob!

— Una *nochecita* me escurrí, y del tirón me jui[6] a Barcelona, donde la carpanta[7] fue tan grande, maestro, que por poco doy las boqueás.[6]

(PÉREZ GALDÓS, *Fortunata y Jacinta*, I, p. 282)

[1] Cf. *ventanilla*. See under -illa.
[2] Cf. *viejecilla* = (miserable) little old woman.
[3] Cf. *paseíto* — similar sense.
[4] Cf. such English expressions as "dear old Blighty"
[5] Needless to say, the speaker is illiterate.
[6] *Sic.* The speaker is illiterate.
[7] See *hambraza*, under -aza.

"One fine night I slipped away, and at one go I made it to Barcelona, where the starvation was so bad,[1] guv'nor, I very nearly took me last gasp."

Por poniente cruzan, lentas, alargadas como *culebrillas*,*[2] unas *nubecitas* rojas, de bordes precisos, bien dibujados.

(CELA, *Viaje a la Alcarria*, p. 87)

Over to the west one or two sharp-edged, clearly defined, (delightful) little red clouds are sailing slowly along, stretched out like small snakes.

[Cf. in the following passage, by the same author, the use, with almost identical sense, of *nubecicas*:

En el cielo, unas *nubecicas* largas y estiradas, unas *nubecicas* blancas... saludaron al vagabundo al punto de entrar en Peñafiel.

(*Judíos, Moros y Cristianos*, p. 79)

In the sky a few long, extended, (sweet) little clouds, (sweet) little white clouds... greeted the tramp as he entered Peñafiel.

In yet another passage from Cela note the subtle, although in this instance certainly very slight difference, in the *-illa* form:

... el viajero... se queda mirando para unas *nubecillas*, gráciles como *palomitas* ...

(*Viaje a la Alcarria*, p. 95)

... the traveller... stands looking towards a few (modest) little clouds, that are as graceful as (pretty) young doves...]

DON J. — ¡Ah sí! Pablo Lobo. Mala *personita* es el tal. *Socarroncito*, *marrullerito*, *ladroncito*. ...

(ALVAREZ QUINTERO, *Puebla de las Mujeres*, p. 15)

DON J. — Oh, yes! Pablo Lobo. He's rather a bad lot, that worthy. A bit of a sly one, a bit of a wheedler and a bit of a thief....

---

[1] Another possible translation, although a free one, would be "where grub was so short".

[2] Note the use here of *-illa*, in tone with the fundamentally pejorative nature of the word *culebra*.

Don J. — [Al mirar una lista de la Lotería] ¡Vaya! Ni un trece mil quinientos siquiera. ¡También es *suertecita* la mía! No salgo de pobre . . ..

(ALVAREZ QUINTERO, *Puebla de las Mujeres*, p. 12)

Don J. — [Looking at a list of lottery results] Just look at that! Not even one thirteen thousand five hundred. I certainly have all the luck! I can't get away from poverty . . ..

— A ti lo que debe interesarte es seguir matando toros . . . ¡Buena *tardecita* se prepara! Me han dicho que el ganado . . .

(BLASCO IBÁÑEZ, *Sangre y Arena*, p. 18)

"What you ought to be concerned with is going on killing bulls . . . There's quite some afternoon ahead! I've been told that the animals . . ."

La abuela no se trataba con nadie. Sólo una antigua criada . . . una vieja *gruñona*★ y de mal humor . . . aparecía por allí . . .. Sentada al lado de la estufa, parecía la abuela Rosa una *viejecita* de cuento; muy *chiquita*★, *arrugadita*★ como una pasa, encogida . . ..

(BAROJA, *La Dama Errante*, p. 21)

The grandmother had nothing to do with anybody. Only a former servant . . . a grumpy, ill-tempered old woman . . . put in an [occasional] appearance at the house . . .. Sitting by the stove Granny Rosa looked like a (dear) little old woman out of a [fairy] tale; a very tiny little creature, all wrinkled-up like a raisin, shrunken . . ..

*-ita (B) NOUN — FEMININE*
*(Changed or specialized sense)*

| | |
|---|---|
| *bolita*[1] | = small round object; pellet; berry. |
| (< bola | = ball) |
| *manita*[2] | = trotter. |
| (< mano | = hand) |

[1] The most common word for "berry", the strictly correct *baya* being little used.

[2] See also under section A. Cf. *manilla*. See under *-illa*. *Manitas de cerdo* = pigs' trotters; *manitas de cordero* = lambs' or sheep's trotters. See note to *alón*, under *-ón*, and to *calabacín*, under *-ín*.

| | | |
|---|---|---|
| †*mañanita*[1] | = | early morning; bed-jacket. |
| (< mañana | = | morning) |
| *mariquita*[2] | = | lady-bird. |
| (< marica | = | magpie) |
| *masita* | = | uniform money or allowance (army). |
| (< masa | = | dough; mass) |
| *mosquita* | | |
| (muerta)[3] | = | hypocritically inoffensive person, person who looks as if butter wouldn't melt in his or her mouth. |
| (< mosca | = | fly) |
| *musiquita*[4] | = | tune. |
| (< música | = | music) |
| *pajarita*[5] | | |
| (corbata de) | = | bow-tie. |
| (< pájara | | |
| (rare) | = | bird) |
| *palomita(s)*[6] | = | popcorn. |
| (< paloma | = | dove) |

[1] The sense "early morning" is not too often found, but its appearance from time to time is interesting. (See Examples from Literature.) Early in the morning = *por la mañana, temprano*. The English expressions "the small hours of the morning" and "the early hours of the morning" are usually rendered by *las altas horas de la noche* and *la madrugada*.

"The first light of day" = *los primeros albores del día* (in Andalusia *las claritas del día*).

[2] The lady-bird is also sometimes called *vaca de San Antón*. For "magpie" see *marica*, under -*ica*. For *mariquita* in the sense of "contemptible little pansy" see *maricón*, under -*ón*.

[3] *Mosquita* alone means, of course, simply "small fly". Cf. *mosquito* = gnat, mosquito.

[4] Both *musiquita* and *musiquilla* are much used colloquially with this meaning. A more literary word for "tune" is *melodía*.

[5] Used in Andalusia as synonym of *mariposa*.

[6] In the singular *palomita* means, of course, "little dove". Cf. *palomilla*. See under -*illa*. Another term for "popcorn" used in some parts of Spain is *rosetas de maíz*. (Cf. the provincial use of *tejeringos* for *churros*.)

| | |
|---|---|
| *tortita*[1] | = pancake; waffle; flap-jack. |
| (< torta | = type of bun, cake or pastry) |
| *varita*[2] | = (fairy) wand. |
| (< vara | = rod, staff) |

## -ita *EXAMPLES FROM LITERATURE* (GROUP B)

Para hacer nuestras excursiones solíamos reunirnos a la *mañanita* en el muelle . . . .

(BAROJA, *Las Inquietudes de Shanti Andía*, p. 47)

We used to meet for our trips early in the morning, on the quay . . . .

Another example:

Era gran madrugador, y por la *mañanita*, con la fresca, se iba a Santa Cruz, . . .

(PÉREZ GALDÓS, *Fortunata y Jacinta*, I, p. 79)

He wasn't one for lying in bed, and bright and early, in the cool morning air, off he would go to Santa Cruz, . . .

[Cf.:

. . . ocurrió que una *mañanita*, cuando los gallos aún dormían, oyó el hermano portero una especie de llanto al pie de la puerta . . . .

(SÁNCHEZ-SILVA, *Marcelino, Pan y Vino*, p. 10)

. . . it came to pass that one fine morning, when the cocks were still asleep, the brother door-keeper heard a sort of crying at the foot of the door . . . .

El vagabundo . . . tomó una *mañanita*, tan temprano que ni aún la mañana se veía, el sendero que dicen la Apretura . . .

(CELA, *Judíos, Moros y Cristianos*, p. 275)

[1] Pancakes of the traditional English type are not usually found in Spain, except in Galicia, where they are called *filloas*. Cf. *tortilla*. See under *-illa*.

[2] Can also mean, of course, simply "small rod or staff". Cf. *varilla*. See under *-illa*.

One fine morning, so early that (even) the morning (itself) was
not yet to be seen, . . . the tramp took the path called the "Tight
Squeeze" . . ..[1]]

## -ita (C) NOUN — MASCULINE
*(Diminutive — frequently with undertones of affection or irony)*

| | |
|---|---|
| *curita*[2] | = small priest; charming little priest; quite a priest. |
| *problemita*[3] | = small problem; delightful (little) problem; proper problem. |
| *telegramita* | = small telegram; delightful (little) telegram; quite a telegram. |

## 2. -ICO, -ICA

## -ico (A) NOUN — MASCULINE
*(Diminutive — generally affectionate)*

| | |
|---|---|
| *besico*[4] | = gentle, nice or sweet little kiss. |
| †*frailecico*[5] | = gentle, humble or sweet friar. |
| *gustico*[6] | = delightful taste or flavour; delightful or lovely feeling or sensation. |
| †*momentico*[7] | = just a moment, instant, jiffy. |

[1] In both these cases it is possible that the meaning is "one morning, in the early hours", but it seems probable that the idea is simply that of "one fine morning", "fine" being used here as in expressions of the type "one fine day they just left without a word". (See *nochecita*, under *-ita* (A), Examples from Literature.) It will be observed that in the two examples in question the indefinite article is used, whereas in those above it is the definite article.

[2] See *curilla*, under *-illa* (m.).

[3] E.g. *a ver qué haces con el problemita este* = let's see what you (can) do with this little lot.

[4] Cf. *besito, besín* — same sense.
   Cf. *besillo.*

[5] Cf. *frailecito, frailuco* — same sense.
   Cf. *frailecillo.*

[6] Cf. *gustito, gustín* — same sense.
   Cf. *gustillo.*

[7] Cf. *momentito, momentín* — same sense.
   Cf. *momentillo.*

| *pajarico*[1] | = cute or sweet little bird. |
| †*solecico*[2] | = gentle or delightful sunshine (when not too strong). |
| *vallecico*[3] | = cute, nice or sweet little valley. |

## -ico EXAMPLES FROM LITERATURE
## (GROUP A)

El trabajo y el amor que los frailes ponían en todo hizo que . . . su convento pareciese un edificio . . . incluso bello; con el agua cerca, los *frailecicos* se dieron trazas de hacer brotar algunos árboles y plantas y flores . . . .

(SÁNCHEZ-SILVA, Marcelino, Pan y Vino, p. 10)

The labour and love that the friars put into everything made . . . of their monastery . . . a building that even looked beautiful; with water near at hand, the humble gentle friars contrived to get a few trees and plants and flowers to spring up . . . ..

. . . Grande fue la sorpresa al encarar . . . con una *mujerona*★ muy *altona*★ y muy *feona*★, vestida de *colorines*★; . . . dijo . . . que don Pepe no estaba, pero que al *momentico* vendría.

(PÉREZ GALDÓS, Fortunata y Jacinta, I, p. 313)

. . . Great was their surprise on coming face to face . . . with a terrifically tall great mountain of a woman, as ugly as they come and dressed in garish colours; . . . she said . . . that Don Pepe was out, but that he would be back in just a jiffy.

La *plazuela*★ de las Vacas, con su *fuentecilla*★ y su cruz, sus *casuchas*★ de escolta, sus viejas silenciosas y trajinadoras, y sus viejos entibiándose al *solecico* mañanero, respira un honesto, un vago aire pueblerino y antiguo . . . ..

(CELA, Judíos, Moros y Cristianos, p. 198)

[1] Cf. *pajarito, pajarín* — same sense.
  Cf. *pajarillo*.
[2] Cf. *solecito* — same sense.
  Cf. *solecillo*.
[3] Cf. *vallecito* — same sense.
  Cf. *vallecillo*.

The small, mean "Plaza de las Vacas", with its modest little fountain and its crucifix, its accompanying poky cottages, its silent, bustling old women and its old men warming themselves in the pleasing, gentle, early-morning sunshine breathes a vague, decorous, old-world, country-village atmosphere . . ..

## -ico (B) ADJECTIVE

| | |
|---|---|
| †apuradico[1] | = in a bit of a fix or jam, in just a wee bit of a tight spot, just a little pressed. |
| malico[2] | = poorly. |
| †medrosico[3] | = timorous. |
| †pobrecico[4] | = poor little . . ., poor, sweet little . . . |
| solico[5] | = all by oneself, all on one's own(some). |

## -ico EXAMPLES FROM LITERATURE
## (GROUP B)

— Vamos a ver, José, tú debes de andar algo *apuradico* de dinero, ¿verdad?

(PALACIO VALDÉS, José, p. 122)

"Look here, Joseph, you must be just a wee bit tight for money, am I right?"

[1] Cf. *apuradito* — same sense.
   Cf. *apuradillo*.
[2] Cf. *malito* — same sense.
*Estar malico (malito)* = to be "poorly".
Cf. *malillo, malejo*. See under -illo, -ejo.
*Es malillo (malejo)* = he's poorish, it's [of] poorish [quality].
[3] Cf. *medrosito* — same sense.
   Cf. *medrosillo*.
[4] Cf. *pobrecito* — same sense.
   Cf. *pobrecillo*.
The form *pobretico* is also found. It may be a metathesis of *pobrecito* or a diminutive of *pobrete*.
[5] Cf. *solito* — same sense.
   Cf. *solillo*.

— No tengas miedo, nena. Verás cómo no nos pasa nada.

Y lo decía ... con la *boquita*\* seca de angustia y el corazón latiéndole más *medrosico* que nunca.

(FRANCÉS, *Revelación*, p. 62)

"Don't be afraid, darling. Nothing's going to happen to us, you'll see."
And she said this ... with her tiny mouth dry from anxiety and her heart throbbing more timorously than ever.

... la senda ... nos sube hasta la *Navazuela*,\*[1] que, por el prado Povea y el regajo del Maillo, lleva al *pobretico* puente de Roncesvalles ... el *pontezuelo*\* de Roncesvalles.

(CELA, *Judiós, Moros y Cristianos*, p. 256)

... the path ... takes us up as far as "la Navazuela",[1] which, via the meadow pasture-ground of Povea and the rivulet of "el Maillo", leads to the sweet, poor little bridge of Roncesvalles ... the humble little bridge of Roncesvalles.


*-ico (C) ADVERB*

*tantico*[2]         = (just) a wee bit.


*-ico EXAMPLE FROM LITERATURE*
(GROUP C)

Miraba desde la foto con los ojos entornados y la mandíbula inferior un *tantico* apretada, como haciendo un gran esfuerzo ...
(ZUNZUNEGUI, *¡Ay, Estos Hijos!*, p. 38)

He looked out from the photo with half-closed eyes and his lower jaw (just) a wee bit tense, as if he were making a great effort ...

---

[1] Diminutive of *nava* = high plain.
[2] E.g. *está un tantico caliente* = it's (just) a wee bit hot.
  Cf. *poquito, poquillo* — similar sense.
  Cf. *poquitín* = (just) a teeny weeny bit.

## -ica (A) NOUN — FEMININE

*(Diminutive — generally affectionate)*

| | |
|---|---|
| †*avecica*[1] | = dear or sweet little bird. |
| *callecica*[2] | = cute or charming little street. |
| †*candelica* (un-<br>    common)[3]<br>*velica* | = cute or humble little candle. |
| *cinturica*[4] | = dainty little waist. |
| *nenica*[5] | = cute or sweet little girl or girlie; darling, sweetie. |
| *nubecica*[6] | = pretty or sweet little cloud. |
| *risica*[7] | = charming or pretty little laugh. |
| *tetica*[8] | = lovely or pretty little breast. |
| *velica*[9] | = delightful or humble little candle. |
| †*vocecica*[10] | = gentle or sweet little voice. |

## -ica EXAMPLES FROM LITERATURE
## (GROUP A)

— Querrás matarte. Entonces, oirás el canto mañanero de una *avecica*, enjaulada, y querrás seguir viviendo.

(PÉREZ DE AYALA, Tigre Juan, p. 147)

[1] Cf. *avecita* — same sense.
  Cf. *avecilla.*
[2] Cf. *callecita* — same sense.
  Cf. *callecilla.*
[3] Cf. *candelita, velita* — same sense.
  Cf. *candelilla, velilla.*
[4] Cf. *cinturita* — same sense.
  Cf. *cinturilla.*
[5] Cf. *nenita* — same sense.
  Cf. *nenilla.*
[6] Cf. *nubecita* — same sense.
  Cf. *nubecilla.*
[7] Cf. *risita* — same sense.
  Cf. *risilla.*
[8] Cf. *tetita* — same sense.
  Cf. *tetilla.*
[9] See *candelica*, above.
[10] Cf. *vocecita* — same sense.
  Cf. *vocecilla.*

"You'll want to kill yourself. Then you'll hear the early-morning song of a sweet little bird in its cage, and you'll want to go on living."

...al entrar en el cuarto de las parturientas y ver la estampa del santo con sus correspondientes *candelicas,* [el catedrático de obstetricia] solía gritar furioso: Señores, o sobro yo o sobra el Santo ....

(Pardo Bazán, Los Pazos de Ulloa, p. 245)

... on coming into the expectant mothers' ward and seeing the picture of the saint with its accompanying set of humble little candles [the professor of obstetrics] used to bellow furiously: "Gentlemen, either I am unnecessary or that Saint is unnecessary ...."

...a la sombra del robledal... el vagabundo, que se ha lavado sus miserias en las aguas del arroyo umbrío y *saltarín**★** que dicen Cobo, escucha la *vocecica* de una niña rubia y misteriosa que canta, zarzalera como el ruiseñor y amorosa y gentil como la zurana ....

(Cela, Judíos, Moros y Cristianos, p. 38)

... in the shadow of the grove of oak trees... the tramp, who has [previously] washed the filth from his body in the water of the shaded, bounding stream called 'el Cobo', listens to the tiny, sweet voice of a fair-haired, weird little girl who is singing, untrammelled as a nightingale and as lovingly and exquisitely as a wild dove ....

*-ica (B) NOUN — COMMON*

*(Pejorative. Most of these words can also be used adjectivally)*

| | |
|---|---|
| acusica[1] | = tell-tale, sneak. |
| antojica[2] | = faddy (individual), individual of fancies or whims. |
| cobardica[3] | = cowardy-cat, funker. |

[1] Cf. *acusón, soplón, chivato.* See under *-ón.*
[2] Uncommon.
   Cf. *antojadizo* (adj.) — same sense, but more common.
   Cf. *caprichudo.* See under *-udo.*
[3] Cf. *cobardón.* See under *-ón.*

| | | |
|---|---|---|
| *cocinica* (m.)[1] | = | man much given to interfering in the kitchen or in domestic affairs. |
| *enfadica*[2] | = | irritable (individual). |
| *gruñica*[3]  *quejica* | = | grumble-guts. |
| *llorica*[4] | = | cry-baby. |
| †*marica*[5] | = | pansy, sissy. |
| *miedica*[6] | = | scaredy-cat. |
| †*mierdica* | = | (little) squirt, twerp, runt. |
| *quejica*[7] | = | grumble-guts. |
| *roñica*[8] | = | stingy blighter, tight-fist. |
| *trampica*[9] | = | cheat. |

## -*ica* EXAMPLES FROM LITERATURE
## (GROUP B)

La cólera de los derrotados se proyectaba unánime sobre el mismo objetivo: la intervención italiana. — ¡El *marica* de Mussolini! — ¡Nos achicharraba como a los *negritos*\*!

(GIRONELLA, *Un Millón de Muertos*, p. 239)

The anger of the defeated was unanimously directed at the same target — the Italian intervention. "That pansy Mussolini!" "He scorched the hide off us just like he did the jolly old blacks!"

---

[1] See *cocinilla*, under -*illa*, section D.
[2] Uncommon.
    Cf. *enfadadizo* (adj.) — same sense, but more common.
    Cf. *geniudo*. See under -*udo*.
[3] Cf. *gruñón*. See under -*ón*.
[4] Cf. *llorón*, *lloricón*, *lloroso*. See under -*ón*.
[5] See note to *maricón*, under -*ón*.
*Marica* also means "magpie". However, it is rarely used in this sense, which is generally conveyed by *picaza* or *urraca*.
[6] Cf. *miedoso* — similar sense.
[7] Cf. *quejoso* — similar sense.
See *gruñica*, above.
[8] Cf. *roñoso* — similar sense.
[9] Cf. *tramposo* — similar sense.

— ¿Oíste, *mierdica*? Te largas de ahí o te abro el alma en canal.

(DELIBES, *El Camino*, p. 70)

"Did you hear, you little squirt? Either you shove off or I'll rip your guts out."

## 3. -ÍN, -INA

*-ín (A) NOUN — MASCULINE*
*(Diminutive — frequently with an affectionate or some other favourable implication)*

| | | |
|---|---|---|
| *besín*[1] | = | (gentle or sweet) little kiss. |
| *comandantín*[2] | = | little major. |
| *chavalín*[3] | = | little or young lad, kid, nipper. |
| †*dedín*[4] | = | (cute) little finger or toe. |
| *estilín*[5] | = | quite a bit of style or fashion-sense. |
| *gustín*[6] | = | slight (but delightful) taste or flavour, slight (but lovely) feeling or sensation. |
| *pajarín*[7] | = | (sweet) little bird. |
| *pañolín* | = | (attractive) little handkerchief. |
| †*pelín*[8] | = | (delightful) little hair. |
| *pillín*[9] | = | little or young rogue, rascal, devil or scamp. |
| †*ventolín*[10] | = | gentle little wind, light breeze. |

[1] Cf. *besito* — similar sense.

[2] Cf. *comandantito* — similar sense.

When General Franco held the rank of major he was affectionately known to some as *el comandantín*.

[3] Cf. *chavalito* — similar sense.

[4] Cf. *dedito* — similar sense.

[5] *Tener estilín* = to be stylish.

Cf. *estilazo*. See under *-azo*.

[6] Cf. *gustirrín, gustico, gustito* — similar sense.

[7] Cf. *pajarito* — similar sense.

[8] Cf. *pelito* — similar sense.

[9] Cf. *pillete, pilluelo* and *pillastre*.

*Pillín* is an affectionate term; *pillete* and especially *pilluelo* tend to have a more pejorative sense and are often used with a meaning akin to that of *golfete, golfillo* = little urchin. *Pillastre* is unreservedly pejorative = miserable scoundrel.

Cf. *diablejo, diablillo* and *granujilla* — all very similar to *pillín* both in basic meaning and in that they are frequently used with a tone of affection.

For a parallel case see *sinvergonzón, sinvergüenzón*, under *-ón*.

[10] An uncommon formation. Compare the widely used *vientecillo*.

## -ín EXAMPLES FROM LITERATURE
## (GROUP A)

... Lituca[1] ... me mandaba callar poniendo un *dedín* muy mono sobre la boca . . ..

(PEREDA, Peñas Arriba, p. 268)

... Lituca ... bade me be silent by putting a delightfully pretty little finger over her mouth . . ..

— ... *Isidrín*, te quiero mucho . . ..

(PASO, Los Pobrecitos, p. 214)

". . . Isidro, my darling, I'm terribly fond of you . . .."

... [el niño] volvió a sacar la lengua, y habló por primera vez ... diciendo muy claro : — *Putona*★.

Ama y criada rompieron a reír, y *Juanín* lanzó una carcajada graciosísima . . ..

(PÉREZ GALDÓS, Fortunata y Jacinta, I, p. 304)

... [the child] again stuck his tongue out, and spoke for the first time... saying quite distinctly: "You great tart."

Mistress and servant both burst into laughter, and little Johnny [also] gave vent to a highly amusing outburst of merriment . . ..

¡Ay, mis hijas *chiquitas*,★ lo que yo os quiero!
Pero,
¡de qué manera
quiero a mi chiquitísima nena tercera!
Es, ¡claro está!, mi tesoro;
tiene los *pelines* de oro
y tiene unas *fuerzotas*★ como un toro.

(GONZÁLEZ CASTELL, Brindis in Mil Mejores Poesías, p. 597)

Oh, my little baby daughters, how much I love you! But how very specially I love my teeny-weeny third baby girl! She's my treasure, of course!; she has delightful little strands of golden hair and the brute strength of a bull.

---

[1] Santander diminutive form of *Lita* ($<$[*So*]*lita* $<$ *Sol* $<$ *Sol*[*edad*]).

El sol ya no pegaba fuerte como en julio; por la mañana soplaba un *ventolín* fresco que anticipaba las brisas de otoño.

(GOYTISOLO, *Fin de Fiesta*, p. 9)

Now the sun no longer burned you fiercely as in July; in the mornings a cool gentle little wind blew, giving a foretaste of the autumn breezes.

## -*ín* (B) NOUN — MASCULINE
*(Change of sense or specialized meaning, often with a diminutive and sometimes with a pejorative implication)*

| | |
|---|---|
| *balancín* | = swing-bar; see-saw. |
| (< balanza | = scales) |
| *baldosín*[1] | = small tile. |
| (< baldosa | = flag-stone) |
| *balín* | = small-calibre bullet. |
| (< bala | = bullet) |
| *batín*[2] | = short dressing-gown; man's dressing-gown. |
| (< bata | = dressing-gown) |
| *bombín*[3] | = bowler hat. |
| (< bomba | = pump; bomb) |
| *borrachín*[4] | = tippler, despicable soaker. |
| (< borracho | = drunk) |
| *botellín*[5] | = small bottle, individual bottle. |
| (< botella | = bottle) |
| *botiquín* | = medicine chest; first-aid kit. |
| (< botica | = apothecary's shop) |

[1] Used especially to indicate the small type of tile often chosen for bathrooms and kitchens.

[2] Nowadays any man's dressing-gown, regardless of length, is referred to as *batín*, *bata* being reserved for the female garment.

[3] Much less used than *(sombrero) hongo*. The connection with *bomba* is that of shape.

[4] For other examples of pejorative force see below the following: *colorín, comodín, folletín, retintín*.

[5] Used in a limited number of cases, notably with *leche, cerveza* and *vermú*: *botellín de leche, botellín de cerveza, botellín de vermú. Botellita* is a more generally applicable form.

74

| †*botín* | = spat. |
| (< bota | = boot) |
| *cafetín*[1] | = small café. |
| (< café | = coffee; café) |
| *calabacín*[2] | = small or baby marrow, courgette. |
| (< calabaza | = pumpkin) |
| *calcetín* | = sock. |
| (< calceta | = hose) |
| *camarín*[3] | = (theatre) dressing room. |
| (< cámara | = chamber) |
| *colín* | = hard toast finger, savoury biscuit finger. |
| (< cola | = tail) |
| *colorín*[4] | = bright, garish colour. |
| (< color | = colour) |
| *comodín*[5] | = joker (cards); (mere) pawn (fig.). |
| (< cómodo | = convenient) |
| *espadín* | = short, ceremonial dress sword. |
| (< espada | = sword) |
| *fajín* | = ceremonial military sash. |
| (< faja | = sash; corset) |
| †*faldellín*[6] | = short skirt; kilt. |
| (< falda | = skirt) |
| *festín* | = feast. |
| (< fiesta | = party, festivity, holiday) |

[1] Cf. *cafetito* = small coffee. The respective meanings are rarely interchanged.

[2] In Spain marrows are invariably picked young for human consumption and hence are small; once they grow large they become tough and unpalatable.

[3] The Italian form *camerino* has become very popular in Spain and is, in fact, more widely used than *camarín*. [Anomalously, *trampolín* (= diving-board), which derives from the Italian *trampolino*, is the only form of the word used in Spain. Cf. *traspontín* (= folding supplementary seat, in trains, buses, etc.) < Italian *strapuntino*.]

[4] Cf. *color llamativo, color chillón* — similar sense.

[5] Cf. *comparsa* = (mere) pawn (fig.).
Cf. *figurón*. See under -*ón*.

[6] This is not a very common word; more natural expressions are *falda (faldita) corta* = short skirt, *falda (faldita) escocesa* = Scottish kilt.

| | |
|---|---|
| *figurín*[1] | = costume (theatre); fashion-plate, fashion magazine; dandy. |
| (< *figura* | = figure) |
| *flautín* | = piccolo. |
| (< *flauta* | = flute) |
| †*folletín*[2] | = penny dreadful; melodrama; cheap serial. |
| (< *folleto* | = pamphlet) |
| *fortín* | = small or low fort. |
| (< *fuerte* | = fort) |
| *futbolín* | = miniature football (game). |
| (< *fútbol* | = football) |
| *labrantín* | = small farmer, smallholder. |
| (< *labrante* | |
| (O. Sp.) | = labourer) |
| *levitín* | = short frock coat or morning coat. |
| (< *levita* | = frock coat or morning coat) |
| *listín* | = short list; telephone directory. |
| (< *lista* | = list) |
| *llavín* | = door-key, latch-key, yale-key. |
| (< *llave* | = key) |
| *maletín* | = small or travelling suitcase. |
| (< *maleta* | = suitcase) |
| *patín*[3] | = skate; scooter. |
| (< *pata* | = leg, foot) |
| *pizarrín* | = child's slate; slate pencil. |
| (< *pizarra* | = slate) |
| *plumín* | = pen nib. |
| (< *pluma* | = feather, pen) |
| *polvorín* | = fine gun-powder; powder magazine; powder-keg (fig.). |
| (< *pólvora* | = gunpowder) |

---

[1] Cf. *figurita, figurilla, estatuita, estatuilla* = figurine.

[2] Cf. *folletón* and *dramón* — similar sense. See under *-ón*.

[3] Cf. *patín* = dimin. of *patio* (very rare).

    Cf. *patinejo, patinillo, patiecito, patiecillo* — more common forms meaning "small courtyard".

    Cf. *patito* (< pato) = duckling.

| | | |
|---|---|---|
| *retintín*[1] | == | sarcasm, sarcastic tone. |
| (< retinte | == | ringing in the ears) |
| *rondín*[2] | == | watchman; policeman, bobby. |
| (< ronda | == | night-patrol, beat) |
| *serrín*[3] | == | saw-dust. |
| (< sierra | == | saw) |
| *sillín* | == | small saddle; saddle (of bicycle or motorcycle). |
| (< silla | == | chair; saddle) |

## *-ín* EXAMPLES FROM LITERATURE (GROUP B)

— Vaya, vaya, con este perdis — decía don Baldomero, ... Siempre tan *extranjerote*.*

– No quiere nada con nosotros — dijo Barbarita, ... — Mira, mira qué levita gris cerrada ... y *botines* blancos ... — Pero Manolo, ¡qué *zapatones** usan por allá! Esos guantes pasarían aquí por guantes de cochero.

(PÉREZ GALDÓS, *Fortunata y Jacinta*, III, p. 78)

"Here's a real rake-about if you like", said Don Baldomero, ... "Always the out and out foreigner."

"He'll have none of us", said Barbarita, ... "Just look at his tight-buttoned grey frock-coat ... and white spats ... .. But Manolo, what thumping great shoes they wear in those foreign parts! The gloves you've got would be taken for a coachman's here."

Ya el paño que cubre en forma de *faldellín* o "kilt" escocés a las mujeres de las cavernas tiene tanto de adorno como de pieza de recato.

(MARAÑÓN, *Vida e Historia*, p. 141)

As early as the caveman era the cloth in the shape of a short skirt or Scottish kilt that covered the women of the time was as much an ornament as a garment of modesty.

[1] Cf. *sorna, tonillo burlón* — similar sense.
[2] This word belongs rather to the nineteenth century than to the present, as does also *guindilla* used in the sense of "bobby".
[3] The form *aserrín* is little used.

... excitó de modo considerable en Pío las lucubraciones fantásticas el ¡Alto! que a su madre y a él les dieron los soldados de la guardia de la Puerta Nueva una madrugada .... Se figuró el muchacho, cuando menos, que era protagonista de una de tantas aventuras con las que tan familiarizado estaba por *novelones**\* y *folletines*, que no dejaba un momento.

(Pérez Ferrero. Vida de Pío Baroja, p. 43)

... Pío's flights of phantasy received considerable stimulus from the (command of) "Halt!" which the soldiers of the guard at the Puerta Nueva shouted at his mother and him in the early hours one morning .... The boy pictured himself as, at the very least, the hero of one of the innumerable adventures with which he was so familiar through (his reading of) highly coloured novels and melodramatic stories, which he never left for a moment.

## -ín (C) ADJECTIVE

| | |
|---|---|
| *aburridín* | = a little bit or a wee bit boring or bored. |
| *bobín*[1] | ⎰ = a little bit or a wee bit silly; (used as subst.) |
| †*tontín* | ⎱ silly boy, silly little chap. |
| †*chiquitín*[2] | ⎱ = tiny, wee, tichy; (used as subst.) tiny chap, wee |
| *pequeñín* | ⎰ fellow. |
| *feuchín*[3] | = a little bit or a wee bit ugly; (used as subst.) ugly little chap or titch. |
| †*pobretín*[4] | = poor little ...; (used as subst.) poor wee laddie. |

[1] Cf. *bobito, tontito* — same sense.

[2] *Chiquitín* = *chico* + *ito* + *ín* (*chiquín* is not used).

Cf. *chiquirritín* = tichy wee, teeny weeny.

Cf. *chiquito* = tiny, wee.

Cf. *chiquitito* = tiny wee, teeny weeny.

There is, naturally, a strong tautological element in such words as *chiquirritín* and in such expressions as *chavalín pequeñín* = tichy wee fellow.

[3] *Feuchín* = *feo* + *ucho* + *ín*.

See *feúcho*, under *-ucho*.

[4] Cf. *pobrecito, pobrecillo* — similar sense.

| | |
|---|---|
| *poquitín* | = just a very little . . .; (used as subst.) just a very little bit. |
| *simplín*[1] | = a little bit or a wee bit naïve; pitifully naïve. |

## -ín EXAMPLES FROM LITERATURE
## (GROUP C)

. . . tengo unos *poquitos*,\* unos minúsculos, unos *chiquirritines* celos de ella; no es envidia. ¡Dios me libre de pecado tan feo! Son . . . otra cosa, *celillos*\* pasajeros engendrados por el gran cariño que le profeso.

(RIVAS, *Tengo una Hermana Solterona*, p. 189)

. . . I'm just a little bit, just a tiny bit, just a teeny weeny bit jealous of her; it isn't envy. May God preserve me from such a hateful sin! It's . . . something else, a little passing jealousy, born of the deep affection I have for her.

. . . ¡*Pobretín*, esa miel no la has catado nunca! . . . ¡El amor! Yo te enseñaré lo que es . . . . No lo sabes, *tontín* . . ., ¡la cosa más rica . . .!

(PÉREZ GALDÓS, *Fortunata y Jacinta*, IV, pp. 326, 327)

."... You poor darling, that's a kind of honey you've never tasted . . . . Love! I'll show you what it is . . . . You don't know, you silly boy, . . . something really tasty . . .!"

## -ín (D) ADJECTIVE
*(Specialized sense, often with augmentative and even pejorative implication)*

| | |
|---|---|
| *andarín*[2] | = (much) given to walking or wandering; (subst.) (great) walker. |

[1] Sometimes used as a stressed rather than a diminutive form, with basically much the same sense as *simplón*, *simplote* (see under -ón, -ote). (For other similar cases of diminutive = augmentative, see Introduction, section 5.)

[2] Cf. *andador*, *andariego* — similar sense. For -iego cf. *mujeriego* = fond of women, much given to wenching. (*Putero* has a similar though even stronger sense, and -ero is, indeed, another suffix often used in this way. A further example: *patatero* = (very) fond of potatoes, given to eating a lot of potatoes.)

| | |
|---|---|
| *bailarín*[1] | = (very) fond of dancing; (subst.) great one for dancing. |
| †*cantarín*[2] | = (very) fond of singing; murmuring (e.g. brook); sing-song (e.g. voice); (subst.) great one for singing. |
| †*parlanchín*[3] | = (very) fond of talking, (excessively) talkative; (subst.) chatterbox, jabberer. |
| †*saltarín* | = (very) fond of jumping, prancing or dancing about, jumpy, bumpy. |

## -*ín* EXAMPLES FROM LITERATURE
## (GROUP D)

Tenía el acento *cantarín* de los montañeses de Orense.

(FERNÁNDEZ FLÓREZ, *El Bosque Animado*, p. 169)

He had the sing-song accent of the natives of the highland districts of Orense.

. . . era una *viejecilla*★ pequeña y *vivaracha*★, irascible, *parlanchina* . . ..

(PÉREZ GALDÓS, *Misericordia*, p. 27)

. . . she was a small, sprightly, irritable little chatter-box of an old woman . . ..

[Los chicos] descendieron *saltarines, chillones.*★

(ZUNZUNEGUI, *¡Ay, Estos Hijos!* p. 46

[The boys] came prancing down, shouting their heads off.

[1] Cf. *bailón*, which has much the same sense. For this similarity of use between -*ín* and -*ón* see other words such as *burlón* (see section -*ón* B). Apart from the colloquial senses given, *bailarín* also has the meaning "professional dancer", for which it is, indeed, the standard term. Cf. *bailador*, usually pronounced *bailaor*, = flamenco dancer. [Cf. "there were some twenty dancers on the floor" = *había unas veinte personas bailando en la pista*. There is no noun in Spanish for this ordinary non-professional sense of "dancer".]

[2] Cf. *cantante*, which is the standard term for "singer". *Cantor* also is used but less generally. Cf. *canta[d]or* = flamenco singer.

[3] Also *hablanchín*, which is, however, less used, except in Andalusia. (Formerly *hablantín* was common but is now rare, except in Spanish America.) Cf. *hablador* — similar sense, but not quite so pejorative.

Cf. *hablistán* — similar sense, but less used.

*-ina NOUN — FEMININE*
*(Changed or specialized sense)*

| | |
|---|---|
| *carnavalina(s)* | = confetti. |
| (<carnaval | = carnival) |
| *chocolatina*[1] | = small bar or packet of chocolate. |
| (< chocolate | = chocolate) |
| *clavellina* | = pink. |
| (< clavel | = carnation) |
| *golondrina*[2] | = swallow. |
| (cf. alondra | = lark) |
| *hornacina* | = (wall) niche. |
| (< horno | = oven) |
| *madrina*[3] | = godmother, sponsor. |
| (< madre | = mother) |
| *neblina*[4] | = mist. |
| (< niebla | = fog) |
| *purpurina* | = metal powder (used, for example, as snow). |
| (< púrpura | = purple, purple dye) |
| *serpentina* | = streamer, paper-ribbon. |
| (< serpiente | = snake) |
| *sobaquina* | = under-arm sweat. |
| (< sobaco | = arm-pit) |
| †*solina* | = sun's glare. |
| (< sol | = sun) |
| *sonatina*[5] | = refrain; same old tune. |
| (< sonata | = sonata) |

[1] Cf. *pastilla de chocolate* = (standard size) bar of chocolate; *tableta de chocolate* = (large size) bar or slab of chocolate.

[2] Does not represent changed sense since it derives basically from L. *hirundo, -inis*, but included here for its interest. The ending *-ina* was added to distinguish the word clearly from *alondra*, with which it was in danger of becoming confused.

[3] Cf. *comadre*, also used popularly for "godmother". Cf. *comadrona* = midwife. Cf. *padrino* = godfather, sponsor, best man, second (in duel).

[4] Cf. *bruma*, used especially in the specific sense of "sea-mist". Cf. *calina* and *vaho* = (heat) haze.

[5] See *estribillo*, under *-illo*.

| | | |
|---|---|---|
| *tesina* | = | short thesis, academic dissertation. |
| (< *tesis* | = | thesis) |
| *tetina* | = | teat (for baby's bottle). |
| (< *teta* | = | teat, breast) |

## -ina EXAMPLE FROM LITERATURE

... un hombre con pinta de ganadero ... se enjugaba el sudor con un *pañolín*★ de seda. Era mediodía y el calor apretaba fuerte. La *solina* se colaba por los ventanales, y el piso de mosaico reverberaba.

(GOYTISOLO, La Isla, p. 8)

... a man who looked like a cattle-breeder ... was wiping the sweat from his face with a small silk handkerchief. It was midafternoon and the heat was fierce. The glare from the sun filtered through the large windows, and the tile floor reflected it off.

### 4. -ILLO, -ILLA, -ILLAS

### -illo (A) NOUN — MASCULINE
*(Diminutive — often with pejorative implication)*

| | | |
|---|---|---|
| *acentillo*[1] | = | slight accent, unpleasant little accent. |
| *ahorrillo(s)* | = | modest or miserable savings. |
| †*airecillo*[2] | = | light wind, (gentle) breeze. |
| *alamillo* | = | small poplar, (modest) little poplar. |
| *ancianillo*[3] | = | (poor) little old man. |
| *apurillo* | = | bit of a tight spot (especially financial). |
| †*arbolillo* | = | small tree, (miserable) little tree. |
| *asuntillo*[4] | = | small piece of business, minor matter. |

[1] Cf. *acentazo*. See under -*azo*.
  Cf. *tonillo*. See below.
[2] Cf. *airote*. See under -*ote*.
  Cf. *vientecillo, brisa* — same sense.
[3] Cf. *ancianito* — similar sense.
[4] Cf. *asuntito* — similar sense.

| | | |
|---|---|---|
| *bachecillo* | = | small or minor pot-hole or air-pocket; bit of a down-hill patch, rather a thin patch (fig.). |
| *bajoncillo* | = | spell of feeling rather low or under the weather. |
| *bosquecillo*[1] | = | small wood, (miserable) little wood. |
| *calculillo(s)* | = | petty calculations or accounts. |
| †*calorcillo*[2] | = | slight sensation of heat, gentle or pleasant warmth. |
| *cochecillo*[3] | = | (modest or wretched) little car. |
| *corrillo* | = | small circle, group or gathering (e.g. for conversation or of spectators). |
| *cuerpecillo*[4] | = | small body, body (of a child); jolly old carcass (humorous). |
| *cursillo* | = | short course. |
| *chiquillo*[5] | = | young boy, kid, lad. |
| *chismecillo(s)* | = | petty gossip, chit-chat. |
| †*descuidillo* | = | minor piece of carelessness, minor oversight. |
| *diablillo*[6] | = | little devil, young rascal or scamp. |
| *dinerillo*[7] | = | bit of money; "pretty penny". |
| *duendecillo* | = | little elf, imp, pixy, sprite or gremlin. |
| *empleíllo*[8] | = | poor or tenth-rate job. |
| †*estudiantillo*[9] | = | two-penny ha'penny student. |
| *febrerillo*[10] | = | little February. |
| †*fenomenillo* | = | minor or petty little phenomenon. |

[1] Cf. *bosquecito* = (cute) little wood, baby wood (children's language).

[2] Cf. *calorcito* — same sense. Despite the strong general tendency of *-illo* to be either simply diminutive or otherwise pejorative, a favourable implication, as seen in this example, is certainly not impossible.

[3] Cf. *cochecito*. See under *-ito*.
See *fotingo*, under *-ingo*.

[4] Cf. *cuerpecito*, *corpezuelo* — similar senses.

[5] Cf. *chiquito* — similar sense.

[6] Cf. *golfillo*, *granujilla* (m.) — similar sense.
See *pilluelo* under *-uelo*.

[7] Cf. *dinerito*, *dinerete* — similar sense.

[8] Cf. *empleíto* : *un empleíllo de mala muerte* = a rotten little job; *un empleíto bastante decente* = quite a fair little job.

[9] Cf. *estudiantito* = budding or dapper young student.

[10] Used in the popular expression *febrerillo loco*, which refers to the inferiority of this month because of its shortness and to the crazy changes of weather associated with it.

| | | |
|---|---|---|
| *fresquillo*[1] | = | slight chilliness. |
| *funcionarillo* | = | minor or petty civil-servant. |
| *gamberrillo* | = | (miserable) little hooligan or larrikin. |
| *gastillo(s)* | = | minor or petty expense(s); incidental(s). |
| *gorrioncillo* | = | (poor) little sparrow. |
| *hombrecillo* | = | (insignificant) little man. |
| *huesecillo* | = | (miserable) little bone. |
| *idolillo* | = | little idol, petty idol. |
| *indiecillo*[2] | = | young or little Indian. |
| *jefecillo*[3] | = | minor or petty leader, little upstart leader. |
| *leoncillo*[4] | = | lion cub. |
| †*mundillo*[5] | = | (small) world, narrow or petty world. |
| *ojillo*[6] | = | small (beady, cunning) eye. |
| *paisillo* | = | (wretched) little country, minor country. |
| *pajarillo*[7] | = | (miserable) little bird. |
| *papelillo*[8] | = | (wretched) little piece of paper. |
| *pastelillo*[9] | = | (miserable) little cake. |
| *patiecillo*[10] | = | small courtyard, (modest) little courtyard. |
| *periodiquillo* | = | modest or minor newspaper. |
| *perrillo*[11] | = | (miserable) little dog. |
| †*personajillo* | = | minor character. |
| *pobrecillo*[12] | = | poor little chap. |
| *politiquillo* | = | modest, minor or two-penny ha'penny politician. |
| †*polvillo* | = | fine dust. |

[1] *Hace fresquillo o fresquete* = it's a bit chilly, on the chilly side.
Cf. *hace fresquito* = it's pleasantly cool, nice and cool.
Cf. *hace un frescazo de mil pares de demonios* = it's infernally chilly.
[2] Cf. *indiecito* — same sense.
[3] Cf. *jefazo*. See under *-azo.*
[4] Cf. *leoncito* — same sense.
[5] E.g. *el mundillo literario* = the literary world; *el mundillo cinematográfico* = the world of (the) cinema.
[6] Cf. *ojito* = (cute, sweet) little eye.
[7] Cf. *pajarito* = (sweet) little bird.
[8] Cf. *papelito* = small piece of paper.
[9] Cf. *pastelito* = (delightful) little cake.
[10] Cf. *patiecito* = (delightful) little courtyard.
[11] Cf. *perrito* = (cute) little dog.
[12] Cf. *pobrecito* = poor little darling.

| | | |
|---|---|---|
| †*pueblecillo*[1] | = | (modest or wretched) little village. |
| *puertecillo*[2] | = | (modest or miserable) little harbour or mountain pass. |
| †*raterillo* | = | petty pick-pocket. |
| †*regalillo*[3] | = | (modest or miserable) little gift. |
| *rojillo*[4] | = | bit of a red; two-penny ha'penny red. |
| *ruidillo*[5] | = | slight sound. |
| *sabihondillo*[6] | = | little know-it-all. |
| *saborcillo*[7] | = | slight (unpleasant) taste or flavour. |
| †*sotillo* | = | (puny) little coppice. |
| †*sueñecillo*[8] | = | short sleep, nap. |
| †*teatrillo*[9] | = | (wretched) little theatre. |
| †*tonillo*[10] | = | slight tone or note, unpleasant little tone or note. |
| †*trabajillo*[11] | = | (modest or poorish) little bit of work. |
| *tufillo* | = | slight odour, pong or stink. |
| *viejecillo*[12] | = | (wretched) little old man. |
| *vientecillo*[13] | = | slight wind, breeze. |
| *vinillo* | = | poorish or weakish wine. |

*-illo* EXAMPLES FROM LITERATURE
(GROUP A)

Un *airecillo* fresco orea las sonrisas a la caída de la tarde.

(CELA, *Judíos, Moros y Cristianos*, p. 25)

[1] Cf. *pueblecito* = (charming) little village.
[2] Cf. *puertecito* = (delightful) little port or mountain pass.
[3] Cf. *regalito* = (nice) little present.
[4] Cf. *comunistilla* (m.) = bit of a commy; minor commy.
  Cf. *rojazo, comunistón*. See under *-azo, -ón*.
[5] Cf. *ruidazo*. See under *-azo*.
[6] Often used adjectivally, e.g. *un niño sabihondillo*; *una niña sabihondilla* (= *una niña redicha, una marisabidilla*).
[7] Cf. *saborcito* = slight (pleasant) taste or flavour.
[8] Cf. *sueñecito* — similar sense.
[9] Cf. *teatrito* = (charming) little theatre.
[10] See *acentillo*, above.
[11] Cf. *trabajito* = (good) little bit of work.
[12] Cf. *viejecito* = (nice) little old man.
[13] See *airecillo*, above.

As evening comes on a cool gentle breeze lends a freshness to people's smiles.

La carretera se extendía, llena de polvo y de carriles hechos por los carros, entre los *arbolillos* enclenques.

(BAROJA, *Camino de Perfección*, p. 47)

The highway, dust-covered and rutted by carts, stretched away between the puny, miserable little trees.

Entró en la cocina Tona, algo tocada también de la murria inverniza, a trajinar en el fogón, donde hablábamos mi tío y yo al *calorcillo* de la lumbre . . ..

(PEREDA, *Peñas Arriba*, p. 189)

Tona, also somewhat affected by the winter blues, came into the kitchen and bustled about at the range, where my uncle and I were talking in the pleasant warmth from the fire . . ..

— No es de extrañar un *descuidillo*, una distracción . . ..

(PÉREZ GALDÓS, *Doña Perfecta*, p. 73)

"There's nothing surprising in a minor oversight, a piece of absent-mindedness . . .."

. . . [estaba] empeñada en casarse, contra viento y marea de su padre, con un *estudiantillo* de medicina, un nadie, hijo de un herrador de pueblo . . ..

(PARDO BAZÁN, *Los Pazos de Ulloa*, p. 148)

. . . against her father's violent opposition, [she was] set on marrying a two-penny ha'penny medical student, a nobody, the son of a village farrier . . ..

El universo es coordinación de infinitos fenómenos heterogéneos. Cada ciencia, en cambio, se conforma con añascar enteco troje de *fenomenillos* homogéneos, y obstínase en no admitir que de fuera, aparte, por debajo y por encima de ellos, exista realidad alguna.

(PÉREZ DE AYALA, *Belarmino y Apolonio*, p. 11)

86

The universe is a coordination of an infinite number of heterogeneous phenomena. Each branch of learning, on the other hand, contents itself with accumulating a puny store of petty little homogeneous phenomena, and persists in refusing to acknowledge the existence of any reality whatsoever outside, apart from, below or above them.

Quien no se acorace a prueba de fracasos en el ponzoñoso *mundillo* literario está perdido.

(BRAVO-VILLASANTE, *Vida y Obra de Emilia Pardo Bazán*, p. 257)

Anyone who does not steel himself against failure in the narrow, venomous little world of the literary is doomed.

Pero he aquí que el autor ... parece querer dejar en ridículo a su héroe, como antes dejó a otros *personajillos*.

(SORDO, in *Baroja y su Mundo*, p. 151)

But lo and behold the author ... seems to wish to make a fool of his hero, as he did earlier with other minor characters.

... antiguos grabados y volúmenes raros, amarillentos ya y con un tenue *polvillo* sobre el papel ....

(POMBO ANGULO, *Hospital General*, p. 192)

... old prints and rare tomes, now yellowed [from age] and with a slight [layer of] fine dust on the paper ....

A la falda de esta loma se encuentra el *pueblecillo*[1] llamado San Juan de Aznalfarache .... Es una *aldehuela** irregular, triste y de ruin caserío.

(PALACIO VALDÉS, *La Hermana San Sulpicio*, p. 376)

On the slope of this hill stands the small village of San Juan de Aznalfarache .... It's a depressing, higgledy-piggledy, poky little place, with mean (little) houses.

Los contrabandistas contemplaban la escuadra en la inquietud y el respeto del *raterillo* que viese desfilar un Tercio de la Guardia Civil.

(BLASCO IBÁÑEZ, *Flor de Mayo*, p. 129)

[1] Note the equation of *pueblecillo* with *aldehuela*. Significantly, Valdés does not use *pueblecito*.

The smugglers watched the fleet with the uneasiness and awe of a petty pick-pocket seeing a division of the Civil Guard march past.

Y todo ello por unas cuantas chucherías y *regalillos* de mala muerte.

(Valera, Juanita la Larga, p. 62)

And all on account of a few baubles and fiddling two-penny ha'penny little gifts.

Quienes procedan del Norte deberán despedirse del árbol tan pronto como rebasen los *sotillos* del Guadalix, hasta el boscaje cultivado de Chamartín de la Rosa.

(Laín Entralgo, La Generación del Noventa y Ocho, p. 72)

Those who come from the north will have to take their leave of trees as soon as they get beyond the miserable little coppices of the Guadalix, until [they reach] the cultivated woodland of Chamartín de la Rosa.

El sol que se encarniza sobre nosotros no favorece el cambio de impresiones, y siento deseos de tumbarme a la fresca y descabezar un *sueñecillo*.

(Goytisolo, Campos de Níjar, p. 20)

The sun which is beating down savagely upon us is not conducive to an exchange of views, and I feel an urge to lie down in the cool and have [a bit of] a nap.

Don Eligio. — ¡Bien! ¡Muy bien! ¡Perfectamente bien! De todo lo cual yo colijo que usted autoriza, en el austero palacio de los Arrayanes, la construcción de ese *teatrillo* . . ..
Doña Sacramento. — *Teatrillo*, no; *teatrito*★. . ..

(Alvarez Quintero, El Genio Alegre, p. 143)

Don Eligio. — Very good! Very well then! Fine! I gather from all this that you give your permission for the construction, in the austere palace of Myrtles, of that wretched little theatre . . . .

Doña Sacramento. — Not wretched little theatre; delightful little theatre.

Su madre le hablaba risueña, pero con cierto *tonillo burlón*★ que la indignaba.

(Palacio Valdés, *La Hermana San Sulpicio*, p. 409)

Her mother spoke to her smilingly, but with a certain mocking, unpleasant little note [in her voice] that infuriated her.

— ¡Qué lejos está ella de que le he descubierto el escondrijo! *Trabajillo* me costó; pero me salí con la mía.

(Pérez Galdós, *Fortunata y Jacinta*, IV, p. 141)

"How little she suspects that I've discovered her hidy-hole! It took me quite a bit of effort; but [finally] I got what I was after."

*-illo (B) NOUN — MASCULINE*
*(Changed or specialized sense)*

| | |
|---|---|
| *ajillo*[1] | = chopped garlic. |
| (< ajo | = garlic) |
| *alguacilillo* | = ceremonial rider (at bull-fight). |
| (< alguacil | = constable) |
| *amorcillo*[2] | = statue of Cupid. |
| (< amor | = love) |
| *armadillo* | = armadillo. |
| (< armado | = armed) |
| *azucarillo* | = hard candy floss. |
| (< azúcar | = sugar) |
| *banquillo*[3] | = small bench; dock (in court). |
| (< banco | = bench) |
| *baratillo* | = second-hand or cheap shop. |
| (< barato | = cheap) |

---

[1] Cf. *picadillo*. See below.
[2] Sometimes used like *angelote*. See under *-ote*.
[3] *El banquillo del acusado (o de los acusados)* = the dock.

| | | |
|---|---|---|
| *barquillo*[1] | = | wafer. |
| (< barco | = | ship) |
| *bocadillo*[2] | = | savoury roll, snack. |
| (< bocado | = | bite) |
| *bolillo(s)* | = | lace-bobbin; bobbin lace. |
| (< bola | = | ball) |
| *bolsillo*[3] | = | pocket. |
| (< bolso | = | bag, handbag) |
| †*bordillo*[4] | = | narrow edge; kerb. |
| (< borde | = | edge) |
| *bordoncillo*[5] | = | refrain; tag, stock phrase; same old tune. |
| (< bordón | = | bourdon) |
| *cabestrillo* | = | sling (arm). |
| (< cabestro | = | halter; bell ox) |
| *calzoncillos* | = | underpants. |
| (< calzones | = | breeches) |
| *caracolillo*[6] | = | winkle. |
| (< caracol | = | snail) |
| *carboncillo* | = | charcoal crayon. |
| (< carbón | = | charcoal, coal) |
| *cardenillo* | = | verdigris. |
| (< cárdeno | = | livid, bluish) |
| *carrillo* | = | jowl. |
| (< cara | = | face) |
| †*cepillo*[7] | = | brush; collection box (in church). |
| (< cepo | = | wooden stock) |

[1] Of type used for ice-cream cornets, which latter are specifically called *cucuruchos*.

[2] Cf. *bocadito* = small bite, tiny morsel.
   Cf. *emparedado* = sandwich.

[3] Cf. *bolsito* = small handbag.
      *bolsillito* = small pocket.
   Cf. *bolsita* = small shopping bag.

[4] *Bordillo de la acera* = kerb.

[5] Cf. *estribillo* — same senses.

[6] Also *bígaro*.
   Cf. *caracolito* = small snail.

[7] *Cepillo de las limosnas* = collection box.

| | | |
|---|---|---|
| *cigarrillo*[1] | = | cigarette. |
| (< cigarro (puro) | = | cigar) |
| *cochinillo*[2] | = | sucking pig. |
| (< cochino | = | pig) |
| *codillo* | = | ham or bacon bone. |
| (< codo | = | elbow) |
| †*conejillo* (de Indias)[3] | = | guinea-pig. |
| (< conejo | = | rabbit) |
| *cuadradillo*[4] | = | lump (of sugar). |
| (< cuadrado | = | square) |
| *cuartillo* | = | pint. |
| (< cuarto | = | fourth) |
| *culillo* | = | small quantity of liquid left in bottom of glass. |
| (< culo | = | bottom, behind) |
| *dedillo*[5] | = | small finger or toe; fingertips (fig.). |
| (< dedo | = | finger, toe) |
| *descansillo*[6] | = | landing (stair). |
| (< descanso | = | rest; interval) |
| *dobladillo*[7] | = | border, hem. |
| (< doblado | = | folded) |
| *estribillo*[8] | = | refrain; tag; same old tune. |
| (< estribo | = | stirrup; running board) |
| *flequillo*[9] | = | fringe (hair). |
| (< fleco | = | fringe, flounce (dress, etc.)) |

[1] Cf. *pitillo* — same sense.

Nowadays *cigarrillo, cigarro* and *pitillo* are all used in the sense of "cigarette", "cigar" being *puro*.

[2] Cf. *cerdito* = piglet. See under *-ito*.

[3] The unsuffixed form *conejo de Indias* is sometimes used.

The synonym *cobayo* is a more technical word.

[4] Cf. *terrón* — same sense. See under *-ón*.

[5] *Saber(se) una cosa al dedillo* = to have something at one's fingertips.

[6] Cf. *meseta, rellano* — same sense, but less common.

[7] Cf. *bastilla* — same sense.

Also *bajo* = hem.

[8] Cf. *bordoncillo* (also *bordón*), *latiguillo, muletilla* — same senses.

Cf. *cantilena, sonatina* — fig. sense only.

[9] Cf. *flequito* = (charming) little flounce (dress, etc.).

| | |
|---|---|
| *frenillo* | = fraenum (of the tongue). |
| (< freno | = brake) |
| *ganchillo* | = crochet, crochet-hook. |
| (< gancho | = hook) |
| *garrotillo* | = croup. |
| (< garrote | = stick, club) |
| *gatillo*[1] | = trigger. |
| (< gato | = cat; jack (vehicle)) |
| *gusanillo*[2] | = miserable little worm; empty feeling; gnawing worry. |
| (< gusano | = worm) |
| †*hatillo* | = possessions, worldly goods, goods and chattels. |
| (< hato | = bundle) |
| †*hilillo*[3] | = small thread; (tiny or thin) trickle. |
| (< hilo | = thread) |
| *hornillo*[4] | = portable spirit-stove; gas or electric ring. |
| (< horno | = oven) |
| *jaboncillo* | = (tailor's and dressmaker's) marking chalk. |
| (< jabón | = soap) |
| *latiguillo*[5] | = refrain; tag, stock phrase; same old tune; clap-trap. |
| (< látigo | = whip) |
| *lazarillo* | = (blind man's) boy guide. |
| (< Lázaro | = Lazarus) |
| *librillo*[6] | = packet of cigarette paper. |
| (< libro | = book) |
| *marmolillo* | = spur-stone; slow heavy person, one like a lump of pudding. |
| (< mármol | = marble) |

[1] *Ser de gatillo fácil* = to be trigger-happy.
  Cf. *gatito* = kitten.
[2] *Matar el gusanillo* = *desayunar* or *beber para olvidar*.
[3] Cf. *hilito* — same senses.
[4] Cf. *hornilla*. See under *-illa*.
[5] Cf. *estribillo* — same senses.
[6] The full phrase is *librillo de papel de fumar*.

92

| | | |
|---|---|---|
| *menudillo(s)* | = | giblet(s); offal. |
| (< menudo | = | small) |
| *molinillo* | = | coffee-grinder. |
| (< molino | = | mill) |
| *moquillo* | = | (animal) distemper. |
| (< moco | = | nasal mucus) |
| *negrillo* | = | elm tree, elm grey. |
| (< negro | = | black) |
| *novillo*[1] | — | young bull. |
| (related to | | |
| nuevo | = | new) |
| *nudillo* | = | knuckle. |
| (< nudo | = | knot) |
| *obispillo*[2] | = | parson's nose (chicken). |
| (< obispo | = | bishop) |
| *organillo* | = | barrel-organ. |
| (< órgano | = | organ) |
| †*palillo*[3] | = | small stick; drum-stick; chop-stick; tooth-pick. |
| (< palo | = | stick) |
| *panecillo* | — | roll (bread). |
| (< pan | = | bread) |
| *pardillo*[4] | = | country-bumpkin, yokel, hick. |
| (< pardo | = | dun-coloured, earth-coloured) |
| *paseíllo* | = | parade (of bull-fighters and attendants prior to corrida). |
| (< paseo | — | stroll, walk) |
| *pasillo*[5] | = | passage, corridor. |
| (< paso | = | step) |

[1] *Hacer novillos* = to play truant (in Spain boys like to play at bull-fighting). *Hacer rabona* has the same sense.

[2] In some areas *obispón*.
Also called *rabadilla*, a term much more commonly used.

[3] *Palillo de tambor* = drum-stick; *palillo chino* = chop-stick; *palillo de (los) dientes* = tooth-pick.

[4] See *berzotas*, under *-otas*.

[5] Cf. *corredor*, which, although it can have the sense of "corridor", is usually used to mean "racing driver".

| | |
|---|---|
| *pecadillo* | = peccadillo, minor fault. |
| (< pecado | = sin) |
| *pelillo*[1] | = small hair; down; downy finish (to cloth). |
| (< pelo | = hair) |
| *pepinillo* | = small cucumber; pickled cucumber, gherkin. |
| (< pepino | = cucumber) |
| *picadillo* | = finely minced meat or fish (for stuffing). |
| (< picado | = chopped) |
| *pitillo*[2] | = cigarette, fag. |
| (< pito | = whistle) |
| †*platillo(s)*[3] | = saucer; trays (of scales); cymbals. |
| (< plato | = plate) |
| *rabillo*[4] | = short tail; corner (of the eye). |
| (< rabo | = tail) |
| *solomillo* | = rump, sirloin. |
| (< solomo (uncommon) | = loin (pork)) |
| *soplillo* | = fire-fan. |
| (< soplo | = blowing, breath) |
| *tornillo* | = screw. |
| (< torno | = lathe; wheel; (dentist's) drill) |
| *tranquillo*[5] | = knack, skill (that opens door to something). |
| (< tranco | = threshold) |
| †*trapillo*[6] | = informal or working dress. |
| (< trapo | = cloth, rag) |

[1] Cf. *pelusa* = down (face, fruit).
   Cf. *pelusilla* = fine down.

[2] See *cigarrillo*, above.

[3] Cf. *platito* = small plate. *Platillo volante* = flying saucer.

[4] *Mirar por el rabillo del ojo* = to look out of the corner of one's eye.
   Cf. *mirar por encima del hombro* = to look down on (to despise).
   Cf. *mirar de reojo* = to look askance.

[5] *Cogerle a algo el tranquillo (el aire, el manejo, el truco)* = to get the knack or hang of something.

[6] *Estar de trapillo* = to be informally dressed, in working garb.

| | |
|---|---|
| *tresbolillo*[1] | = triangular or staggered formation. |
| (< trébol | = clover, shamrock) |
| *tresillo* | = card game (for three); three-piece suite. |
| (< tres | = three) |
| *ventanillo*[2] | = poky little window; peep-hole. |
| (< ventano | = small window) |
| *veranillo* (de | |
| San Martín)[3] | = Indian summer. |
| (< verano | = summer) |
| *visillo* | = (lace) window-curtain. |
| (< viso | = view point, vantage point) |

## -illo EXAMPLES FROM LITERATURE (GROUP B)

De repente, los truenos sonaron sin interrupción y la lluvia se transformó en un aguacero de gotas gruesas.... Desde el balcón, veía bajar el agua, desbordando los *bordillos* de las aceras.... Olía todo a humedad y a *carbonilla**\* de tren.

(GARCÍA HORTELANO, *Tormenta de Verano*, p. 303)

Suddenly the thunder started to crash without a pause, and the rain turned into a downpour of heavy drops.... From his balcony he could see the water running down, overflowing the kerbs.... Everything smelled damp and like coal smoke and smuts from a train.

...en aquella época el *cepillo* de las limosnas solamente recogía alguna *calderilla.\**

(GIMÉNEZ-ARNÁU, *El Canto del Gallo*, p. 187)

...in those days all that used to appear in the collection-box was a little small change.

---

[1] Used in the expression *colocar a tresbolillo* = to place in triangular formation, to stagger. The *s* is due to the influence of *tres*.

[2] Cf. *mirilla*. See under -illa.

[3] Cf. *el calorcito del membrillo* (Andalusia) — same sense.

...y añadía, con petulancia: Mis amigos son los *conejillos de Indias* que yo utilizo para la vivisección espiritual.

(BAROJA, *La Dama Errante*, p. 44)

...and he added arrogantly: "My friends are the guinea-pigs I use for spiritual vivisection."

...y de Salamanca, con el parvo *hatillo* del Estado español naciente sobre los hombros, hemos de pasar a Burgos....

(SERRANO SUÑER, *Entre Hendaya y Gibraltar*, p. 55)

...and from Salamanca, with the meagre goods and chattels of the nascent Spanish State on our shoulders, we must pass on to Burgos....

Por entre sus dedos brotaba un *hilillo* de sangre....

(BLASCO IBÁÑEZ, *Flor de Mayo*, p. 29)

A thin trickle of blood seeped between her fingers.

[Cf. *hilito*:
— ¡Melón, melón! — pedía (la enferma) con un *hilito* de voz.

(ZUNZUNEGUI, *¡Ay, Estos Hijos!*, p. 200)

"Melon, melon!" (the sick girl) beseeched in the barest whisper of a voice.]

...miss Annie suele hacerle observaciones agripunzantes cuando le ve tirar al suelo la *colilla** del cigarro, o apagarla en el *platillo* de su taza de café, o escarbarse con el *palillo* las encías....

(PARDO BAZÁN, *La Sirena Negra*, p. 1048)

...Miss Annie is wont to direct cutting remarks at him when she sees him throw a cigarette-end on the floor, or stub one out on the saucer of his cup of coffee, or poke his gums with a toothpick....

Refugio ... estaba aquel invierno muy mal de ropa, y no iba al café del Siglo, sino al del Gallo, ... porque la sociedad modesta que frecuentaba aquel establecimiento permitía presentarse en él de *trapillo* o con *mantón** y *pañuelo** a la cabeza.

(PÉREZ GALDÓS, *Fortunata y Jacinta*, IV, p. 216)

Refugio ... was very badly off for clothes that winter, and she did not go to the Century Café but to the Cock, ... because the unpretentious type of people who regularly patronized the place made it possible for one to go there in ordinary house apparel or in a shawl and with a scarf on one's head.

## -illo (C) ADJECTIVE
*(and past participle used adjectivally)*

| | |
|---|---|
| alegrillo[1] | = quite cheerful, gay, lively or merry; a little on |
| animadillo | the merry or high side (from drink); pretty high. |
| ambiciosillo | = rather ambitious, on the self-seeking side. |
| apartadillo[2] | = a bit out of the way, rather off the beaten track; pretty out of the way. |
| †apuradillo | = rather embarrassed; a little hard-pressed; rather hard-up. |
| atacantillo[3] | = rather irritating, inclined to get on one's nerves. |
| †atrevidillo[4] | = rather bold, a little forward, on the forward side; pretty bold. |
| barrigoncillo | |
| triponcillo | = a little pot-bellied, a bit paunchy. |
| canijillo[5] | = weakly, sickly, rather weak, rather poor in health; pretty weakly, pretty poor in health; rather behind in physical growth. |
| cansadillo[6] | = rather tired; rather tiring; pretty tired or tiring. |

[1] E.g. *¡qué animadillo estamos!* = what a very lively mood we're in! (This refers to one person; note the idiomatic mixture of singular *(animadillo)* and plural *(estamos)*).
Cf. *alegrete, animadete* — similar sense.

[2] E.g. *es un sitio algo apartadillo* = it's a spot (that's) a wee bit out of the way. Cf. *es un sitio apartadito* = it's a spot (that's) nicely off the beaten track.
Cf. *retiradillo*, below.

[3] See *cargantillo*, below.

[4] Cf. *atrevidito* = rather forward (but attractively so), a little daring (in an attractive way). Cf. *pillín* and *sinvergonzón*. See under *-ín, -ón*.
Cf. *atrevidete* — similar sense.

[5] Cf. *debilucho, endeblucho*, etc. See under *-ucho*.

[6] Cf. *cansadito*. See under *-ito*.

| | |
|---|---|
| *cargantillo*[1] | = inclined to get on one's nerves; pretty irritating. |
| *ceboncillo*[2] | = a bit on the fat or tubby side; pretty tubby. |
| *complicadillo* | = quite or rather complicated; pretty complicated. |
| *costrosillo* | = rather mouldy or tatty, on the dilapidated or seedy side; pretty seedy. |
| *creidillo*[3] ⎫ *presumidillo* ⎭ | = rather conceited, on the conceited side; pretty conceited. |
| †*curiosillo*[4] | = rather inquisitive, inclined to be inquisitive; pretty inquisitive. |
| *chulillo*[5] | = rather pugnacious, a bit bellicose; pretty bellicose. |
| †*delicadillo* | = a bit sickly, on the weak(ly) side. |
| *descaradillo* | = a wee bit cheeky or impudent; pretty impudent. |
| †*desmedradillo* | = a bit puny or frail, rather sickly or thin. |
| *desnutridillo*[6] | = a little undernourished; pretty undernourished. |
| *despistadillo*[7] | = rather off the track, a bit lost or vague. |
| *dificilillo*[8] | = a bit difficult, on the awkward side; pretty awkward. |
| †*durillo* | = a bit hard, toughish, stiffish. |
| *enamoradillo*[9] | = half in love, infatuated. |
| *envidiosillo* | = on the envious side, inclined to be envious. |
| *escamadillo*[10] | = on the wary side; pretty suspicious. |
| *escandalosillo*[11] | = a little or rather scandalous; spicyish; pretty spicy. |

1 See *atacantillo*, above.

2 Cf. *ceboncete* — similar sense.

3 Cf. *creidete*, *presumidete* — similar sense.

4 Cf. *curiosón*. See under *-ón*.

5 Cf. *chulito* = on the pugnacious or bellicose side (but in a witty way, with a saving grace). Both forms are commonly used as nouns. (For *chulo* see *bravucón*, under *-ón*.)

6 Cf. *desnutridete* — similar sense.

7 Cf. *despistadete* — similar sense.

8 Cf. *facilito*. See under *-ito*.

9 Cf. *enamoradito*.

Cf. *el chico está enamoradillo nada más* = the boy's merely infatuated; *¡están tan enamoraditos!* = they're so very much in love, they're so delightfully in love!

10 Cf. *escamadete* — similar sense. See *escamón*, under *-ón*.

11 E.g. *un libro bastante escandalosillo* = a (really) pretty spicy book, a pretty spicyish book.

| | |
|---|---|
| *feíllo* | = a bit ugly, uglyish; homely, plain (f.). |
| *flojillo*[1] | = rather weak, weakish; pretty weak or feeble; loosish. |
| †*fuertecillo*[2] | = strongish; pretty strong; heavyish. |
| *graciosillo* | = quite amusing or funny, having a certain amount of wit. |
| *guapillo*[3] | = quite handsome, handsomish; pretty handsome. |
| *guasoncillo* | = quite or pretty witty. |
| *insignificantillo* | = quite or rather insignificant; pretty unimpressive. |
| *malillo*[4] | = rather poor, poorish, baddish; pretty bad or poor, not much cop. |
| †*mamoncillo*[5] | = sucking or suckling, breast-fed, of the tenderest age. |
| *mimosillo* | = rather pettish, a bit pettish. |
| *perezosillo*[6] | = rather or a bit lazy, on the lazy side; pretty lazy. |
| †*pobrecillo*[7] | = rather poor. |

[1] Much used figuratively, e.g. *una traducción flojilla* = a rather feeble translation.

[2] E.g. *es una película fuertecilla* = it's a film that's pretty strong meat; *fue una comida fuertecilla* = it was a pretty heavy meal.

[3] E.g. *es bastante guapillo* = he's really quite handsome, he's really pretty handsome, he's really quite a handsome laddie, he's really a pretty handsomish laddie.

Cf. *guapito*. See under *-ito*.

Cf. *guapete*. See under *-ete*.

Cf. *guapazo, guapote*. See under *-azo, -ote*.

[4] Cf. *malejo* — similar sense. See under *-ejo*.

E.g. *es una tela bastante malilla (maleja)* = it's a pretty poorish cloth.

Cf. *malito*. See under *-ito*.

Cf. *malón, malote*. See *-ón, -ote*.

Cf. *regularcillo*. See below.

[5] Often used substantivally, e.g. *un mamoncillo* = *un niño mamoncillo* = child at the breast, infant. See *mamón* under *-ón*. Cf. *cochinillo*. See under *-illo* (noun).

[6] Cf. *perezosón*. See under *-ón*.

[7] *Pobrecillo* is widely used as a noun, e.g. *el pobrecillo se ha hecho daño* = the poor little chap has hurt himself.

Cf. *pobrecito, pobrecico, pobretico*. See under *-ito, -ico*.

| | |
|---|---|
| *preocupadillo*[1] | = rather or a bit worried; pretty worried. |
| *presumidillo*[2] | = rather or pretty conceited. |
| *puñeterillo*[3] | = rather or a bit awkward or difficult (persons), inclined to be cantankerous or bloody-minded; pretty bloody-minded or bitchy. |
| *quemadillo*[4] | = rather or a bit burnt; pretty burnt. |
| *regularcillo*[5] | = rather or pretty so so, (definitely) on the middling or poorish side. |
| *rencorosillo* | = rather spiteful, inclined to be spiteful, a (wee) bit spiteful; pretty spiteful. |
| †*retiradillo*[6] | = rather or a little set back or withdrawn; pretty withdrawn. |
| *sueltecillo*[7] | = rather loose, on the loose side, loosish; pretty loose. |
| *teatralillo* | = rather theatrical, inclined to be (a bit) dramatic; pretty theatrical or dramatic. |
| *triponcillo*[8] | = a bit or rather pot-bellied; quite or pretty pot-bellied. |
| *vanidosillo* | = rather vain, on the vain side; pretty vain. |
| *vulgarcillo*[9] | = rather ordinary, on the ordinary side; pretty commonplace. |

[1] E.g. *está algo preocupadillo* = he's just a little worried.

[2] See *creidillo*, above.

[3] From *puñetero* = awkward, cussed, irritating, cantankerous, bloody-minded, bloody. See *puñeta*, under *-eta*.

*Puñetero* and *puñeterillo* are frequently used as nouns, e.g. *es un puñeterillo* = he's an awkward little basket, he's a cantankerous little perisher.

Although stronger still, *cabrón* and *cabroncete* are very similar in sense. See under *-ón, -ete*.

For another somewhat allied meaning see *chulillo*, above.

[4] E.g. *sabe a quemadillo* = it tastes a (wee) bit burnt.

[5] Cf. *malillo* — similar sense. See above.

[6] Cf. *apartadillo* — similar sense. See above.

[7] Cf. *flojillo* — similar sense in some cases. See above.

[8] See *barrigoncillo*, above.

[9] Cf. *vulgarcejo* — similar sense.

## -illo EXAMPLES FROM LITERATURE
## (GROUP C)

*Apuradillo* se vio el maestro de escuela para impugnar el nuevo argumento del boticario.

(VALERA, Juanita la Larga, p. 149)

The school-master found himself quite hard-pressed to refute the apothecary's fresh argument.

Resumen: que tuvo que abandonar Bailón aquel acomodo, y después de rodar por ahí dando *sablazos,*★ fue a parar a la redacción de un periódico muy *atrevidillo*; como que su misión era echar *chinitas*★ de fuego a toda autoridad.

(PÉREZ GALDÓS, Torquemada en la Hoguera, pp. 51, 52)

To cut a long story short, Bailón had to leave that employment, and after wandering about touching people for money, he ended up on the editorial staff of a very boldish newspaper — boldish because its object was to take really sharp (little) digs at all forms of authority.

— Y tú, ¿tienes miedo, di?
— Unas veces sí ·y otras veces no.
— ¿En este momento lo tienes?
— ¡ Ah, qué *curiosilla* eres! — exclamó.

(PALACIO VALDÉS, Marta y María, p. 118)

"Tell me, are *you* (ever) frightened?"
"Sometimes I am, sometimes I'm not."
"Are you right now?"
"Oh, what an inquisitive little thing you are!" he exclaimed.

De niño había sido encanijado[1] y *desmedradillo*, objeto de la burla de sus compañeros, lo que desarrollara en su interior un enfermizo sentimiento de lo ridículo, ...

---

[1] It is interesting to note the high incidence of adjectives such as *encanijado, canijo, enfermizo, enteco* and *enclenque* accompanying terms in *-illo*. Cf. phrase *arbolillos enclenques,* quoted from Baroja in section A.

Creció Pachico *delicadillo* y enteco, (e) hízose notar en el colegio por su timidez . . ..

(UNAMUNO, *Paz en la Guerra*, pp. 21, 48)

As a child he had been weakly and on the puny side, a figure of fun to his school-mates, and this had given rise in him to a morbid sensitivity about foolish behaviour, . . .

Pachico grew up rather sickly and infirm, (and) became noted at school for his shyness . . .

El repecho hasta el paso de la Puerta Falsa es *durillo* y algo trabajoso.

(CELA, *Judíos, Moros y Cristianos*, p. 276)

The rise up to the pass of "Puerta Falsa" is stiffish and somewhat of a trudge.

— Sí, hija, el compromiso es *fuertecillo* . . ..
— Si estuviera aquí la señora, no pasaría usted esos *apurillos*★. . ..

(PÉREZ GALDÓS, *La de Bringas*, pp. 250, 254)

"Yes, my dear, the matter is (just) a wee bit pressing . . .."
"If Madam were here you wouldn't (have to) go through these nasty little financial squeezes . . .."

. . . empapó un trozo de tela blanca en agua y se la dio a chupar al *mamoncillo*[1]. . .. El *chiquitín*★ había cerrado sus ojos y al *calorcillo*★ del áspero hábito del buen hermano se había dormido.

(SÁNCHEZ-SILVA, *Marcelino, Pan y Vino*, p. 12)

. . . he soaked a piece of white cloth in water and gave it to the little baby to suck . . .. The wee fellow had closed his eyes and with the comforting warmth of the good friar's rough habit had fallen asleep.

MARIBEL. — No entiendo.
PAULA. — ¡*Pobrecilla* ![1] Pero ¡qué *inocentona*!★

(MIHURA, *Maribel y La Extraña Familia*, p. 159)

[1] Substantival use.

M. — I don't understand.

P. — Poor little thing! But what an utterly guileless creature!

En Muñochas, pueblo algo *retiradillo* de la carretera, el vagabundo tuvo una novia . . ..

(CELA, *Judíos, Moros y Cristianos*, p. 212)

In Muñochas, a village set back some little way from the main road, the tramp [at one time] had a girl-friend . . ..


## -*illo* (D) ADVERB

†*tardecillo* = (pretty) latish.


## -*illo* EXAMPLE FROM LITERATURE
## (GROUP D)

— *Tardecillo* vino usted anoche. A las once no había vuelto usted todavía.

(PÉREZ GALDÓS, *Fortunata y Jacinta*, II, p. 31)

"You were [pretty] latish getting in last night. You still hadn't got back at eleven."


## -*illo* (E) PRESENT PARTICIPLE[1]

| | |
|---|---|
| *creciendillo*[2] | = gradually growing or coming on. |
| *habiendillo*[3] | = gradually being more, increasing. |
| *lloviznandillo*[4] | = gently drizzling. |
| *notandillo*[5] | = gradually noticing. |
| †*silbandillo* | = gently, softly whistling. |

[1] Also found with -*ito*, e.g. *callandito* = very quietly or softly.

[2] E.g. *ya va creciendillo* = he's gradually growing, coming on now. (Cf. *ya va empezandillo a crecer* = he's gradually beginning to grow, come on now.)

[3] E.g. *va habiendillo más* = there is, are gradually beginning to be more about.

[4] E.g. *está lloviznandillo* = it's gently drizzling, it's drizzling [just] a wee bit (i.e. *está lloviznando un poco*).

[5] *se va notandillo más* = it's gradually becoming more noticeable.

## -illo EXAMPLE FROM LITERATURE
## (GROUP E)

...el vagabundo ... desgrana, *pasito*\* a paso y *silbandillo*, la
pagana y dulce letanía de las Navazuelas.....

(CELA, Judíos, Moros y Cristianos, p. 261)

...the tramp ... hums out, very slowly and whistling softly,
the gentle pagan litany of *Las Navazuelas*.....


## -illa (A) NOUN — FEMININE
*(Diminutive — often with pejorative implication)*

| | |
|---|---|
| *arenilla(s)* | = fine grain(s) of sand, small grain(s) of sand. |
| †*aventurilla* | = (petty) little adventure or escapade. |
| *cancioncilla*[1] | = (modest) little song or ditty. |
| *carreterilla*[2] | = (wretched) little road, small or minor road. |
| *coquetilla*[3] | = little flirt, bit of a flirt. |
| *cortinilla*[4] | = little or short curtain. |
| *culturilla*[5] | = bit of culture, superficial culture. |
| *chaquetilla*[6] | = small or short jacket. |
| *chiquilla*[7] | = young girl, lass. |
| *escocesilla* | = wee Scots lassie. |
| *esperancilla*[8] | = slender or slight hope. |
| *estatuilla*[9] | = small statue, figurine. |

---

[1] Cf. *cancioncita* = (sweet) little song.

[2] Cf. *carreterita* = (attractive or delightful) little road. See under -*ita*.
Cf. *caminillo* = (wretched) little lane or track; *caminito* = (attractive or
delightful) little lane or path. See under -*illo*, -*ito*.

[3] Cf. *coquetuela* — similar sense.

[4] Cf. *cortinita* = (cute) little curtain.

[5] Cf. *un barnicillo de cultura* = a thin veneer of culture. Cf. *barnicito*. See
under -*illo*, -*ito*.

[6] Cf. *chaquetita* = (attractive) little jacket.

[7] Cf. *chicuela* — similar sense.
    Cf. *chiquita* = (sweet) little girl.

[8] Cf. *Esperancita* = young Esperanza.

[9] Cf. *estatuita* — same sense. See *figurín,* under -*ín*.

| | | |
|---|---|---|
| *esterilla* | = | small mat. |
| *florecilla*[1] | = | (poor) little flower, (modest or delicate) little bloom. |
| †*francesilla*[2] | = | little French girl; little French piece or bit. |
| *fuentecilla*[3] | = | (modest) little fountain, spring. |
| †*gentecilla*[4] | = | (petty) riff-raff. |
| *gitanilla*[5] | = | little or young gipsy girl. |
| †*gorrilla* | = | small cap. |
| *grasilla* | = | bit of grease or fat, thin film of grease or fat. |
| †*hierbecilla(s)*[6] | = | (miserable) little bit of grass, (wretched) little weed(s). |
| †*honrilla* | = | modest (code of) honour. |
| †*iglesilla*[7] | = | (modest) little church. |
| †*marejadilla* | = | slight swell. |
| *mentirilla*[8] | = | small lie, white lie. |
| *modistilla* | = | young or little dressmaker, midinette, seamstress. |
| *novelilla*[9] | = | (miserable) little novel, two-penny ha'penny novel. |
| *nubecilla*[10] | = | (modest) little cloud. |
| †*obrilla* | = | (modest) little work. |
| †*palabrilla*[11] | = | (fiddling) little word. |
| *paredilla* | = | (flimsy) little wall. |
| *pasioncilla* | = | (wretched or base) little passion, passion of little account. |
| *pelusilla(s)* | = | little bit(s) of fluff or down. |
| †*pensioncilla* | = | modest pension, meagre allowance. |

---

[1] Cf. *florecita* = (sweet) little flower.
[2] Cf. *francesita* = (delightful) little French girl, charming French girl.
[3] Cf. *fuentecita* = (delightful) little fountain, spring.
[4] Cf. *gentezuela* — similar sense. See *gentuza* under *-uza*.
[5] Cf. *gitanita* = (delightful) little gipsy girl.
[6] Cf. *hierbecita(s)* = (delightful) little bit of grass.
[7] Cf. *iglesuela* — similar sense, but more pejorative and less common.
[8] Cf. *mentirijilla* — same sense.
[9] Cf. *novelón* and *novelucha*. See under *-ón* and *-ucha*.
[10] Cf. *nubecita* and *nubecica*. See under *-ita* and *-ica*.
[11] Cf. *palabrita* = (delightful) little word.

| | |
|---|---|
| *personilla*[1] | = insignificant little person, person of little importance. |
| *placilla*[2] | = (modest) little square. |
| *politiquilla* | = petty politics or scheming. |
| *propinilla* | = modest tip, wretched little tip. |
| *putilla* | = bit of a tart, (miserable or wretched) little whore. |
| *resaquilla* | = slight under-tow (sea); slight hang-over, bit of a hang-over (after drink). |
| *risilla*[3] | = (nasty) little laugh, giggle, snigger, titter. |
| *sonrisilla*[4] | = (nasty) little smile, smirk, grin. |
| *suertecilla*[5] | = (just) a bit of luck, a little or wee bit of luck. |
| *telilla*[6] | = flimsy or poorish cloth. |
| *tosecilla* | = slight cough, (nasty) little cough. |
| †*vidilla* | = (miserable) little life or existence. |
| *vocecilla*[7] | = (thin) little voice, (nasty) little voice. |
| *zorrilla* | = (wretched) little vixen or fox; (miserable) little tart or whore. |

## *-illa* EXAMPLES FROM LITERATURE

## (GROUP A)

No dudaba ni tanto así del amor de su marido, pero quería . . . enterarse de ciertas *aventurillas*.

(PÉREZ GALDÓS, *Fortunata y Jacinta*, I, p. 107)

She did not have the slightest doubt of her husband's love, but she wanted . . . to find out about certain petty little escapades.

---

[1] *Una mala personilla* = a bit of a bad lot, rather a nasty customer, a nasty little piece of work. Also *mala personita* (iron.).

[2] Cf. *plazuela* — similar sense.
   Cf. *placita* = (charming) little square.

[3] Cf. *risita* = (pleasant) little laugh, or as *risilla*, according to context.

[4] Cf. *sonrisita* = (nice) little smile.

[5] Cf. *suertecita* = similar sense.

[6] Cf. *tela malilla (maleja)* — similar sense.

[7] E.g. *no me gusta esa vocecilla de mal humor* = I don't like that nasty, bad-tempered little tone of voice. Cf. *vocecita* = (sweet) little voice.

— ...Y lo que es esa *francesilla* asquerosa, no se ríe de mí....
(Pérez Galdós, *Fortunata y Jacinta*, IV, p. 293)

"... And as for that disgusting little French piece, she isn't going to laugh at me...."

[Cf. *francesota*, referring to the same person:

-- ...El revólver es para matar ... a la *francesota*, infame, traicionera....
(*Ibid*, p. 339)

"...the revolver is to kill ... the French bitch with, the vile, treacherous creature...."]

— ...antes los caballeros ... apaleaban a los sastres, a los zapateros y a la demás *gentecilla menuda**; pero ahora esa *gentecilla* se nos ha subido a las barbas....
(Baroja, *Paradox, Rey*, p. 39)

"... Formerly the gentry ... used to thrash tailors, shoemakers and all the other petty riff-raff; but now the riff-raff has got above itself...."

El hombre era un tipo flaco, amojamado, de *gorrilla*, gabán viejo, con el cuello subido, y una guitarra a la espalda. Las mujeres iban vestidas de claro.... El de la guitarra preguntó al doctor si no les podría dar alguna *cosilla* para comer. Con una peseta les bastaba.
(Baroja, *La Dama Errante*, pp. 187, 188)

The man was a thin, shrivelled-up specimen, wearing a (miserable) little cap and an old overcoat with the collar turned up, and carrying a guitar on his back. The women were dressed in light colours.... The fellow with the guitar asked the doctor if he couldn't give them just a little something to buy food with. A peseta was all they needed.

...un peón caminero ... daba lánguidos *azadonazos** en las *hierbecillas* nacidas al borde de la cuneta.
(Pardo Bazán, *Los Pazos de Ulloa*, pp. 22, 23)

... a roadman ... was taking languid swipes with his hoe at the miserable little weeds growing beside the ditch.

B. — Vete a otro barrio.

M. — ¡El mío es éste! Y yo no le quito el pan a ningún compañero de industria en el suyo. ¡Tengo mi *honrilla*!

(BUERO VALLEJO, *Un Soñador para un Pueblo*, p. 209)

B. — Clear off to another district.

M. — *This* is my district right here! And *I* don't deprive anybody in the same trade as myself of a living in *his* area. I have my code of honour, even if it is a modest one!

... La *Iglesuela*[*1] — *iglesilla* donde las mozas rezan a Santa María de la Oliva — es tierra talaverana . . ..

(CELA, *Judíos, Moros y Cristianos*, p. 297)

... La Iglesuela, a modest little church where the country girls pray to Saint Mary of the Olive, lies in the province of Talavera.

El mar había desplegado todas las gradaciones en que es tan fértil su seno versátil: *marejadilla*, marejada, mar picada, mar gruesa, mar arbolada y temporal deshecho.

(PÉREZ DE AYALA, *El Anticristo*, p. 183)

The sea had displayed all the vicissitudes (or moods) in which her fickle breast is so fertile: slight swell, swell, choppy sea, heavy sea, high sea and raging storm.

Con todo, la Pardo Bazán escribe sin temer a los nuevos *Calvinillos*[*] que preparan la hoguera con ramas verdes . . ..

Como el cuentista que lee a Cervantes, a Shakespeare, a Tolstoy, y luego encuentra despreciable su pequeña *obrilla*, así el pintor se desvanece a la vista de Rubens . . ..

(BRAVO-VILLASANTE, *Vida y Obra de Emilia ̄ :rdo Bazán*, pp. 222, 225)

Despite everything, Pardo Bazán writes undaunted by the new petty Calvins who are preparing the execution pyre with green wood . . ..

---

[1] Name of a church and of the village to which it belongs.

Just like the story-writer who reads Cervantes, Shakespeare or Tolstoy, and then finds his own modest little works despicable, so the painter feels his heart sink at the sight of Rubens ....

... había sonrisas y besos y *palabrillas* de enamorados ....
(MAEZTU, *Don Quijote, Don Juan y La Celestina*, p. 89)

... there were smiles and kisses and lovers' sweet nothings ....

He sacado en limpio que Rita vive de una *pensioncilla* que le pasa su abuela materna ....
(PARDO BAZÁN, *La Sirena Negra*, p. 1017)

This much I've got straight, that Rita lives on a modest allowance from her maternal grandmother ....

— Y cuando llega la hora de la muerte, ¿qué importa ni de qué sirve haber pasado un poco más alegre y tranquila esta *vidilla* perecedera y despreciable?
(PARDO BAZÁN, *Los Pazos de Ulloa*, p. 381)

"And when the hour of death comes, what does it matter, what purpose does it serve to have had a little more of a gay and untroubled time in this transient, contemptible, wretched little episode that is human life?"

*-illa (B) NOUN — FEMININE*
*(Changed or specialized sense)*

| | |
|---|---|
| ahogadilla[1] | = ducking. |
| (< ahogado | = drowned; stifling) |
| alcantarilla | = drain. |
| (< alcántara | = bridge, arch) |
| alfombrilla[2] | = rug; measles. |
| (< alfombra | = carpet) |

[1] Cf. *aguadilla* — same sense, but little used.
*Darle a uno una ahogadilla* = to give someone a ducking.
Cf. *chapuzón*. See under *-ón*.
[2] Cf. *alfombrita* = (attractive) small carpet.
The first meaning given is the most common, the word generally used for "measles" being *sarampión*.

| | | |
|---|---|---|
| †*almohadilla* | = | head-rest; cushion (esp. at bull-fight). |
| (< almohada | = | pillow) |
| *ardilla*[1] | = | squirrel. |
| (< (h)arda | | |
| O. Sp. | = | squirrel or marten) |
| *arenilla* | = | abrasive (for cleaning). |
| (< arena | = | sand) |
| *avanzadilla*[2] | = | out-post, forward post. |
| (< avanzado | = | advanced) |
| *banderilla*[3] | = | banderilla (bull-fight). |
| (< bandera | = | flag) |
| *barandilla*[4] | = | railing, banister. |
| (< baranda | = | rail) |
| *barbilla*[5] | = | chin. |
| (< barba | = | beard) |
| *bastardilla*[6] | = | italics. |
| (< bastardo | = | bastard) |
| *bastilla* | = | hem. |
| (< basta | = | basting) |
| *bombilla*[7] | = | bulb (electric light). |
| (< bomba | = | pump; bomb) |
| *boquilla*[8] | = | mouth-piece (pipe); cigarette-holder. |
| (< boca | = | mouth) |

[1] In modern Spanish the distinction is clear: *ardilla* = squirrel; *garduña* = marten.

[2] Cf. *avanzada* — same sense, but less common.

[3] Cf. *banderita* = (cute) little flag.

[4] *Barandilla* and *baranda* are, however, sometimes used synonymously; the former tends to be the more common word.

[5] Cf. *barbita* = small beard.
*Barbilla doble* (also *papada*) = double chin.
The gallicism *mentón* is rarely used.

[6] The full term is *letra bastardilla*.

[7] Cf. *bombita* = small pump or bomb.
Cf. *perilla*. See below.

[8] Cf. *boquita* = small mouth, (cute) little mouth.
*Hablar de boquilla* = to talk a lot or big (but do little).

| | |
|---|---|
| *buhardilla*[1] | = attic, garret, loft. |
| (< buharda | = skylight) |
| *cabrilla*[2] | = burn mark (on the leg, from sitting too near a fire). |
| (< cabra | = female goat) |
| *cabritilla*[3] | = dressed kid, kidskin. |
| (< cabrita | = small female goat) |
| †*cajetilla*[4] | = packet (of cigarettes). |
| (< cajeta | = small box) |
| *calderilla* | = small change, petty cash, coppers. |
| (< caldera | = cauldron, boiler, copper) |
| *camarilla* | = palace clique or pressure group. |
| (< cámara | = chamber) |
| *camilla*[5] | = stretcher; round table covered with a long cloth and with a brazier under it to give warmth. |
| (< cama | = bed) |
| *campanilla*[6] | = small bell; electric chime; blue-bell (flower); uvula. |
| (< campana | = bell) |
| *canastilla* | = layette. |
| (< canasta | = basket) |
| *carbonilla* | = fine coal; smuts, dense smoke (from railway engine). |
| (< carbón | = coal) |

[1] Cf. *guardilla, desván* — same sense.
Cf. *ático* = top flat.

[2] Cf. *cabrita* = small female goat.

[3] Cf. *cabrito* = kid, young goat. See under *-ito*.
*Guantes de cabritilla* = kid gloves. Cf. *trato(s) de guante blanco* = kid-glove treatment.

[4] Cf. *cajita* = small box, (cute) little box.
Anomalously, one says *una caja de cerillas*, despite the fact that Spanish match-boxes are particularly small.

[5] Cf. *camita* = (sweet) little bed.
In the second sense given *cámilla* stands for *mesa de camilla* or *mesa-camilla*.

[6] Cf. *campanita* = (cute) little bell.
Cf. *gal(l)illo, úvula* (< uva) = uvula.
*De muchas campanillas* = very grand or superior.

| | |
|---|---|
| *carrerilla*[1] | = rapid motion (in a Spanish dance). |
| (< carrera | = race) |
| *carretilla* | = wheelbarrow. |
| (< carreta | = cart, waggon) |
| †*cartilla*[2] | = spelling book; telling off. |
| (< carta | = letter) |
| *casilla*[3] | = hut; pigeon hole. |
| (< casa | = house) |
| *centralilla*[4] | = sub or private telephone exchange. |
| (< central | = telephone exchange) |
| *cerilla*[5] | = match; ear wax. |
| (< cera | = wax) |
| *cocinilla*[6] | = (wretched) little kitchen or stove; portable spirit-stove. |
| (< cocina | = kitchen; kitchen-stove) |
| *coletilla* | = tail-piece, foot-note, postscript. |
| (< coleta | = pigtail) |
| *colilla*[7] | = cigarette end or stub. |
| (< cola | = tail; queue) |
| †*comidilla*[8] | = poor or wretched food or meal; (tasty bit of gossip, talk (of the town, etc.). |
| (< comida | = food or meal) |

[1] *Decir de carrerilla* = to string off (say quickly one after the other a list of things). Cf. *decir de un tirón* = to say all at one go, to say all in one breath.

[2] Cf. *cartita* = (delightful) little letter.
*Leerle a uno la cartilla* = to read someone the riot act, to give someone a good talking to.
*Cartilla de racionamiento* = ration book.

[3] Cf. *casita* = (charming) little house, cottage.
*Sacar a uno de sus casillas* = to get someone's goat.

[4] *Centralita* is also so used.

[5] Spanish matches are usually made of wax. Those made of wood are called *fósforos*. The technical term for "ear wax" is *cerumen*.

[6] Cf. *cocinita* = (cute) little kitchen or stove.
Cf. *hornillo, infernillo* = portable spirit-stove. See *hornilla*, below.

[7] Cf. *colita* = (sweet) little tail.

[8] Cf. *comidita* = (tasty) food.
Cf. *comideja* = poor or wretched food or meal. See under *-eja*.

| | | |
|---|---|---|
| *comilla(s)* | = | inverted comma(s). |
| (< coma | = | comma) |
| *coronilla*[1] | = | crown (of the head). |
| (< corona | = | crown; wreath) |
| *costanilla* | = | short sloping street. |
| (< cuesta | = | slope, incline) |
| †*cotilla* | = | stays, corset; gossip. |
| (< cota | = | coat of mail) |
| *criadilla(s)*[2] | = | bull's testicle(s). |
| (< criado | = | raised, bred) |
| *cuadrilla* | = | bull-fighting team, team. |
| (< cuatro | = | four) |
| *cuartilla* | = | sheet of writing paper. |
| (< cuarta | = | fourth part) |
| *cucharilla*[3] | = | tea-spoon. |
| (< cuchara | = | spoon) |
| *empanadilla*[4] | = | small savoury pie (of the Cornish pasty type). |
| (< empanada | = | savoury pie) |
| *ensaladilla*[5] | = | Russian salad. |
| (< ensalada | = | salad) |
| †*escalerilla*[6] | = | gangway (ship, plane). |
| (< escalera | = | stairway) |
| *escobilla* | = | bush (tech.). |
| (< escoba | = | broom) |
| †*escuadrilla* | = | (air-force) squadron. |
| (< escuadra | = | (naval) squadron or fleet) |

[1] Especially used in the phrase *estar hasta la coronilla* = *estar harto* = to be fed up (to the teeth). Also in *andar de coronilla* = *andar de cabeza* = to be extremely busy, not to know whether one is on one's head or one's heels.

[2] Cf. *criadita* = (sprightly) young servant girl.
*Criadillas* are a highly esteemed delicacy of the Spanish cuisine, as are also *mollejas* (= sweetbreads) and *sesos* (= brains).

[3] Cf. *cucharita* = small spoon.

[4] Cf. *empanadita* = small empanada.
(Cf. *empanada* (< pan) = pie, with *emparedado* (< pared) = sandwich.)

[5] Cf. *ensaladita* = (nice) little salad.

[6] Cf. *escalerita* = small stairway.

| | |
|---|---|
| *espinilla*[1] | = black-head. |
| (< espina | = thorn) |
| *falsilla* | = sheet of guide lines (for writing). |
| (< falso | = false, sham) |
| *fierecilla* | = shrew, little terror. |
| (< fiera | = wild creature) |
| *flotilla*[2] | = flotilla; fishing fleet. |
| (< flota | = fleet) |
| *gargantilla*[3] | = necklace. |
| (< garganta | = throat) |
| *gomilla*[4] | = elastic band. |
| (< goma | = rubber) |
| *guerrilla*[5] | = guerrilla war(-fare), partisan war(-fare). |
| (< guerra | = war) |
| *guindilla*[6] | = dried red pepper, chilli. |
| (< guinda | = mazard cherry; glacé cherry) |
| *hablilla(s)* | = talk, chit-chat, gossip. |
| (< habla | = speech) |
| *hornilla*[7] | = kitchen stove. |
| (< horno | = oven) |
| *horquilla* | = hair-pin. |
| (< horca | = pitch-fork) |

[1] Cf. *espinita* = small or tiny thorn.

[2] E.g. *flotilla de destructores* = destroyer flotilla; *flotilla pesquera* = fishing fleet.

[3] Now a somewhat antiquated term. The usual word is *collar*.

[4] *Gomita* also is sometimes used with the sense of "elastic band", but generally means either "small (erasing) rubber" or "small rubber object" (in general).

[5] Cf. *Guerrita* = young Guerra (surname).
*Guerrillero* = guerrilla or partisan fighter.

[6] For masculine see section D.

[7] Cf. *cocina* = kitchen stove or kitchen.
Cf. *hornillo* = portable spirit-stove; gas (or electric) ring.
Cf. *infernillo* (or *infiernillo*) = portable spirit-stove.
Cf. *hogar* = gas (or electric) ring.
*Una hornilla (cocina) de cuatro hogares (hornillos)* = a stove with four rings. See *cocinilla*, above.

| | | |
|---|---|---|
| *lamparilla*[1] | = | small lamp; night light. |
| (< lámpara | = | lamp) |
| *lentilla(s)*[2] | = | contact lens(es). |
| (< lente | = | lens) |
| *manilla*[3] | = | hand (watch or clock); curtain-ring. |
| (< mano | = | hand) |
| *masilla* | = | putty. |
| (< masa | = | dough; mass) |
| *mantequilla* | = | butter. |
| (< manteca | = | lard; cooking fat; dripping) |
| *mantilla*[4] | = | Spanish mantilla, head-shawl. |
| (< manta | = | blanket) |
| *manzanilla*[5] | = | camomile (tea). |
| (< manzana | = | apple) |
| *maquinilla* (de | | |
| afeitar)[6] | = | razor. |
| (< máquina | = | machine, apparatus, engine) |
| *marisabidilla* | = | (little) know-it-all, (little) blue-stocking. |
| (< María + | | |
| p. p. of saber) | | |
| *mascarilla*[7] | = | death-mask; anaesthetic mask. |
| (< máscara | = | mask) |

[1] *Lamparilla de aceite* = night-light. (Also called *mariposa*.)

[2] The full expression is *microlentillas de contacto*.

[3] Cf. *manecilla* = hand (watch or clock).
   Cf. *manita, manecita* = small hand (human).

[4] Cf. *mantita* = (cute) little blanket.
   Cf. *mantón*. See under *-ón*.

[5] Cf. *manzanita* = (attractive or nice) little apple.
Camomile tea is so called in Spanish because of the resemblance of the
ud of the camomile plant to an apple.
Manzanilla wine owes its name to its place of origin: the village of *Manza-
illa* in the province of Huelva.

[6] *Maquinilla eléctrica* = electric razor.
   Cf. *navaja de afeitar* = cut-throat razor.
   Cf. *maquinita* = (cute) little machine, etc.

[7] The most general terms for "mask" are *máscara* (e.g. *baile de máscaras*)
ad *antifaz*. See *careta*, under *-eta*.
   Cf. *mascarón (de proa)* = figure-head (ship).

| | | |
|---|---|---|
| *mesilla* (de noche)[1] | = | bedside table. |
| (< *mesa* | = | table) |
| *mezclilla* | = | tweed cloth. |
| (< *mezcla* | = | mixture) |
| †*mi(a)jilla*[2] | = | spot, speck; little bit, wee bit. |
| (< *miga* | = | crumb) |
| *mirilla*[3] | = | peep-hole (in a door). |
| (< *mira* | = | sight (gun); watch or lookout tower (obsolete sense)) |
| *morcilla* | = | black-pudding. |
| (< *morcón* (uncommon) | = | stuffed intestine) |
| *muletilla*[4] | = | refrain; catch phrase. |
| (< *muleta* | = | crutch) |
| *mulilla* | = | (small) mule (form always used for mules of *arrastre* team in bull-fighting). |
| (< *mula* | = | mule) |
| *muñequilla* | = | rubbing- or polishing-rag or bag. |
| (< *muñeca* | = | wrist; doll) |
| *natilla(s)* | = | custard. |
| (< *nata* | = | cream) |
| *navajilla*[5] | = | small clasp-knife; penknife. |
| (< *navaja* | = | clasp- or jack-knife) |
| *octavilla*[6] | = | leaflet. |
| (< *octava* [parte] | = | eighth) |

---

[1] Cf. *mesita* = (attractive) little table, small table.

[2] Cf. *mi(a)jita* — same sense. These are Andalusian dialect forms which have become of fairly general use.

Cf. *miaja*, *miaja* — similar sense. *Mi(a)jilla* < *mi(a)ja* < *migaja* < *miga*.

[3] Cf. *ventanillo*, which is a larger type of peep-hole in the shape of a small window.

[4] See *estribillo*, under -*illo*.

[5] *Navajita* also is commonly used in the sense of "penknife". *Cortaplumas* is scarcely found in the Spanish of today.

[6] Cf. *folleto* = pamphlet. Cf. *panfleto* = lampoon.

| | |
|---|---|
| *pacotilla*[1] | = rubbish, trash. |
| (derivation | |
| dubious) | |
| *palomilla*[2] | = strut, support. |
| (< paloma | = dove, pigeon) |
| *pandilla* | = gang. |
| (< banda | = band, faction) |
| *papilla* | = pap, baby-food. |
| (< papa | = pap) |
| *parrilla* | = grill; grill-room; dance-room (hotel). |
| (< parra | = vine) |
| *pastilla*[3] | = tablet; pastille; bar (of chocolate or soap). |
| (< pasta | = paste) |
| *patilla(s)*[4] | = side-whisker(s), side-board(s); spectacle leg(s). |
| (< pata | = foot, leg) |
| *peladilla* | = small pebble; sugar almond. |
| (< pelado | = bare) |
| *pelotilla*[5] | = small ball of wax incrusted with pieces of glass (used by flagellants); act of toadying. |
| (< pelota | = ball) |
| *perilla*[6] | = goatee; light bulb. |
| (< pera | = pear) |
| *pesadilla* | = nightmare. |
| (< pesado | = heavy, tedious) |
| *pescadilla*[7] | = (small) haddock. |
| (< pescada | = haddock, (small) hake) |
| *plantilla*[8] | = shoe sock; staff, list of staff. |
| (< planta | = sole (foot); floor, storey) |

[1] *Ser de pacotilla* = to be rubbishy or jerry-built.

[2] Cf. *palomita* = (charming) little dove.

[3] Cf. *tableta* = tablet, (large) bar (of chocolate).

[4] Cf. *patitas* = (delightful or cute) little feet or legs (usually non-human).

[5] *Hacerle a uno la pelotilla* = *darle a uno coba* = to toady to, to butter up, to suck up to someone.

[6] Cf. *bombilla* = light bulb.

[7] Cf. *merluza* = (large) hake.

[8] Cf. *nómina* = staff list; payroll.
   Cf. *personal* = staff.

| | |
|---|---|
| *puntilla*[1] | = point lace; small nail; small dagger (bull-fighting); final stroke, last straw (fig.). |
| (< punta | = tip, end) |
| *redecilla*[2] | = hair-net. |
| (< red | = net) |
| *rejilla*[3] | = criss-cross work; luggage rack (train). |
| (< reja | = [iron] grille) |
| *seguidilla*[4] | = seguidilla (flamenco); popular poetic metre. |
| (< seguido | = continuing, continuous) |
| *sombrilla*[5] | = sun-shade. |
| (< sombra | = shade) |
| *taleguilla*[6] | = breeches (of bull-fighter). |
| (< talega | = bag, sack) |
| *taquilla* | = box-office, booking-office; window or grill (in banks, etc.). |
| (< taca (uncommon) | = small cupboard) |
| *tetilla* | = male nipple. |
| (< teta | = teat, breast) |
| *toldilla* | = round-house (naut.); canvas cover (for cart). |
| (< toldo | = awning) |
| *toquilla*[7] | = kerchief, small shawl. |
| (< toca | = head-dress) |
| *torrecilla* | = turret. |
| (< torre | = tower) |

[1] Cf. *encaje* = lace.
 Cf. *clavito* = small nail.
 Cf. *cachetero* = small dagger (bull-fight).
 *Dar la puntilla a* = to finish off, to put an end to.
[2] Cf. *redecita* = small net.
[3] Cf. *rejita* = small grille, grating.
 Cf. *baca* = luggage rack (car, coach).
[4] Cf. the phrase *en seguidita* = in just a moment.
[5] Cf. *sombrita* = (pleasant) bit of shade.
[6] Cf. *taleguita* = (nice) little bag.
[7] Cf. *toquita* = (charming) little head-dress.

| | |
|---|---|
| *tortilla*[1] | = omelette. |
| (< torta | = bun, cake or pastry) |
| *trabilla* | = strap. |
| (< traba | = hobble (for horses); fastening) |
| *trencilla* | = thin ornamental ribbon, braid. |
| (< trenza | = plait, plat) |
| *vainilla*[2] | = vanilla. |
| (< vaina | = sheath) |
| *varilla*[3] | = rib (fan, umbrella); dip-stick (for oil level); float (fisherman's); (pl.) whisk. |
| (< vara | = rod, staff) |
| *ventanilla*[4] | = window (vehicle); counter position (bank, post office, etc.); nostril. |
| (< ventana | = window) |
| *zancadilla*[5] | = trip (wrestling); trick, deceit. |
| (< zancada | = long, swift stride) |
| *zapatilla*[6] | = slipper; beach shoe; low flat motor-boat; washer. |
| (< zapato | = shoe) |

-illa *EXAMPLES FROM LITERATURE*
(GROUP B)

— Yo lo tengo afeitado la mar de veces, y sabía ser un tío cordial cuando quería.... Me acuerdo que cada vez que decía una broma

[1] Cf. *tortita* = pancake; waffle; flap-jack.
   *Tortilla, tortilla francesa, tortilla a la francesa* = omelette; *tortilla de patata(s)* = Spanish or potato omelette.
   Cf. *tortillita* = small omelette.
[2] Cf. *vainita* = little sheath.
[3] Cf. *varita* = (attractive) little stick; (fairy's) wand.
[4] It is curious that, whereas the window of a vehicle is always referred to as *ventanilla* and not *ventana*, the door of a vehicle is nowadays usually called *puerta*, the word *portezuela*, once obligatory in such cases, being less and less used.
[5] *Echarle (ponerle) a uno la zancadilla* = to trip up, to queer someone's pitch, to thwart. (Cf. *contrariar* = to thwart.)
[6] Cf. *zapatito* = small shoe.

o un chascarrillo cualquiera, en seguida ... levantaba la cabeza de la *almohadilla* y se volvía a todas partes, ...para ver cómo había caído el chiste....

(SÁNCHEZ FERLOSIO, *El Jarama*, p. 69)

"I've shaved him masses of times, and he could be a cheery bloke when he liked.... I remember that whenever he told a joke or made some quip or other, he used to raise his head ... at once from the rest and look all round, ...to see how it had been received...."

— ...tus faltas nacen del amor y no del interés; y los mismos disparates que haces por un hombre poderoso que te da grandes cantidades, los harías si fuera un pobre pelagatos y tuvieras que comprarle tú a él una *cajetilla.*

(PÉREZ GALDÓS, *Fortunata y Jacinta*, IV, p. 65)

"... your sins stem from love and not from self-interest; and the same crazy things that you do for a wealthy man who gives you large sums of money you would do also if he were a poor wretch and *you* had to buy *him* a packet of cigarettes."

Para tener compañía y servicio, tomó por criada a una niña.... Llamábase Encarnación, y parecía muy *formalita.*★ Su ama le leyó la *cartilla* el primer día, diciéndole: — Mira: si algún sujeto que tú no conoces ... te pregunta en la calle si vivo yo aquí, dices que no. No abras nunca la puerta a ninguna persona que no sea de la casa.... Conque fíjate bien en lo que te mando.

(PÉREZ GALDÓS, *Fortunata y Jacinta*, IV, p. 206)

She took on a young girl as a maid for the company and the help.... Her name was Encarnación and she seemed a regular little model of good behaviour. Her mistress read her the riot act on the first day, saying to her: "Look here, if an individual you don't know ... asks you when you're out if I live here, you're to say I don't. Never open the door to anyone who doesn't belong to the house.... So take good note of my instructions."

Por el andén pasa un mendigo *barbudo*★ recogiendo *colillas* ...
Un hombre le dice: — Ven, León, que te tengo mucho cariño.
¿Quieres un *pitillo*★? — Cuando León se le acerca, [el hombre] le
da una *bofetada*★ que suena como un *trallazo*.★

(Cela, Viaje a la Alcarria, p. 39)

A heavily-bearded beggar goes along the platform picking up
cigarette-ends.... A man says to him: "Come here, Leo, you
know I'm very fond of you. Want a fag?" When Leo goes up to
him, [the man] gives him a swipe that rings out like a whip-lash.

Entrando en la cuestión palpitante, diré a usted que su famoso
brindis ha sido *comidilla* general de España por espacio de medio
mes.

(Pardo Bazán, in letter quoted by C. Bravo-Villasante in Vida<br>y Obra de Emilia Pardo Bazán, p. 66)

Coming to the burning question I will tell you that your celebrated
toast has been the talk of all Spain for a period of half a month.

Es verdad que la Guindilla mayor se tenía bien ganado su apodo
por su *carita*★ redonda y *coloradita*★ y su carácter picante y agrio
como el aguardiente. Por añadidura era una *cotilla*. Y a las *cotillas*
no les viene mal todo lo que les caiga encima.

(Delibes, El Camino, p. 56)

It's true that the elder "Red Pepper" thoroughly deserved her
nickname because of her round, very ruddy little face and because
her nature was as biting and sharp as unrefined brandy. In addition
she was a gossip. And gossips are really due for anything they get.

Las ruedas tocaron el suelo, y, al fin, el aparato se detuvo y se
abrió la puerta.... Miguel descendió la *escalerilla* metálica ....

(Sampedro, Congreso en Estocolmo, p. 9)

The wheels touched the ground, and the machine finally came
to rest and the door opened.... Miguel came down the metal
gang-way ....

121

Factor decisivo, sin duda, fue la llegada a Mallorca de una *escuadrilla* de aviones italianos que se adueñaron del aire...

(GIRONELLA, *Un Millón de Muertos*, p. 239)

Undoubtedly a decisive factor was the arrival in Majorca of a squadron of Italian aircraft which took control of the sky...

... Sor Facunda.. era la *marisabidilla* de la casa, muy leída y escribida... Llevaba siempre tras sí, en las horas de recreo, un hato de niñas precozmente místicas, *preguntonas*★, *rezonas*★. ...

(PÉREZ GALDÓS, *Fortunata y Jacinta*, II, pp. 280, 281)

... Sister Facunda... was the convent's (little) know-it-all, a regular blue-stocking... At play-time she always had following after her a bevy of little girls with precocious mystic tendencies and an excessive fondness for asking questions and for praying....

— Esas cosas no se arreglan en un día, ni tampoco en quince. Ten una *miajilla* de paciencia.

(GOYTISOLO, *Campos de Níjar*, p. 113)

"Things like that can't be fixed in a day, or in a fortnight for that matter. Have a wee bit of patience."

*-illa (C) NOUN — MASCULINE*
*(Diminutive — often with pejorative implication)*

| | | |
|---|---|---|
| comunistilla[1] | = | bit a communist; miserable little communist. |
| curilla[2] | = | little priest; miserable little priest. |
| chuletilla[3] | = | rather pugnacious type, cocky little individual. |
| †granujilla[4] | = | little rascal or scamp, bit of a rogue; miserable little scamp. |

[1] Cf. *rojillo* — similar sense. See under *-illo*.
 Cf. *comunistón, rojazo*. See under *-ón, -azo*.
[2] Cf. *curita* and *curete*. See under *-ita* (m.), *-ete*.
 Cf. *curángano* and *curazo*. See under *-ángano, -azo*.
[3] See *bravucón*, under *-ón*.
[4] See *pillín*, under *-ín*. The root-word *granuja* (lit. sense [fem.] "loose grapes") is used in the same way: — *un granuja* = a rascal, scamp.

| | |
|---|---|
| *hipocritilla*[1] | = bit of a hypocrite; miserable little hypocrite. |
| *horterilla*[2] | = modest shop assistant, two-penny ha'penny shop assistant. |
| *maletilla*[3] | = complete beginner, regular greenhorn, wretched novice (especially in bullfighting). |
| *sinvergüencilla* | = bit of a rascal, rogue or devil; miserable little bounder. |

## -illa EXAMPLE FROM LITERATURE
## (GROUP C)

— Este *granujilla* lo que tiene es pocas ganas de estudiar, ¿verdad?
(ZUNZUNEGUI, *¡Ay, Estos Hijos!* p. 21)

"All that's wrong with this little scamp is that he doesn't feel much like studying, am I right?"

## -illa (D) NOUN — MASCULINE
*(Changed or specialized sense)*

| | |
|---|---|
| *cabecilla*[4] | = ring-leader, rebel leader, partisan leader. |
| (< cabeza | = head) |
| *cocinilla*[5] | = man much given to interfering in the kitchen or in domestic affairs in general. |
| (< cocina | = kitchen, stove) |
| *fuguilla*[6] | = restless, jittery, impetuous, hustling or quick-tempered individual. |
| (< fuga | = flight) |

[1] Cf. *hipocritón*. See under *-ón*.
[2] Cf. *dependientucho* — similar sense. See under *-ucho*.
[3] The root-word *maleta* (lit. suitcase) is used in the same way: *un maleta* = a rotten bull-fighter or performer.
  Cf. *torerillo* = (modest, poor or wretched) little, novice or young bull-fighter.
[4] Cf. *cabecita* = small head. See under *-ita*.
[5] Cf. *cocinita* = small kitchen, small stove. See under *-ita*. See also under *-illa* (B) and under *-ica* (B).
[6] Also *fuguillas*.

†*guindilla*[1]  = policeman, bobby (nineteenth century).
(< guinda  = mazard cherry)

## -*illa* EXAMPLE FROM LITERATURE
## (GROUP D)

Increpaba con facilidad a los guardias . . .. Los *guindillas* eran aún, casi todos, entrados en edad, *bonachones*★ y *pacienzudos*★.

(PÉREZ FERRERO, *Vida de Pío Baroja*, p. 138)

He was easily able to chide the police . . .. The bobbies were still, almost all of them, getting on in years, thoroughly good-natured and long-suffering in the extreme.

## -*illas* ADVERB

(*en*) *cuclillas*[2]  = squatting.
(*a*) *hurtadillas*  = furtively, stealthily.
(*de*) *puntillas*  = on tip-toe.
(*a*) *las vistillas*  = peeping surreptitiously.

### 5. -EJO, -EJA

-*ejo* (A) NOUN — MASCULINE
(*Diminutive — often with pejorative implication*)

†*animalejo*[3] ⎱ = wretched little animal; wretched or hapless little
†*bichejo* ⎰   creature; pest.
†*apurejo*[4]  = rather a tight spot, spot of trouble, bit of a jam, bit of a fix.

---

[1] This special sense is said to have arisen as a result of the use by the town police of a red ornament in their ceremonial caps.

For feminine see section B.

[2] Derives originally from *clueca* = broody (said of hens).

[3] The two words are often used synonymously, but *bichejo* is nevertheless more fundamentally pejorative than *animalejo*.

Cf. *animalillo*, *animalucho* — similar sense.

Cf. *bichillo*, *bichucho* — similar sense.

Cf. *bestezuela* — similar sense.

[4] Cf. *apurillo* — same sense.

| | | |
|---|---|---|
| *articulejo* | = | wretched or modest little article. |
| †*bichejo*[1] | = | wretched little creature or insect. |
| †*caballejo* | = | wretched or modest little horse. |
| *caminejo*[2] | = | wretched or narrow little path. |
| *castillejo* | = | miserable or modest little castle. |
| †*corralejo*[3] | = | miserable or modest little yard. |
| †*diablejo*[4] | = | little devil, little rascal. |
| *discursejo* | = | wretched or modest little speech. |
| †*gracejo* | = | light humour, gentle wit. |
| †*gusanejo*[5] | = | wretched little worm. |
| *hermanejo*[6] | = | young brother, little perisher of a brother. |
| *ladroncejo*[7] | = | thieving little rascal or perisher. |
| *librejo*[8] | = | miserable or modest little book. |
| *lugarejo*[9] | = | miserable or modest little village. |
| *milloncejo(s)*[10] | = | perishing million(s). |
| †*pellejo*[11] | = | coarse, rough, thick or loose skin; scruff. |
| †*rinconcejo* | = | small corner, modest little spot. |
| *rocinejo* | = | wretched or poor old nag. |
| *sobrinejo* | = | young nephew, perishing nephew. |
| *tipejo*[12] | = | bit of a queer type; rather a bad lot; wretched individual. |

[1] See *animalejo*, above.
[2] Cf. *caminillo, caminucho, senderuelo* — similar sense.
[3] Cf. *corralillo* — same sense.
[4] Cf. *diablillo* — same sense. See *pillín*, under *-ín*.
[5] Cf. *gusanillo*. See under *-illo*.
[6] Cf. *hermanete* — similar sense.
[7] Cf. *ladronzuelo* — similar sense.
[8] Cf. *librillo* — similar sense.
[9] See *poblacho*, under *-acho*.
[10] E.g. *está podrido de milloncejos* = he's rotten with perishing money, he's a perishing millionaire.
[11] Cf. *pelleja* — similar sense, but less common.
*Salvar el pellejo (la pelleja)* = to save one's skin, hide or bacon.
*jugarse el pellejo (la pelleja)* = to risk one's skin, hide or neck.
*un viejo pellejo* = an old codger.
*una vieja pelleja* = an old dame.
[12] Cf. *tiparraco*. See under *-aco*.

(GROUP A)

... un loro ... se mantenía allí con la seriedad y circunspección propias de estos *animalejos*, observándolo todo.

(PÉREZ GALDÓS, *Doña Perfecta*, p. 43)

... a parrot ... was perched there watching everything with the gravity and circumspectness typical of these wretched (little) creatures.

[Cf. *bichejo*:

Contempló pensativamente una araña que frotaba sus patas, larguísimas y sutiles, como si temiese que se le helasen; y aquel *bichejo* le dio más que nada la impresión del frío.

(FERNÁNDEZ FLÓREZ, *El Bosque Animado*, p. 108)

He gazed thoughtfully at a spider which was rubbing its extremely long, fine legs, as if it were afraid that they might become frozen; and that wretched little creature gave him a greater sensation of cold than anything else.]

— ... ando en un *apurejo* del que usted me puede sacar.

(CELA, *Judíos, Moros y Cristianos*, p. 103)

"I'm in a bit of a fix, and you can get me out of it."

... [son] *caballejos* menudos, omnívoros y despeinados, ... que no galopan nunca pero no se cansan jamás.

(FERNÁNDEZ FLÓREZ, *El Bosque Animado*, p. 7)

... [they are] small, shaggy, modest little horses, which can live on anything ... which never gallop, but which never get tired either.

La poderosa mula de don Ramón ... se hallaba en un *corralejo* o pequeño cercado contiguo a la *casilla*.★

(VALERA, *Juanita la Larga*, p. 253)

Don Ramón's powerful mule ... was in a modest little yard or small enclosure adjoining the hut.

Su *cachazudo** hermano se apelotonaba en un rincón para dejar espacio a aquel *diablejo*, que, a pesar de su debilidad, le trataba como un déspota.

(BLASCO IBÁÑEZ, *Flor de Mayo*, p. 56)

His phlegmatic brother huddled up in a corner in order to leave (plenty of) room for that little devil who, despite his weakness, treated him tyrannically.

... se recomienda ... por el garbo y donaire con que está escrito y cierto *gracejo zumbón,** muy de cepa gallega, que le sazona.

(UNAMUNO, *Mi Religión*, p. 108)

... it is made attractive ... by the jauntiness and wittiness with which it is written and by a certain light, waggish humour which is very typically Galician and which gives it piquancy.

Contemplando desde la sierra lo que se veía del panorama del puerto, habíame comparado yo, por la fuerza del contraste, con un mísero *gusanejo*.

(PEREDA, *Peñas Arriba*, p. 36)

Gazing down from the mountains on what could be seen of the panorama of the pass I had compared myself, because of the violent contrast, with a miserable, wretched little worm.

Cogiólos uno a uno Chisco por el *pellejo* del *cerviguillo** y los fue arrojando a la barranca.

(PEREDA, *Peñas Arriba*, p. 230)

One by one Chisco grabbed them by the loose skin of the scruff of the neck and flung them into the ravine.

El vagabundo ... sigue camino hasta Urueñas, donde se premia con dos *cuartillos** de vino ... y se busca un *rinconcejo* para posar.

(CELA, *Judíos, Moros y Cristianos*, p. 105)

The tramp ... continues on his way as far as Urueñas, where he treats himself to two pints of wine ... and finds himself a modest little spot to rest.

*-ejo (B) NOUN — MASCULINE*
(*Changed or specialized sense*)

| | | |
|---|---|---|
| abadejo | = | (fresh) cod-fish; (orn.) goldcrest. |
| (< abad | = | abbot) |
| marmolejo | = | (small) marble column. |
| (< mármol | = | marble) |

*-ejo (C) ADJECTIVE*

| | | |
|---|---|---|
| apuradejo[1] | = | a little hard pressed, in a bit of a fix or jam. |
| escuchimiza-<br>dejo[2] | = | on the stunted side, a bit runtish. |
| †malejo[3] | = | poorish, on the bad, poor or weak side, not much cop. |
| †medianejo[4] | = | fairish only, middling. |
| mimadejo[5] | = | rather spoilt, on the spoilt side. |
| rubiejo[6] | = | fairish (in complexion), having fairish hair. |

*-ejo EXAMPLES FROM LITERATURE*
(GROUP C)

El vagabundo, en el camino de Bohoyo, amigó con un pastor muchacho que se entretenía en tirar lejos su cachava para que el *perrillo** se la trajese . . . .
— Parece bueno, el perro . . . .
— Sí, señor; para lo ruin que es, no me salió *malejo* del todo.
(CELA, *Judíos, Moros y Cristianos*, pp. 237, 238)

On the way to Bohoyo the tramp struck up a friendship with a shepherd lad who was amusing himself by flinging his staff far from him for his miserable little dog to fetch . . . .
"He seems O.K., that dog of yours . . . ."

[1] Cf. *apuradillo, apuradete* — similar sense.
[2] Cf. *escuchimizadillo, escuchimizadete* — similar sense.
[3] Cf. *malillo* — similar sense.
[4] Cf. *medianillo, medianete* — similar sense.
[5] Cf. *mimadillo, mimadito, mimadete* — similar sense.
[6] Cf. *rubillo* — similar sense.

"Yes, you're right; considering what a poor object he is, he hasn't turned out to be altogether a bad little perisher."

A diferencia del gaditano o malagueño, el almeriense es poco aficionado a la bebida. La culpa se la echo yo a los caldos del país, por lo general muy *medianejos*. El que bebo ahora — *vinagrón** y algo repuntado — difiere apenas del desbravado y zurraposo de Garrucha.

(GOYTISOLO, *Campos de Níjar*, p. 26)

Unlike the natives of Cadiz and Malaga those of Almeria are not very keen on drink. *I* lay the blame [for this] on the area's wines — for the most part very middling [affairs]. The one I'm drinking now — vinegary stuff and on the sour side — is scarcely different from Garrucha's roughly refined, dreggish product.

## *-eja (A) NOUN — FEMININE*
*(Diminutive — often with pejorative implication)*

| | |
|---|---|
| *calleja*[1] | = little or narrow street, modest or wretched street, lane, alley. |
| *comideja*[2] | = poor or wretched food or meal. |
| *copeja* | = wretched glass, jolly old glass or drink. |
| †*copleja*[3] | = modest or poor little verse or song, ditty, jolly old verse. |
| *libreja* | = miserable pound, paltry quid. |
| †*palabreja*[4] | = wretched word, queer or affected word. |

[1] Cf. *callejón, callejucha, callejuela* = narrow lane, wretched little lane or alley.
  Cf. *callecita* = (delightful) little street.
  Cf. *callejita* = (attractive) little lane.
[2] Cf. *comidilla* — similar sense.
  Cf. *comistrajo* — similar sense. See under *-ajo*.
[3] Cf. *coplilla, coplucha* — similar sense.
[4] Cf. *palabrota* = crude, coarse or vulgar word. See under *-ota*.

| *patateja*[1] | = miserable potato, perishing spud, jolly old spud. |
| †*pelleja*[2] | = coarse skin. |
| †*propineja* | = modest tip; perishing tip; jolly old tip. |

*-eja* EXAMPLES FROM LITERATURE
(GROUP A)

> *Cerquita*\* de los Galayos
> está el nogal del Barranco,
> donde acampan los turistas
> en el rigor del verano.

La *copleja* . . . es *malilla*\*, pero el vagabundo no se siente culpable.

(CELA, *Judíos, Moros y Cristianos*, p. 275)

> Hard by "The Slabs"
> stands the Ravine walnut tree,
> where the tourists camp
> in the fierce heat of summer.

The jolly old verse is . . . poorish, but the tramp does not consider himself to blame for that.

> — . . . ¡Pobre nena!

Al oír esta exclamación de cariño . . . Jacinta arrugó el ceño. Ella había heredado la aplicación de la *palabreja*, que ya le disgustaba por ser como desecho de una pasión anterior . . . .

(PÉREZ GALDÓS, *Fortunata y Jacinta*, I, p. 111)

> ". . . Poor girlie!"

On hearing this exclamation of affection . . . Jacinta frowned. She had inherited the wretched word, which had been used for another and which was now displeasing to her because it was like a left-over from a previous love-affair . . . .

> — ¿Alguno de vosotros se encargaría de un negocio difícil en que hay que exponer la *pelleja*?

(BAROJA, *Zalacaín el Aventurero*, p. 87)

---

[1] E.g. *carne con unas patatejas* = meat with a few miserable spuds.
[2] Cf. *pellejo*. See under *-ejo*.

"Would any of you be interested in undertaking a difficult piece of business that involves risking one's neck?"

... los criados, en la cocina, calculaban ya a cuánto ascendería la *propineja* nupcial.

(Pardo Bazán, Los Pazos de Ulloa, p. 156)

... in the kitchen the servants were already working out how much the jolly old wedding tip would amount to.

## -eja (B) NOUN — FEMININE
### (Changed or specialized sense)

| | | |
|---|---|---|
| *candileja(s)* | = | foot light(s); lime light. |
| (< candil | = | oil lamp) |
| *comadreja*[1] | = | weasel, stoat. |
| (< comadre | = | godmother; old wife) |
| *molleja(s)*[2] | = | sweetbread(s). |
| (< molla[3] | = | lean meat) |
| *moraleja* | = | moral (of story, etc.). |
| (< moral | = | morals, morality) |

## o. -UELO, -UELA

## -uelo (A) NOUN — MASCULINE
### (Diminutive — often with pejorative implication)

| | | |
|---|---|---|
| *arroyuelo*[4] | = | (poor or modest) little stream. |
| *autorzuelo* | = | wretched author, third-rate author. |

---

[1] For *comadrona* see *madrina*, under *-ina*.
[2] See *criadilla(s)*, under *-illa*.
[3] This derivation is dubious.
[4] Cf. *riachuelo*. See below.
*Arroyuelo* is not necessarily pejorative but tends to be so, whereas *riachuelo* is nearly always definitely contemptuous in tone. See *riacho*, under *-acho*.
Cf. *arroyito* = (delightful) little stream or brook.
Cf. *regajito, regatito* = (charming) little brook.
Cf. *regajillo, regatillo, riatillo* = (poor or modest) little brook.

| | | |
|---|---|---|
| †*barquichuelo*[1] | = | (miserable) little boat. |
| *ceguezuelo* <br> *cieguezuelo* } | = | (poor) little blind boy. |
| *corderuelo*[2] | = | (poor) little lamb. |
| *corpezuelo*[3] | = | small body, jolly old carcass. |
| †*escritorzuelo* | = | wretched little writer, petty writer. |
| †*farsantuelo* | = | wretched little humbug or play-actor. |
| †*ingratuelo* | = | ungrateful little wretch or devil. |
| *jovenzuelo*[4] <br> *mozuelo* <br> *rapazuelo* } | = | young lad, youngster, young un, young whipper-snapper. |
| †*ladronzuelo* | = | thieving young rascal, thieving little devil or perisher, thieving little monkey. |
| *mozuelo*[5] | = | young lad. |
| *nietezuelo*[6] | = | little grandson. |
| *ojuelo(s)*[7] | = | (beady) little eye(s). |
| *patizuelo* | = | modest, poor or wretched little court-yard. |
| *pequeñuelo* | = | little chappie, wee mite. |
| *piecezuelo*[8] | = | (poor) little foot. |
| †*pilluelo*[9] | = | little or young rascal, rogue, scamp or urchin. |
| *politicuelo* | = | petty or two-penny ha'penny politician. |

[1] Note double ending.

  Cf. *barquito* = (attractive) little boat.

[2] Cf. *corderillo* — similar sense.

  Cf. *corderito* — similar sense, but more favourable tone.

[3] Cf. *cuerpecillo, cuerpecito* — distinction as for *corderillo, -ito.*

*Hay que trabajar el corpezuelo* = one must give the jolly old carcass some exercise.

[4] Cf. *jovencillo, jovencito* — distinction as for *corderillo, -ito,* but little difference.

  Cf. *mocito, mocete* — very similar sense.

[5] See *jovenzuelo,* above.

[6] Cf. *nietecillo, nietecito* — distinction as for *corderillo, -ito,* but very little difference.

[7] *Ojuelo(s)* is almost always used in a pejorative context with some such idea as "beady, cunning or nasty little eye(s)". It is thus close to *ojillo* and different rom *ojito.*

[8] Rare. *Piececillo* is much more common. Cf. *piececito* = charming little foot.

[9] See *pillín,* under *-ín.*

| | | |
|---|---|---|
| *polluelo*[1] | = | chick, young one. |
| *rapazuelo*[2] | = | youngster. |
| *reyezuelo*[3] | = | petty king, princeling. |
| †*riachuelo*[4] | = | (wretched) little stream. |
| *senderuelo*[5] | = | (narrow) little path. |
| ††*tiranuelo* | = | petty tyrant. |
| *viejezuelo*[6] | = | (wretched) little old man. |

## -*uelo* EXAMPLES FROM LITERATURE
## (GROUP A)

... sobre la mesa (había) dos grandes caracoles de mar, y, en medio de ellos, un *barquichuelo* de cristal toscamente labrado.

(PALACIO VALDÉS, *José*, p. 37)

... on the table (were) two large conch shells and, between them, a wretched little, clumsily fashioned glass boat.

Ved que nosotros, pobres *escritorzuelos*, mendigos de la fama, cargados del bagaje de nuestros *libracos*★, andamos por el mundo ... recogiendo afanosos, de aquí y de allá, piropos que nos den la medida de nuestro valer.

(BENAVENTE, *Cartas de Mujeres*, p. 332)

Remember that we poor petty writers, beggars after fame loaded down with the burden of our wretched books, go about

---

[1] Cf. *pollito* — similar sense.
Cf. *hijuelo* (uncommon) — also used in this way, e.g. *una gallina y sus hijuelos* = a hen and her young ones.
[2] See *jovenzuelo*, above.
[3] Cf. *régulo* — same sense.
[4] Note double ending. See *arroyuelo*, above.
[5] Cf. *caminillo, caminucho* — similar sense.
Contrast *caminito*. See under -*ito*.
[6] Also *vejezuelo*.
Cf. *viejecillo* — similar sense.
Contrast *viejecito*. See *viejezuela*, under -*uela*.

the world . . . eagerly gathering up from one place and another flattering remarks which will give us the measure of our worth.

— ¿Me engañarás otra vez, *farsantuelo*?
(PÉREZ GALDÓS, Fortunata y Jacinta, III, p. 355)

"Will you deceive me again, you precious little humbug?"

— . . . si no discurriera tanto como discurro . . . ¿qué habría sido de ti, *ingratuelo*?
(PÉREZ GALDÓS, Fortunata y Jacinta, II, p. 123)

". . . if I didn't give things as much thought as I do . . . what would have become of you, you ungrateful [young] puppy?"

Rápidamente, como un *ladronzuelo*, salvó la cortina de la alcoba.
(ZUNZUNEGUI, ¡Ay, Estos Hijos!, p. 19)

Quickly, like a petty little thief, he slipped through the curtain leading to the bedroom recess.

. . . [el ratón] miraba a Sor Marcela con sus *ojuelos* negros y *pillines*.*
(PÉREZ GALDÓS, Fortunata y Jacinta, II, p. 270)

. . . [the mouse] looked at Sister Marcela with its mischievous, [beady] little black eyes.

De las techumbres de paja de las barracas salían las bandadas de gorriones como un tropel de *pilluelos* perseguidos.
(BLASCO IBÁÑEZ, La Barraca, p. 11)

The flocks of sparrows were emerging from the thatched roofs of the huts like a mob of young urchins in flight from a pursuer.

El viajero se queda . . . a la sombra de un *grupito** de álamos escuálidos que hay a la orilla del Solana, un *riachuelo* casi sin agua que viene arrastrando su miseria desde la Sierra de Umbría Seca.
(CELA, Viaje a la Alcarria, pp. 133, 134)

The traveller stays ... in the shade of a small cluster of emaciated poplars growing on the bank of the *Solana*, a fiddling, almost waterless little stream that trickles impoverishedly down from the *Umbría Seca* hills.

La *pandilla** a que pertenecían los Baroja tenía su *jefecillo**, naturalmente, que obligaba a su acompañamiento a imitarle en sus fechorías. Una de éstas consistía en ir pasando, primero el *tiranuelo* y después sus vasallos, ante un escaparate donde había unas cuantas pelotas amontonadas junto al cristal, en el que ellos daban sucesivos *golpecitos** hasta conseguir que las pelotas se desparramaran.

(PÉREŻ FERRERO, *Vida de Pío Baroja*, p. 40)

The gang to which the Baroja boys belonged naturally had its little upstart leader who forced those with him to follow suit in the misdeeds he perpetrated. One of these took the following form: first the petty tyrant and then his vassals would go past a shop-window where there were a number of balls piled against the glass, on which one after another they would all give taps until they made the pile collapse.

## -*uelo* (B) NOUN — MASCULINE
(*Changed or specialized sense*)

| | |
|---|---|
| *brazuelo* | = upper part of foreleg (animals). |
| (< brazo | = arm) |
| *gazpachuelo* | = Andalusian cold soup made mainly of potato and mayonnaise. |
| (< gazpacho | = Andalusian cold soup made mainly of tomato, vegetable pepper, bread crumbs and vinegar) |
| *hoyuelo*[1] | = dimple. |
| (< hoyo | = hole, hollow) |
| *mochuelo*[2] | = (night-)owl, owlet. |
| (< mocho | = short-cropped, cut off) |

[1] The form *hoyito* is now being increasingly used to replace *hoyuelo* in this sense.

[2] Cf. *buho* = (eagle-)owl, *lechuza* = (barn-)owl, *estrige* = screech-owl.

| | |
|---|---|
| *pañuelo*[1] | = handkerchief; head scarf. |
| (< paño | = cloth) |
| *reyezuelo* | = (orn.) kinglet, wren; goldcrest. |
| (< rey | = king) |

## -uelo (C) ADJECTIVE

| | |
|---|---|
| †*chiquituelo* | = insignificantly or miserably small. |
| *estrechuelo*[2] | = small and narrow, wretchedly narrow. |
| †*gordezuelo*[3] | = small and fat, small and chubby. |
| *locuelo* | = a bit crazy, a little on the mad-cap side. |
| *pedantuelo* | = on the pedantic side; foolishly pedantic. |
| *pequeñuelo* | = tiny, weeny, very young. |
| †*respondonzuelo* | = a (wee) bit given to answering back. |
| *traidorzuelo* | = a bit or a mite treacherous. |

## -uelo EXAMPLES FROM LITERATURE
## (GROUP C)

— En la menor no se reparaba, porque es tan *chiquituela* y consumida que parece un gusarapo.

(VALERA, *Juanita la Larga*, p. 125)

"People didn't notice the younger one because she's such a wasted-away, miserable little thing that she looks like a water-worm."

— ... tienes unas *manitas*\* *gordezuelas* de confitero.

(ZUNZUNEGUI, *¡Ay, Estos Hijos!*, p. 141)

". . . you have the chubby little hands of a pastry-cook."

— ... ¡Usted ha cenado fuerte!
— He cenado lo que me ha dado la gana.

[1] Cf. *pañoleta*. See under *-eta*.
[2] E.g. *un sendero estrechuelo* = a wretchedly narrow path. **A very similar** sense is conveyed by *senderuelo* and *caminucho*.
[3] Cf. *gordito* = nice and chubby or plump. See *regordete*, under *-ete*.

— *Respondonzuelo* se va haciendo el *mocito.*\*
— Me hago lo que quiero.

(VALERA, Pepita Jiménez, p. 188)

"... You've had a hefty supper!"
"I have had the sort of supper I jolly well pleased."
"Quite a little one for answering back the laddie's becoming!"
"I'm becoming what I like."

---

*-uela (A) NOUN — FEMININE*
*(Diminutive — often with pejorative implication)*

| | |
|---|---|
| †*aldehuela*[1] | = wretched or miserable little village, apology for a village. |
| †*bestezuela*[2] | = little animal or creature, wretched or hapless little animal or creature, wee beastie (Scots). |
| *callejuela*[3] | = wretched little lane or alley, narrow lane or alley. |
| †*coquetuela*[4] | = coquettish little creature or monkey. |
| †*covachuela*[5] | = narrow little cave; poky or miserable little government office. |
| †*chicuela*[6] <br> *mozuela* <br> *muchachuela* | = young girl, lass; mere slip of a girl. |
| †*gentezuela*[7] | = petty riff-raff, wretched scum. |
| *intrigüela* | = petty little intrigue. |
| *mozuela*[8] | = lass. |

[1] See *poblacho*, under *-acho*.
[2] See *animalejo*, under *-ejo*.
[3] See *calleja*, under *-eja*.
[4] Cf. *coquetilla* — similar sense.
[5] More used of the past than of the present. See Examples from Literature.
[6] Cf. *chiquilla* — similar sense.
Contrast *chiquita, mocita, muchachita* = delightful young girl.
[7] See *gentuza*, under *-uza*.
[8] See *chicuela*, above.
*Mozuela* is used regionally with the meaning "unmarried girl or woman", this being especially common in Granada (cf. *mocita* in Seville): *Y que yo me la llevé al río — creyendo que era mozuela — pero tenía marido.* (GARCÍA LORCA, *La Casada Infiel*).

| | | |
|---|---|---|
| *muchachuela*[1] | = | lass. |
| †*mujerzuela*[2] | = | wretched woman or creature; slut, trollop. |
| *plazuela*[3] | = | modest or mean little square. |
| *portezuela*[4] | = | small or narrow door; door (of a vehicle). |
| †*tontuela* | = | silly little girl or creature. |
| †*viejezuela*[5] | = | wretched little old woman. |

## -uela EXAMPLES FROM LITERATURE
## (GROUP A)

... fue estrechándose el valle ... y cuando quedó convertido en un saco angosto, dimos en una *aldehuela* que llenaba todo el fondo de él.

(PEREDA, *Peñas Arriba*, p. 30)

... the valley gradually became narrower and narrower ..., and when [finally] there was no more than a narrow defile left, we came upon a wretched little village which filled the whole of the bottom of it.

Don Fabián acarició la cabeza de un niño esquivo como una *bestezuela*.

(CELA, *Judíos, Moros y Cristianos*, p. 99)

Don Fabián stroked the head of a little boy who was as evasively reserved as a small wild creature.

[1] See *chicuela*, above.

[2] Cf. *mujercilla* — similar sense.
Contrast *mujercita* = delightful little woman. *Mi mujercita* = my darling wife.

[3] Cf. *placilla* — similar sense.
Contrast *placita* = charming little square. See *plazoleta*, under -*eta*.

[4] More used formerly than at present. See note to *ventanilla*, under -*illa*.

[5] Also *vejezuela*.
Cf. *viejecilla* — similar sense.
Contrast *viejecita* = attractive or charming little old woman.

En una ocasión tropezaron mis ojos con los de la hermana, y me miró alegremente. *¡Coquetuela!* exclamé para adentro.

(PALACIO VALDÉS, *La Hermana San Sulpicio*, p. 83)

Once my eyes met those of the nun, and she looked at me gaily. Coquettish little monkey! I exclaimed inwardly.

... aquel Don Quixote de *covachuela* que fue Felipe II.

(UNAMUNO, *Andanzas y Visiones Españolas*, p. 56)

... that Don Quixote of poky bureaucracy who was Philip II.

... me dio a entender claramente que su interés estaba por encima de las antipatías inmotivadas de una *chicuela*.

(BAROJA, *La Ciudad de la Niebla*, p. 117)

... he gave me clearly to understand that his interests were above the foundationless dislikes of a mere slip of a girl.

*Gentezuelas* desconsideradas y groseras solían añadir al nombre familiar algún mote infamante: Doña Paca la tramposa, ...

(PÉREZ GALDÓS, *Misericordia*, p. 74)

Thoughtless, uncouth people, petty scum, were in the habit of adding to her popular name some abusive expression such as "la tramposa": Madam Francis, the trickster, ...

— Tu mujer, tus hijos, nunca te ven.... Te gastas lo que ganas con *mujerzuelas* y en los garitos ....

(BUERO VALLEJO, *Un Soñador para un Pueblo*, p. 227)

"Your wife and children never see you.... You spend what you earn on your own amusement — on whores and in the gambling dens ...."

— Pero ¿vas a llorar ahora, *tontuela*?

(LAFORET, *Nada*, p. 53)

"But are you going to cry now, you silly little thing?"

Doña Pitusa era una *viejezuela* pequeña, de nariz corva, ojos muy vivos y boca de sumidero ....

Don Cleto ... era un *viejecito** *bajito** y flaco, muy limpio, muy arreglado ... ..

(BAROJA, El Arbol de la Ciencia, p. 489)

Doña Pitusa was a wretched little old woman, with a bent nose, very lively eyes and a sunken mouth ... ..

Don Cleto ... was a shortish, thin, very clean, very neat, nice little old man ... ..

## -uela (B) NOUN — FEMININE
*(Changed or specialized sense)*

| | |
|---|---|
| *castañuela(s)* | = castanet(s). |
| (< *castaña* | = chestnut) |
| *cazuela*[1] | = earthenware bowl; stew. |
| (< *cazo* | = saucepan) |
| *habichuela*[2] | = French bean. |
| (< *haba* | = bean) |
| *lentejuela* | = spangle, sequin. |
| (< *lenteja* | = lentil) |
| *sanguijuela*[3] | = leech. |
| (< *sangre* | = blood) |
| *triquiñuela* | = trick, dodge, catch. |
| (< *trique* | |
| (rare) | = crack, slight report) |
| *zarzuela*[4] | = light or comic-opera (Spanish). |
| (< *zarza* | = bramble) |

[1] See *cazoleta*, under *-eta*. Cf. *cacerola* = twin-handled metal stewing-pan.

[2] Widely used in many provinces, but not the standard term, which is *judía (verde)*; also very common is *alubia*.

[3] Not strictly speaking derived from *sangre*, but probably from a Vulgar Latin diminutive formed on *sanguis*. Nevertheless, given thus for convenience.

[4] Probably so-called because the first performance of such a work in Spain is reputed to have taken place at *La Zarzuela*, a spot which had presumably once been covered in brambles, although *zarzal* would accord better with this than *zarzuela*.

Cf. *opereta* = light or comic-opera (non-Spanish).

*-ete (A) NOUN — MASCULINE*

*(Diminutive, frequently used to indicate jocularity, irony, scorn and also ironic affection)*

| | | |
|---|---|---|
| †*caballerete*[1] | = | fine (young) gentleman, spruce (young) gentleman, (little) Lord Fauntleroy. |
| *cerdete*[2] | = | jolly old pig or pork, fine young pig, fine pork, some pig or pork. |
| *cuñadete*[3] | = | jolly old brother-in-law, fine brother-in-law. |
| *curete*[4] | = | jolly old priest, fine priest, some priest. |
| *dinerete*[5] | = | jolly old money, jolly old cash. |
| †*discursete*[6] | = | jolly old speech, fine speech, some speech. |
| †*durete*[7] | = | jolly old five-peseta piece. |
| *estofadete*[8] | = | jolly old stew, good old stew. |
| *fresquete*[9] | = | rather chilly weather. |
| *galancete* | = | bright young beau, smart young blade, spruce young chappie. |
| *golfete*[10] | = | (proper) little urchin. |
| *jarrete*[11] | = | jolly old jug; (modest) little jug. |
| *librete*[12] | = | jolly old book; (modest) little book. |

[1] Cf. *caballerito* (iron.) — similar sense.
  Cf. *señoritingo* — similar sense. See under *-ingo*.
[2] Cf. *cerdito* (iron.) — similar sense.
[3] Cf. *cuñadito* (iron.) — similar sense.
[4] Cf. *curita* (iron.) — similar sense. See under *-ita* (m.).
  Cf. *curilla*. See under *-illa* (m.).
  Cf. *curazo*. See under *-azo*.
[5] Cf. *dinerito* (iron.) — similar sense. See under *-ito*.
  See also *dinerillo*, under *-illo*.
[6] Cf. *discursito* (iron.) — similar sense.
[7] Cf. *durito* (iron.) — similar sense. See under *-ito*.
[8] Cf. *estofadito* (iron.) — similar sense.
[9] See *fresquillo*, under *-illo*.
[10] Cf. *golfillo* — similar sense. See *pillín* under *-ín*.
[11] Cf. *jarrito* (iron.) — similar (first sense).
  Cf. *jarrillo* — similar (second sense).
[12] Cf. *librito* (iron.) — similar (first sense).
  Cf. *librillo* — similar (second sense).

| | |
|---|---|
| *maridete*[1] | = jolly old hubby, good old hubby. |
| *mozalbete* | = (mere) youngster, young shaver. |
| †*oficialete*[2] | = budding, dapper, dashing or spruce young offieer, officious young officer. |
| †*pillete*[3] | = (regular) young rascal, (proper) little rogue or scamp. |
| †*pobrete*[4] | = miserable pauper, poor devil. |
| †*realete* | = jolly old *real*. |
| *sabadete* | = jolly old Saturday, good old Saturday. |
| *sombrerete*[5] | = jolly old hat; (modest) little hat. |
| *tiete*[6] | = miserable little twerp; uppish little perisher. |
| *torete*[7] | = jolly old bull, fine bull, (poor) little bull; (miserable) little bull. |
| †*traguete* | = jolly old swig, good old swig; (modest) little swig. |
| *vejete*[8] | = little old boy or chap, little old codger or dodger, (sprightly) old gaffer, (lively or nimble) old fellow or old-timer; silly old boy. |

*-ete EXAMPLES FROM LITERATURE*
(GROUP A)

— ¿Es decir, que a la hora de comprar mineral estos *caballeretes* regatean como en el Rastro madrileño?

(ZUNZUNEGUI, *¡Ay, Estos Hijos!*, p. 150)

[1] Cf. *maridito* (iron.) — similar sense.
[2] Cf. *oficialito* — similar sense.
Cf. *tenientito*. See under *-ito*.
[3] See *pillín*, under *-ín*.
[4] An adejctive, of course, but more often than not used substantivally.
[5] Cf. *sombrerito* — similar (first sense).
Cf. *sombrerillo* — similar (second sense).
[6] Cf. *chulillo* and *puñeterillo* for not dissimilar meanings. For the contemptuous implication of *-ete* cf. its force in *cabroncete* and *mariconcete*. See *cabrón* and *maricón*, under *-ón*.
[7] Cf. *torito* (iron.) — similar (first group of senses).
Cf. *torillo* — similar (last sense).
[8] Cf. *viejecito* — similar sense.

"You mean that when the moment to buy ore comes these fine (young) gentlemen haggle the same as (the people) in the Rastro in Madrid?"

En la plaza del Coro, el vagabundo, que quiere probar sus mañas de cómico, congrega a los *mirones**\* con una *campanilla,**\* les echa un *discursete,* y les recita ...

(Cela, Judíos, Moros y Cristianos, p. 79)

In the Square of the Choir the tramp, who wants to try out his skill as a performer, gathers together the lookers-on with a small hand-bell, trots them out a jolly old speech and recites to them ...

— ... porque un joven se retira tarde y se gasta algún *durete*[1] en picos pardos, me le llaman monstruo ....

(Pérez Galdós, Fortunata y Jacinta, IV, p. 69)

"... because a young fellow gets home late and lashes out the odd jolly old five-peseta piece[1] on enjoying himself painting the town red they call the poor chap a monster ...."

... ahora los guardacostas estaban mandados por *oficialetes* recién salidos de la escuadra de instrucción, con muchos humos ....

(Blasco Ibáñez, Flor de Mayo, p. 104)

... now the coastguards were commanded by spruce[2] young officers fresh from training school, cocky[2] youngsters with a very good opinion of themselves ....

... lo veía más robusto ... y tan *bondadosote**\* como siempre, a pesar de su continuo roce con los "gatos" de barca, *pilletes* capaces de las mayores malicias...

(Blasco Ibáñez, Flor de Mayo, p. 61)

... she found him lustier ... and as thoroughly good-natured as ever, despite his constant contact with the ship's "lads", young rascals who were capable of the worst mischief...

---

[1] Considerably more, of course, in the nineteenth century than today.
[2] Both these ideas are implied in *oficialete*.

— Si no me ha querido cuando tenía algunos cuartos, ¿cómo me ha de querer hoy, que soy un *pobrete* y tengo sobre los hombros tanta familia?

(Palacio Valdés, José, p. 118)

"If she wouldn't have me when I had a bit of cash, how can I expect her to have me now that I'm a miserable pauper and weighed down with such a load of responsibility to my family?"

— ¡Tres mil reales! — dijo el usurero, poniendo la cara de duda reflexiva que para los casos de benevolencia tenía; ... — ¡Tres mil *realetes*! ... Hija de mi alma, mire usted...

(Pérez Galdós, Torquemada en la Hoguera, p. 112)

"Three thousand "reales"!", said the money-lender, putting on the expression of thoughtful dubiety which he used in cases calling for charity; ... "Three thousand jolly old "reales"! ... My dear girl, really ..."

Los mozos portadores del equipaje se habían adelantado mucho, deseosos de ... echar un *traguete* en la taberna.

(Pardo Bazán, Los Pazos de Ulloa, p. 125)

The village lads who were carrying the luggage had got far ahead, being eager to ... to have a jolly old swig at the inn.

*-ete (B) NOUN — MASCULINE*
*(Change of meaning or specialized sense)*

| | |
|---|---|
| *arete*[1] | = ear-ring. |
| (< aro | = ring) |
| *banquete* | = banquet. |
| (< banco | = bench) |
| *boquete* | = narrow opening, hole. |
| (< boca | = mouth) |

[1] Although still found regionally, neither *arete* nor its synonym *zarcillo* is normally used today by educated Spaniards, having been replaced by *pendiente*.

| | | |
|---|---|---|
| *bracete*[1] | = | linked arm. |
| (< brazo | = | arm) |
| *caballete* | = | trestle; easel. |
| (< caballo | = | horse) |
| *clarete* | = | claret wine. |
| (< claro | = | light) |
| *clarinete* | = | clarinet. |
| (< clarín | = | bugle) |
| *cojinete*[2] | = | bearing. |
| (< cojín | = | cushion) |
| *colorete*[3] | = | rouge. |
| (< color | = | colour) |
| *chupete* | = | baby's comforter, dummy. |
| (< chupar | = | to suck) |
| *filete* | = | fillet (of fish); steak. |
| (< filo | | |
| O. Sp. | = | thread) |
| *grumete* | = | cabin boy, ship's boy. |
| (< groom[4] | | |
| Eng.) | | |
| †*molinete* | = | whirling motion, flourish (especially of the *capote* in bull-fighting); turnstile. |
| (< molino | = | mill) |
| †*palacete* | = | mansion, large private residence. |
| (< palacio | = | palace) |
| *poyete* | = | low stone or brick bench. |
| (< poyo | = | stone bench) |
| *ramillete* | = | small bunch of flowers, bouquet, posy, nosegay. |
| (< ramo | = | branch; bunch of flowers) |
| *rodete*[5] | = | bun, chignon. |
| (< rueda | = | wheel) |

[1] Used almost exclusively in the expression *ir del bracete* = to go arm in arm.
[2] *Cojinete de bolas* = ball bearing.
[3] Cf. *colorcete*, as in *¡qué colorcetes tiene!* = what a jolly good colour he's got! (i.e. complexion).
[4] The Spanish for "groom" is *mozo de cuadra*.
[5] Not a very generally used word; much more common is *moño*.

| | | |
|---|---|---|
| *salmonete* | = | red mullet. |
| (< salmón | = | salmon) |
| †*soniquete*[1] ⎫ | = | slight, monotonous sound. |
| *sonsonete* ⎭ | | |
| (< son | = | sound) |
| *templete*[2] | = | shrine; band-stand. |
| (< templo | = | temple) |
| *tenderete*[3] | = | stall, stand (e.g. market). |
| (< tender | = | to stretch or spread out) |
| *volquete* | = | tip-up lorry. |
| (< volcar | = | to tip up, upset) |

*-ete* EXAMPLES FROM LITERATURE

(GROUP B)

Alguno, avezado en estos lances, hacía *molinetes* con la garrocha, y lograba remansar un espaciado círculo en la ciega y bramadora fuga de hombres y bestias.

(VALLE-INCLÁN, *¡Viva mi Dueño!* p. 146)

Here and there individuals who were accustomed to these incidents whirled their goading-poles round and managed to create about themselves a broad circle of calm in the blind, roaring stampede of men and animals.

— ... Todos los banqueros y hombres de negocios a quienes sus asuntos no permiten alejarse de la capital tienen aquí sus *palacetes*...

(ZUNZUNEGUI, *¡Ay, Estos Hijos!*, p. 181)

"... All the bankers and business men whose work does not allow them to go far from the capital have their residences here..."

---

[1] Cf. *sonecillo, ruidillo* = slight or faint sound or noise.
Curiously, the word *sonido*, which is of infinitely more general use than *son*, is very rarely given a diminutive form.

[2] *Templete (quiosco) de la música* = band-stand.

[3] Gives a rather pejorative impression, whereas the most general word, *puesto*, does not.

... ocurrió que una *mañanita*★, cuando los gallos aún dormían, oyó el hermano portero una especie de llanto al pie de la puerta.... Anduvo el hermano unos pocos pasos guiado por aquel *soniquete*, cuando vio algo así como un bulto.... Se acercó; de allí salían los *ruidillos*★....

(SÁNCHEZ-SILVA, Marcelino, Pan y Vino, pp. 10, 11)

... it came to pass that one fine[1] morning, when the cocks were still asleep, the brother door-keeper heard a sort of crying at the foot of the door.... The friar walked a few steps guided by that slight, monotonous sound, and suddenly saw something that looked like a bundle.... He moved closer; that was where the faint noises were coming from....

## *-ete (C) ADJECTIVE*

| | |
|---|---|
| †*aduloncete* | = a bit or a little given to flattery, quite or rather toadying; pretty toadying, despicably toadying. |
| *alegrete*[2] ⎤<br>*animadete* ⎦ | = a bit gay or merry, quite or rather merry or high (from drink); pretty high. |
| *atrevidete*[3] | = a bit forward or bold; pretty bold. |
| *ceboncete*[4] | = a bit on the fat side, tubby; pretty weighty. |
| *creidete*[5] ⎤<br>*presumidete* ⎦ | = quite or rather conceited; pretty conceited. |
| *desnutridete*[6] | = on the undernourished side; pretty undernourished. |
| *despistadete*[7] | = a bit off the track, lost or vague, not altogether with it; pretty out of touch. |
| *entrampadete* | = a bit in debt, rather in the red; pretty in the red. |

---

[1] Or, possibly, "early one morning". See under *-ita* (B).
[2] See *alegrillo* and *animadillo*, under *-illo*.
[3] See *atrevidillo*, under *-illo*.
[4] See *ceboncillo*, under *-illo*.
[5] See *creidillo* and *presumidillo*, under *-illo*.
[6] See *desnutridillo*, under *-illo*.
[7] See *despistadillo*, under *-illo*.

| | | |
|---|---|---|
| *escamadete*[1] | = | rather wary; pretty suspicious. |
| *guapete*[2] | = | quite handsome, handsomish; pretty handsome. |
| *mimadete* | = | a bit or rather spoilt; pretty spoilt. |
| *peladete* | = | a bit or rather close-cropped; pretty shorn. |
| *presumidete*[3] | = | rather conceited; pretty conceited. |
| *regordete*[4] | = | fattish, chubby, tubby. |
| *rendidete* | = | a bit or rather whacked; pretty well fagged out. |
| *tacañete* | = | on the mean side; pretty stingy, despicably stingy. |
| †*tristoncete* | = | on the depressed or depressing side; pretty dreary. |
| *vulgarcete* | = | quite or rather ordinary; pretty commonplace. |

## *-ete* EXAMPLES FROM LITERATURE (GROUP C)

... cuando el profesor explicaba la asignatura, "Chupito" fingía prestar una gran atención, moviendo la cabeza *aduloncete*,[5] como haciéndose cargo. Era el más "pelotillero" del curso.

(ZUNZUNEGUI, *¡Ay, Estos Hijos!*, p. 32)

... when the master was teaching the lesson, "Chupito" would pretend to pay great attention, nodding in a contemptibly fawning fashion, as if he were understanding [everything]. He was the biggest "toady" in his year.

— Lo que he visto es muy hermoso. Yo pensé que todo iba a ser más *tristoncete* ....

(MIHURA, *Maribel y la Extraña Familia*, p. 157)

"What I've seen is very beautiful. I thought everything was going to be more on the dreary side...."

[1] See *escamadillo*, under *-illo*.
[2] See *guapillo*, under *-illo*.
[3] See *creidete*, above.
[4] Cf. *gordinflón, rechoncho, rollizo* — similar sense. See *gordezuelo*, under *-uelo*.
[5] See *adulón*, under *-ón*, and *pelotilla*, under *-illa*.

148

*-eta* (A) NOUN — *FEMININE*
(*Diminutive, often with slightly pejorative or jocular implications*)

| | |
|---|---|
| *anqueta*[1] | = small rump or haunch. |
| †*cadeneta* | = small or short chain. |
| *caleta* | = small bay or cove, creek, inlet. |
| †*comedieta* | = short play, insubstantial comedy. |
| *isleta*[2] | = small island, islet. |
| *pandereta* | = small tambourine. |
| *pileta*[3] | = small trough or basin. |
| *placeta*[4] | = small square. |
| *saleta*[5] | = small drawing room. |
| *vigueta* | = small beam or girder. |

*-eta* EXAMPLES FROM LITERATURE
(GROUP A)

De pronto se ha oído un crujido en la boca de papá, y una imprecación mayor, seguida de una *cadeneta* de tacos y *taquillos**, es pronunciada ... media muela, partida en trozos minúsculos, sale rodando por el suelo ... ..

(NEVILLE, *La Familia Mínguez*, p. 89)

Suddenly a crack is heard in dad's mouth, and a considerable oath is uttered, [to be] followed by a [whole] little string of swear-words and minor swear-words ... half a back-tooth, broken in tiny pieces, comes out and rolls across the floor ... ..

Contradigo aquí a muchos que, según textos de *comedietas* y *cuentecillos** franceses, tratan de aligerar la carga del matrimonio

---

[1] Used especially in the phrase *estar de media anqueta* = to be seated or positioned in an awkward, lop-sided or tilted manner.

[2] Not unlike *islote* but less specifically pejorative. See *islote,* under *-ote.*

[3] Used in Spanish America as synonym of *piscina* = swimming-pool.

[4] Cf. *plazoleta (plaza + uela + eta )* = tiny little square.

[5] A word belonging more to the past than to the present and used mainly in the context of royal palaces.

despojándolo de toda gravedad y trascendencia.... Aconsejan los tales el empleo de toda clase de especiería picante en el aderezo del para ellos *desabridote** guiso matrimonial.

(BENAVENTE, *Cartas de Mujeres*, p. 345)

Here I contradict many who, according to texts from insubstantial plays and petty tales by French authors, attempt to lighten the load of marriage by stripping it of all seriousness and importance.... These people advise the use of all kinds of spicy seasoning in the garnishment of what is for them the thoroughly insipid dish of matrimony.


## -*eta* (B) NOUN — FEMININE

*(Changed or specialized meaning)*

| | |
|---|---|
| *agujeta(s)*[1] | = muscular aches and pains, fatigue pains, sensation of being knocked-up. |
| (< aguja | = needle) |
| *aleta* | = fin (fish); side (nose); wing (car). |
| (< ala | = wing) |
| *avioneta* | = light aeroplane, monoplane, trainer. |
| (< avión | = aeroplane) |
| *banqueta*[2] | = stool, foot-stool. |
| (< banco | = bench) |
| *bragueta* | = fly (trousers). |
| (< braga(s) | = breeches; underpants) |
| *calceta*[3] | = knitting. |
| (< calza(s) | = breeches; hose) |
| *camioneta* | = van. |
| (< camión | = lorry) |
| *camiseta* | = vest. |
| (< camisa | = shirt) |

[1] Cf. *hormigueo, hormiguillo* = pins and needles.
[2] Cf. *taburete* = stool, high stool.
[3] *Hacer calceta* = *hacer punto* = to knit.

| | |
|---|---|
| *careta*[1] | = mask. |
| (< cara | = face) |
| *carreta* | = long narrow cart, waggon. |
| (< carro | = cart) |
| *caseta* | = bathing or beach hut; booth (fair). |
| (< casa | = house) |
| *cazoleta* | = bowl (pipe). |
| (< cazuela[2] | = earthenware bowl) |
| *cebolleta* | = shallot; spring onion. |
| (< cebolla | = onion) |
| *colchoneta*[3] | = metal mattress. |
| (< colchón[4] | = mattress) |
| *coleta*[5] | = pig-tail. |
| (< cola | = tail) |
| *corneta* | = bugle. |
| (< cuerno | = horn) |
| *chincheta* | = drawing-pin. |
| (< chinche | = bed-bug) |
| *furgoneta* | = van; estate car, shooting brake. |
| (< furgón | = goods-waggon, luggage van) |
| *gacheta*[6] | = glue-paste, gloy. |
| (< gacha(s) | = paste, pap) |
| *garceta* | = egret. |
| (< garza | = heron) |
| *glorieta*[7] | = small square or circus, street roundabout. |
| (< gloria | = glory) |
| *historieta* | = short tale, episode; strip-cartoon; comic paper. |
| (< historia | = history, story) |

[1] Used especially in the term *careta antigás* = gas mask, and in the phrase *quitarse la careta* = to show one's true colours, to stop putting on a show. See *mascarilla*, under -*illa*.

[2] See under -*uela*.

[3] Not in very general use, the most common term being the borrowed French *sommier*.

[4] See under -*ón*.

[5] *Cortarse la coleta* = to retire (bullfighters).

[6] Not in very general use, the most common term being *engrudo*.

[7] As in *La Glorieta de Bilbao* (square in Madrid).

| | | |
|---|---|---|
| *jugarreta*[1] | = | dirty trick. |
| (< juego | = | game) |
| *lengüeta* | = | shoe-tongue; flap, tab. |
| (< lengua | = | tongue) |
| *libreta* | = | note-book. |
| (< libro | = | book) |
| *loseta*[2] | = | floor-tile, marble tile. |
| (< losa | = | flag-stone) |
| *meseta*[3] | = | table-land, plateau. |
| (< mesa | = | table) |
| *metralleta*[4] | = | sub machine-gun. |
| (< metralla | = | grape-shot, shrapnel) |
| *muleta* | = | crutch; muleta (bull-fight). |
| (< mula | = | she-mule) |
| *paleta* | = | trowel; paddle-board; palette; front tooth. |
| (< pala | = | shovel) |
| *pañoleta*[5] | = | small shawl. |
| (< pañuelo | = | [hand]kerchief) |
| *papeleta* | = | slip of paper; ticket (e.g. for raffle) or receipt portion; pawn ticket; result paper (examination); tricky or unpleasant matter or situation. |
| (< papel | = | paper; role) |
| *peineta* | = | back- or side-comb. |
| (< peine | = | comb) |
| *peseta* | = | peseta. |
| (< peso | = | weight; peso (coin)) |
| *puñeta*[6] | = | annoyance, irritation, pest. |
| (< puño | = | fist) |

[1] Cf. *mala jugada* — same sense.
[2] Cf. *baldosín* — similar sense. See under *-ín*.
[3] Cf. *mesetilla* = small plateau.
  Cf. *altiplanicie* and *altiplano* (S.A.) = high plateau.
[4] Cf. *ametralladora* = machine-gun.
[5] Cf. *toquilla* — similar sense.
See *mantón*, under *-ón*.
For *pañuelo* see under *-uelo*.
[6] This word is very widely used in modern Spanish, although certainly not in polite speech. It has much the same force as English expressions of the

| | |
|---|---|
| *rabieta* | = fit of temper, tantrum. |
| (< rabia | = rage) |
| *roseta*[1] | = rosette. |
| (< rosa | = rose) |
| *sardineta*[2] | = chevron. |
| (< sardina | = sardine) |
| *soleta*[3] | = departure. |
| (< suela | = sole) |
| *tableta*[4] | = tablet, bar. |
| (< tabla | = board, plank) |
| *tarteleta* | = individual fruit tart or pie. |
| (< tarta | = cake, tart) |
| *tijereta* | = vine tendril; ear-ring. |
| (< tijera(s) | = scissors) |
| *torreta* | = turret (tank); conning-tower (submarine). |
| (< torre | = tower) |
| *trompeta* | = trumpet; trumpeter (m.). |
| (< trompa | = [French] horn) |
| *vagoneta* | = small open goods truck. |
| (< vagón | = carriage, truck) |
| *veleta* | = weather-vane or cock; fickle person. |
| (< vela | = sail) |
| *vinagreta* | = vinegar sauce. |
| (< vinagre | = vinegar) |

---

"bloody nuisance" type. It is thus a vulgar equivalent of such words as *lata* and *pesadez*. *Estar hecho la puñeta* = to be browned-off or cheesed-off. *Vete a hacer puñetas* = go to blazes. See *puñeterillo*, under *-illo*.

[1] In some parts of Spain, notably the south, the expression *rosetas de maíz* is used for "pop-corn", although the most common term is *palomitas*.

Cf. *escarapela* = rosette (badge of political party, football team, etc.).

[2] Cf. *galón* = stripe.

[3] Used in slang expression *tomar soleta* = to clear off, to hop it, to light out.

[4] *Tableta de chocolate* = (large) block of chocolate.

Cf. *pastilla de chocolate* = (medium-size) bar of chocolate.

Cf. *chocolatina* = small bar of chocolate.

*voltereta*[1]    = somersault.
(< vuelta    = turn, spin)


*-eta EXAMPLE FROM LITERATURE*
(GROUP B)

  — Yo comprendo que, para ti, la *papeleta* se las trae.
                    (MIHURA, *Maribel y la Extraña Familia*, p. 156)

"I realize that, for you, the situation is a pretty tricky one."

---

[1] The most general word. Cf. *salto mortal* — used especially in circus contexts, and *vuelta de campana* — used particularly of cars involved in accidents.

# Chapter II. Augmentatives

*-ón (A) NOUN — MASCULINE (PERSONS)*
*(Generally augmentative and/or pejorative, but sometimes with attenuative implication. Many of these nouns are also used in the feminine and adjectivally)*

| | |
|---|---|
| *abusón*[1] | = one who abuses or takes advantage, one given to taking liberties or making free. |
| †*acusón*[2] | = sneak, tale-bearer, tell-tale. |
| *aprovechón*[3] | = one with an eye to the main chance, one who takes advantage. |
| *beatón* | = atrociously sanctimonious, pious or goody-goody individual, Bible-puncher. |
| *besucón* | = one much given to kissing, excessively demonstrative person, slobberer. |
| *bravucón*[4] *jaquetón* *valentón* | = blustering, boasting, bullying individual. |
| †*cabrón*[5] | = cuckold; bugger, bastard, swine. |

[1] Cf. similar sense of *aprovechón*, below.

[2] Cf. *acusica, chivato, soplón*. All four words have the same sense, but *acusón* and *acusica* belong to the language of children, whereas *chivato* and *soplón* tend to be associated with the world of the criminal.

[3] Cf. similar sense of *abusón*, above.

[4] See *fanfarrón, fantasmón* and *matón*, below.
Cf. *chulo, chulapo* (aug. *chulapón*), *chuleta* = bellicose or pugnacious individual, "do-you-want-a-fight?" type.

[5] This highly vulgar word is probably the strongest personal insult in Spanish. It means "cuckold" (approximate equivalent), but is frequently used as a more general term of abuse with just about the same force as the English "bugger". In its etymological sense of "he-goat" *cabrón* has been completely replaced by *macho cabrío*. The form *cabro*, although found in Italian and some South American Spanish, is not used in Spain.
Cf. the augmentative form *cabronazo* = real bugger, first-class bugger, and the diminutive *cabroncete* = despicable little bugger, miserable little basket.
Cf. *cornudo*. See under *-udo*.

| | | |
|---|---|---|
| *cacicón* | = | big boss (in local politics), blasted political boss. |
| *cagón*[1] | = | shitter; funker; despicable object. |
| *capitalistón* | = | bloated capitalist. |
| †*carlistón*[2] | = | rabid Carlist, Carlist blighter. |
| *cientificón*[3] | = | essentially or hopelessly academic type, regular egg-head; blasted scientist. |
| †*cobardón*[4] | = | great coward. |
| *comilón*[5] | = | heavy eater. |
| *comodón* | = | comfort-lover; one reluctant to put himself out. |
| *comunistón*[6] | = | real or rabid communist, communist blighter. |
| *copión* | = | copy-cat, one given to copying others. |
| *criticón*[7] | = | fault-finder, grumbler, one given to criticizing. |
| *curiosón* | = | nosy individual, inquisitive blighter, one given to prying. |
| *chicarrón* | = | burly, hefty, sturdy chap, fellow, lad. |
| *chulapón*[8] | = | really pugnacious individual, "do-you-want-a-fight?" type. |
| †*chupón* | = | sponger, parasite. |
| *derrochón* | = | spendthrift, squander bug. |
| *dormilón* | = | sleepy-head, one very fond of sleep. |
| *egoistón*[9] | = | selfish blighter, selfish devil. |
| *empollón* | = | swot, excesively studious pupil. |

---

[1] Very vulgar. Cf. *meón*. (See under adjective section.) *Cagueta* is another vulgar term of like meaning.

[2] For example see section B.

Cf. the words *carcunda* and *carca* — pejorative expressions for *carlista* — the use of which is similar to that of the English "Tory" or "reactionary" for "conservative", i.e. they are terms of political-social abuse.

[3] See *cientificote*, under *-ote* (adj.).

[4] For example see section B.

Cf. *cobardica*. See under *-ica*.

Cf. *mandilón, temerón* — similar sense.

[5] Cf. *glotón, tragón, zampón* — similar sense.

[6] Cf. *rojazo* — similar sense. See under *-azo*.

Cf. *comunistilla* and *rojillo*. See under *-illa* (m.) and *-illo*.

[7] Cf. *protestón*. See following section.

[8] See *bravucón*, above.

[9] *Un egoistón de marca* = an utterly selfish blighter, a first-class egoist.

| | |
|---|---|
| †espadón[1] | = big shot, big gun, military big noise or strong man. |
| estudiantón | = slow, plodding student, plodder. |
| faltón[2] | = unreliable blighter; abusive, disrespectful or objectionable devil. |
| fanfarrón[3] | = boaster, braggart. |
| fantasmón[4] | = braggart, play-actor, showman. |
| farolón[5] | = bluffer, blusterer; show-off. |
| figurón | = exaggerated, outlandish or ridiculous figure; (mere) representative figure or figure-head, puppet. |
| fisgón[6] | = one (much) given to prying, nosy individual. |
| gandulón[7] | = great lay-about, lazy hound. |
| gigantón | = great giant. |
| †gorrón[8] | = sponger. |
| gruñón[9] | = groaner, grouser, grumbler, one who grunts or growls. |
| hambrón[10] | = hungry-guts, hungry-gutted individual. |
| hampón[11] | = member of the underworld, crook, rogue. |
| hipocritón | = complete hypocrite, out and out hypocrite, regular hypocrite. |

[1] The notable nineteenth-century figure General Narváez was known as *El Espadón de Loja* (his birthplace).
  Cf. the now more common *jefazo*. See under *-azo* (A).
[2] Cf. *informal* — the usual word for "unreliable".
[3] See *bravucón*, above.
[4] Cf. *farsantón* = utter humbug or hopeless play-actor.
[5] The form *farolero* is considerably more common than *farolón*.
[6] Cf. *curiosón*, above.
[7] Cf. *gandulazo* — same sense.
  Cf. *perezosón* — similar sense.
[8] Cf. the phrase *de gorra* — *comer de gorra* = to eat for nothing or at someone else's expense.
[9] Cf. *gruñica*. See under *-ica*.
  Cf. *protestón* — similar sense.
[10] Cf. *hambriento*, *famélico* = ravenous, starving, i.e. same sense, but literary tone.
[11] Cf. *el hampa* = the underworld.

| | |
|---|---|
| *hombrón*[1] <br> *hombretón* } | = burly man, hefty great fellow. |
| *ignorantón* | = really ignorant fellow, really dim type, regular ignoramus. |
| *inocentón*[2] | = completely naïve person, regular simpleton. |
| *jaquetón*[3] | = boaster, braggart, bully. |
| *jesuitón* | = big noise among the Jesuits; damned or blasted Jesuit. |
| *logrón* | = profiteer, one out for all he can get. |
| *llorón*[4] | = cry-baby, sniveller. |
| †*mandilón*[5] | = cowardy-cat, funker, sissy. |
| *maricón*[6] | = pansy, fairy, homosexual; bugger, sod (general term of violent abuse). |
| *mariposón* | = flirt, flighty fellow; pansy, homosexual (less used in this sense). |
| *matón* | = bully. |
| *millonarión* | = bloated millionaire. |
| †*mirón*[7] | = gawper, starer; looker-on. |

[1] Cf. *hombrazo, hombrote* — same sense.

[2] Cf. *simplón, simplote* — same sense. See *simplón*.

[3] See *bravucón*, above.

[4] Cf. *llorica*. See under *-ica*.

Cf. *lloricón* (adj.).

Cf. *lloroso* (adj.).

*Llorón* and *llorica* are both used with the sense of "cry-baby". *Llorón* is also used adjectivally, e.g. in the expression *sauce llorón* = weeping willow (tree). The adjectives *lloricón* and *lloroso* have the sense of "weepy", "tearful", "watery".

[5] For example see section B.

See *cobardón*, above.

Cf. *canguelo* and *mieditis* (m.) (slang) = funk.

[6] The basic word is *marica* (m.) (< *María* — female name par excellence).

*Maricón* is generally used as a plain variant of this, without augmentative force, the augmentative function being filled by *mariconazo* = complete or confirmed homosexual. Correspondingly, there are two scornful diminutive forms *mariquita* (m.) (< *marica*) and *mariconcete* (< *maricón*) = despicable or miserable little pansy. All these terms are naturally offensive in the extreme.

[7] *Mirón* usually means "one who gawps or gazes excessively" (especially at women). The meaning of "looker-on" is rather less common. Cf. *espectador* = onlooker. The translation "looker-on" has been chosen deliberately to bring out the more colloquial nature of *mirón* as opposed to *espectador*.

| | |
|---|---|
| *mozón*[1] | = hefty, lusty, strapping lad. |
| †*novatón* | = hopeless or utter novice or beginner. |
| *pedantón* | = out and out, hopeless or insufferable pedant. |
| *perdilón*[2] | = loser, hopeless loser. |
| *perezosón* | = really lazy blighter, regular lazybones. |
| *pidón*[3] | = worry-guts, one who keeps on asking for things. |
| *pobretón* | = miserable pauper. |
| *politicón*[4] | = blasted politician; one keen on dabbling in politics. |
| †*practicón* | = doctor of long experience but little knowledge; hack, plodder (in any profession). |
| *progresistón* | = rabid, red-hot progressive. |
| *protestón*[5] | = grouser, grumbler, one given to excessive complaining. |
| *remendón* | = repairer, shoe-mender. |
| †*santón*[6] | = holy-man; sanctimonious person, hypocrite; grand old man, doyen, high priest (fig.). |
| *segundón*[7] | = second- (or later) born son. |
| *señorón* | = fine or grand gentleman; one of the bloated gentry, regular nob. |
| *simplón*[8] | = utterly naïve person, regular simpleton. |
| †*sinvergonzón*[9] | = real bounder, out and out rascal or rogue; proper devil. |

[1] Cf. *mozallón, mozarrón, mozancón, pollancón, mocetón, mozo grandullón* — all with very much the same sense.
Cf. *chicazo, chicote, chicarrón, muchachote.* (See under *-azo, -ote.*) These latter forms are, in general, more common than those based on *mozo.*

[2] Word confined exclusively to the language of children.

[3] Cf. *pedigón, pedilón* — same sense.

[4] Cf. *politicastro* — similar sense, but rather more pejorative.

[5] Cf. *gruñón, gruñica* — similar sense.

[6] Cf. *santurrón* — same sense.

[7] Always in an inferior position in matters of inheritance — hence the pejorative form.

[8] Cf. *simplote, inocentón* — same sense.
Cf. *simplín.* See under *-ín.*

[9] The form *sinvergüenzón* is also common. Although the basic idea is essentially pejorative — *un sinvergüenza = uno que no tiene vergüenza* — these two augmentative forms particularly are often used in a quite affectionate way, meaning "a real rogue, but a rather likeable one", "a proper devil".

| | | |
|---|---|---|
| *solterón*[1] | = | hopeless or confirmed bachelor. |
| †*soplón*[2] | = | informer, squealer, one who spills the beans, gives the game away or blows the gaff. |
| *tardón* | = | real slow-coach, very slow person. |
| *tragón*[3] | = | greedy-guts, one who bolts or gulps down his food. |
| *trapalón* | = | liar, deceiver, one who takes people in or has people on. |
| *tumbón*[4] | = | lazy-bones, one excessively fond of sitting or lying down. |
| *valentón*[5] | = | blustering, boasting, bullying individual. |
| *zampón*[6] | = | greedy-guts. |

## -ón EXAMPLES FROM LITERATURE
## (GROUP A)

— ¡ *Acusón* ! — le dijo por lo bajo la *chicuela*★ al coger la lámpara; ¡ *feón* !

(PÉREZ GALDÓS, Fortunata y Jacinta, II, p. 38)

"Sneak!", the slip of a girl said to him in a whisper as she took hold of the lamp; "ugly mug!"

[Cf. Lucío. — ¿Quién ha zío er *chivato*?★
Doña S. — ¿Qué *palabrota*★ es ésa?
Lucío. — *Chivato*★ quié decí *soplón*, con permizo de la señora.

(ALVAREZ QUINTERO, El Genio Alegre, p. 85)

Lucío. — Who was the "squealer"?
Doña S. — What is that crude expression?
Lucío. — By your leave, m'am, "squealer" means informer.]

— Oiga usté, señor Llagostera, ¿su padre de usté era de Cabra?
— No señor; ¿por qué lo pregunta?

---

[1] Cf. *solterón empedernido* = utterly or hopelessly confirmed bachelor.
[2] See *acusón*.
[3] See *comilón*.
[4] Cf. *perezosón* — similar sense.
[5] See *bravucón*.
[6] See *comilón*.

— Por na . . .. Es que a los de Cabra los suelen llamar *cabrones*.[1]
(PALACIO VALDÉS, *La Hermana San Sulpicio*, p. 128)

"I say, Mr. Crabbe, was your father from Bucks.?"
"No, sir, why do you ask?"
"No reason. . .. Just that natives of Bucks. are usually called buggers".[2]

[Cf. the augmentative form *cabronazo* in the following passage:

Lulú ... se insultó con la mujer de Manolo; la llamó tía zorra, borracha, perro, y añadió que su marido era un *cabronazo*.
(BAROJA, *El Arbol de la Ciencia*, p. 485)

Lulu ... exchanged insults with Manolo's wife; she called her a whore, a boozer, a bitch, and added that her husband was a first-rate bugger.]

En estas condiciones el orden público se va convirtiendo más y más en un fantasma que sólo logran resucitar efímeramente los generales rebelados que asumen poderes prácticamente dictatoriales: Los "*Espadones*", y la intervención del ejército en la vida política del país se convierte en un mal endémico.
(EGUIAGARAY, *Historia Contemporánea de España*, p. 113)

Under these conditions law and order gradually became more and more of an illusion, and was briefly restored from time to time only by the efforts of the generals in revolt who took on to all intents and purposes dictatorial powers. Army strong-men and military intervention in the country's political life became an endemic ill.

Dos solitarios echan en un rincón una partida de ajedrez. . ..
A su lado . . . están sentados tres o cuatro *mirones* con cara de cobistas; cuando uno de los jugadores saca un *pitillo*\*, el *mirón* más próximo

---

[1] The natives of *Cabra* are, in fact, called *egabrenses*.
[2] This translation, though far from satisfactory, does give a similar impression in English to that produced by the original in Spanish. Needless to say, no offence whatsoever is meant to the natives of Buckinghamshire.

se lo enciende; . . . cuando un peón, o un alfil, o un caballo ruedan debajo de la mesa, el *mirón* de turno se apresura a recogerlo.

(CELA, *Viaje a la Alcarria*, p. 185)

Two solitary individuals are playing a game of chess in a corner. . . . Sitting beside them are three or four lookers-on with a toadying expression on their faces; when one of the players gets out a cigarette, the nearest looker-on lights it for him; . . . when a pawn or a bishop or a knight rolls under the table the looker-on whose turn it is rushes to pick it up.

— La conducta de usted es incalificable. Se conduce usted como un *novatón*; olvida usted que toda prudencia es poca. El Indalecio es un irresponsable, usted no, usted sabe la enorme responsabilidad que pesa sobre nuestras cabezas.

(VALLE-INCLÁN, *Baza de Espadas*, p. 144)

"Your conduct is unspeakable. You behave like a complete beginner; you forget that we cannot be too careful. Friend Indalecio is an irresponsible individual; you are not; you know the tremendous responsibility that lies upon us."

— ¡Ande usted, *pobretón*! . . . Ande, váyase y no vuelva, ¡*gorrón*!, ¡*pegote*★!, ¡*chupón*!

(PALACIO VALDÉS, *José*, p. 162)

"Off with you, you miserable pauper! . . . Off with you, clear out and don't come back, sponger, parasite, blood-sucker!"

DON E. — ¡Blasfemo! ¿Qué dices?
A. — ¡Que tengo a Velázquez por una máquina de pintar! ¡Por un *practicón*! . . . ¡Abajo *idolillos*★!

(ALVAREZ QUINTERO, *El Genio Alegre*, p. 81)

DON E. — Blasphemer! What are you saying?
A. — I'm saying that I consider Velázquez a painting machine. A hack! . . . Down with petty idols!

El General Prim, con bravatas cuarteleras y grandes gestos de teatro levantino, . . . *temerón*★ y con reservas mentales, entre humorismos biliosos, declaraba que las revoluciones no se hacen con santos ni con *santones*. . ..

— Más que a los santos con novena y fiesta, temo a los *santones* de la democracia. Esos apóstoles de todas las disidencias son intratables.

(VALLE-INCLÁN, *Baza de Espadas*, p. 181)

General Prim, with barrack-room bravado and grand, Mediterranean, theatrical gestures, . . . blustering and with mental reservations, declared in the middle of jaundiced witticisms that revolutions cannot be carried out with either priests or high-priests. . ..

"I'm less worried about the novena and holy-day type of priest than I am about the high-priests of democracy. Dealings with such apostles of every kind of dissension are impossible."

— ¿Pero cómo os habéis puesto así, *sinvergüenzones*, indecentes, puercos, marranos. . .!?

(PÉREZ GALDÓS, *Fortunata y Jacinta*, I, p. 260)

"But how have you got yourselves into such a state, you utterly shameless little devils, you foul, dirty, filthy brats?"


*-ón (B) ADJECTIVE (especially referring to persons)*
*(Generally augmentative and/or pejorative, but sometimes with attenuative implication. Many of these adjectives are also used substantivally)*

| | |
|---|---|
| *adulón*[1] | = (much) given to fawning or toadying. |
| *babión*[2] | = (much) inclined to having one's head in the clouds, hopelessly out of touch with reality. |
| †*bailón* | = very fond of dancing, crazy on dancing; dancing, bouncing. |
| *barrigón*[3]  *tripón* | = big-bellied, pot-bellied. |

[1] Often used substantivally (= fawner, toady).
   Cf. *cobista, pelotillero* — same sense. See *pelotilla* under *-illa*.
[2] Cf. the phrase *estar en Babia* = to have one's head in the clouds.
[3] Cf. *barrigudo* — same sense. See under *-udo*.

| †*bonachón*[1] | = thoroughly good-natured, really kindly, kindly to a fault. |
| *burlón*[2] *chungón* *guasón* *zumbón* | = (much) given to mocking, fond of joking, facetious. |
| *cabezón*[3] | = having a large head; stubborn. |
| *calentón*[4] | = unpleasantly warm or hot, tepid; highly sexy. |
| *camastrón* | = fly, sly, tricky. |
| *cazurrón* | = really or hopelessly sullen or dour and wily. |
| *cebón*[5] *fondón* | = really fat or hefty; obese. |
| *clasicón*[6] | = utterly or exasperatingly classical or traditional, hopelessly conservative or old-fashioned. |
| *coquetón*[7] | = really flirty or flighty; (really) cute, ducky, sweet. |
| †*contentón* | = really contented, really pleased or pleased with oneself, highly satisfied or self-satisfied. |
| *contestón*[8] *replicón* *respondón* | = (much) given to answering back, cheeky in one's replies. |
| *cornalón* | = having large horns (bulls). |
| *cotorrón*[9] | = trying to be young, affecting youth. |
| *culón* | = having a large behind or posterior. |

---

[1] Cf. *buenazo* — similar sense. See under -*azo*.

[2] Often used substantivally (= joker, funny-man, funny-cuts). Cf. *bromista* — similar sense.

[3] Cf. *cabezudo, cabezota* — same senses. See under -*udo*.

[4] For first sense cf. *calentorro, calentucho*. See under -*orro*, -*ucho*. For second sense note that *caliente* often means "sexy". Cf. *cachondo*, which has the same meaning. Cf. *calentito* = nice and warm or hot; a bit sexy, nice and sexy.

[5] Cf. *gordorro, gordote* — similar sense.

[6] Note that, in modern Spanish, *clásico* is often used in the figurative sense of "traditional", "conservative", "old-fashioned".

[7] E.g. *¡qué sombrero más coquetón!* = what a really cute hat!

[8] All three forms are in common use.

[9] From *cotorra* = small parrot, parakeet.

| | |
|---|---|
| *cursilón* | = very much given to snobbery, affectation and putting-it-on; very much inclined to bad taste or vulgar ostentation. |
| *chafón* | = (much) given to putting on the damper or to being a wet-blanket. |
| *chillón* | = shrill (voice); loud, garish, gaudy (colour). |
| *chungón*[1] | = (much) given to joking. |
| *dentón*[2] | = big-toothed, toothy. |
| *desobedientón* | = really or hopelessly disobedient. |
| *destrozón*[3] | = destructive, (much) given to smashing things to pieces; hard on one's clothes, shoes, etc. |
| *dulzón*[4] | = over-sweet, sickly-sweet, cloying, over-rich, terribly rich. |
| *elegantón* | = really smart or stylish, very natty; over-dressy. |
| *escamón*[5] | = distrustful, wary. |
| *exigentón*[6] | = very exacting or demanding, over-fussy, choosy or particular. |
| *facilón*[7] | = really easy, easy as pie, simplicity itself, a walk-over, a push-over. |
| †*feón*[8] | = really ugly, plain in the extreme. |

[1] See *burlón*, above.

[2] Cf. *dentudo*. See under *-udo*.

[3] Especially used to refer to children: *un niño destrozón, ¡qué niña más destrozona!* The form *destructivo* tends to be used in more literary and technical contexts: *poder destructivo*. *Destructor*, although it can be used adjectivally, is generally found as a noun with the meaning "destroyer" (naval vessel).

[4] Cf. *dulzarrón* — similar sense.

[5] *Escama*, the literal sense of which is "scale" (as of fish), can also mean "distrust". Hence *ser escamón* = to be distrustful, to be of a suspicious nature. Cf. *estar escamado* = to be suspicious (for some specific reason).

[6] Two synonyms of *ser exigentón*, widely used in colloquial speech, are: *ser (muy) chinche* and *ser (muy) hueso*, the second being applied especially to teachers and examiners.

[7] It is interesting to compare *facilón* with *facilito*. Both have the same basic sense of "very easy", but in *facilón* the tone is strongly contemptuous, whereas in *facilito* the feeling conveyed is rather one of affection: "nice and easy". See under *-ito*.

[8] For example see section A.

Cf. *feote*, *feúcho* — similar sense. See under *-ote*.

| | |
|---|---|
| *fondón*[1] | = really fat, really hefty, obese. |
| *gachón* | = sweet and attractive or fetching, cute and flirtatious, woosome and spoony; spoiled and demanding of fuss. |
| *grandón*[2] | = really big, outsize. |
| †*grandullón* | = really big, strapping, gawky. |
| †*guapetón* | = really handsome; really well got-up, really well decked-out. |
| †*guasón*[3] | = (much) given to joking, facetious, flippant. |
| *inglesón*[4] | = typically, utterly, hopelessly or irredeemably English. |
| *juguetón* *retozón* } | = playful, (much) given to frolicking about. |
| *ligón*[5] | = (much) given to getting off, making contact or clicking with members of the opposite sex. |
| †*lloricón* †*llorón* } | = weepy, tearful, watery. |
| †*machacón*[6] | = terribly insistent or importunate, given to keeping on and on, given to harping on and on. |
| *malón*[7] | = really bad; naughty. |

[1] See *cebón*, above.

[2] Cf. *grandote* — similar sense. See under *-ote*.

[3] See *burlón*, above.

[4] When a Spaniard describes an Englishman as *inglesón* he implies that that Englishman embodies for him the most typical traits and faults of the English character. Similarly *españolón* = typically Spanish (in the pejorative sense). Such words are frequently used substantivally: — *un inglesón, un escocesón, un britanicón, un españolón,* etc. Cf. *alemanote, inglesote,* etc. See under *-ote*.

For *alemanón, -ote* and *italianón, -ote* cf. English expressions such as "Jerry", "Heinie", "Hun", "Boche" and "Eye-tie", "Wop". Cf. *franchute* (also *gabacho*) = "Frenchie", "Froggy".

[5] A very recent formation. The verb *ligar* and the noun *ligue* are used with corresponding meanings.

[6] Cf. *remachón*. See below.

[7] Cf. *malote* — same sense.

*Malón* (and also *malote*) are used with particular frequency as attenuatives: — *no seas malón (malote)* (e.g. to a child) = don't be a naughty little perisher. There is thus often a close approximation in these forms to *malillo*. See under *-illo*.

| | | |
|---|---|---|
| *mamón*[1] | = | suckling; very fond of sucking, over-fond of sucking. |
| *mandón* | = | bossy, domineering. |
| †*meón*[2] | = | piddling, pissing. |
| †*mordelón* | = | given to biting, snappy. |
| †*moscón* | = | fly-like; buzzing, droning. |
| *narigón*[3] | = | big-nosed, having a large nose. |
| †*noblón*[4] | = | noble, generous or selfless to a fault. |
| *pagón* | = | (much or excessively) given to or insistent on being the one who pays (e.g. of standing drinks). |
| *patarrón*[5] | = | utterly or frightfully clumsy, awkward or gawky. |
| *pegón*[6] | = | (much) given to hitting or striking people. |
| *peleón* | = | (much) given to scrapping; very ordinary (wine). |
| †*pobretón* | = | hard-up. |
| †*preguntón*[7] | = | inquisitive, nosy, snoopy, (much) given to asking questions. |
| *ramplón* | = | heavy, clumsy; coarse, crude, vulgar. |
| *refunfuñón*[8] | = | querulous; (much) given to grumbling. |
| *regalón*[9] | = | self-indulgent, comfort-loving. |
| *regañón* | = | (much) given to scolding. |
| *regatón* | = | (much) given to haggling. |
| *remachón*[10] | = | (much) given to ramming ideas home with excessive repetition. |

[1] E.g. *un niño mamón, un cerdito mamón*. With this latter cf. *lechón* and *cochinillo*. See *cerdito* under –*ito*, *cochinillo* under –*illo*, and *lechón* under –*ón* (dimin.).

[2] E.g. *un niño meón* = a child who is always piddling. The word is also frequently used figuratively as in the phrase *Santiago meón* = pouring Santiago (Santiago de Compostela in Galicia has an extremely high annual rainfall).

[3] Rarely used nowadays. See *narigudo*, under –*udo*.

[4] Cf. *noblote* — same sense.

[5] Cf. *patoso* = clumsy, awkward.
Cf. *meter la pata* = to put one's foot in it, blunder.

[6] Word applied almost exclusively to children.

[7] E.g. *niño preguntón, policía preguntón*.
Cf. *curiosón*. See preceding section.

[8] Cf. *gruñón, protestón* — similar sense. See preceding section.
Cf. *quejica, quejumbroso, quejumbrón* (little used) — similar sense. See –*ica*.

[9] Cf. *comodón*. See preceding section.

[10] Cf. *machacón*. See above.

| | | |
|---|---|---|
| remolón[1] | = | (much) given to putting things off, dragging one's feet or shirking, sluggish, work-shy. |
| replicón[2] | = | (much) given to answering back, cheeky. |
| reservón[3] | = | highly reserved, close or secretive. |
| respondón[4] | = | (much) given to answering 'ck, cheeky. |
| retozón[5] | = | frisky, frolicksome, playful. |
| reventón[6] | = | (much) given to spoiling people's enjoyment by telling them the end of a film, joke, story, etc.; bulging. |
| rompilón | = | (much) given to breaking, tearing or wearing out, terribly hard on (e.g. clothes). |
| saltón[7] | = | (much) given to hopping or jumping; dancing; prominent, protruding, starting. |
| †secatón[8] | = | extremely dry or short, curt to the point of harshness. |
| sensualón | = | extremely sensual. |
| simpaticón[9] | = | really nice, extremely likeable, very friendly indeed, very easy to get on with. |
| †sobón | = | much given to petting or pawing. |
| sosón[10] | = | utterly insipid; dull in the extreme. |
| suavón[11] | = | unpleasantly soft, slimily soft. |
| †temblón[12] | = | (very) quivering, shaking, tremulous. |

[1] Cf. *perezosón* — similar sense.
  Cf. *gandulón*. See preceding section.
[2] See *contestón*, above.
[3] Cf. the more literary and less forceful *reservado* = reserved.
[4] See *contestón*, above.
[5] Cf. *juguetón*. See above.
[6] Much used as a substantive in phrases such as: *es un reventón*; *me ha reventado la película* = he's a spoil-sport; he's spoiled the picture for me (by telling me the end).
  *Reventón* is sometimes found in the expression *ojos reventones*, but is considerably less common in this use than *saltón*. See below.
[7] Used especially in the phrase *ojos saltones* = goggle eyes. The first sense given is found much more commonly in *saltarín*. See under *-ín*.
[8] Also *secarrón*.
[9] Cf. *simpaticote* — similar sense.
[10] Cf. *sosote* and *sosaina* — similar sense.
[11] Cf. *blandorro, blanducho*. See under *-orro, -ucho*.
[12] Cf. *tembloroso* and *trémulo* — very similar in sense, but more literary in tone.

| | | |
|---|---|---|
| *temerón* | = | bluffing, blustering. |
| *tontón*[1] | = | completely foolish or daft; big silly. |
| †*torpón* ⎱ | = | hopelessly clumsy, really dull- or slow-witted, |
| *torparrón* ⎰ | | lumbering; clumsy great goof. |
| *tripón*[2] | = | big-bellied, pot-bellied. |
| *tristón*[3] | = | (pretty) miserable, mournful or depressing; on the dejected, gloomy or dreary side; moody. |
| *viciosón*[4] | = | thoroughly or utterly depraved. |
| *zepelinón* | = | having the shape of a Zeppelin, (hideously) sausage-shaped. |
| *zumbón*[5] | = | ironic, joking, mocking, waggish. |

## -*ón* EXAMPLES FROM LITERATURE
## (GROUP B)

El farol aprisionaba en su círculo *bailón* las figuras, y correteaban por el muro, con intriga de marionetas, las tres sombras.

(VALLE-INCLÁN, *La Corte de los Milagros*, p. 147)

The lantern imprisoned the figures in its bobbing circle, and the three shadows scurried back and forth across the wall like puppets performing a drama of intrigue.

. . . como Matilde tenía un carácter más firme, o era más *tiesecilla*,★ según la expresión vulgar, pronto llegó a dominar a su dócil y *bonachona* amiga.

(PALACIO VALDÉS, *La Hermana San Sulpicio*, p. 121)

. . . as Matilda had a firmer character, or was a bit more strait-laced as the popular expression has it, she soon came to control her amenable and thoroughly good-natured friend.

---

[1] Cf. *tontote* (little used) and *tontaina* — similar sense.
[2] Cf. *tripudo* — same sense. See *barrigón*, above.
[3] Almost always attenuative. Cf. *tristoncete* — substantially same sense as *tristón*. See under -*ete*.
[4] Cf. *viciosote* — same sense.
[5] See *burlón*, above.

Ahora sí que estarás *contentona,*
*Carlistona, mandilona ;*
Ahora sí que estarás *contentón,*
*Carlistón, mandilón, cobardón.*
(Words of song quoted by BAROJA in *Zalacaín el Aventurero*, p. 129)

*Now* you'll be good and satisfied, you Carlist bitch, you funker;
*now* you'll be good and satisfied, you Carlist blighter, you funker,
you great coward.

Era un buen muchacho, *grandullón,* con los ojos azules.....
(BAROJA, *Las Inquietudes de Shanti Andía,* p. 190)

He was a good lad, a strapping boy, with blue eyes.....

— Conozco señoras, de empleados que están cesantes la mitad
del año, y da gusto verlas tan *guapetonas.* Parecen duquesas, y los
niños *principitos*★.
(PÉREZ GALDÓS, *La de Bringas,* p. 251)

"I know wives of Civil Service clerks who are out of a job half
the year, and it's a pleasure to see how very handsomely they get
themselves up. They look like duchesses, and the children like
(regular) little princes."

La segunda vez, el doctor — mirándome con escama algo *guasona,*
sorprendido de mi interés por aquella desmirriada — amplió las
noticias.
(PARDO BAZÁN, *La Sirena Negra,* p. 1015)

The second time, the doctor — regarding me with somewhat
quizzical mistrust, surprised at my interest in that scrawny creature —
elaborated on his information.

... vio sentada ante sí a la *mujerzuela*★, que, con ojos esquivos y
*lloricones,* a causa del picor producido por el espeso sahumerio,
le miraba.
(PÉREZ GALDÓS, *Misericordia,* p. 56)

... he saw the slatternly woman sitting before him; she was looking at him with shifty eyes, made watery by the smarting from the thick aromatic smoke.

... el ama, *viejecilla** *llorona*, estorbosa e inútil.

(PARDO BAZÁN, *Los Pazos de Ulloa*, p. 87)

... the housekeeper, a useless little old woman, always crying about something and more of a hindrance than a help.

[An example of figurative use:

... en todo el trayecto hasta Barcelona no cesó de llover. . ... Jacinta estaba contenta, y su marido también, a pesar de la melancolía *llorona* del paisaje.

(PÉREZ GALDÓS, *Fortunata y Jacinta*, I, pp. 120, 121)

... during the whole trip right to Barcelona it never stopped raining. . ... Jacinta was happy, and so was her husband, in spite of the dripping mournfulness of the countryside.]

— No es aquí donde debe combatirse la tuberculosis — afirmaba Von Börse con *machacona* insistencia.

(POMBO ANGULO, *Hospital General*, p. 143)

"It is not here that tuberculosis should be combated", declared Von Börse with tedious insistence.

— ... *Meona* se presenta la otoñada.

(PÉREZ DE AYALA, *Tigre Juan*, p. 152)

". . . It looks like the autumn season is going to be a (real) soaker."

... no se le oían aquellos refunfuños de perro *mordelón* . . ..

(PÉREZ GALDÓS, *Torquemada en la Hoguera*, p. 68)

... none of that growling typical of a snappy dog was heard from him . . ..

Me veo limosneando a los pintorescos y joviales mendigos, cuya salmodia zumbadora, *moscona*,[1] me despierta el domingo antes del toque de misa.

(PARDO BAZÁN, *La Sirena Negra*, p. 1054)

[1] Used adjectivally this word is rare.
Cf. the noun *moscón* = blue-bottle, which is in common use. For a similar case see note on *siestona*, below.

I can see myself distributing alms among the colourful and cheery beggars, whose buzzing, droning litany wakes me up on Sunday before the peals of the bell calling to mass.

— ... es el vecino más *noblón* del pueblo y el mejor amigo de sus amigos.... Lleva el corazón en la mano, y dará la piel cuando no tenga capa que partir con el pobre.

(PEREDA, *Peñas Arriba*, p. 56)

"... he's the most thoroughly generous-hearted inhabitant in the village and the best friend his friends have got.... He wears his heart on his sleeve, and when he has nothing else left to share he'll give a beggar the coat off his own back".

[Cf. the use of *noblote* in this passage from the same work:

... el *ochentón*\* ..., con ser tan grande y tan feo, no era desagradable ... por el fondo *noblote* y honrado que se descubría a través de los poros de su corteza silvestre.

(*Ibid.*, p. 111)

... the old man of eighty odd ..., despite his great size and ugliness, was not unpleasant ... because behind his rough exterior one could perceive a completely generous and honest nature.]

... decían que era uno de esos estudiantes *pobretones* que, a fuerza de fuerzas, pueden ir aprobando cursos.

(BAROJA, *Camino de Perfección*, p. 5)

... they said he was one of those hard-up students who, by means of a stiff struggle, are able gradually to get through University.

Lázaro era muy *preguntón*, y desde que llegaba poníase a examinarnos ... acerca de todo cuanto habíamos hecho, hablado y aun pensado durante su ausencia.

(ALARCÓN, *El Escándalo*, p. 85)

Lázaro was very inquisitive, and from the moment he arrived he would begin to subject us to an examination ... concerning everything we had done, spoken about and even thought about during his absence.

Como la señorita se disponía a besarle en los carrillos, miss Annie se interpuso rápidamente, dando una orden *secatona*:

— Baby ..., shake hands.

(PARDO BAZÁN, La Sirena Negra, p. 1064)

On seeing that the young lady was making ready to kiss him on the cheeks, Miss Annie [the governess] quickly intervened by issuing an injunction which was curt to the point of harshness:

"Baby ..., shake hands."

En la *siestona*[1] tarde de verano, los viajeros apenas intercambiaban desganadamente suspensivos retazos de frases.

(IGNACIO ALDECOA, La Despedida, p. 23)

In the profoundly siesta-steeped summer afternoon the passengers barely exchanged a few odd, reluctant and unfinished sentences.

Por el Retiro paseaban los niños ricos y los novios pobres: aquéllos, displicentes y soñadores; éstos, ilusionados y *sobones*.

(CELA, Don Pío Baroja, p. 48)

Through the Retiro (park) strolled the sons of well-to-do families and young men without money who wanted to get married; the former with a dreamy, supercilious air; the latter full of vague hopes and intent on petting their girls as much as possible.

... el Mediterráneo, el golfo azul y *temblón*....

(BLASCO IBÁÑEZ, Entre Naranjos, p. 47)

...the Mediterranean, the blue, shimmering bay....

Una bandada de perdices levanta el vuelo, raso, *torpón*, de pájaro poco fogueado....

(CELA, Viaje a la Alcarria, p. 131)

[1] This is by no means a common use of the word. The adjective *siestón, -ona* is, at the very least, rare, and has in all probability been coined by the author. We have here an excellent example of the immense scope offered by the Spanish suffixes for personal invention. *Siestona* is, however, of fairly frequent occurrence as a noun with the meaning "immensely long or heavy siesta".

Cf. *siestecita* = short siesta, nice little siesta. See under -*ita*.

Cf. *sueñazo, sueñecito*. See under -*azo*, -*ito*.

A covey of partridges take to the air, flying low and lumberingly, in the manner of birds little accustomed to being shot at....

*-ón (C) NOUN — MASCULINE (THINGS)*
*(Augmentative, neutral or with favourable or unfavourable implications)*

| | |
|---|---|
| †*alegrón* | = great joy, immense delight, feeling of being really bucked. |
| *bigotón*[1] | = whacking big moustache. |
| *bodón* | = magnificent, grand or slap-up wedding. |
| *calorón*[2] | = terrible or terrific heat. |
| *carrerón*[3] | = terrific race or rush, hell of a race or rush; magnificent or outstanding university or professional record. |
| *cartelón* | = whacking great placard or poster. |
| *caserón*[4] | = big house, vast house, barn of a place. |
| *corridón* | = big or great bull-fight; magnificent bull-fight. |
| *corrientón*[5] | = terrible or terrific draught. |
| *cortinón* | = large, thick or heavy curtain. |
| *costurón* | = large, crude seam, whacking great seam; big scar, irregular scar. |
| *cuartelón* | = rambling great barracks, barn of a place. |
| *culebrón* | = huge snake, hell of a big snake. |
| *ejemplarón* | = magnificent specimen (e.g. animal or child). |
| *esquilón* | = large cattle bell. |
| *facón* | = large knife or dagger. |
| *faenón*[6] | = great piece of work, magnificent performance, fine show (bull-fighting); really dirty trick. |

[1] Cf. *bigotazo* — same sense.
[2] Cf. *calorazo* — same sense.
[3] Cf. *carreraza*. See under *-aza*.
[4] Always tends to have a pejorative tone, e.g. *un caserón destartalado* = a ramshackle or rambling great house. Cf. *casaza* = superb big house. The forms *casón* and *casona* are less widely used.
[5] E.g. *un corrientón de mil pares de demonios* = a hell of a great draught.
[6] Used in connexion with the behaviour of a bull-fighter in the ring. For second sense cf. the phrase *hacerle a uno una faena* = to play a rotten trick on someone.

| | |
|---|---|
| *familión* | = huge family, whacking big family. |
| *fiebrón* | = high temperature, fierce temperature (in illness). |
| *fiestón* | = superb or smashing party; magnificent festivity. |
| *fortunón* | = huge fortune, whopping great fortune. |
| *garrafón* | = hell of a big carafe or decanter. |
| †*goterón*[1] | = heavy leak; large stain (caused by dampness); large rain-drop. |
| *gotón*[2] | = heavy or huge drop. |
| *gripón*[3] | = hefty dose of 'flu, hell of a dose of 'flu. |
| †*lagartón* | = huge lizard. |
| *lagrimón* | = huge tear. |
| †*lugarón*[4] *pueblón* †*poblachón* | = over-grown village, out-size village. |
| †*manchón* | = big stain, hell of a stain; large patch (e.g. of vegetation). |
| †*memorión*[5] | = fabulous or phenomenal memory. |
| *mentirón* | = whopping big lie. |
| *murallón* | = big, great or high (fortress-)wall. |
| *novelón* | = tediously long novel; highly coloured or absurdly romantic novel. |
| *nubarrón*[6] | = big, dark, lowering cloud. |

[1,2] The two phrases *goterones de lluvia (o de agua)* and *gotones de lluvia (o de agua)* can both have the same meaning of "large rain-drops", although *goterón* is not very widely used in this sense. For *agua = lluvia* see *airote*, under -*ote*. For "gutter" see *canalón*, under -*ón* (diminutive).

[3] Cf. *gripazo* — same sense.

[4] The three words are fundamentally equal in meaning, although a fuller translation of *poblachón*, rendering the double suffix, would be "ugly, over-grown village". The idea of ugliness is, nevertheless, implicit in all three forms. Cf. *aldeota* — same sense. See under -*ota*.

[5] E.g. *tiene un memorión fantástico* = he has a really phenomenal memory. Also *memoriona*.

[6] Cf. other double suffix forms such as *sueñarrón*, *ventarrón* and *vozarrón*. See below.

| | |
|---|---|
| *palizón*[1] | = real beating or hiding; hell of a knocking-up. |
| *paredón*[2] | = huge wall, damn great wall; isolated wall (standing amongst ruins); wall used for execution by firing-squad. |
| †*pastelón* | = huge cake, whacking big cake. |
| *patadón* | = hefty great kick, hell of a kick. |
| *peliculón*[3] | = long film; magnificent or superb film. |
| *pelotón* | = big ball. |
| *peñón*[4] | = big rock. |
| *pilón* | = large basin or trough. |
| *poblachón*[5] | = over-grown village. |
| *problemón*[6] | = hefty problem, hell of a problem, real corker of a problem. |
| *programón* | = big or long programme; terrific programme. |
| *pueblón*[7] | = over-grown village. |
| *resacón* | = terrific under-tow; hell of a hang-over. |
| *salón* | = large drawing or reception room, big hall. |
| *sueñarrón*[8] | = tremendously heavy sleep, tremendous feeling of drowsiness. |
| *tablón*[9] | = big, heavy or thick plank or board. |
| *tormentón* | = heavy or terrific storm. |
| *torreón* | = big, main or fortified tower. |
| *uñón* | = whacking great finger- or toe-nail. |

[1] E.g. *le dieron (pegaron) un palizón* = they gave him a real pasting; *el viaje fue un palizón* = the journey was utterly exhausting, really knocked us up, really played them out.

[2] E.g. *un paredón feísimo* = a hideously ugly great wall.

[3] E.g. *es un peliculón larguísimo, y no demasiado bueno* = it's an immensely long film, and not all that good; *es un peliculón fantástico* = it's a really phenomenal picture.

[4] Cf. *peñasco* — similar sense.
*El peñón de Gibraltar* = the Rock of Gibraltar.

[5] See *lugarón*, above.

[6] Cf. *problemazo* — same sense.

[7] See *lugarón*, above.

[8] Cf. *sueñazo*. See under *-azo*.
See *nubarrón*, above.

[9] Used especially in the expression *tablón de anuncios (avisos)* = notice-board.

| | |
|---|---|
| *ventarrón* | = terrifically strong wind, hell of a wind. |
| *visitón* | = visitors or callers who are a hell of a bore or pain-in-the-neck. |
| *vozarrón* | = terrifically loud or powerful voice. |
| *zapatón* | = huge or heavy shoe, clumsy great shoe. |

## -*ón* EXAMPLES FROM LITERATURE
## (GROUP C)

— Dígale que viene de parte del Sanlúcar. Se llevará un *alegrón*.
> (GOYTISOLO, *Campos de Níjar*, p. 18)

"Tell him old Sanlúcar sent you. He'll be really bucked."

Seguidamente se limpió una lágrima, redonda y apretada como un *goterón* de lluvia.
> (DELIBES, *El Camino*, p. 62)

Immediately after she wiped away a tear which was as round and dense as a heavy rain-drop.

... un *lagartón* verdibermejo de dos palmos de largo.
> (CELA, *Judíos, Moros y Cristianos*, p. 117)

... a huge reddy-green lizard two hand's breadths in length.

... fue preciso que todo Madrid se transformase; ... que el marqués de Pontejos adecentase este *lugarón*.
> (PÉREZ GALDÓS, *Fortunata y Jacinta*, I, pp. 49, 50)

... it was necessary for the whole of Madrid to be transformed; ...for the Marqués de Pontejos to clean up this over-grown village.

[Cf. *aldeota* in the same work:

... esta orgullosa Corte iba a pasar en poco tiempo de la condición de *aldeota* indecente a la de capital civilizada.
> (*Ibid.*, p. 55)

... this proud seat of the Court was going to pass in a brief space of time from the state of a filthy, out-size village to that of a civilized capital city.

Cf. *poblachón*:

— Madrid es otra cosa desde hace seis años. ¡Antes era una basura! ... un *poblachón*. Apestaba....
(BUERO VALLEJO, Un Soñador para un Pueblo, p. 223)

"In the last six years Madrid has become a different town. Previously it was a filthy mess... an ugly over-grown village. It stank...."]

... miraba contristado el paisaje ameno, el huerto con su *dormilón**estanque, el umbrío *manchón* del soto....
(PARDO BAZÁN, Los Pazos de Ulloa, p. 117)

... he gazed dejectedly at the pleasant landscape, at the garden with its drowsy pond, at the big, shady patch made by the copse....

Su cabeza ... es un almacén, y, cosa más insólita, al lado de tanta noticia, fecha y hecho, sobre el matorral espeso del *memorión* atestado, salta un chisporroteo de ideas, ... algunas realmente originales.
(PARDO BAZÁN, La Sirena Negra, p. 1044)

His head ... is a storehouse, and, what is more unusual, side by side with so much information, with so many dates and facts, above the thick undergrowth of his crammed, phenomenal memory, you get a darting, crackling sparkle of ideas, ... some of them genuinely original.

— ... hace poco le mandó ... un *pastelón* así, mirad, del tamaño del brasero de doña Calixta, que tenía dentro muchas pasas *chiquirrininas**....
(PÉREZ GALDÓS, Fortunata y Jacinta, I, pp. 31, 32)

"... recently he sent him ... a whacking great cake like this, look — the size of Doña Calixta's fire-pan — with a (whole) lot of teeny weeny raisins in it...."

*-ón* (D) *NOUN — MASCULINE*
*(Action or result of action — often of a pejorative nature)*

| | |
|---|---|
| *abollón* | = dent, indentation, bashing in. |
| †*acelerón* | = act of accelerating or revving (hard), act of jamming down accelerator. |
| *achuchón* *estrujón* | = squeeze, hug. |
| †*apagón*[1] | = black-out, power-cut. |
| *apretón*[2] | = squeeze, shake, grip. |
| *atracón*[3] | = heavy dose, bellyful, blow-out. |
| *bajón*[4] | = falling-off, going down-hill, turn for the worse. |
| †*bofetón*[5] | = slap, swipe, wallop. |
| *borrón*[6] | = blot, blur, blotch. |
| *chafarrinón* | = blotch, splodge. |
| *chamuscón*[7] | = scorch; scorch-mark; singe, singeing. |
| *chapuzón*[8] | = dip, plunge; ducking. |
| *desconchón* | = patch from which wall-paper has flaked or peeled off; patch from which plaster has fallen. |

[1] Cf. the more literary and technical *restricciones* = power-cuts.

[2] Used generally of the hands: — *apretón de manos* = hand-shake, grip of the hands; *se dieron un apretón de manos* = they shook or gripped each other by the hand(s).
An *achuchón* or *estrujón* is given with the arms.
Cf. *chichón* = bump or lump (on the head).

[3] E.g. *se dio un auténtico atracón de pasteles* = he had a veritable blow-out of cakes; *se dio un verdadero atracón de trabajo, de estudiar* = he put in a really heavy session of work, of studying, he had a real bellyful of work, of studying.

[4] *Dar (pegar) un bajón* = to fall off, go off, go down-hill.
*Ha pegado un gran bajón* = he's gone right down-hill, he's taken a turn very much for the worse.
Cf. *dar (pegar) una vejada* = (suddenly) to become (look) old or much older.

[5] Cf. *bofetada* — same sense, equally common.

[6] Cf. *borrador* = rough copy, first draft.

[7] Cf. *chamusquina* — similar sense.

[8] *Darse (pegarse) un chapuzón* = to take (go for) a dip; *darle a uno un chapuzón* = to give someone a ducking. *Remojón* is also used in these two senses. Cf. *ahogadilla*. See under *-illa*.

| | | |
|---|---|---|
| *desgarrón*[1] *rasgón* | = | rent, rip, tear; wrench. |
| *empellón* | = | (violent or rude) push or shove. |
| †*empujón* *envión* | = | push, shove, thrust. |
| †*estirón*[2] | = | act of stretching; act of growing quickly. |
| *estrujón*[3] | = | squeeze, hug. |
| *lametón*[4] | = | (fierce or strong) lick. |
| *limpión*[5] | = | quick clean, rough clean-up, quick wipe-over. |
| †*madrugón*[6] | = | act of rising or getting up early, early rise. |
| *moratón* | = | bruise, black and blue mark. |
| †*parón*[7] | = | act of stopping or halting. |
| *pellizcón* | = | hell of a pinch or nip. |
| *pescozón*[8] | = | thump or swipe on the neck. |
| *pisotón*[9] | = | act of treading or stamping (on someone's foot). |
| *planchón*[10] | = | act of passing an iron; great disappointment or embarrassment. |
| *plantón*[11] | = | act of standing someone up. |
| *rasgón*[12] | = | rent, rip, tear. |
| *remojón* | = | dip, plunge; ducking; drenching, soaking. |

[1] Both words are used in the literal sense, only *desgarrón* in the figurative.

[2] *Dar (pegar) un estirón* = to shoot up, suddenly to grow taller. *Este año Enrique ha dado un gran estirón* = Henry has shot right up, grown very much taller this year.

[3] See *achuchón*, above.

[4] Cf. *lengüetazo* — similar sense.

[5] *Dar (pegar) un limpión a* = to give (something) a quick or rough clean-up. *Le voy a pegar un limpión* = I'm going to give it a quick wipe-over.

[6] *Darse (pegarse) un madrugón* = to get up at an early hour in the morning. *Me vi obligado a pegarme un madrugón de miedo* = I was forced to get up at a fearful hour, at an ungodly hour or unearthly hour, at the crack of dawn.

[7] E.g. *me dio un parón* = he stopped me, he pulled me up.

[8] Also *pescozada*, but much less common.

[9] E.g. *me dio un pisotón de mil pares de demonios* = he gave me a hell of a stamp on the foot.

[10] See *planchazo*, under -*azo*.

[11] E.g. *en dos ocasiones le dio (un) plantón* = she twice stood him up. Cf. *esquinazo*. See under -*azo*.

[12] See *desgarrón*, above.

| | | |
|---|---|---|
| *repentón* | = | sudden impulse or urge. |
| *resbalón*[1] | = | slip, skid. |
| *reventón*[2] | = | burst; tyre-burst, blow-out; real knocking-up. |
| *revolcón* | = | spill, throw, tumble. |
| *socavón* | = | (ground) subsidence, sinking. |
| *sofocón*[3] | = | nasty surprise, nasty turn, unpleasant sensation. |
| *sopetón*[4] | = | cuff, slap. |
| †*tiritón* | = | shiver, shudder. |
| *tirón*[5] | = | pull, tug, yank. |
| *tropezón*[6] | = | stumble, trip. |
| *vacilón* | = | act of staggering or swaying. |
| *valsón*[7] | = | act of waltzing about. |

## -ón EXAMPLES FROM LITERATURE
## (GROUP D)

Dio unos *acelerones* antes de hacer entrar la velocidad.
— No hagas carreras con el coche a la vuelta.
— Descuida, padre.
(García Hortelano, Tormenta de Verano, p. 260)

He revved the engine (hard) a few times before engaging gear.
"Don't go racing the car on your way back."
"Don't worry, father."

En ese momento hubo un *apagón* de la luz en toda la casa.
(Zunzunegui, ¡Ay, Estos Hijos!, p. 60)

Just then there was a black-out of all the lights in the house.

---

[1] Cf. *patinazo*. See under -*azo*.
[2] Cf. *pinchazo* = puncture.
In the last sense given — that of utter exhaustion — *reventón* is not very extensively used. Cf. the far more common *palizón*.
[3] E.g. *se llevó un gran sofocón* = he got a very nasty surprise, he had a very nasty turn.
[4] Most commonly found in the phrase *de sopetón* = suddenly, unexpectedly, out-of-the-blue.
[5] Much used in the phrase *de un tirón* = right-off, straight-off pat, at one go.
[6] *Dar tropezones* = to stumble.
[7] Usually used in the plural in the phrase *dar valsones* = to waltz about.

. . . lo tiró sobre el empedrado y principió a darle de *bofetones*.
(ALARCÓN, *El Sombrero de Tres Picos*, p. 180)

. . . he threw him onto the paved ground and began to give him a drubbing.

— Había venido a ver si conseguía que dieran un *empujón* a las obras del pantano . . . .
(CALVO-SOTELO, *La Muralla*, p. 37)

"I had come to see if I could manage to persuade them to get a move-on with work on the reservoir . . . ."

Aquel otoño fue cuando Luisito dio el gran *estirón*. Acababa de cumplir los doce años. La abuela . . . quedó asustada del cambio.
(ZUNZUNEGUI, *¡ Ay, Estos Hijos !*, p. 33)

It was that autumn that young Luis really shot up (in growth). He had just had his twelfth birthday. His grandmother . . . was staggered by the change.

Se le hizo duro acostumbrarse a los *madrugones*. A las seis y media . . . las *madrugadas*\* húmedas metían por los resquicios de la ventana álgidos y lóbregos cuchillos.
(ZUNZUNEGUI, *¡ Ay, Estos Hijos !*, p. 84)

He found it hard to get used to rising early. At half-past six . . . the damp mornings slipped dark, icy knives through the chinks round the window.

— . . . En la guerra tenía que haber visto usted este tren. A cada legua le daban el *parón* y todo el mundo abajo. En la guerra . . . .
Se quedó un instante suspenso. Sonaron los frenos del tren y fue como un *encontronazo*\*.
(IGNACIO ALDECOA, *La Despedida*, p. 26)

". . . You should've seen this train during the war. Every three miles or so they called it to a stop and it was a case of everybody out. During the war . . . ."

He sat for a moment with his words hanging in the air. The train's brakes were heard and suddenly it was like a collision.

Murmuró Feliche:
— ¿Pero está desahuciada? ...
La Marquesa Carolina, recogiéndose con un *tiritón* bajo su abrigo de pieles, interrogó:
— ¿Usted sabe si la enfermedad es de contagio?
(VALLE-INCLÁN, La Corte de los Milagros, p. 118)

Feliche whispered:
"But has all hope for her been given up?" ...
Marchioness Caroline, huddling up inside her fur coat with a shiver, enquired:
"Do you know if the disease is infectious?"

*-ón (E) NOUN — MASCULINE*
*(Change of meaning or specialized meaning)*

| | |
|---|---|
| *abejón*[1] | = drone. |
| (< abeja | = bee) |
| *alón*[2] | = wing of chicken. |
| (< ala | = wing) |
| *asperón* | = abrasive stone. |
| (< áspero | = rough) |
| *avispón* | = hornet. |
| (< avispa | = wasp) |
| *balón* | = ball (esp. football); (oxygen)balloon. |
| (< bala | = bullet) |
| *bodegón* | = still-life painting (of food, bottles of wine, etc. |
| (< bodega | = wine cellar) |

[1] This word is not widely used, the usual term being *zángano*. Cf. *abejorro*. See under *-orro*.
[2] A wing of chicken for eating tends always to be called *alón*, regardless of its size. Thus, a large wing of chicken is *un alón grande*. A large wing of a live bird is *un ala grande*.

| | |
|---|---|
| *butacón* | = high straight dining-chair. |
| (< *butaca* | = arm-chair) |
| *cajón* | = large box, chest; drawer. |
| (< *caja* | = box) |
| *camisón* | = night-shirt, night-dress. |
| (< *camisa* | = shirt) |
| *cañón* | = cannon, gun; gun-barrel; canyon, ravine. |
| (< *caño* | = tube, spout) |
| *cascarón* | = egg-shell. |
| (< *cáscara* | = shell, peel) |
| *cinturón* | = belt. |
| (< *cintura* | = waist) |
| *colchón* | = mattress. |
| (< *colcha* | = bedspread) |
| *chaquetón* | = short overcoat (usually lady's). |
| (< *chaqueta* | = jacket) |
| *dramón*[1] | = melodrama, blood-and-thunder stuff. |
| (< *drama* | = drama, play) |
| *faldón* | = coat-tail, shirt-tail. |
| (< *falda* | = skirt) |
| *filón* | = seam (of ore). |
| (< *filo* O. Sp. | = thread) |
| *fresón*[2] | = (cultivated) strawberry. |
| (< *fresa* | = (wild) strawberry) |
| *guión* | = cross, standard; hyphen, dash; script. |
| (< *guía* | = guide; guidebook, directory) |
| *hormigón* | = concrete. |
| (< *hormigo*(s) | = paste of ground almonds and honey) |
| *lamparón* | = oil-stain, grease-spot. |
| (< *lámpara* | = lamp) |

---

[1] Cf. *folletón, folletín* — similar sense. See under -*ín*.

[2] The word *fresón* signifies a cultivated strawberry of more or less any size; a particularly large cultivated strawberry would thus be called *fresón grande*.

*Fresa* is the word used to indicate the wild variety of strawberry, which tends to be very small. However, *fresa* can have either meaning, the full term for wild strawberry being *fresa silvestre*.

| | | |
|---|---|---|
| *lanchón*[1] | = | barge, lighter. |
| (< lancha | = | launch, small boat) |
| *latón* | = | brass, yellow brass; tin-plate. |
| (< lata | = | tin, tin-plate) |
| *marmitón* | = | scullion, kitchen-boy. |
| (< marmita | = | pot) |
| †*mascarón*[2] | = | figurehead (naut.). |
| (< máscara | = | mask) |
| *medallón*[3] | = | medallion. |
| (< medalla | = | medal) |
| *moscón*[4] | = | blue-bottle. |
| (< mosca | = | fly) |
| *notición*[5] | = | excellent or magnificent piece of news; surprising or unexpected piece of news. |
| (< noticia | = | piece of news) |
| *papelón*[6] | = | poor performance or show, poor figure (fig.). |
| (< papel | = | part, role) |
| *pimentón*[7] | = | sweet red pepper (powder). |
| (< pimiento | = | pepper (vegetable)) |
| *portón* | = | main door or gate; courtyard door or gate; prison door or gate. |
| (< puerta | = | door, gate) |
| *pulgón* | = | green-fly. |
| (< pulga | = | flea) |
| *ropón*[8] | = | wide loose cassock or sack. |
| (< ropa | = | clothes) |

[1] Cf. *barcaza, gabarra* — same sense. See under *-aza.*

Cf. *gabarrón* = large barge or lighter.

[2] See *mascarilla*, under *-illa.*

[3] *Medallón* is not used in the sense of "big medal", which is simply *medalla grande.*

[4] Cf. *moscardón, moscarda* = blow-fly. *Moscardón* is also sometimes used in the same sense as *abejorro*, i.e. to mean "bumble-bee". *El vuelo del moscardón* = The Flight of the Bumble-bee (the music by Rimsky-Korsakov).

[5] Cf. *noticias importantes* = big news.

[6] *Hacer un papelón* = to play a sorry role, to cut a sorry figure.

[7] Cf. *pimentón picante* = hot red pepper, Cayenne pepper (powder).

[8] Cf. *ropaje* = robes. Cf. *hopa* — similar sense to that of *ropón* ; both are used to refer to the sack worn by condemned criminals.

| | | |
|---|---|---|
| *salchichón* | = | salame sausage. |
| (< salchicha | = | sausage) |
| *salpicón*[1] | = | medley. |
| (< salpicar | = | to splash, sprinkle, strew) |
| *sillón* | = | arm-chair. |
| (< silla | = | chair) |
| *tacón* | = | heel (shoe). |
| (< taco | = | wooden plug) |
| *telón*[2] | = | curtain (cinema, theatre). |
| (< tela | = | cloth) |
| *toallón* | = | bath towel (large), beach towel (large). |
| (< toalla | = | towel) |
| *trenzón* | = | pyjama cord. |
| (< trenza | = | plait, plat) |
| *velón* | = | brass lamp. |
| (< vela | = | candle) |

## -ón EXAMPLE FROM LITERATURE
## (GROUP E)

Quisiera, pues, buscar otro Don Juan que el de Zorrilla, porque éste, psicológicamente, me parece un *mascarón* de proa, un *figurón*★ de feria, pródigo en ademanes chulescos y petulantes, que sólo pueden complacer a la plebe suburbana.

(ORTEGA Y GASSET, *Introducción a un Don Juan*, p. 46)

I should like, then, to seek a Don Juan other than Zorrilla's, because the latter's creation seems to me to be, from a psychological point of view, a figurehead, a (mere) fair-ground puppet character who is a mass of bellicose and arrogant gestures that can be pleasing only to the rabble of the slums.

---

[1] Used especially in the phrase *salpicón de mariscos* (= *mariscada*) = dish of mixed fish and especially shell-fish. The word *zarzuela* is used with like meaning.

[2] *El telón de acero* = the Iron Curtain.

*(With diminutive and sometimes pejorative sense or a specialized or changed meaning implying diminution in relation to the root-word)*

| | |
|---|---|
| *callejón*[1] | = narrow or wretched lane or alley. |
| (< *calleja* | = lane or alley) |
| †*canalón*[2] | = (rain or roof) gutter. |
| (< *canal* | = channel, canal) |
| *carretón*[3] | = hand-cart, station waggon. |
| (< *carreta* | = cart, waggon) |
| *cerrejón* | = small hill, hillock. |
| (< *cerro* | = hill) |
| *cordón*[4] | = cord; (shoe-)lace. |
| (< *cuerda* | = string, rope) |
| *cronicón*[5] | = short chronicle. |
| (< *crónica* | = chronicle) |
| *escalón*[6] | = step (one of a flight); rung (of a ladder). |
| (< *escala* | = rope-ladder) |
| *lechón*[7] | = sucking-pig. |
| (< *leche* | = milk) |

[1] See *calleja*, under *-eja.*
*Callejón sin salida* = dead-end (lit., fig.).
Cf. *callejoncillo* = miserably narrow alley.
[2] Cf. *gotera* = leak; damp-stain. See note to *goterón.*
Cf. *arroyo (de la calle)* = (street) gutter.
[3] See *carreta*, under *-eta.*
Cf. *carretoncillo* = small hand cart or station waggon.
Cf. *carretilla* = wheelbarrow. See under *-illa.*
[4] Cf. *cordelillo, bramante, guita* = twine.
*Cordones de zapatos* = shoe laces.
Cf. *cordoncillo* = (miserable) little cord.
[5] This word is naturally of historical rather than contemporary interest, but is given here because of its form.
[6] Cf. *escalerilla* = gangway (ship, aircraft). See under *-illa.*
[7] Cf. *lechoncillo* = little sucking-pig.
The most common word for "sucking pig" is, however, *cochinillo.* (See under *-illo.*) Cf. *cerdito* = piglet. (See under *-ito.*)
For *lechazo* and *cordero lechal* = sucking lamb, see *corderito*, under *-ito.*
See also *mamón.*

| | | |
|---|---|---|
| *mantón*[1] | = | woollen shawl. |
| (< manto | = | cloak) |
| *montón* | = | heap, pile. |
| (< monte | = | hill, mountain) |
| *mosquetón* | = | (short) musket or rifle. |
| (< mosquete | = | musket) |
| *perdigón* | = | young partridge; (buck-)shot. |
| (< perdiz | = | partridge) |
| *piñón* | = | pine-kernel. |
| (< piña | = | pine-cone) |
| *plantón* | = | scion, shoot. |
| (< planta | = | plant) |
| †*plumón* | = | down. |
| (< pluma | = | feather) |
| *ratón*[2] | = | mouse. |
| (< rata | = | rat) |
| *requesón* | = | cream cheese. |
| (< queso | = | cheese) |
| *serrijón* | = | short chain of mountains. |
| (< sierra | = | saw; mountain chain) |
| *tapón* | = | plug, stopper; traffic jam; buffer (state). |
| (< tapa | = | lid) |
| *terrón* | = | clod, lump (of earth); lump, cube (of sugar). |
| (< tierra | = | earth) |
| *torrejón* | = | (modest or crooked) little tower or turret. |
| (< torreja | = | small tower) |

## -ón EXAMPLES FROM LITERATURE
(GROUP F)

Todo este panorama de tejados daba una impresión de grandeza y de melancolía. De vez en cuando se aclaraba el cielo, y luego comenzaba a llover y se oía el ruido del agua que caía de los *canalones*.

(BAROJA, *La Ciudad de la Niebla*, p. 176)

[1] *Mantón de Manila* = silk shawl.
Cf. *mantilla* = Spanish mantilla, lace head-shawl. See under *-illa*.
Cf. *toquilla* = small woollen shawl.
[2] Cf. *ratoncillo* = little mouse.

All this panorama of roofs conveyed a sensation of grandeur and mournfulness. Now and again the sky became lighter, and then it would begin to rain and the sound of the water running from the gutters would be heard.

   . . . las orillas de la rubia canasta se poblaron de cabezas de *pollitos** de atusado *plumón* . . ..

(Miró, Libro de Sigüenza, p. 122)

   . . . round the edges of the flax-coloured basket there (suddenly) appeared the heads of a series of delightful little smooth-downed chicks . . ..

## -ón (G) ADJECTIVE
### (Diminutive–Pejorative)

| | |
|---|---|
| mogón[1] | = having a broken-off horn; lacking one of its horns (cow or bull). |
| †pelón[2] | = having little hair; hairless, bald. |
| rabón | = having a very short tail; tailless. |
| volantón[3] | = nestling, fledgeling, newfledged (bird). |

## -ón EXAMPLE FROM LITERATURE
## (GROUP G)

   Era un muchacho como de diecisiete años, rapado . . . parecidísimo a Nucha y a Carmen, cuando puede parecerse un *pelón* a dos señoritas con buenas trenzas de pelo.

(Pardo Bazán, Los Pazos de Ulloa, p. 137)

He was a lad of about seventeen, with a close-cropped head . . . and an extremely strong resemblance to Nucha and Carmen, in so far as a hairless male can resemble two young women with generous plaits of hair.

[1] A not very common, technical word.
[2] A colloquial word which is also used substantivally: *un pelón* = a baldie. Cf. *calvorota*. See under *-ota*.
Cf. *motilón* — same sense, but now rare.
[3] Also used substantivally: *un volantón* = a fledgeling.

## -ón (H) NOUN-ADJECTIVE
### (Age)

| | |
|---|---|
| *cuarentón* (*-ona*) (cuadragenario-a)[1] | = (person) in his, her forties, forty years old. |
| *cincuentón* (*-ona*) (quincuagenario-a) | = (person) in his, her fifties, fifty years old. |
| *sesentón* (*-ona*) (sexagenario-a) | = (person) in his, her sixties, sixty years old. |
| *setentón* (*-ona*) (septuagenario-a) | = (person) in his, her seventies, seventy years old. |
| *ochentón* (*-ona*) (octogenario-a) | = (person) in his, her eighties, eighty years old. |
| *noventón* (*-ona*) (nonagenario-a) | = (person) in his, her nineties, ninety years old. |

## -ona (A) NOUN — FEMININE
*(Augmentative and/or pejorative, but can, on occasion, be used attenuatively)*

| | |
|---|---|
| *carpetona* | = hefty great file. |
| *carterona* | = hell of a big brief-case or wallet. |
| *casona*[2] | = (rambling) big house, (ugly) great place. |
| †*comilona* | = heavy meal, slap-up meal. |
| *embusterona* *mentirosona* | } = terrible one for lying, shocking liar. |
| *fregona* | = kitchen-maid or scrubbing girl. |

---

[1] The forms in *-ón* are by far the commoner, and, although there is sometimes a slightly pejorative tinge about them, this is by no means always the case. The forms in *-ario* are markedly academic.

[2] *Casona* is a comparatively uncommon word, the form *caserón* being much more widely used. See under *-ón*.

Cf. *casaza* = magnificent big house. See under *-aza*.

It is interesting to compare the similar case of *salona* (= drawing-room) and *sillona* (= arm-chair), which are logical feminine formations, derived from *sala* and *silla*, and yet are rare in comparison with *salón* and *sillón*. See under *-ón*.

| | | |
|---|---|---|
| *lagartona* | = | really artful or crafty creature or besom. |
| *mentirosona*[1] | = | shocking liar of a woman. |
| *mujerona* | = | hefty great woman, hell of a big woman, strapping woman. |
| *panfilona* | = | completely dim-witted or guileless creature. |
| *patatona* | = | whacking great potato, hell of a big spud. |
| *repipona*[2] | = | terribly precocious child, proper little grown-up. |
| *sargentona* | = | terribly bossy woman, regular battle-axe. |
| †*señorona* | = | big or formidable woman; grand lady. |
| *sisona* | = | woman (much) given to pilfering, pilferer. |
| †*solterona* | = | real old-maid, proper spinster-type. |
| *teatralona* | = | terribly theatrical or dramatic creature. |
| *vergüenzona* | = | terrible feeling of shame or embarrassment; shocking disgrace. |
| *vomitona* | = | violent fit of sickness. |

## *-ona* EXAMPLES FROM LITERATURE
## (GROUP A)

— ... es un *tragón*\* y tiene un empacho de las *comilonas* que se atiza.

(BUERO VALLEJO, *Un Soñador para un Pueblo*, p. 222)

"... he's a greedy-gutted individual and he's got indigestion from the outsize meals he packs away."

Una pobre ... voluble, egoísta o adúltera, le parecía una cosa monstruosa; pero esto mismo en una *señorona* lo encontraba disculpable.

(BAROJA, *El Arbol de la Ciencia*, p. 487)

That a poor woman ... should be fickle, selfish or an adulteress she thought was something monstrous; but these same things she considered pardonable in a grand lady.

[1] See *embusterona*, above.
[2] From the very colloquial *repipi* = (child) old before his or her time, (insufferable) little know-it-all. Both the basic word and the augmentative are used either substantivally or adjectivally; they are found much more commonly in the feminine than in the masculine.

Era esta señora *buenaza*★ y amable, sin gran talento ni comprensión, pero con un fondo de buena voluntad para todo. La cuñada de Belén, en cambio, ... era un basilisco. A mala intención no le ganaba nadie. *Solterona*, flaca, seca, de color cetrino, tenía la actitud fiera y el gesto desdeñoso.

(BAROJA, La Dama Errante, p. 30)

This lady was pleasant and kind to a fault, with no great intelligence or understanding, but with an underlying good will in everything. Belen's sister-in-law, on the other hand, ... was a fire-brand. When it came to spitefulness there was no one to beat her. A proper old maid, skinny, dried-up, with a sallow complexion, she had a fearsome presence and her expression was one of contempt.

## -ona (B) NOUN — FEMININE
*(Changed or specialized sense)*

| | |
|---|---|
| encerrona | = treacherous snare, under-hand trap; brief voluntary confinement. |
| (< encierro | = locking up, confinement, encirclement) |
| †*intentona*[1] | = foolhardy, rash or wild attempt, crack or try; unsuccessful attempt; military revolt (especially if a failure), (frustrated) rebellion. |
| (≶ intento | = attempt) |
| jamona | = fleshy or beefy middle-aged woman. |
| (< jamón | = ham) |
| pelucona | = gold doubloon. |
| (< peluca | = wig) |
| pepona | = large cardboard doll. |
| (< Pepa | = popular form of *Josefa*) |
| tumbona | = easy chair (in which to recline). |
| (< tumbón | = lazybones) |

[1] See *cuartelazo*, under -*azo*.

The word *intentona* is invariably used in connexion with two notably unsuccessful risings which took place in Spain in the latter part of the nineteenth century — those of the Captain-General of the Balearic Islands, Ortega *(la intentona de San Carlos de la Rápita)*, and of Brigadier-General Villacampa *(la intentona de Villacampa)*.

(GROUP B)

... los árboles de Miraflores ... recibieron *balazos*★ del fusilamiento de los infelices cogidos en Basurto y complicados en la trama que produjo la *intentona* de San Carlos de la Rápita.

(UNAMUNO, Paz en la Guerra, p. 23)

... the trees of Miraflores ... were hit by shots from the execution of the wretches caught at Basurto and implicated in the plot which gave rise to the (ill-fated) revolt at San Carlos de la Rápita.

## 2. -AZO, -AZA, -AZAS

### *-azo* (A) NOUN — MASCULINE
*(Augmentative, with either pejorative or favourable implication)*

| | |
|---|---|
| *acentazo*[1] | = terribly strong accent. |
| *animalazo*[2] | = great big animal, hulking great brute, whacking great creature. |
| †*artistazo* | = terrific artist or actor; hopeless or incorrigible play-actor. |
| *besazo* | = hell of a big kiss, long-drawn-out kiss. |
| *bigotazo(s)* | = flowery great moustache, handle-bar moustache; great big whisker(s). |
| *bochornazo* | = terribly sultry or heavy weather; frightful feeling of shame, disgrace or embarrassment. |
| *bromazo* | = something beyond a joke, unpleasant or practical joke. |
| *broncazo*[3] | = hell of a ticking-off or bawling-out; real row. |
| *buenazo*[4] | = really decent chap; person good or kind to a fault. |
| *calambrazo* | = hell of a cramp or electric shock. |

[1] Cf. *acentillo*. See under *-illo*.

[2] Cf. *animalote* — same sense.

[3] *Un broncazo de no te menees, un broncazo de padre y muy señor mío* = a really rip-roaring ticking-off or row.

[4] *Buenazo* is more commonly used substantivally than as an adjective: *es un buenazo* = he's a chap who's kind to a fault.

Cf. *buenote, bondadosote* — similar sense. See under *-ote*.

Cf. for sense *hijazo, maridazo, padrazo*, below.

| | |
|---|---|
| *calorazo*[1] | = terrific heat. |
| †*cambiazo* | = violent change; (quick or sudden) switch or switch-over. |
| *camionazo* | = hell of a big lorry, whacking great truck; fine big lorry. |
| †*capitalazo*[2] | = hell of a lot of money, mint of money, fortune, packet. |
| *catarrazo*[3] | = hell of a cold. |
| *cerebrazo* | = terrific brain. |
| *cochazo*[4] | = hell of a big car; (ostentatious) great car; (fine) big car. |
| *complejazo* | = hell of a complex. |
| *coñazo*[5] | = hell of a bind or bore. |
| *copazo*[6] | = great big wine-glass or glass of wine; whacking big snow flake. |
| *curazo*[7] | = hefty great priest; confounded or blasted priest; magnificent or superb priest. |
| *chicazo*[8] | = hefty big chap; tomboy. |
| †*chispazo*[9] | = violent flash, outburst or spark. |
| †*discursazo* | = lengthy great discourse; superb speech. |

[1] Cf. *calorón* — same sense. *Hace un calorazo (calorón) de miedo* = it's really fearfully hot.

[2] Cf. *dineral, fortunón, millonada* — same sense. See under *-al*.

[3] See *gripazo*, below.

[4] *Un cochazo llamativo* = a flashy great bus; *un cochazo estupendo* = a magnificent or smashing car.

[5] Extremely vulgar but very common equivalent of *latazo* (see this word below).

[6] In the first sense *copazo* derives from *copa* and has a synonymous feminine form *copaza*; in the second sense the derivation is from *copo*. Thus *copazos (copazas) de vino* = great big wine-glasses or glasses of wine; *copazos de nieve* = whacking great snow flakes.

[7] *Los malditos curazos de la censura* = the blasted priests on the board of censorship; *un curazo de pelo en pecho* = a real he-man priest, a superb, real man of a priest.
See *curángano*, under *-ángano*.

[8] Cf. *chicarrón, chicote*, which have the same sense, although only *chicazo* is regularly used with the figurative meaning of "tomboy". See under *-ote*.

[9] *El chispazo que originó la guerra* = the spark that set the war off; *en un chispazo comprendió* = in a (sudden) flash he understood or realized.

| | | |
|---|---|---|
| *empachazo*[1] | = | hell of a blow-out or cramming, terrific indigestion. |
| *empalagazo*[2] | = | great blow-out, terrific surfeit (of sweet food). |
| *escandalazo* | = | rip-roaring scandal; terrific din or uproar. |
| *escotazo*[3] | = | very open, very low or plunging neck-line. |
| *esquinazo* | = | ugly great corner; magnificent corner (site). |
| *estilazo*[4] | = | terrific style, elegance or fashion-sense. |
| *estrenazo* | = | terrific first-night, grand première. |
| *estupendazo*[5] | = | really handsome devil, real smasher. |
| *exitazo* | = | colossal or terrific success. |
| *filosofazo*[6] | = | two-penny ha'penny or café philosopher; fine or great philosopher. |
| *frescazo*[7] | = | marked chilliness, hellish chilliness. |
| *gandulazo*[8] | = | great loafer or idler, hell of a lay-about. |
| *gatazo* | = | hell of a big cat, whopping great cat. |
| †*geniazo*[9] | = | absolute genius; violent temper. |
| *golosazo*[10] | = | real devil for sweet things. |
| *golpazo* | = | hell of a blow or wallop, real corker. |
| *gringazo*[11] | = | great gangling Yank or foreigner, blasted Yank or foreigner. |

[1] Cf. *atracón* — similarly used. See under *-ón*. Cf. *empalagazo*, below.

[2] See *empachazo*, above.

[3] Cf. *escotito*. See under *-ito*.

[4] Cf. *estilín*. See under *-ín*.

[5] For substantival use cf. *buenazo*, above.

[6] *Un filosofazo de tres al cuarto* = a tin-pot philosopher; *un filosofazo magnífico* = a superb philosopher.

[7] *Hace un frescazo de mil pares de demonios* = it's infernally chilly. Cf. *fresquillo*. See under *-illo*.

[8] See *gandulón*, under *-ón*.

[9] For the second sense cf. *geniudo* : *tener un geniazo* = *ser geniudo* = to have a violent temper, to be violently bad-tempered. See *geniudo* and *corajudo* under *-udo*.

[10] Cf. *golosón* — same sense.

[11] Cf. *gringote* — same sense. These two expressions are Spanish-American, but well-known in Spain.

| | |
|---|---|
| *gripazo*[1] *trancazo* | = heavy dose of 'flu, really hefty attack of 'flu. |
| *groserazo*[2] | = rude great oaf, atrociously rude fellow. |
| *guapazo*[3] | = really handsome devil. |
| *guerrazo* | = tremendous or colossal war. |
| †*gustazo*[4] | = immense or terrific pleasure, satisfaction or thrill, hell of a kick. |
| *haigazo*[5] | = flashy great car; magnificent big car. |
| †*hijazo* | = hefty great son or boy; really good or doting son; beloved or darling son. |
| †*humazo* | = dense smoke. |
| *jefazo*[6] | = big boss, big bug, one of the top brass. |
| *juergazo* | = uproarious party, tremendous binge, terrific do. |
| *kilazo*[7] | = hefty great two and a quarter pounds. |
| *latazo*[8] *pelmazo* *rollazo* *tostonazo* | = hell of a bore, thundering bore, crashing bore, prize pain-in-the-neck. |

[1] *Trancazo* refers especially to the aches and pains which are associated with influenza and which, in this word, are likened to the effect produced by a blow from a cross-bar or club.

Cf. *catarrazo*, *muermazo* = hell of a dose of catarrh, hell of a cold.

[2, 3] For substantival use of adjectives see under *buenazo* and *estupendazo*, above.

[4] E.g. *se dio el gustazo de decirle cuatro verdades* = she treated herself to the immense satisfaction of giving him a piece of her mind.

[5] *Haigazo* was formed on the popular expression *haiga* = flashy car; magnificent car. The term is said to have arisen in the following way: on the analogy of such forms as *caiga* and *traiga* the illiterate often use, as the subjunctive of *haber*, *haiga* for *haya*. Thus it may well be that more than one moneyed but uneducated person has entered a car showroom and asked for *el mejor coche que haiga*.

Cf. *cochazo*. See above.

[6] *El jefazo de arriba* = the big boss at the top; *los jefazos* = the top brass.

Cf. the phrase *pájaro gordo* : *es un pájaro gordo* = he's a big noise.

[7] *Se sentó con sus cien kilazos* = he sat down with all the weight of his two hundred and twenty-five pounds (approx.).

[8] *Latazo* is used only of things, *pelmazo* only of persons; *rollazo* and *tostonazo* can be used for either.

| | | |
|---|---|---|
| *liquidazo*[1] | = | hell of a lot of liquid. |
| *lomazo* | = | whacking great or magnificent loin (meat) |
| *lujazo* | = | terrific luxury. |
| *llenazo* | = | really packed house (theatre, cinema, etc.). |
| *maridazo* | = | hefty great husband; doting or over-indulgent husband. |
| *muermazo*[2] | = | heavy attack of glanders; hell of a cold. |
| *multazo*[3] | = | hell of a fine, hefty fine. |
| *negociazo* | = | really big deal, terrific piece of business, tremendously profitable business. |
| *negrazo*[4] | = | hefty or burly great negro; blasted great negro; fine big negro. |
| *nieblazo*[5] | = | hell of a thick fog. |
| *noviazo* | = | burly great fiancé, boy-friend; blasted fiancé; magnificent or smashing fiancé. |
| †*ojazo(s)* | = | great big eye(s), large (round) eye(s), fine big eye(s). |
| *osazo* | = | whacking great bear. |
| *padrazo*[6] | = | hefty great father; doting or over-indulgent father. |
| *panazo*[7] | = | huge quantity of bread; hell of a big loaf. |
| *partidazo* | = | wonderful match, marvellous catch (for marriage) |
| *pelmazo*[8] | = | hell of a bore. |
| *perrazo* | = | hell of a big dog; whacking great hound; fine big dog. |
| *personajazo*[9] | = | really important figure, big name, big noise. |

[1] *Bebió tanto liquidazo, que se puso enfermo* = he drank such a terrific quantity of liquid that he was ill after it. Cf. *panazo*, below.

[2] See *gripazo*, above.

[3] Also *multaza*, but less common.

[4] *Un negrazo gigantesco* = a towering great negro.

[5] Also *nieblaza*, but less common.

[6] Cf. *padrastro*. See under *-astro*.

[7] *Come tanto panazo, que se va a poner gordísimo* = he eats such huge quantities of bread that he's going to get a shocking size. Cf. *liquidazo*, above.

[8] See *latazo*, above.

[9] Cf. *jefazo*, above.

| | | |
|---|---|---|
| *piezazo(s)* | = | whacking great foot, feet. |
| *pisazo* | = | huge flat; magnificent flat. |
| *platazo* | = | damn great plate(ful). |
| †*pleitazo* | = | really big lawsuit. |
| *problemazo*[1] | = | hell of a problem, really hefty problem. |
| *profesoradazo* | = | huge or magnificent teaching staff. |
| *puentazo* | = | hell of a big bridge; magnificent bridge. |
| *puestazo* | = | magnificent post, plum job. |
| *ratazo* | = | quite a while, hell of a long time. |
| *rojazo*[2] | = | real red, red-hot communist. |
| *rollazo*[3] | = | hell of a bore. |
| *ruidazo*[4] | = | terrific noise, hell of a din. |
| *solazo*[5] | = | terrific amount of sunshine; fierce or magnificent sun. |
| †*sueldazo* | = | fat great salary, whacking great salary. |
| *sueñazo*[6] | = | terrific (feeling of) sleepiness, tremendous sleep. |
| †*talentazo*[7] | = | super-intelligence; highly intelligent, talented or gifted person. |
| *tiempazo*[8] | = | atrocious weather; magnificent weather. |
| *torazo* | = | hell of a big bull; damn great bull; fine big bull. |
| *torerazo* | = | hefty great bull-fighter; magnificent bull-fighter. |
| *tormentazo*[9] | = | hell of a storm, terrific storm. |

[1] Cf. *problemón* — same sense.
[2] Cf. *comunistón* — same sense.
   Cf. *rojillo, comunistilla*. See under *-illo, -illa* (m.).
[3] See *latazo*, above.
[4] Cf. *estrépito, estruendo* — similar sense, but more literary tone.
[5] Cf. *sol de justicia* = pitiless or ferocious sun.
[6] See *suenarrón*, under *-ón*.
[7] *Es un talentazo* = he's a highly talented or intelligent person.
[8] *Un tiempazo espantoso* = foul weather; *un tiempazo imponente* = glorious weather. Cf. *tiempecito* in its ironic sense. See under *-ito*.
[9] Cf. *tormentón* — same sense.

| | |
|---|---|
| *tortazo* | = hell of a clout, slap, wallop. |
| *tostonazo*[1] | = hell of a bore. |
| *traficazo* | = hell of an amount of traffic, tremendous weight of traffic. |
| *trancazo*[2] | = hefty attack of 'flu. |
| *viajazo*[3] | = terrific journey, magnificent tour. |
| *vinazo* | = coarse wine; magnificent wine. |

## -*azo* EXAMPLES FROM LITERATURE
## (GROUP A)

— La Sofi ... no me parece que reúna encantos como para justificar esa obcecación criminal.
— ¡ La Sofi es una diosa!
— Y tú un *artistazo*. La has idealizado y no eres capaz de la fría reflexión.

(VALLE-INCLÁN, Baza de Espadas, p. 108)

"Sophie ... does not appear to me to have charms sufficient to justify such criminal blindness."
"Sophie's a goddess!"
"And you're a hopeless play-actor. You've idealized her and you're incapable of cool thinking."

Cuando el niño estudiaba los últimos años de su carrera, verificóse en él uno de esos *cambiazos* críticos que tan comunes son en la edad juvenil. De travieso y alborotado volvióse tan *juiciosillo**, que al mismo Zalamero daba quince y raya.

(PÉREZ GALDÓS, Fortunata y Jacinta, I, p. 7)

When the lad was in the last years of his university course he underwent one of those violent and decisive changes which are so common in youth. From a wild, mischievous boy he turned into such a little model of level-headedness that he even knocked spots off Zalamero.

---

[1] See *latazo,* above.
[2] See *gripazo,* above.
[3] Cf. *viajecito.* See under –*ito.*

— ... Mira el doctor Perpiñá.... Ha hecho un *capitalazo* con ese jarabe....

(PÉREZ GALDÓS, *Fortunata y Jacinta*, IV, p. 9)

"... Just look at Doctor Perpiñá.... He's made a mint of money with that syrup of his...."

... de improviso, sintiendo uno de aquellos *chispazos* de cólera repentina y momentánea, que no era dueño de refrenar, ... soltó unas cuantas asperezas y severidades que hicieron enmudecer a la asamblea.

(PARDO BAZÁN, *Los Pazos de Ulloa*, pp. 96, 97)

... unexpectedly feeling one of those violent flashes of sudden and fleeting anger which he was incapable of checking, ... he uttered a few harsh remarks and strictures which silenced the assembled company.

— Habló después Castelar. ¡Qué *discursazo*! ¡Qué valor de hombre!

(PÉREZ GALDÓS, *Fortunata y Jacinta*, I, p. 405)

"Then Castelar spoke. What a superb speech! What a talented man!"

— ¡Y qué *geniazo* va sacando!

(PÉREZ GALDÓS, *Fortunata y Jacinta*, II, p. 159)

"And what a violent temper he's developing!"

¿... quién le quitaba el *gustazo* de juzgar a su modo la conducta del amo y las señoritas, de alardear de discreción, censurando ... algunos actos que ella, si fuese señora, no realizaría jamás?

(PARDO BAZÁN, *Los Pazos de Ulloa*, p. 147)

... why should she deprive herself of the immense satisfaction of passing her own kind of judgement on the behaviour of her master and his daughters, the immense satisfaction of showing off her good sense by criticizing ... certain things which she, if she were a lady of position, would never dream of doing?

— ... Los hijos no sabéis nunca lo que las madres os queremos; si os lo figurarais, no seríais así.

— Anda, no seas *chiquilla*\*, tranquilízate . . . . Tendrás carta del *hijazo* todas las semanas; te lo prometo . . . .

(ZUNZUNEGUI, *¡ Ay, Estos Hijos !*, p. 154)

"... You boys never know how much we mothers love you; if you had any realization of it, you wouldn't behave the way you do."

"Get away with you, don't talk like a silly girl, calm down . . . . You'll get a letter from your darling son every week, that's a promise . . . ."

... se metieron en la cocina, al lado del fuego, que despedía un *humazo* que impregnaba las ropas y hacía llorar.

(BAROJA, *La Dama Errante*, p. 177)

... they went into the kitchen [and settled themselves] by the fire, which was giving out a dense smoke that impregnated their clothes and made their eyes water.

Joven aún, sólo revelaban su edad aquellos *ojazos* claros de virgen, *inocentones*\* y tímidos.

(BLASCO IBÁÑEZ, *La Barraca*, p. 17)

She was still young, but you could only tell this by those light, shy, utterly guileless eyes, the big, (round) eyes of a virgin.

Perdíase en un dédalo de ... *pleitecillos*\* menudos de atrasos y *pleitazos* gordos de partijas.

(PARDO BAZÁN, *Los Pazos de Ulloa*, p. 61)

He became lost in a labyrinth of ... petty little lawsuits dealing with payments in arrears and big, really important suits concerning partitions of inheritances.

... con tal que tengamos muchos secretarios y oficinas, con secciones y subdivisiones y *sueldazos* bestiales, ... poquísimo importa que expire la labranza entera.

(AZORÍN, *Lecturas Españolas*, p. 239)

... as long as we have a lot of secretaries and offices, with departments and subsections and terrific, whacking great salaries ... it (really) matters very little indeed if the whole of the country's farming dies out.

— ... si me pusiera a disputar contigo, tú, con tu *talentazo* descomunal, me confundirías mil veces ....

(PÉREZ GALDÓS, *Doña Perfecta*, p. 75)

". . . if I were to start arguing with you, you with your vast super-intelligence, you would get the better of me right, left and centre."

## -azo (B) NOUN — MASCULINE
*(Action or result of action — often of a pejorative nature)*

| | |
|---|---|
| *abanicazo* | = blow or swipe with a fan. |
| †*aldabonazo* | = thump with a door-knocker, hammering on door or on conscience. |
| *aletazo(s)* | = beating or flapping (of wings). |
| *alfilerazo*[1] | = jab with a pin; pin-prick, dig (fig.). |
| *almohadillazo* | = blow with a cushion. |
| *arañazo* | = scratch (given by person or animal). |
| †*balazo* | = shot; bullet wound. |
| *bancazo*[2] | = blow with a bench. |
| *baquetazo*[3] | = blow with a ramrod; knock, cropper. |
| *barquinazo(s)*[4] = | (violent) swaying, jolt, jolting (of ship, vehicle). |
| *bastonazo* | = blow or swipe with a stick. |
| *batacazo*[5] | = thud, bump ; cropper. |
| †*bayonetazo* | = bayonet thrust. |
| †*bocinazo* | = blast on a horn, honk. |

[1] Cf. *puyazo* in figurative sense. See below.

[2] *Bancazo* also has the meaning "magnificent bank."

[3] *Se ha dado muchos baquetazos en la vida ; la vida le ha dado muchos baquetazos ; se ha llevado muchos baquetazos en la vida* = he's taken lots of knocks in life; he's come many a cropper in life.

[4] *Dar barquinazos* = to sway or jolt (violently) from side to side.

[5] *Darse un batacazo* = to come a cropper (lit. and fig.).

| †*boñigazo* | = blow from a piece of dried cow-dung. |
| *botellazo* | = clout, wallop with a bottle. |
| *braguetazo*[1] | = act of marrying a woman with money or for her money. |
| *brochazo*[2] | = stroke of a (paint-)brush. |
| *cabezazo*[3] | = butt with the head; knock on the head. |
| *cacharrazo* | = clout or wallop with a pot or pan. |
| *campanillazo(s)* | = clang(ing) of bell(s). |
| *cantazo*[4] | = blow with a stone or pebble. |
| *cañazo* | = blow with a cane or reed. |
| *cañonazo(s)* | = gunfire, detonation(s) of artillery. |
| *capotazo* | = flourish or pass with a cape (bull-fighting). |
| *carpetazo*[5] | = act of filing away, shelving. |
| *castañazo* | = blow from a chestnut; clout, wallop (in general). |
| †*codazo*[6] | = jab, dig with the elbow; nudge. |
| *coletazo* | = lash or swish of a tail. |
| *cordonazo*[7] | = blow with a cord or rope. |
| *cristazo*[8] | = blow with a crucifix. |
| *cuartelazo*[9] | = barrack mutiny, military revolt or coup. |

[1] *Dar el braguetazo* = to marry money (of man).

[2] Cf. *brochada* — same sense, but rare.

[3] Cf. *cabezada* = nod (prior to sleep).

*Me dio un cabezazo* = he butted me with his head; *se dio un cabezazo* = he banged himself on the head; *daba cabezadas* = his head was nodding.

[4] Cf. *pedrada* — same sense.

Cf. *chinazo* and *chinarrazo*, below.

[5] *Dar(le) carpetazo a un asunto* = to shelve a matter.

[6] *Me dio un codazo* = he jabbed me with his elbow; he nudged me; *abrirse paso a codazo limpio* = to elbow one's way through brazenly or unrestrainedly. (Cf. *se desasió a puñetazo limpio* = he broke loose by lashing out punches right, left and centre; *vive a sablazo limpio* = he lives by unashamedly touching people for money. See *puñetazo* and *sablazo*, below.)

[7] *El cordonazo de San Francisco* = autumn equinoctial squall(s) or storm(s).

[8] As in the phrase *hacer cristianos a cristazos* = to bludgeon people into Christianity.

[9] Other terms of like meaning are: *golpe militar, golpe de fuerza, intentona militar, militarada, generalada, pronunciamiento*. Also *cuartelada*.

| †*culatazo* | = blow with the butt (of a fire-arm); recoil. |
| *chinarrazo* | = blow with a large pebble. |
| *chinazo*[1] | = blow with a pebble. |
| *derechazo*[2] | = blow or stroke delivered with right hand; right-handed pass in bull-fighting. |
| *encontronazo*[3]<br>*topetazo*<br>*trompazo* | = bump, knock, crash. |
| †*escobazo* | = blow or swipe with a broom. |
| *escopetazo*[4] | = shot or wound from a shot-gun; nasty, sudden shock. |
| *espaldarazo* | = blow on the back; accolade, act of recognition or acknowledgement of merit. |
| *esquinazo*[5] | = act of avoiding or dodging a person. |
| †*estacazo*[6] | = blow or swipe with a stake or cudgel. |
| *flechazo*[7] | = arrow-shot or wound; love-at-first-sight. |

[1] See *cantazo*, above.

[2] Cf. *zurdazo*, below.

[3] *Encontronazo*, despite its double suffix form *(encuentro + ón + azo)*, does not, in fact, have any greater force of meaning than *topetazo* or *trompazo*. Thus "a terrific bump" or "a hell of a crash" would be *un encontronazo (topetazo, trompazo) tremendo, un encontronazo (topetazo, trompazo) de mil pares de demonios.*

These expressions are frequently used to refer to a collision between vehicles and are usually found with the verbs *darse* and *pegarse*: — *se ha dado un topetazo con (en) el coche* = he's had a crash with the car. The technical expression for collision is *choque*. The form *encontrón* is very little used. *Topetazo* has two rather less common synonyms in *topetada* and *topetón*. *Trompazo* also has a less common synonym in *trompada*.

[4] *Le dieron (largaron) un escopetazo* = they gave him a nasty or violent shock or surprise.

[5] Literally "act of dodging round a corner to avoid someone", but used in the sense of "avoiding" or "dodging" in general. *Le di (un) esquinazo* = I avoided or dodged him, I gave him the slip. Cf. *plantón*. See under *-ón*.

Cf. the expression *hacerse el encontradizo* = to bump into someone (apparently by accident, but in fact) on purpose.

[6] Cf. *garrotazo, mazazo, porrazo* — similar sense. See below. Cf. *estacada* = fence, palisade. *Dejar en la estacada* = to leave in the lurch. Note completely different sense from *estacazo*.

[7] *Fue un flechazo* = it was love-at-first-sight.

| | |
|---|---|
| *fogonazo* | = powder-flash. |
| †*frenazo*[1] | = (sharp, sudden) braking. |
| †*garrotazo*[2] | = blow or swipe with a club or stick. |
| *golletazo* | = blow on neck of a bottle; violent cutting off (e.g. of dealings); thrust into lungs (bull-fighting). |
| *guantazo*[3] | = blow delivered with a glove, slap. |
| †*guarrazo*[4] | = clout, cropper, wallop. |
| *hachazo*[5] | = stroke of an axe. |
| *ladrillazo* | = blow from a brick. |
| †*latigazo*[6] *trallazo* *vergajazo* | = whip-lash; pick-me-up, life-saver (drink). |
| †*lengüetazo*[7] | = lick, act of licking, stroke of tongue. |
| *linternazo*[8] | = blow or swipe delivered with a lantern or torch; blow (in general). |
| *manotazo*[9] | = blow or swipe from the hand. |
| *martillazo*[10] | = blow from a hammer, hammer stroke. |
| †*mazazo*[11] | = blow from a mace or club. |
| *metrallazo* | = blast of shrapnel. |
| *navajazo*[12] | = slash or thrust of a (clasp-) knife; knife-wound. |
| *paletazo*[13] *varetazo* | = glancing blow from a bull's horn. |
| *palmetazo* | = swipe of a fly-swatter. |

[1] *Dio un frenazo* = he jammed on the brakes.

[2] See *estacazo*, above.

[3] Cf. *guantada* — same sense.

[4] A vulgar and not very common term. Cf. *trastazo*, below.

[5] *Le mató a hachazos* = he hacked him to death with an axe; *le mató de un hachazo* = he killed him with a blow from an axe.

[6] Of the three words *latigazo* alone has the second or figurative sense.

[7] Cf. *lametón* — similar sense.

[8] Cf. *trastazo*, below.

[9] Cf. *manotada, manotón* — same sense, but less used.

[10] *Le mató a martillazos* = he pounded him to death with a hammer; *le mató de un martillazo* = he killed him with a blow from a hammer.

[11] Cf. *mazada* — same sense, but little used. See *estacazo*, above.

[12] Cf. *navajada* — same sense, but little used.

[13] *Varetazo* is the more common word.

| | | |
|---|---|---|
| *patinazo*[1] | = | skid; blunder, faux pas. |
| *pianazo*[2] | = | bang or thump on piano key(s). |
| *picotazo* | = | (savage) peck (of a bird). |
| *pinchazo*[3] | = | puncture; jab (injection). |
| *planchazo*[4] | = | stroke or blow with an iron; great disappointment; great embarrassment. |
| †*plumazo*[5] | = | stroke of the pen (lit., fig.). |
| *porrazo*[6] | = | blow with a truncheon or club; clout, wallop, bash. |
| †*portazo*[7] | = | act of slamming a door. |
| *pucherazo* | = | blow or clout with a pot; cooking or rigging (of election results). |
| *puñetazo*[8] | = | blow with the fist, punch. |
| *puyazo*[9] | = | prick with a goad, jab; dig (fig.). |
| *ramalazo* | = | sudden unexpected outburst, flash (e.g. of anger, madness or inspiration). |
| †*trasponazo* | = | act of harsh scraping, rasping. |

[1] *Patinazo* is used of both persons and vehicles and in both literal and figurative senses. *Dar (pegar) un patinazo* = to skid; to blunder. Cf. *resbalón*, which also means "skid", but is used only of persons and in the literal sense.

[2] Cf. *teclazo*, below.

[3] *Tener un pinchazo* = to have a puncture; *hemos tenido un pinchazo* = we have had a puncture.

[4] Cf. *planchón*. See under *-ón*. Both words are used with the literal sense of "act of passing an iron", e.g. *le voy a pegar un planchazo (planchón) a esta camisa* = I'm going to run the iron over this shirt. In addition, however, *planchazo* is used figuratively in two ways which are illustrated by the following examples: — *yo creí que me iban a pagar 2.000 pesetas, pero sólo fueron 500. ¡ Menudo planchazo !* = I thought they were going to pay me 2,000 pesetas, but (in the event) it was only 500. A real let-down (disappointment)!; *creyéndome que era la señora de la casa, le besé la mano, pero ¡ resultó que era la muchacha ! ¡ Vaya planchazo que me llevé !* = under the impression that she was the lady of the house, I kissed her hand, but it turned out that she was the maid! You can imagine what an utter fool I felt (how horribly embarrassed I was)!

[5] *De un plumazo* = with a stroke of the pen. Cf. *plumada* — same sense, but rare.

[6] See *estacazo*, above.

[7] *Dar un portazo* = to slam or bang the door.

[8] Cf. *puñada* — same sense, but less common.

[9] *Darle, echarle, largarle, meterle a uno un puyazo* = to have, take a dig at someone. Cf. *alfilerazo*, above. Cf. *puntada* — same sense.

| | | |
|---|---|---|
| *regletazo* | = | stroke, swipe or rap with a ruler. |
| *rodillazo* | = | jab of the knee. |
| *sablazo*[1] | = | sabre thrust or wound; act of sponging, cadging or touching for money. |
| *sartenazo* | = | blow, clout, wallop with a frying-pan. |
| †*taconazo* | = | stamp, rap produced with the heel. |
| *taponazo* | = | pop, report (on opening a bottle). |
| *teclazo*[2] | = | act of striking piano or typewriter key. |
| *telefonazo*[3] | = | telephone call, ring. |
| *tijeretazo*[4] | = | cut, slash made with scissors. |
| †*timbrazo*[5] | = | (shrill) ring (of a bell). |
| *topetazo*[6] | = | bump, knock, crash. |
| *trallazo*[7] | = | whip-lash. |
| *trancazo*[8] | = | blow with a cross-bar or heavy stick. |
| *trastazo*[9] | = | clout, thump, whack, blow (in general). |
| *trompazo*[10] | = | bump, knock, crash. |
| *varetazo*[11] | = | glancing blow from a bull's horn. |
| *ventanazo* | = | act of slamming shut a window. |
| *vergajazo*[12] | = | whip-lash. |
| *vistazo*[13] | = | look, glance. |
| *zarpazo* | = | gash, rent made by a paw. |
| *zurdazo* | = | blow or swipe with left hand. |

[1] *Darle, pegarle, largarle, meterle a uno un sablazo* = to touch someone for money.

[2] *Dar teclazos* = to bash or thump away on a piano or typewriter.

[3] *Darle, pegarle a uno un telefonazo* = to give someone a ring, to ring someone up. Cf. *llamada (telefónica)* = (telephone) call.

[4] Also *tijeretada*, but much less common.

[5] Cf. *llamada* — similar sense, but weaker — "call".

[6] See *encontronazo*, above.

[7] See *latigazo*, above.

[8] Generally used with its figurative sense of " 'flu". See under *gripazo*.

[9] Cf. *linternazo*, above.

[10] See *encontronazo*, above.

[11] See *paletazo*, above.

[12] See *latigazo*, above.

[13] *Dar, echar un vistazo* = to take a look, gander; *abarcar de un vistazo* = to take in at a glance.

Cf. *mirada, ojeada* — same sense.

... dando sobre la puerta un par de *aldabonazos* capaces de despertar a los siete durmientes.

(PALACIO VALDÉS, *La Hermana San Sulpicio*, p. 144)

... delivering on the door a couple of thumps with the knocker that were enough to wake the dead.

[Cf. example of figurative use:

Cruzamos una serranía desierta . . .. En mitad de la paramera, los muros derruidos de una *casucha** recogen — y es un *aldabonazo* en todas las conciencias — la dramática invocación del paisaje: MÁS ÁRBOLES, MÁS AGUA.

(GOYTISOLO, *Campos de Níjar*, p. 18)

We are going through a desolate mountain district . . .. In the midst of the wilderness the crumbling walls of a hovel record a message which represents a hammering on everyone's conscience — the dramatic appeal from the countryside: MORE TREES, MORE WATER.]

Los reyes que salen a *balazos* acaso volverán; pero aquellos que salen a *escobazos*, ésos no volverán.
(Verse written at the time of the ignominious expulsion of Isabel II from Spain (1868).

Monarchs who are shot out of the country with a volley of bullets may possibly come back again; but those who are swept out on the end of a broom will certainly not come back again.

— A *bayonetazos* acabamos con todos — dijo el hombre, sonriendo.

(BAROJA, *Zalacaín el Aventurero*, p. 103)

"We finished them all off at bayonet point", the man said, grinning.

Un gitano se cruza con nosotros montado sobre un borrico. El chófer (del camión) da un *bocinazo* y el animal se espanta. Por la *ventanilla*★ de atrás, a medida que nos alejamos, le veo trotar envuelto en una nube de polvo.

(GOYTISOLO, *Campos de Níjar*, p. 122)

A gipsy passes us riding an ass. The driver (of the lorry) gives a blast on his horn and the animal shies. As we draw away I can see him out of the back window, trotting along shrouded in a cloud of dust.

¿Sería él más libre en el colegio, o en la Universidad, que cuando el Moñigo y él se peleaban a *boñigazo* limpio en los prados del valle?

(DELIBES, *El Camino*, p. 53)

Would he be freer at school or University than when "Shitty-pants" and he had a scrap in the valley meadows, flinging lumps of dried cow-dung at each other for all they were worth?

... en fin, que *pasito*★ a paso y a *codazo* limpio, se habían ido metiendo en la clase media, en nuestra *bonachona*★ clase media, toda necesidades y pretensiones ....

(PÉREZ GALDÓS, *Torquemada en la Hoguera*, p. 39)

... in short, very gradually, and by brazenly elbowing their way, they had pushed themselves into the middle class, our thoroughly easy-going middle class, which is just one mass of straitened circumstances and (excessive) aspirations ....

La Guardia Civil, fiera de sol en charoles y fusiles, acudía poniendo paz a *culatazos*.

(VALLE-INCLÁN, *¡Viva mi Dueño!*, p. 129)

The Civil Guard, with the sun flashing savagely on their weapons and patent-leather helmets, moved in, restoring order with their rifle-butts.

... el muchacho cogió la vara con las dos manos y le arrimó un *estacazo* a la yegua ... el pobre animal, con el recuerdo del *garrotazo*, ya no volvió a pararse.

(BAROJA, *La Dama Errante*, p. 163)

... the boy took the stick in both hands and gave the mare a swipe ... the poor creature, remembering this whack, did not stop again.

En la curva de Axpe, por poco acaba el viaje yéndose [el coche] contra un tranvía. Un *frenazo* brutal, y adelante.

(ZUNZUNEGUI, *¡ Ay, Estos Hijos !*, p. 163)

At the bend at Axpe the journey very nearly came to an end [with the car] crashing into a tram. A violent slamming-on of the brakes, and then away again.

... una de las chicas patinó sobre el limo y se quedó sentada . . ..
— También fue de los que hacen época el *guarrazo* que se pegó Fernando el día que fuimos a Navacerrada.

(SÁNCHEZ FERLOSIO, *El Jarama*, pp. 27, 28)

... one of the girls slipped on the mud and ended up in a sitting position . . ..
"That was a fine old cropper Fernando came too, the day we went to Navacerrada."

... le grité, restallando las palabras como *latigazos* . . ..

(VALLE-INCLÁN, *Sonata de Estío*, p. 163)

... I yelled at him, snarling out the words like whip-lashes . . ..

Acababan de chapuzarse, y un *vientecillo** ahilado les secaba el cuerpo a fríos *lengüetazos*.

(DELIBES, *El Camino*, p. 76)

They had just been in for a dip, and a gentle breeze licked coldly round their bodies as it dried them.

Hombre impresionable, Luis salió de la lectura como si le hubiesen dado un *mazazo* en la cabeza.

(ZUNZUNEGUI, *¡ Ay, Estos Hijos !*, p. 107)

Being easily affected by things, Luis felt, when he emerged from reading the book, as if he had been clubbed on the head.

La vida de esos grotescos personajes, las costumbres de esa vieja porción española, están descritas con la sequedad despiadada, con el ácido *plumazo* rápido, tan propios del estilo barojiano . . ..

(SORDO, in Baroja y su Mundo, p. 151)

The lives of those grotesque characters [and] the customs of that ancient bit of Spain are described with the ruthless asperity [and] the swift, acid stroke of the pen which are so typical of Baroja's style . . ..

— Se ha marchado dando un *portazo*.

(NEVILLE, La Familia Mínguez, p. 123)

"He left slamming the door behind him."

Hablaban en el jardín del palacio de Algorta. En aquel momento Luisito derrapó con la "bici" al tomar la curva de un sendero y estuvo en un tris que no se diera una morrada.[1]

La abuela, al oír el *rasponazo* de las ruedas . . ., se alzó como despedida del asiento.

— ¡Este chico! . . . se ha debido de dar un *golpazo* . . ..

(ZUNZUNEGUI, ¡Ay, Estos Hijos!, p. 24)

They were talking in the garden of the Algorta mansion. Just then young Luis skidded on his "bike" as he was rounding a bend in a path and very nearly took a header face-first into the ground.

His grandmother, on hearing the harsh scraping of the tyres . . ., shot out of her seat. "That boy! . . . he must have got an awful thump . . .."

. . . comenzaron a bailar, dando fuertes *taconazos* sobre los azulejos.

(PALACIO VALDÉS, La Hermana San Sulpicio, p. 387)

. . . they began to dance, stamping violently with their heels on the coloured glazed tiles.

El silencio fue agujereado por los *timbrazos* de un teléfono mudo durante días enteros.

(GIMÉNEZ-ARNÁU, El Canto del Gallo, p. 13)

The quiet was (suddenly) rent by the (shrill) ringing of a telephone which had been silent for days on end.

---

[1] Cf. *morrón* — same sense (lit. "wallop on the snout").

## -azo (C) NOUN — MASCULINE
### (Changed or specialized sense)

| | | |
|---|---|---|
| *espinazo* | = | spine, back-bone. |
| (< *espina* | = | thorn; fish-bone) |
| *lechazo* | = | sucking lamb. |
| (< *leche* | = | milk) |
| *sargazo*[1] | = | sargasso, gulf-weed. |
| (< *sarga* | = | osier, willow) |
| *trancazo*[2] | = | (heavy) attack of 'flu. |
| (< *tranca* | = | cross bar, club) |

## -azo (D) ADVERB

| | | |
|---|---|---|
| *antañazo* | = | way back in by-gone days or in days of yore. |

## -aza (A) NOUN — FEMININE
### (Augmentative with either pejorative or favourable implications)

| | | |
|---|---|---|
| *barbaza(s)* | = | whacking great beard, great mass of face-fungus. |
| *bestiaza*[3] | = | hefty great creature, coarse great female. |
| *bocaza* | = | huge great mouth, whacking great gate. |
| *bodaza*[4] | = | magnificent, grand or slap-up wedding. |
| *cajaza* | = | whacking great box, hell of a big box; fine big box. |
| *carnaza(s)* | = | coarse heavy flesh. |
| *carreraza*[5] | = | terrific race or rush; magnificent university or professional record. |

[1] *El mar de los Sargazos* = the Sargasso Sea.

[2] See *gripazo*, under section A.

[3] Cf. *hembràza*, below.

*Bestiaza* has a strong pejorative tone, whereas *hembraza*, though crude, is often favourable in implication.

[4] Cf. *bodón* — same sense.

Cf. such phrases as *boda de postín, boda por todo lo alto*.

[5] Cf. *carrerón*. See under *-ón*.

Both words have the same two senses, although *carreraza* is much more commonly used with the second meaning than with the first. E.g. *para ser tan joven, ha hecho (tiene) una carreraza (un carrerón) imponente* = for such a young man he has done really phenomenally well. [Cf. *ha hecho estupendamente*, which does not mean "he has done magnificently", but "he has done absolutely right or absolutely the right thing".]

Cf. *expedientazo* — same sense. *Tener un expedientazo* = to have a magnificent university or professional record.

| | |
|---|---|
| *casaza*[1] | = hell of a big house; magnificent big house. |
| †*cochinaza* | = utterly filthy creature. |
| *colaza* | = devil of a big tail or queue. |
| *cosaza* | = hefty great thing, whacking great object. |
| *españolaza* | = heavy, very dark Spanish woman; magnificent example of a Spanish woman. |
| *hambraza*[2] | = tremendous or ravenous hunger, colossal appetite. |
| *hembraza*[3] | = hell of a big female; magnificent big female. |
| *ladronaza* | = (vile) thieving creature, thieving bitch. |
| *lavaza(s)* | = slops, dirty soapy water from washing. |
| †*lenguaza* | = (vile) great tongue. |
| *lunaza* | = magnificent large moon; superb big piece of plate glass. |
| *madraza*[4] | = over-indulgent mother. |
| *manaza* | = (clumsy) great hand, paw or fist; (powerful) big hand. |
| †*miradaza* | = powerful or passionate look. |
| *olaza* | = hell of a big wave; superb large wave. |
| *piernaza* | = hefty great leg. |
| *piscinaza* | = hell of a big swimming-pool; fine large swimming-pool. |
| *playaza* | = hell of a big beach; magnificent large beach. |
| †*sangraza* | = thick or heavy black blood. |

*-aza EXAMPLES FROM LITERATURE*
(GROUP A)

— ¿También fumas, *cochinaza?*

(PÉREZ GALDÓS, *La de Bringas*, p. 255)

"You smoke too, do you, you utterly filthy creature?"

[1] Cf. *caserón*. See under *-ón*.
 Cf. *casona*. See under *-ona*.
 Cf. *pisazo*. See under *-azo*.
[2] In Andalusia the forms *hambrera* and *hambrina* are used with the same sense.
[3] See *bestiaza,* above.
[4] Cf. *padrazo*. See under *-azo*.

... de buena gana le hubiera cortado a Papitos toda aquella *lenguaza* que sacaba.

(PÉREZ GALDÓS, *Fortunata y Jacinta*, II, p. 37)

... he would gladly have cut off the whole of that [vile] great tongue Papitos was sticking out.

— ... Hay chicas muy guapas. — De eso ya me he enterado ... contestó el primo, echando a Rita una *miradaza*.

(PARDO BAZÁN, *Los Pazos de Ulloa*, p. 139)

"... We have some very beautiful girls here." "So I have discovered ...", the cousin answered, giving Rita a powerful look.

... vaciaba su morral, del cual salieron dos *perdigones*★ y una liebre muerta, con los ojos empañados y el pelaje maculado de *sangraza*.

(PARDO BAZÁN, *Los Pazos de Ulloa*, p. 35)

... he was emptying his game-bag, and out of it came two young partridges and a dead hare with its eyes filmed-over and its fur stained with thick black blood.


*-aza (B) NOUN — FEMININE*
*(Changed or specialized sense)*

| | |
|---|---|
| *barcaza*[1] | = barge. |
| (< barca | = boat) |
| *cachaza* | = phlegm. |
| (< cacha | = buttock) |
| *gallinaza* | = hen-dung. |
| (< gallina | = hen) |
| *linaza* | = linseed. |
| (< lino | = flax) |

[1] Cf. *gabarra* and *lanchón* — same sense. See under *-ón*.

| melaza | = molasses. |
|--------|-----------|
| (< miel | = honey) |
| mostaza | = mustard. |
| (< mosto | = must) |

## -azas NOUN — MASCULINE
*(Augmentative and/or pejorative)*

| †*bragazas*[1] | = hen-pecked husband, man dominated by his wife; coward, funker. |
|---------------|-----|
| *bocazas* | = loud-mouthed individual, loud-mouthed braggart. |

## -azas EXAMPLE FROM LITERATURE

Lo malo era que el Moñigo entendía que el valor de un hombre puede cambiar de la noche a la mañana.... Hoy podía ser uno un valiente y mañana un *bragazas*, o a la inversa.

(DELIBES, *El Camino*, p. 98)

The worst of it was that "Shittypants" considered that a man's courage could change overnight.... One day a fellow might be a hero and the next a funker, or vice versa.

### 3. -OTE, -OTES, -OTA, -OTAS

## -ote (A) NOUN — MASCULINE
*(Augmentative and frequently pejorative, but also capable of attenuative use)*

| †*airote*[2] | = strong wind, hell of a blast. |
|-------------|-----|
| *alemanote*[3] | = big hefty German, great oaf of a German; blessed or blasted German. |

[1] Cf. *calzonazos* — same first sense.
[2] *Airote* = *ventarrón*. See under *-ón*.
[3] Cf. *inglesote* = gawky great Englishman, blessed Englishman; *vascote* = hulking great Basque, oafish great Basque.
Cf. *gringote* (also *gringazo*) — used in Spanish America to mean "gawky great Yank", "blasted (great) Yank". See *gringazo*, under *-azo*.
Cf. *inglesón*, *españolón*, etc. See *inglesón*, under *-ón*.

| | | |
|---|---|---|
| †*amigote*[1] | = | buddy, crony, (wretched) pal, chum, mate. |
| †*angelote*[2] | = | big hefty angel; big chubby child. |
| †*animalote*[3] | = | hefty great animal, whacking great brute. |
| *chicote*[4] *muchachote* | = | hefty big lad, strapping fellow. |
| *discursote* | = | long-winded speech. |
| *gamberrote* | = | real hooligan, proper larrikin. |
| *gringote*[5] | = | blasted Yank. |
| †*herejote* | = | out and out heretic. |
| *liberalote* | = | out and out liberal. |
| †*librote*[6] | = | clumsy, cumbersome great tome; dull old book. |
| *machote* | = | he-man, tough guy. |
| *materialistote* | = | base or out and out materialist. |
| *militarote* | = | real army type, dyed-in-the-wool soldier, member of the thick-headed military, blimp. |
| *muchachote*[7] | = | hefty big lad. |
| *negrote* | = | hulking great negro. |
| *niñote*[8] | = | big hefty child; over-grown child (fig.). |
| †*papelote(s)*[9] | = | old paper, paper trash, rubbish, wretched paper(s). |
| *pasmarote*[10] | = | real dim-wit, terribly slow type. |
| *quesote*[11] | = | whacking great cheese. |
| *seriote* | = | terribly serious or solemn individual, regular sober-sides. |
| †*viciosote* | = | utterly depraved individual. |

[1] Cf. *amigacho* — same sense, but less common. Cf. *amiguito* — sometimes used ironically with a similar meaning (e.g. fine friend). See under *-acho, -ito*.

[2] Cf. *angelón* — similar sense, but little used.

[3] Cf. *animalazo* — same sense.

[4] Cf. *chicarrón* — same sense. See under *-ón*.

 Cf. *chicazo*, which is much used in the figurative sense of "tomboy": *María es un chicazo*. See under *-azo*.

[5] See *alemanote*, above.

[6] Cf. *libraco* — similar sense. See under *-aco*.

[7] See *chicote*, above.

[8] Cf. *niñón* — similar sense, but little used.

[9] Cf. *papelajo(s), papelorio(s), papelucho(s); papeleo, papelería*. See under *-ajo*.

[10] Cf. *pasmón* — same sense.

[11] Cf. *quesazo* — same sense.

(GROUP A)

... entró Ballester diciendo que se había levantado un *airote*
muy fuerte y amenazaba tormenta.

(PÉREZ GALDÓS, Fortunata y Jacinta, IV, p. 29)

... Ballester came in saying that a very fierce, strong wind had
sprung up and [that] a storm was threatening.

... y fue que el *pillete*★ del *sobrinito*★, confabulado con sus *amigotes*,
logró embriagarle.

(PÉREZ GALDÓS, Fortunata y Jacinta, I, p. 77)

... and what happened was that his rascally young nephew,
in league with his wretched cronies, managed to get him intoxicated.

[Cf. the different shade of meaning in this passage:

— Por lo bonito que eres, no quiero reñirte ni enfadarme contigo.
¡Quia! Vamos a ser muy *amigotes* tú y yo.

(PARDO BAZÁN, Los Pazos de Ulloa, p. 209)

"Because you're such an attractive little chap I don't want to
scold you or get angry with you. Certainly not! We're going to
be jolly good pals you and I."]

— ¡Ay, que es Neluco! — exclamó ... con su *carita*★ de *angelote*
de Rubens inundada de alegría ... y mirándome un *tantico*★ rubo-
rizada.

(PEREDA, Peñas Arriba, p. 110)

"Goodness, it's Neluco!" she exclaimed ... her [delightful] little
face — like that of one of Rubens' chubby angels — [was] filled
with joy ... and [she was] looking at me with [just] a wee bit of
a blush [on her cheeks].

Pues en cuanto me quedé dormido, ¡qué sueños! Manadas de
osos por todas partes, y osos de todos los tamaños ... tres de los más
*lanudos*★ y graves sentados en una peña ... tres *animalotes* ....

(PEREDA, Peñas Arriba, p. 218)

Well, as soon as I fell asleep, what dreams I had! Hordes of bears on all sides, and bears of every size ... three of the shaggiest and most solemn-looking sitting on a rock ... three hulking great brutes ....

[Cf. *animalazo* in the same work:

... no me impidió el frío nervioso que corrió por todo mi cuerpo estimar la exactitud con que Pito había calificado el lucir de los ojos de aquel *animalazo*.

(*Ibid.*, p. 227)

... the nervous chill that ran all through my body did not prevent me from appreciating the accuracy with which Pito had described the hulking great brute's blazing eyes.]

— Cada uno me tiene que dar el veinticinco por ciento para mi obra ... si no, Dios y San José les amargarán el premio.
— El veinticinco es mucho .... Consúltalo con San José y verás cómo me da la razón.
— ¡Hereje! ... *¡ herejote !* ...
Samaniego se empeñó en que Guillermina había de tomar una copa de champagne.
— ¿Pero tú qué has creído de mí, *viciosote?* ¡Yo beber esas porquerías! ...

(PÉREZ GALDÓS, *Fortunata y Jacinta*, I, pp. 333, 334)

"Each of you has to give me twenty-five per cent for my [charity] work ... otherwise God and Saint Joseph will spoil the prize for you."
"Twenty-five is a great deal .... Put it to Saint Joseph and you'll see how he agrees with me."
"You heretic...! You out and out heretic...!"
Samaniego insisted that Guillermina should have a glass of champagne.
"But what do you think I am, you utterly depraved fellow? Do you imagine I could drink that revolting stuff?"

— ¿Qué es el esplín más que soberbia? Sí, lo que usted tiene es soberbia, el usted satánico. Esos *inglesotes* se figuran que el mundo

se ha hecho para ellos . . .. No, señor mío, hay que ponerse en fila
y ser como los demás.

(Pérez Galdós, Fortunata y Jacinta, IV, p. 105)

"What is spleen but overweening pride? Yes, what's the matter
with you is overweening pride, Satan's "I". Those blessed English
imagine the world was created for them . . .. Well, it just wasn't;
people have got to get in line and be like everybody else."

— Veo a Belarmino leyendo *librotes* y escribajeando *papelorios**
lo más del día, y creía que esto no podía por menos de martirizarle
los sesos y volverle más loco de lo que está.

(Pérez de Ayala, Belarmino y Apolonio, p. 81)

"I see Belarmino reading great tomes and covering old bits of
paper with scrawl for most of the day, and I thought this could
not but be a torment to his brain and drive him crazier than he
[already] is."

— Son copias de escrituras . . ., cuentas viejas de particiones de
bienes y otros *papelotes* de familia . . ..

(Pereda, Peñas Arriba, p. 197)

"They are copies of title deeds . . ., old accounts relating to
partitions of property and other old family papers . . .."

*-ote (B) NOUN — MASCULINE*
*(Changed or specialized sense, often with diminutive implication)*

| | |
|---|---|
| *anclote* | = small kedge or stream anchor, grapnel. |
| (< ancla | = anchor) |
| *barrote* | = short thick iron bar (esp. cell, prison). |
| (< barra | = bar) |
| *camarote* | = cabin, berth (on ship-board). |
| (< cámara | = chamber) |
| *capote* | = military or bullfighting cape or cloak. |
| (< capa | = cape, cloak) |

| *cascote(s)*[1] | = rubble, debris. |
| (< casco(s) | = pieces of broken china or glass) |
| †*islote*[2] | = small barren island; pocket (fig.). |
| (< isla | = island) |
| *palote* | = pot-hook, stroke (in writing). |
| (< palo | = stick) |

## -ote EXAMPLE FROM LITERATURE
## (GROUP B)

De la espesa masa indiferenciada que henchía el café a toda hora, sobresalía, por las noches, el arriscado *islote* de los artistas y asimilados, bajo la dirección de Valle-Inclán.

(FERNÁNDEZ ALMAGRO, *Vida y Literatura de Valle-Inclán*, p. 119)

Amidst the dense indeterminate mass that packed the café at all hours there stood out in the evenings the embattled island of artists and camp-followers, under the leadership of Valle-Inclán.

## -ote (C) ADJECTIVE
*(Many of these words are also used substantivally)*

| *alegrote*[3] | = really cheery or hearty. |
| *altote*[4] | = excessively or over-tall, towering great. |
| *anchote* | = very broad, really broad-in-the-beam, excessively wide. |
| *barbarote* (i)[5] }  | = (i) completely uncivilized, really oafish; |
| *brutote* (ii) | (ii) hopelessly clumsy or slow-witted. |

[1] Cf. *cascajo(s)* — similar but rather more pejorative sense: old or wretched rubble.

Cf. *escombro(s)* — same general sense as *cascote(s)*.

[2] An example of the figurative use: *este pueblo constituye un islote de influencia catalana incrustado dentro de un territorio fundamentalmente castellano* = this village represents a pocket of Catalan influence forming an enclave inside basically Castilian territory.

[3] Cf. *alegrón* = great joy. See under *-ón*.

[4] Cf. *altón* — same sense, but less common.

[5] Grouped together because of the strong similarity of meaning. Note, however, that the sense, though close, is not identical. (Note similar groupings below.)

| | | |
|---|---|---|
| *bastote* (i) | ⎫ | = (i) completely or thoroughly coarse, crude or |
| *groserote* (ii) | ⎬ | rough; (ii) coarse or rude in the extreme; |
| *ordinariote* (iii)[1] | ⎭ | (iii) hopelessly common or vulgar, as common |
| | | as they come, as common as they make 'em. |
| *blancote*[2] | | = excessively, crudely or harshly white; un- |
| | | pleasantly pallid. |
| *bondadosote*[3] | ⎫ | = good, kind or kindly in a completely natural |
| *buenote* | ⎭ | or rough and ready fashion; good or kind to |
| | | a fault. |
| †*brutote*[4] | | = terribly rough; hopelessly clumsy, heavy- |
| | | handed or slow-witted. |
| †*buenote*[5] | | = good or kind to a fault. |
| *campechanote*[6] | ⎫ | = really open, completely informal, quite free |
| *francote* | ⎭ | and easy, of the really hale-fellow-well-met |
| | | type, really bluff or hearty. |
| *cientificote*[7] | | = really learned, excessively or hopelessly aca- |
| | | demic, completely wrapped up in the pursuit |
| | | of knowledge. |
| †*coloradote*[8] | ⎫ | = really ruddy, really red-faced; really fresh- |
| *frescote* | ⎭ | looking, really blooming with health. |
| †*descaradote*[9] | ⎫ | = impudent or cheeky to an extreme, having |
| *frescote* | ⎭ | a real nerve, having the cheek of the |
| | | devil. |

---

[1] *Ordinariote* has a less common synonym *ordinarión*.

[2] Cf. *blancucho, blancuzco, paliducho* — similar sense. See under *-ucho*.

[3] Cf. *bonachón*. See under *-ón*.

[4] See *barbarote*, above.

[5] See *bondadosote*, above.

For special sense of feminine form *buenota* see under Examples from Literature.

[6] See *llanote* and *sencillote*, below.

Cf. *confianzudo* = excessively informal, over-familiar. See under *-udo*.

[7] Cf. *cientificón* — same sense. Both words are commonly used as sub-stantives, with such meanings as "essentially or utterly academic type".

[8] See *frescote* and *sanote*, below.

[9] See *frescote*, below.

Cf. *frescales* — same sense.

See *carota*, under *-ota*.

| | |
|---|---|
| *desgalichadote* | = excessively gawky or gangling. |
| †*docilote*[1] | = utterly docile or meek. |
| *enormote* | = really huge. |
| *feote*[2] | = really ugly, ugly with a vengeance. |
| *formalote* | = thoroughly well-behaved; completely reliable. |
| *francote*[3] | = really open, completely free and easy. |
| †*frescote*[4] | = really fresh, positively blooming (with health); utterly impudent. |
| *gordote*[5] | = really fat or hefty. |
| *grandote*[6] | = really big, positively hefty or hulking. |
| *groserote*[7] | = coarse or rude in the extreme. |
| *guapote* hermosote | = really handsome or lovely, of really fine, healthy appearance, flagrantly handsome or lovely. |
| †*hermosote*[8] | = really handsome or healthy-looking. |
| †*honradote*[9] | = honest as the day, honest to a fault. |
| *independientote* | = really independent or stand-offish. |
| *infelizote*[10] | = utterly hapless or luckless. |
| †*liberalote* | = thoroughly liberal, liberal to a fault, over-liberal, exaggeratedly liberal. |
| †*llanote*[11] sencillote | = completely or utterly straight-forward, unaffected or natural. |

[1] Cf. *docilón* — same sense.

[2] Cf. *feón* — same sense.

[3] See *campechanote*, above.

[4] The masculine form *frescote* almost invariably has the second or figurative sense. See *descaradote*, above. The feminine form *frescota*, on the other hand, is frequently used in the first sense, less frequently perhaps with the figurative meaning. See *coloradote*, above, and *sanote*, below.

[5] Cf. *gordorro* — same sense.

[6] Cf. *grandón* — same sense.

[7] See *bastote*, above.

[8] E.g. *¡ qué niño más hermosote !* = what a really fine, healthy-looking child!

See *guapote*, above, and *sanote*, below.

[9] Cf. *honradito*. See under –*ito*.

[10] Often used substantively: *es un infelizote* = he's a really hapless devil, he's a really poor fish or mutt.

Also *infelizón*, but much less common.

[11] Cf. *campechanote*, above.

| | |
|---|---|
| *mayorzote*[1] | = really big, properly grown-up. |
| *morenote*[2] | = really dark or swarthy. |
| *noblote*[3] | = noble, generous or selfless to a fault. |
| †*ordinariote*[4] | = thoroughly common or vulgar. |
| *pesadote*[5] | = really heavy; really wearisome, tedious to an extreme. |
| *provocativote*[6] | = extremely provocative, flagrantly provocative. |
| *sabiote*[7] | = really learned or erudite. |
| †*sanote*[8] | = in really rude or blooming health, revoltingly healthy. |
| *sencillote*[9] | = completely simple or straight-forward, totally unassuming. |
| *simpaticote*[10] | = really likeable or agreeable. |
| †*simplote*[11] | = completely or utterly artless or naïve. |
| *sosote*[12] | = utterly insipid or dull. |
| *templadote*[13] | = excessively mild, balmy. |

[1] E.g. *ya es un chico mayorzote* = he's a really big or grown-up fellow now. Cf. *mayorcito* — similar sense. E.g. *ya eres mayorcito para esos juegos* = you're a big [little] chap now for games like that.

[2] E.g. *es un tío morenote* = he's a really dark or swarthy bloke or customer.
Cf. *morenazo, morenón* — similar sense. *Morenote* is probably the most common form, followed by *morenazo,* which tends to convey an additional implication of handsomeness; *morenón* is rather less used.

[3] Cf. *noblón* — similar sense.

[4] See *bastote,* above.

[5] Cf. *pesadón* — similar sense.
Cf. *pesadito.* See under *-ito.*

[6] Cf. *descaradote,* above — often used similarly, especially in the feminine — *una mujer provocativota* = a flagrantly provocative woman; *una mujer descaradota* = an utterly shameless or brazen woman, hussy.

[7] Often used substantivally: *es un sabiote* = he's a really learned chap or customer.

[8] Cf. *frescote* and *hermosote,* above.

[9] See *llanote,* above.

[10] Cf. *simpaticón* — same sense.

[11] Cf. *simplón* — same sense.

[12] C.f. *sosón* — same sense.

[13] E.g. *una noche templadota* = a balmy night. Cf. *templaducho, calentucho.* See under *-ucho.*

| | | |
|---|---|---|
| *vagote* | = hopelessly lazy. |
| *viciosote*[1] | = utterly depraved. |

## *-ote* EXAMPLES FROM LITERATURE
## (GROUP C)

Platero ... pasa ... del patio de mármol al de las flores y de éste al corral, como una flecha, rompiendo — *¡ brutote !* — en su corta fuga, la enredadera azul.

(JIMÉNEZ, Platero y yo, p. 105)

Like an arrow Platero ... races ... from the marble courtyard to the one with the flowers and then into the outer yard, breaking down, in his brief flight, the blue creeper — clumsy great oaf!

La Tere ... meneaba el bullarengue con poderío ...; estaba *buenota*, pero no era demasiado lista.

(CELA, Judíos, Moros y Cristianos, p. 205)

Old Terese ... swayed her behind powerfully ...; she looked a real bit of all right, but she wasn't too smart.

... las manos *coloradotas* y plebeyas de los mercaderes.

(VALLE-INCLÁN, Sonata de Estío, p. 113)

... the coarsely ruddy, plebeian hands of the merchants.

CONCHA. — ¿No sabes que está el señorito rabiando como un perro?
GUITARRA. — Yo, sí, señora; la que paese que no lo sabe es usté.
CONCHA. — ¡Calla, *descaradote*!

(ALVAREZ QUINTERO, Puebla de las Mujeres, p. 45)

CONCHA. — Don't you know the master is hopping mad?
GUITARRA. — *I* do, m'am; the one who doesn't seem to know is you.
CONCHA. — Hold your tongue, you utterly impudent devil!

---

[1] Cf. *viciosón* — same sense.

Considerábanla de poco entendimiento, *docilota* y fácilmente gobernable.

(PÉREZ GALDÓS, *Fortunata y Jacinta*, II, p. 265)

They considered her to be not very intelligent, thoroughly docile and easily led.

— ... se ha casado con la hija de un rico labrador de aquí, sana, *frescota*, colorada como las amapolas.

(VALERA, *Pepita Jiménez*, p. 208)

"... he's married the daughter of a well-to-do local farmer, a healthy, really blooming girl, red-faced as a poppy."

Encarnación aprobaba estas afirmaciones con rudos gestos de su rostro *hermosote* y bravío.

(BLASCO IBÁÑEZ, *Sangre y Arena*, p. 63)

Encarnación gave approval to these statements with energetic expressions of her wild and flagrantly beautiful face.

... el *honradote* Retor [era] incapaz de desobedecer a lo que le previniese el alguacil del pueblo. ...

(BLASCO IBÁÑEZ, *Flor de Mayo*, p. 96)

"El Retor", as honest as the day, was incapable of disobeying anything the village constable might indicate to him. ...

[Cf. *honradito*:

— Es tan *honradito* el pobre Ponce, que todo lo que escribe es de conciencia, y hasta cuando elogió el *dramón*★ aquel que a mí me sacaba de quicio, lo hizo porque le salía de dentro.

(PÉREZ GALDÓS, *Fortunata y Jacinta*, IV, pp. 261, 262)

"Poor Ponce is such a little model of honesty that everything he writes is scrupulously his genuine opinion, and even when he praised that [frightful] melodrama that I couldn't stand he did so because that's how he really felt about it."]

ALFONSO. — ... me escribió Cánovas a Sandhurst diciéndome que el manifiesto que yo firmé allí había producido una magnífica impresión en España.

ISABEL. — Pues la habrá producido en España, pero a mí no. Está lleno de expresiones *liberalotas*. Salmerón no lo hubiera escrito de otra manera, y a mí no me ha gustado nada....

(LUCA DE TENA, *¿Dónde vas, Alfonso XII?*, p. 153)

ALFONSO. — ... Cánovas wrote to me at Sandhurst telling me that the manifesto I signed there had made an excellent impression in Spain.

ISABEL. — Well it may have made an excellent impression in Spain, but it hasn't done so on me. It's full of exaggeratedly liberal phrases. Salmerón wouldn't have made a better job of it, and I didn't care for it at all....

... en aquella forma y con aquellos aires campechanos y *llanotes* se desborda siempre el espíritu generoso y hospitalario de las damas de aquella agreste región montañesa.

(PEREDA, *Peñas Arriba*, p. 127)

... the hospitable and open-hearted spirit of the ladies of that wild mountain region always generously displays itself in that fashion and with that frank, completely unaffected air.

— Pueblo nací y pueblo soy; quiero decir, *ordinariota* y salvaje....

(PÉREZ GALDÓS, *Fortunata y Jacinta*, III, p. 110)

"I was born one of the people and I [still] am one of the people; I mean wild and as common as they come...."

Era un jesuita alto y *sanote* de ojos claros y color sonrosado.... Espaldas campesinas y manos poderosas y *peludas*.*

(ZUNZUNEGUI, *¡Ay, Estos Hijos!*, p. 90)

He was a tall Jesuit with light-coloured eyes and a pink complexion, brimming over with health.... [He had] a peasant's back and powerful hairy hands.

Un verdadero héroe; tímido, encogido y *simplote*, como todos los fuertes.

(BLASCO IBÁÑEZ, Sangre y Arena, p. 104)

A real hero; shy, bashful, and completely naïve, like all strong men.

### -otes ADVERB

lejotes      = a really long way (off), a hell of a long way (off).

### -ota (A) NOUN — FEMININE
*(Augmentative — pejorative. Often used also as masculine and adjectivally)*

aldeota[1]    = ugly, sprawling village, over-grown village, out-size village.

cabezota[2]   = (i) hell of a big head, damn great head (f.);
                (ii) having a damn great head (adj.);
                (iii) pig-headed individual (m. and f.);
                (iv) pig-headed (adj.).

calvorota[3]   = (i) whacking great or damn great bald head or pate (f.);
                (ii) having a damn great bald head, bald-headed or bald-pated (adj.);
                (iii) bald-headed man, baldie (m.).

carota[4]     = (i) damn great face (f.);
                (ii) person with the cheek of the devil, thick-skinned blighter or creature (m. and f.);
                (iii) having a real nerve, thick-skinned (adj.).

---

[1] See *lugarón, pueblón* and *poblachón,* under *-ón.*
Cf. *aldehuela, aldeúcha, poblacho,* etc. See *poblacho,* under *-acho.*
[2] See *cabezón,* under *-ón,* and *cabezudo,* under *-udo.*
[3] See *pelón,* under *-ón.*
[4] See *descaradote* and *frescote,* under *-ote.*
See also *frescales,* under *-ales,* and *sinvergonzón, sinvergüenzón,* under *-ón·*

| | |
|---|---|
| *cenota*[1] | = hell of a big supper, real slap-up supper. |
| *charlota(s)*[2] | = completely silly or idiotic talk, utterly idle or senseless drivel. |
| *grasota* | = thick, heavy fat or grease. |
| *narizota*[3] | = (i) damn great nose, hell of a big conk (f.);<br>(ii) person with a whacking big nose (m. and f.);<br>(iii) having a big nose, big-nosed (adj.). |
| †*niñota*[4] | = gawky great child, big over-grown child. |
| †*palabrota*[5] | = coarse or crude word or expression, oath, obscenity. |
| *pandillota* | = wretched gang, set or mob. |
| *picorota*[6] | = hell of a big peak. |
| †*tiota*[7] | = revolting or disgusting creature; old whore. |

*-ota EXAMPLES FROM LITERATURE*
(GROUP A)

... la blanquísima greña se le desbordaba por todo el perímetro de la *cabezota*.

(PEREDA, Peñas Arriba, p. 54)

... the brilliantly white mass of hair splayed out all round the edge of his huge head.

... [era] un sujeto *calvorota* y nervioso ... cartero [que había sido] expulsado del cuerpo por *marica*.*

(CELA, Judíos, Moros y Cristianos, p. 112)

... [he was] a jittery, bald-pated individual ... a postman [who had been] dismissed from the Post Office for being a homosexual.

---

[1] Cf. *cenaza* — same sense, although perhaps less common.

[2] Cf. the diminutive form *charlotita(s)* = petty talk or chat (not unpleasant perhaps, but quite pointless).

[3] Senses (ii) and (iii) are much more commonly conveyed by the form *narizotas* than by *narizota*. See under *-otas*.

Cf. *narigudo, narigón, narizón*. See under *-udo*.

[4] Cf. *niñona* — similar sense.

[5] Cf. *palabreja* and *terminucho*. See under *-eja* and *-ucho*.

[6] Cf. *picacho* — similar sense.

[7] Cf. *tiona, tiorra* — similar sense.

Le tomó por los hombros, *mandona*.★
— Estás loca, mujer, ¿qué tienes? . . .
Se abandonó *querendona*,★ sobre su hombro.
— Eres una *niñota* grande.
                              (ZUNZUNEGUI, *¡Ay, Estos Hijos!*, pp. 292, 293)

She took him domineeringly by the shoulders.
"You're crazy, woman, what's the matter with you?" . . .
She let herself sink amorously onto his shoulder.
"You're [just] a big over-grown kid."

— Por decir esas *palabrotas* no van a tener más fuerza los caballos,
¿verdad?
                              (ZUNZUNEGUI, *¡Ay, Estos Hijos!*, p. 20)

"Using those coarse expressions won't make the horses have any
more energy, will it?"

. . . resultaban ser unas *tiotas* relajadas, *comilonas*,★ borrachas y
ávidas de dinero.
                              (PÉREZ GALDÓS, *Fortunata y Jacinta*, I, p. 19)

. . . they turned out to be loathsome, dissolute creatures, with
voracious appetites, drunken and greedy for money.


*-ota* (B) NOUN — FEMININE
(Changed sense)
  capota       = hood (usually flat-topped and separate from any
                 coat); lady's bonnet; car hood.
  (< capa      = cape, cloak)


*-ota* (C) ADVERB
  arribota[1]  = right at the top, at the blinking top, a hell of a
                 long way up.

[1] Está *arribota del todo* = it's right at the very top, it's right at the blasted top.

## -otas NOUN — COMMON
*(Augmentative — pejorative and vulgar)*

| | |
|---|---|
| *berzotas*[1] | = real clod or country bumpkin, regular hick, proper yokel or oaf. |
| *gafotas*[2] | = real four-eyes. |
| *narizotas*[3] | = proper big-nose, one with a real conk. |

### 4. -UDO

## -udo ADJECTIVE
*(Augmentative and often pejorative in implication)*

√ †*barbudo*[4]   = thickly bearded, heavily bearded.

†*barrigudo*[5]
*panzudo*
*tripudo*   } = big-bellied, pot-bellied.
*ventrudo*

*bezudo*[6]   = thick- or blubber-lipped.

†*bigotudo*[7]   = bewhiskered, heavily moustached, having a bushy moustache.

*cabelludo*[8]
*melenudo*
*peludo*   } = hairy, long-haired.
*velludo*

---

[1] From *berzas*: *un berzas* = a country bumpkin (< *berza* = cabbage).
Cf. *tufarros* = utter clod (< *tufo* = smell, stink).

[2] From *gafas*: *un gafas* = a four-eyes.

[3] See *narigudo*, under *-udo. El Rey Narizotas* = Fernando VII.

[4] Cf. *barbado* = having or wearing a beard.

[5] Cf. *barrigón, tripón* — same sense.

[6] Uncommon. More natural expressions are *de labios gruesos, de labios abultados*.

[7] Cf. *abigotado* = having or wearing a moustache.

[8] *Cabelludo* is rarely used except in the phrase *cuero cabelludo* = scalp. *Melenudo* refers to the hair of the head, *peludo* and *velludo* to that of the body.

| | | |
|---|---|---|
| *cabezudo*[1] | = | large-headed; pig-headed. |
| †*cachazudo* | = | phlegmatic, stolid. |
| *cachetudo*[2] | | |
| *carrilludo* | } = | thick-faced, thick- or puff-cheeked. |
| *mofletudo* | | |
| *campanudo*[3] | = | bell-shaped; pompous. |
| †*caprichudo*[4] | = | head-strong, wilful. |
| *carrilludo*[5] | = | thick-faced, thick- or puff-cheeked. |
| *cejudo*[6] | = | thick-browed, having thick eye-brows. |
| *ceñudo* | = | frowning, scowling; louring, threatening. |
| *cogotudo*[7] | = | bull-necked. |
| *cojonudo*[8] | } = | great, smashing, hot stuff. |
| *pistonudo* | | |
| *complejudo*[9] | = | that gives one a complex, depressing. |
| †*concienzudo* | = | conscientious. |
| *conchudo*[10] | = | shell-covered; wary. |

[1] Cf. *cabezón* and *cabezota*, both of which are used with the same two meanings of (i) having a large head, and (ii) stubborn.

Cf. *testarudo, tozudo* = pig-headed, stubborn.

*Cabezudo* is much used also as a noun with the sense "large-headed dwarf figure", as in the phrase *gigantes y cabezudos,* an essential element of many Spanish festival processions.

[2] Of these three words only *mofletudo* is in common use.

[3] The word is rare in the first sense, which is much more naturally expressed by *de forma de campana* or *campaniforme*. In the second sense it is fairly common, being more or less equivalent to *altisonante, rimbombante, engolado*.

[4] Cf. *voluntarioso* — same sense.

[5] See *cachetudo,* above.

[6][7] Both words are uncommon. More natural expressions are *de cejas muy pobladas, de cogote grueso.*

[8] Both these words are highly colloquial and vulgar. They are used with the same meaning as *estupendo, imponente, soberbio,* etc.

Cf. *macanudo* and *morrocotudo,* below.

[9] Neologism. *Es complejudo = da complejo = es de complejo = es deprimente.*

Cf. *acomplejado*: — *está acomplejado* = he's suffering from an [inferiority] complex, he's depressed.

[10] Uncommon. More natural expressions are *lleno de conchas, cubierto de conchas* = shell-covered; *cauto, prudente* = wary. Cf. *tener [muchas] conchas* = to be [very] close, wary. See *escamón,* under *-ón*.

| | | |
|---|---|---|
| †*confianzudo*[1] | = | familiar, over-familiar, inclined to take liberties; trusting. |
| †*copudo* | = | having a thick top, having thick foliage (of trees). |
| *corajudo*[2] *geniudo* | = | quick-tempered. |
| †*cornudo*[3] | = | horned. |
| *dentudo*[4] | = | big-toothed, toothy. |
| *embadanudo* | = | shrivelled-up, wizened. |
| *fachudo*[5] | = | who looks a sight. |
| *forzudo* *membrudo* | = | brawny, lusty, stalwart. |
| *ganchudo* | = | hooked, hook-shaped. |
| *geniudo*[6] | = | bad or quick-tempered. |
| *greñudo* | = | having tangled or dishevelled hair. |
| *hocicudo*[7] *morrudo* | = | large-snouted, having a big snout. |
| †*huesudo*[8] | = | bony. |
| *juanetudo* | = | having (large) bunions, afflicted with bunions. |
| *lanudo* | = | woolly, shaggy. |
| †*linajudo* | = | of (most) noble lineage, of great nobility. |
| *macanudo*[9] †*morrocotudo* | = | great, huge, fantastic, formidable, terrific. |
| *machotudo*[10] | = | he-mannish. |
| *melenudo*[11] | = | long-haired. |

[1] In present-day Spanish this word almost invariably has the first sense given, the meaning "trusting" being conveyed by *confiado*.

[2] *Geniudo* is a neologism and very colloquial. See *geniazo*, under *-azo*.

[3] Frequently used as a noun with the same sense as *cabrón*. See under *-ón*.

[4] Little used. Cf. *dentón* — same sense and more common.

[5] Little used. Cf. *fachoso* — same sense and more common.

[6] See *corajudo*, above.

[7] *Hocicudo* is little used. Cf. *hocicón* — same sense and more common.

[8] Cf. *osudo, huesoso, ososo* — same sense, but little used. The word found in technical medical parlance is *óseo*.

[9] Highly colloquial and humorous words of Spanish-American origin.

[10] Extremely colloquial and not very common. See *machote*, under *-ote*.

[11] See *cabelludo*, above.

| | | |
|---|---|---|
| *membrudo*[1] | = | big-limbed, brawny. |
| *menudo*[2] | = | small, petite (f.). |
| †*mofletudo*[3] | = | thick-faced, thick- or puff-cheeked. |
| *morrudo*[4] | = | large-snouted, having a big snout. |
| †*narigudo*[5] | = | big-nosed, having a large nose. |
| *nervudo*[6] | = | sinewy, having strong sinews, tough, wiry (person). |
| *orejudo*[7] | = | big-eared, having large ears. |
| *pacienzudo*[8] | = | patient in the extreme, long-suffering. |
| *pantorrilludo*[9] | = | large-calved (leg). |
| *panzudo*[10] | = | big-bellied, pot-bellied. |
| *patilludo*[11] | = | having long side-boards (face). |
| —†*peludo*[12] | = | hairy. |

[1] See *forzudo*, above.

[2] E.g. *es un hombre menudo* = he's a man of slight build; *es una chica menudita* = she's a dainty little creature.

From L. *minutu* and not properly an augmentative at all, but given for a highly idiomatic use which is illustrated by the following examples:

*¡ Menudo !* = a fine one!

*¡ Menudo dineral le habrá costado !* = a (right) pretty penny it must have cost him!; *¡ menuda hipocritona está hecha ésa !* = a fine old hypocrite she's turned out to be!; *¡ menuda marcha le ha dado su novia !* = a merry dance his fiancée has led him!; *¡ menudo multazo le han puesto !* = a real hell of a fine they've given him!; *¡ menudo ricacho será !* = a real money-bags he must be!

Cf. colloquial English "half", e.g. he isn't half lucky! ( = *¡ menuda suerte tiene!*)

[3] See *cachetudo*, above.

[4] See *hocicudo*, above.

[5] Cf. *narigón, narizón* — same sense, but rare in modern Spanish. See *narizota(s)* under *-ota(s)*. Cf. the parallel case of *orejudo, orejón*. See below.

[6] Cf. *tener mucho nervio* = to have a lot of sinew or gristle (meat), to be pretty tough or wiry (person).

Cf. *nervioso* = nervous, nervy, jittery.

[7] Cf. *orejón* — same sense, but rarely used. See *narigudo, narigón,* above, for parallel case.

Cf. *orejones* = circular pieces of dried fruit or vegetable, especially peach, apricot and tomato.

[8] Cf. *sufrido* — same sense.

[9] Not very common; a more natural expression is *de pantorrillas grandes*.

[10] See *barrigudo*, above.

[11] Not very common; a more natural expression is *de patillas largas*.

[12] See *cabelludo*, above.

| | | |
|---|---|---|
| *pellejudo*[1] | = | having a lot of loose skin. |
| *pestañudo*[2] | = | having thick eye-lashes. |
| *picudo*[3] | = | beaked, large-beaked; pointed. |
| *pistonudo*[4] | = | great, terrific. |
| *rabudo*[5] | = | large-tailed, having a long tail. |
| *repolludo*[6] | = | cabbage-shaped; squat. |
| *sañudo* | = | cruel, sadistic. |
| *sesudo* | = | (excessively, tediously) sensible, level-headed (to a fault). |
| *talentudo* | = | brainy, clever, gifted. |
| †*talludo* | = | tall; grown-up; getting long in the tooth. |
| *tesonudo* | = | dogged, tenacious. |
| *testarudo*[7] *tozudo* | = | pig-headed, stubborn. |
| *tripudo*[8] | = | big-bellied, pot-bellied. |
| — *velludo*[9] | = | hairy. |
| *ventrudo*[10] | = | big-bellied, pot-bellied. |
| *zancudo*[11] | = | long-shanked. |
| *zapatudo* | = | wearing hefty great shoes; leathery, tough. |

## -udo *EXAMPLES FROM LITERATURE*

... unos mozos se divierten enseñando la instrucción al bobo del pueblo. Es un *hombrecillo*★ barbudo, de labios caídos y orejas en forma de asa. Su *mosquetón*★ es una vara de fresno.

(GOYTISOLO, *Campos de Níjar*, pp. 14, 15)

[1] Not very common; a more natural expression is *que tiene (tenía) much-pellejo.*

[2] Not very common; a more natural expression is *de pestañas muy pobladas.*

[3] Cf. *puntiagudo* = sharp-pointed.

[4] See *cojonudo,* above.

[5] Not very common; a more natural expression is *de rabo largo.*

[6] Not very common; more natural expressions are *de forma de repollo* ; *achaparrado.*

[7] See *cabezudo,* above.

[8] See *barrigudo,* above.

[9] See *cabelludo,* above.

[10] See *barrigudo,* above.

[11] Cf. *zancón* — same sense, but little used.

... a few lads are amusing themselves teaching the village idiot drill. He's an insignificant little man with a thick beard, drooping lips and handle-shaped ears. His rifle is a switch from an ash-tree.

Su gran *amigote*\* el secretario del Ayuntamiento era un hombre muy *bajito*\*, *barrigudo*, calvo y muy chato; ... las uñas y las yemas de los dedos siempre las tenía amarillas ... de tanto apurar las *colillas*.\*

(GUTIÉRREZ-SOLANA, *Florencio Cornejo*, p. 57)

His great buddy the Town Council secretary was a bald, very shortish, pot-bellied little man, with a very flat nose; ... his nails and fingertips were always yellow ... as a result of his smoking his cigarettes right down to their ends.

... un tío tremendo y *bigotudo* que parecía el jefe de una *cuadrilla*\* de cómicos.

(CELA, *Judíos, Moros y Cristianos*, p. 51)

... a huge, heavily-moustached fellow who looked like the leader of a troop of actors.

... oponía un *cachazudo* escepticismo a las afirmaciones del marinero ....

(FERNÁNDEZ FLÓREZ, *El Bosque Animado*, p. 26)

... he countered the sailor's statements with stolid scepticism ....

Quien es *voluntarioso*\* de joven, no dejará de ser *caprichudo* de viejo ...

(PÉREZ DE AYALA, *Tigre Juan*, p. 155)

A person who is wilful in youth will not fail to be (thoroughly) head-strong in old-age ....

La exposición seria y *concienzuda* que nos hizo ... duró cerca de una hora.

(PALACIO VALDÉS, *La Hermana San Sulpicio*, p. 15)

The solemn and conscientious explanatory lecture which he gave us ... lasted nearly an hour.

. . . trataba con miramiento a la Casiana, con respeto al cojo, y únicamente se permitía trato *confianzudo*, aunque sin salirse de los términos de la decencia, con el ciego llamado Almudena . . ..

(PÉREZ GALDÓS, *Misericordia*, p. 32)

. . . she was considerate in her dealings with "La Casiana", respectful to the lame man, and only in the case of the blind [Moor] called Almudena did she allow herself familiarity, although without overstepping the bounds of propriety . . ..

Los olmos son los que acaban en punta y las olmas son las que tienen un ramaje *copudo*, redondo, maternal.

(CELA, *Viaje a la Alcarria*, p. 180)

The "olmos" are the elms which grow to a tip, and the "olmas" are the ones that have a thick top with round, motherly foliage.

Aquella noche el *cornudo* monarca del abismo encendió mi sangre . . .

(VALLE-INCLÁN, *Sonata de Primavera*, p. 57)

That night the horned monarch of hell inflamed my blood . . .

James Fry era un hombre alto, *huesudo*, de cara larga algo *caballuna*,★ de pelo *rojizo*★. . ..

(BAROJA, *La Ciudad de la Niebla*, p. 183)

James Fry was a tall, bony man, with a long, somewhat horse-like face, [and] gingery hair . . ..

No se conocía en todo el contorno . . . casa *infanzona*★ más *linajuda* ni más vieja, y a cuyo nombre añadiesen los labriegos con acento más respetuoso el calificativo de pazo-palacio, reservado a las moradas hidalgas.

(PARDO BAZÁN, *Los Pazos de Ulloa*, p. 217)

In all the surrounding district . . . no stately house was known that was older or of greater nobility, no house to the name of which the peasants added in more respectful tones the designation "pazo-palacio," which is reserved for aristocratic residences.

. . . el pobre chico no caía en la cuenta de que se iba pareciendo a los poetas *melenudos* . . ..

(PÉREZ GALDÓS, *Fortunata y Jacinta*, IV, p. 40)

... the poor chap didn't realize that he was beginning to look increasingly like a long-haired poet....

... *coloradote,*\* *mofletudo,* con las cejas unidas y muy *peludas* sobre unos *ojazos*\* de buey.

(PEREDA, Peñas Arriba, p. 178)

... ruddy-complexioned, puff-cheeked, with really shaggy, close-together brows over two great ox-like eyes.

... abalanzándose sobre el joven Ohando, le dio una bofetada *morrocotuda.*

(BAROJA, Zalacaín el Aventurero, p. 15)

... hurling himself upon [the] young Ohando he gave him a whopping swipe.

... se ve un hombre gordo, moreno y chato, al lado de una mujer gorda, morena y chata, pues es un hombre petulante y seguro de sí mismo; pero si el hombre gordo, moreno y chato tiene una mujer flaca, rubia y *nariguda,* es que no tiene confianza en su tipo ni en la forma de su nariz.

(BAROJA, El Arbol de la Ciencia, p. 559)

... you see a fat, dark man with a flat nose beside a fat, dark woman with a flat nose, well that's an arrogant, self-confident man; but if the fat, dark man with a flat nose has a thin, fair wife with a large nose, that means that he hasn't any confidence in his figure or in the shape of his nose.

Su señoría bautizó a los niños ... y confirmó a los no confirmados, que se contaban a centenares, entre ellos no pocos harto *talludos.*

(VALERA, Juanita la Larga, p. 84)

His Grace baptized the children ... and confirmed those [members of the community] who had not already been; of the latter there were some hundreds, and amongst them not a few who were pretty grown-up.

*-al* NOUN — *MASCULINE*
*(Augmentative)*

†*dineral*[1]    = hell of a lot of money, mint of money, (small) fortune, packet.

## *-al* EXAMPLE FROM LITERATURE

— ... El pescado y la verdura están por las nubes; no se puede comer nada sin gastar un *dineral* ....

(ZUNZUNEGUI, *¡Ay, Estos Hijos!*, p. 246)

"... [The prices of] fish and vegetables are sky-high; you can't get anything to eat without spending a mint of money ...."

---

[1] See *dinerete, dinerillo, dinerito,* under *-ete, -illo, -ito.*
Cf. *capitalazo, fortunón, millonada* — similar sense.

# Chapter III. Pejoratives

## -aco NOUN — MASCULINE
### (Pejorative)

| | |
|---|---|
| †*bicharraco*[1] | = loathsome or odious creature or insect. |
| †*chismarraco* | = wretched bit of stuff or junk, wretched thingumajig. |
| *hombraco*[2] | = (great) gawky fellow. |
| †*libraco*[3] | = wretched old book, (cumbersome) old tome. |
| †*pajarraco* | = loathsome, ugly or ungainly bird; strange, queer or rummy bird; dodgy or shady customer, nasty-looking piece of work. |
| *tiparraco*[4] | = loathsome type, revolting individual. |

## -aco EXAMPLES FROM LITERATURE

. . . los *animalejos*★ se derraman como una tromba por el arruinado palacio de Leoncio, ·devoran cuanto encuentran, y gracias a que el muerto se ha llevado ya al impío en cuerpo y alma, que si no, los tales *bicharracos*, de puro agradecidos, no dejan casta de él.

(MAEZTU, *Don Quijote, Don Juan y La Celestina*, p. 84)

. . . the wretched creatures swarm like a flood over Leoncio's ruined palace, devouring everything they find, and it's a good job the dead man has by this time carried off the godless villain body

---

[1] -*aco* is used particularly in combination with -*arro*. Cf. *pajarraco* (contraction of *pajararraco*) and *tiparraco*, below.
  Cf. *bichejo*, *bichucho* — similar sense, though milder. See under -*ejo*, -*ucho*.
[2] Not widely used. See *hombracho*, under -*acho*.
[3] Cf. *librote* — similar sense. See under -*ote*.
[4] Cf. *tipejo* — similar sense, though milder. See under -*ejo*.

and soul, for, otherwise, the aforementioned loathsome vermin, out of sheer gratitude, wouldn't leave a trace of him.

— ... Yo pensé que vivías en un apartamento.... Pero ¡qué burrada! ¡Qué de *chismarracos*!... ¡Jolín! ¡Pero si hay hasta un loro!

(MIHURA, *Maribel y la Extraña Familia*, p. 94)

"... I thought you lived in an apartment.... But what a hell of a lot of stuff! What a load of odds and ends of old junk ...! Crikey! There's even a parrot, how do you like that!"

... había puestos de libros en donde se congregaban los bibliófilos a revolver y a hojear los viejos volúmenes llenos de polvo. Hurtado solía pasar todo el tiempo que duraba la feria registrando los *libracos*....

(BAROJA, *El Arbol de la Ciencia*, p. 461)

... there were bookstands where the bibliophiles gathered to rummage and browse among the old, dust-covered tomes. Hurtado used to spend the whole time, as long as the fair lasted, examining the wretched (old) books.

Casi rozando nuestras cabezas volaban torpes bandadas de feos y negros *pajarracos*.

(VALLE-INCLÁN, *Sonata de Estío*, p. 116)

Ungainly flocks of ugly, black, weird [great] birds were flying over our heads almost grazing us.

[Another example, in which the word refers to an old man:

A aquel *pajarraco* de mal agüero todo el mundo le odiaba.

(BAROJA, *Las Inquietudes de Shanti Andía*, p. 192)

That queer [old] bird of ill-omen was hated by everyone.]

*-acho* (*A*) *NOUN* — *MASCULINE*
(*Pejorative and, sometimes, augmentative*)

| | |
|---|---|
| *amigacho*[1] | = wretched pal, crony. |
| †*corpacho*[2] | = ugly or revolting carcass. |
| †*dicharacho*[3] | = crude or vulgar expression. |
| *hilacho*[4] | = loose, straggly or odd thread. |
| *hombracho*[5] | = ugly, gawky (great) fellow. |
| *picacho* | = ugly (great) peak. |
| *poblacho*[6] | = ugly village, wretched or tin-pot village, dump of a village. |
| †*populacho*[7] ⎫ *vulgacho* ⎭ | = common herd, rabble, mob, scum. |
| *riacho*[8] | = ugly or wretched river or stream. |

---

[1] See *amigote*, under *-ote*.

[2] Cf. *corpachón* = ugly great carcass.

[3] Cf. *terminacho* (uncommon) and *terminucho*, *palabreja* and *palabrota* — similar sense. See under *-ucho*, *-eja* and *-ota*.

[4] Two feminine forms exist — *hilacha* and *hilaza*, but they are rare.

[5] Cf. *hombrazo* (rare), *hombrón*, *hombretón*, *hombrote* — similar sense. See under *-ón*, *-ote*.

[6] A form *poblazo* exists, but is rare.

Cf. *pueblucho* — same sense, but rather less common than *poblacho*.

Cf. *pueblecillo*. See under *-illo*.

Cf. *poblachón*. See under *-ón*.

Cf. *aldehuela* and *aldeúcha* — same sense.

Cf. *aldeorrio* — same sense, but less common. Similarly *villorrio*.

Cf. *aldeota*. See under *-ota*.

Cf. *lugarejo* — same sense.

Cf. *lugarón*. See under *-ón*.

[7] A form *populazo* exists, but is rare. *Vulgacho* is less common than *populacho*. See *gentuza*, under *-uza*.

[8] Not very widely used. Much more common is the diminutive form *riachuelo* = wretched or miserable little stream.

*ricacho*[1]  = excessively or ostentatiously wealthy man, money-
bags, one who is filthy rich.

*vulgacho*[2]  = scum.


*-acho EXAMPLES FROM LITERATURE*
(GROUP A)

— ... Si no están allí las condenadas modistas, me paseo por
encima de su *corpacho* como por esa sala ....
$\qquad$ (PÉREZ GALDÓS, *Fortunata y Jacinta*, IV, p. 312)

"... If the blasted dressmakers hadn't been there, I'd have trodden
all over her ugly carcass as if it had been (the floor of) that drawing-
room ...."

... [éstos] dan la última palabra sobre lo que se dabate, soltando
un juicio doctoral y reduciendo a su verdadero valor las bromas
y los *dicharachos*.
$\qquad$ (PÉREZ GALDÓS, *Fortunata y Jacinta*, III, p. 12)

... [the latter] have the last word about what is being argued
over, uttering an authoritative opinion and deflating the jokes and
crude expressions to their real value.

Su admiración era la misma del *populacho*, que sólo reconoce la
sabiduría de un hombre mal pergeñado y con rarezas de carácter ....
$\qquad$ (BLASCO IBÁÑEZ, *Sangre y Arena*, p. 17)

His admiration was the same as that of the common herd, who
only recognize learning in a man who is badly turned-out and has
an eccentric character ....


*-acho (B) NOUN — MASCULINE*
(*Changed sense*)
*bombacho(s)*[3]  = ballooned trousers, plus-fours.
(< bomba  = pump; bomb)

[1] Rather more common is the augmentative *ricachón* = real money-bags.
[2] See *populacho*, above.
[3] The connexion with *bomba* is that of shape.

| | | |
|---|---|---|
| *gazpacho*[1] | = | Andalusian cold soup. |
| (< caspa | = | dandruff) |

## -acho (C) ADJECTIVE

| | | |
|---|---|---|
| *vivaracho*[2] | = | really lively or spritely, darting. |

## -acha NOUN — FEMININE
### (Pejorative)

| | | |
|---|---|---|
| *covacha*[3] | = | unpleasant or wretched cave; beastly hovel. |

### 3. -AJO, -AJA

## -ajo (A) NOUN — MASCULINE
### (Pejorative)

| | | |
|---|---|---|
| *bebistrajo*[4] | = | rotten drink, wretched concoction. |
| †*cintajo* | = | blasted, miserable or tawdry ribbon. |
| *colgajo(s)* | = | wretched hanging stuff, miserable or tawdry hanging ornaments. |
| *comistrajo*[5] | = | rotten food, wretched mess. |
| *escupitajo*<br>*escupitinajo*<br>*gargajo*<br>*salivajo* | = | (revolting) spit or spittle. |

[1] The semantic link between *gazpacho* and *caspa* appears to lie in the idea of small particles, one of the main ingredients of *gazpacho* being breadcrumbs.

[2] E.g. *ojuelos vivarachos* = very lively or darting, (beady) little eyes.

The word *pizpireta* (fem. only.) = lively and jaunty, is not dissimilar to *vivaracha*.

[3] Cf. *covachón* = really wretched cave or hovel.

Cf. *covachuela*. See under -*uela*.

Cf. *cuevona* = big cave; ramshackle place.

[4] Cf. *comistrajo*, below.

[5] See *comideja*, under -*eja*.

Cf. *bebistrajo*, above.

| †*espumarajo(s)*[1]= | (ugly) spume, (dirty) froth. |
| *gargajo*[2] | = (revolting) spittle. |
| †*hierbajo(s)* | = miserable, straggly grass or weed(s). |
| †*latinajo(s)* | = (bit of) Latin jargon, (bit of) gibberish in Latin, dog Latin. |
| *papelajo(s)*[3] | = blasted or wretched paper(s), dirty or untidy (old) paper(s). |
| *pingajo*<br>*trapajo* | }= wretched (old) rag or tatter. |
| *pintarrajo*[4] | = rotten painting, daub. |
| *salivajo*[5] | = (disgusting) saliva, spit or spittle. |
| *trapajo*[6] | = wretched (old) rag or tatter. |

## -*ajo* EXAMPLES FROM LITERATURE
## (GROUP A)

Era viuda ... a la vera de los sesenta años, gorda, con unos peinados estrambóticos que ... se los cambiaba todos los días, arbolando la cabeza de *cintajos* y bigudís.

(Zunzunegui, *¡ Ay, Estos Hijos !*, p. 242)

She was a widow ... bordering on sixty, fat, with an eccentric taste in hair-styles, which ... she changed every day, covering her head with a forest of tawdry ribbons and curlers.

[1] *Espumarajo* is used in preference to the simple *espuma* whenever there is any sort of pejorative implication, e.g. in the phrase *echar (arrojar) espumarajos por la boca* = to foam at the mouth.

[2] *See escupitajo*, above.

[3] Cf. *papelorio(s), papelote(s), papelucho(s)* — same sense.

Cf. *papeleo, papelería* — also used similarly, but in addition often with the meaning "(wretched) forms", "(infernal) red-tape". Also *papelamen*.

[4] Cf. the verb *pintarrajear* = to daub or bedaub. (Cf. also *escribajear* = to scrawl or scribble.)

[5] There also exists a form *salivazo*. See *escupitajo*, above.

[6] See *pingajo*, above.

Los hombres ... se fijaron ... en la avanzada escollera de Levante, rojos *pedruscos*★ sobre los cuales comenzaban a romperse las primeras moles de agua, cubriéndose de hirvientes *espumarajos*.

(BLASCO IBÁÑEZ, *Flor de Mayo*, p. 42)

The men ... fixed their gaze ... on the jutting Eastern breakwater, rough, red-coloured chunks of rock, which, as the first masses of water began to crash over them, were becoming covered in ugly, seething spume.

[Another example in a different context:

... repuestos del susto, volvieron hechos basiliscos, arrojando *espumarajos* por la boca.

— ¡Ese *vejestorio*★ está insultando al pueblo! — ¡Es un carcunda rabioso! — ¿Por qué no matáis a ese bribón?

(PALACIO VALDÉS, *Marta y María*, p. 157)

... having recovered from their fright, they came back in a state of fury, foaming at the mouth.

"That old fossil is insulting the people!" "He's a raving Carlist!" "Why don't you kill the blighter?"]

El viajero ... se encuentra con una fuente ... cubierta por una losa hendida por los años ... y en las grietas de la losa nacen unos *hierbajos* desgarbados.

(CELA, *Viaje a la Alcarria*, p. 213)

The wayfarer ... comes upon a spring of water ... covered over with a slab of stone cracked with age ... and in the crevices of the stone a few ungainly, straggly weeds are growing.

Constantemente repetía un *latinajo* que, si no recuerdo mal, era "similia similibus curantur", lo que yo, en verdad, no sé qué quiere decir.

(BAROJA, *Las Inquietudes de Shanti Andía*, p. 192)

He continually repeated a piece of Latin jargon, which, if I remember aright, was "similia similibus curantur", and what this means, to be quite honest, I don't know.

## -ajo (B) NOUN — MASCULINE
### (Changed or specialized sense)

| | | |
|---|---|---|
| cascajo(s)[1] | = | rubble, old or wretched rubble. |
| (< casco(s) | = | piece(s) of broken china or glass) |
| escobajo[2] | = | wretched old broom; bare stalk (of a bunch of grapes). |
| (< escoba | = | broom) |
| espantajo[3] | = | scarecrow (lit. and fig.), outlandish or grotesque object, sight (person). |
| (< espanto | = | fright, terror) |
| estropajo | = | kitchen scourer. |
| (< estopa | = | tow, coarse hemp) |
| horcajo | = | fork (made by two streams or hills); mule yoke. |
| (< horca | = | pitch-fork) |
| lagunajo | = | rain puddle or pool. |
| (< laguna | = | small lake, lagoon) |
| sombrajo | = | shack, shanty (constructed to give shade). |
| (< sombra | = | shade) |

## -ajo (C) ADJECTIVE

| | | |
|---|---|---|
| pequeñajo[4] | = | miserably small. |

## -aja (A) NOUN — FEMININE
### (Pejorative — diminutive)

| | | |
|---|---|---|
| migaja(s)[5] | = | miserable little crumb(s) or small piece(s) of bread |

[1] Cf. *cascote(s)* — similar sense. See under -*ote*.

[2] Cf. *raspajo* — same (second) sense, but little used.

[3] Little used in the literal sense, which is usually expressed by *espantapájaros*.

[4] Sometimes used with a tone of affection: pitifully (but not unattractively) small.

Cf. *pequeñujo*.

[5] Cf. *migajón* (also *miga*) = pap (of bread).

*-aja (B) NOUN — FEMININE*
*(Changed or specialized sense)*

| | | |
|---|---|---|
| rodaja | = | slice (esp. of fish). |
| (<rueda | = | wheel) |
| sonaja | = | rattle (esp. child's). |
| (<son | = | sound, note) |
| tinaja | = | large earthenware vessel. |
| (< tina | = | jar) |

### 4. -ALES

*-ales (A) NOUN — MASCULINE*
*(Pejorative, but often with strong implication of affection. Noun forms are also frequently used adjectivally)*

| | | |
|---|---|---|
| frescales[1] | = | cheeky devil, cheeky hound, fellow with a regular nerve. |
| †rubiales | = | blondie, blond-top. |
| viejales[2] | = | old boy, old chap, old-timer or son of a gun. |
| vivales | = | sharp customer, smart operator, slick or spivvy type. |

*-ales EXAMPLE FROM LITERATURE*
(GROUP A)

El Marqués de Torre-Mellada ... era un *vejete*★ *rubiales*, pintado y perfumado, con malicias y melindres de monja boba.

(VALLE-INCLÁN, *La Corte de los Milagros*, p. 24)

The Marquis of Torre-Mellada ... was a fair-topped old boy, wearing make-up and perfume, and as tricky and mincing as a dim nun.

*-ales (B) ADJECTIVE*

| | | |
|---|---|---|
| mochales | = | cracked, potty, having a screw loose. |

[1] Cf. *frescote.* See under *-ote.*
[2] Cf. *vejete.* See under *-ete.*

## -alla NOUN—FEMININE
*(Pejorative or augmentative.)*

| | |
|---|---|
| antigualla[1] | = ancient object, thing of the past, piece of out-moded junk or rubbish; old-fashioned person, old fogey, has-been. |
| canalla[2] | = rabble, scum; cur, cad, heel, rotter (m.). |
| clerigalla[3] | = mob of wretched priests, pack of blasted clergy-men. |
| gentualla[4] | = rabble, scum. |
| morralla[5] | = small fry, rag-tag and bob-tail. |
| muralla | = high or fortress wall. |

## -alla EXAMPLES FROM LITERATURE

— ¡Oh! los hombres del día, ¿para qué habían de entretenerse en estudiar *antiguallas*?

(PÉREZ GALDÓS, *Doña Perfecta*, p. 70)

"Oh! Why should up-to-date men waste their time studying out-moded old stuff?"

[An example of the personal use:

— ... [este papel] no viene del pueblo, sino de nuestros enemigos: de todas las *antiguallas* que nos odian porque ocupamos puestos que ellos ya no merecen.

(BUERO VALLEJO, *Un Soñador para un Pueblo*, p. 217)

"... [this paper] does not come from the people, but from our enemies; from all the old fogeys who hate us because we hold positions which they no longer deserve."]

[1] Cf. *vejestorio*. See under *-orio*. In *antigualla* the predominant idea is that of being out-moded; in *vejestorio* it is that of age.

[2] Masculine in second sense: *un canalla* = a rotter.
See *gentuza*, under *-uza*.

[3] Neither this word nor its synonym *cleriguicia* (Galdós uses *cleriguicio*) is in common use today. See *curángano*, under *-ángano*.

[4] Now little used. See *gentuza*, under *-uza*.

[5] See *gentuza*, under *-uza*.

## 6. -ÁNGANO, -ÁNGANA

*-ángano NOUN — MASCULINE*
*(Pejorative)*

| †*curángano*[1] | = miserable or blasted priest. |
| *perrángano*[2] | = wretched or blasted dog, hound or mongrel. |

*-ángano EXAMPLE FROM LITERATURE*

— ¡Pues me gusta la santidad de estas *traviatonas*★ de iglesia! ...
Se encierran aquí por retozar a sus anchas con los *curánganos* de
babero . . ..

(PÉREZ GALDÓS, *Fortunata y Jacinta*, II, p. 235)

"Well, a fine sort of sanctity you get in these religious "stray
sheep" ...! They shut themselves up here so as to be able to romp
about freely with the blasted bib-and-tucker young priests . . .."

*-ángana NOUN — FEMININE*
*(Pejorative)*

| *telángana* | = wretched dibs or dough, blasted shekels. |

## 7. -ANGO, -ANGA

*-ango NOUN — MASCULINE*
*(Pejorative)*

| †*querindango*[3] | = contemptible paramour, miserable lover, blasted lover. |

---

[1] Cf. *clerigucho, clerizonte* — same sense, but little used.
See *curazo*, under *-azo*.
[2] Cf. *chucho* = pooch.
[3] Cf. *querindolo* (Galician) — same sense.
Cf. *querendón* (adj.) = amorous.

— Eso de que un hombre se consuma en el trabajo para dar pan a la mujer y a los hijos y cuando vuelve a su casa se la encuentre abrazada al *querindango*, francamente, es para hacer una barbaridad....

(BLASCO IBÁÑEZ, *Flor de Mayo*, p. 177)

"For a man to wear himself out at work in order to feed his wife and children and then when he gets home to find her hugging a blasted lover, honestly, it's enough to make a fellow do something really wild...."

*-anga* NOUN — FEMININE
(Pejorative)

| | |
|---|---|
| †*fritanga* | = coarse fried food, slap-up fry. |
| †*pendanga*[1] | = miserable tart, wretched whore. |

*-anga* EXAMPLES FROM LITERATURE

... como ambos amantes habían convenido en enaltecer y restaurar prácticamente la hispana cocina, hacía [Fortunata] unos *guisotes*★ y *fritangas* cuyo olor llegaba más allá de San Francisco el Grande.

(PÉREZ GALDÓS, *Fortunata y Jacinta*, III, p. 128)

... since the two lovers had agreed to exalt Hispanic cooking and to restore it in a practical way, [Fortunata] used to prepare some really full-blooded stews and slap-up frys, the smell of which reached beyond the Church of San Francisco el Grande.

— Dicen que es una santa. ¡Sí, una santa que anda suelta! ... ¡Mira qué *ojillos*★ hipócritas pone la *pendanga*!

(PALACIO VALDÉS, *Marta y María*, p. 156)

"They say she's a saint. A saint on the loose, more like it...! Just look at the hypocritical (beady) little eyes she puts on, the miserable whore!"

[1] Cf. *pendeja, pindonga, pendón* (m.), *pingo* (m.), *pingajo* (m.) — similar sense.

## -astre (A) NOUN — MASCULINE
(Pejorative)

| †pillastre[1] | = miserable or petty rogue or scoundrel. |
| †pollastre | = miserable or petty young blood. |

## -astre EXAMPLES FROM LITERATURE
(GROUP A)

— ... en fin, que el pueblo español está ineducado y hay que impedir que cuatro *pillastres* engañen a los inocentes . . ..
(PÉREZ GALDÓS, Fortunata y Jacinta, IV, p. 254)

". . . in short, the Spanish people are [politically] uneducated, and we must see to it that a few petty rogues don't take in those who are easily duped. . . ."

En el [grupo] masculino figuraban el médico . . ., el ingeniero Suárez y . . . cuatro o cinco *pollastres*, que por lo simples e insignificantes no merecen especial mención.
(PALACIO VALDÉS, Marta y María, p. 127)

In the male [group] figured the doctor . . ., Suárez the engineer and . . . four or five petty young bloods, who, because of their fatuousness and insignificance do not deserve any special mention.

## -astre (B) ADJECTIVE
(Pejorative)

| †fulastre[2] | = really hapless or useless. |

---

[1] See *pillín,* under *-ín.*

[2] Sometimes used substantivally — really hapless or useless creature or object.

Cf. *fulastrona* = whore.

*-astre* EXAMPLE FROM LITERATURE
(GROUP B)

... Aquel cuitado, aquella calamidad de chico, aquella inutilidad,
tan *fulastre* y para poco....

(PÉREZ GALDÓS, *Fortunata y Jacinta*, II, p. 100)

... That wretch, that calamity of a youth, that useless object,
such a really hapless, diffident creature....

## 9. -ASTRO, -ASTRA

*-astro* (A) NOUN — MASCULINE
(*Pejorative*)

| | |
|---|---|
| †*camastro* | = wretched bed, rotten old bed. |
| *criticastro*[1] | = blasted, rotten or third-rate critic. |
| †*medicastro*[2] | = blasted, rotten or third-rate doctor. |
| *poetastro*[3] | = blasted, rotten or third-rate poet. |
| †*politicastro*[4] | = blasted, rotten or third-rate politician. |

*-astro* EXAMPLES FROM LITERATURE
(GROUP A)

Un día, al visitar una *buhardilla*★ de barrios bajos, al pasar por el
corredor de una casa de vecindad, una mujer vieja ... se le acercó
y le dijo que si quería pasar a ver a un enfermo. Andrés ... entró
en el tabuco. Un hombre demacrado, famélico, sentado en un
*camastro*, cantaba y recitaba versos.

(BAROJA, *El Arbol de la Ciencia*, p. 557)

[1] Not widely used.
Cf. *criticón*. See under *-ón*.
[2] Not widely used.
See *medicucho*, under *-ucho*.
[3] Not widely used.
[4] Not widely used.
See *politicucho*, under *-ucho*.
Cf. *politicón*. See under *-ón*.

One day, when he was visiting a garret in a slum area, as he was going along the passage-way of a tenement building, an old woman ... came up to him and asked him if he would go in and see a sick man. Andrew ... went into the poky little room. An emaciated, starving man, sitting on a wretched old bed, was singing and reciting poetry.

... el médico, probablemente aburrido de espiritualidad y de romanticismo, se volvió a casar, con una labradora, lo cual para Luisa Fernanda y Laura, fue y sigue siendo un verdadero crimen, la prueba palmaria de la grosería y de la torpeza de sentimientos de ese *medicastro* cerril.

(Baroja, Camino de Perfección, p. 180)

... the doctor, probably weary of spirituality and romanticism, re-married, choosing a farm-girl, and for Luisa Fernanda and Laura this was and still is a veritable crime, palpable proof of the coarseness and base feelings of that uncouth, third-rate medical practitioner.

— Seamos prácticos, señores, seamos prácticos, y no confundamos las *pandillas*\* de *politicastros* con el verdadero país.

(Pérez Galdós, Fortunata y Jacinta, IV, p. 253)

"Let us be practical, gentlemen, let us be practical, and let us not mistake the cliques of third-rate politicians for the real Spain."

-astro, -astra (B) NOUN — SPECIAL GROUP
*(Pejorative implication)*

| | |
|---|---|
| *hermanastro* | = step-brother. |
| *hermanastra* | = step-sister. |
| *hijastro* | = step-son. |
| *hijastra* | = step-daughter. |
| *padrastro*[1] | = step-father; bad father. |
| *madrastra*[1] | = step-mother; bad mother. |

[1] Colloquially, *padrastro* and *madrastra* are often used in the sense of *mal padre* and *mala madre*, and this is even more the case with the augmentative forms *padrastrón* and *madrastrona*.
Cf. *padrazo, madraza*. See under *-azo, -aza*.

*-engue ADJECTIVE*
*(Pejorative)*

†*blandengue*[1]   = contemptibly soft, feeble.

*-engue EXAMPLE FROM LITERATURE*

... Currito, que no valía para nada y era un *blandengue*, ... no defendió a su amigo.

(VALERA, *Pepita Jiménez*, p. 130)

... Currito, who was good for nothing and a feeble object, ... did not defend his friend.

## 11. -INGO

*-ingo NOUN — MASCULINE*
*(Pejorative)*

†*fotingo*[2]     = crate, (little) old crock, wretched old jalopy.
†*señoritingo*[3]   = fine young gentleman (iron.), his lordship (iron.), little Lord Fauntleroy.

*-ingo EXAMPLES FROM LITERATURE*

El vagabundo, que había oído hablar del auto-stop, quiere probar fortuna y hace señas a un coche .... El dueño del coche, un señor más serio de lo preciso para el cochino *fotingo* que lleva, ... ni mira para el vagabundo.

(CELA, *Judíos, Moros y Cristianos*, p. 151)

---

[1] Almost always used in a figurative sense and often substantivally.

[2] Probably derived from "Ford". It is a word which is not widely used today, belonging rather to the recent past. Much more common is the expression *cacharro*.

[3] Cf. *caballerete* — similar sense, although not quite so pejorative. See under *-ete*.

The tramp, having heard of hitch-hiking, wishes to try his luck and signals to a car . . .. The owner of the car, a gentleman with a more solemn expression than necessary considering the punk (little) old crock he's driving, . . . doesn't even look in the tramp's direction.

[Cf. the sense of *cochecillo* in this passage from the same work :

. . . son pueblos . . . *fresquitos** y llenos de veraneantes de manga corta y familia numerosa, *cochecillo* renqueante, los afortunados, y buena voluntad y dos pagas extraordinarias los más. (*Ibid.*, p. 20)

. . . they are villages . . . which are pleasantly cool, and full of summer residents, men in short sleeves with large families and — the lucky ones — modest, halting little cars, and most of them with (just) good intentions and a couple of bonuses.]

— No hagas más que unas sopas de ajo. El *señoritingo* no vendrá a almorzar, y si viene, le acusaré las cuarenta.
(PÉREZ GALDÓS, *Fortunata y Jacinta*, II, p. 121)

"Just make a bit of garlic soup. His lordship won't be in to lunch, and if he is, I'll give him a piece of my mind."

[Another example, interesting for its context:

— (Me dirán después) quién acude con el alivio y maneja mejor el arte de la medicina, si este curandero o esos *señoritingos* licenciados.
(PÉREZ DE AYALA, *Tigre Juan*, p. 62)

"(You'll tell me afterwards) who comes (more quickly) with relief and handles better the art of medicine, whether this [old] quack or those fine young gentlemen with their University degrees."]


12. -INGUE

*-ingue NOUN — MASCULINE*
*(Pejorative)*

potingue = brew, concoction, foul mixture.

## *-orio* NOUN — *MASCULINE*
### *(Pejorative and/or jocular)*

| | |
|---|---|
| casorio[1] | = poor or second-rate marriage or wedding. |
| envoltorio | = bundle, untidy bundle, poorly made or badly tied package. |
| jolgorio[2] | = jollification, merry-making, living-it-up. |
| lavatorio[3] | = washing, superficial or disorderly washing. |
| †papelorio(s)[4] | = old paper(s), rubbishy paper(s), disorderly or wretched paper(s). |
| requilorio(s)[5] | = unnecessary formalities; beating about the bush. |
| †vejestorio[6] | = piece of old junk; old wreck, old crock; old codger or geezer, old fogey or fossil, doddering old fool, ancient character. |

## *-orio* EXAMPLES FROM LITERATURE

... [por todas partes] había más papeles, más legajos, amarillentos, vetustos, carcomidos, arrugados y rotos; .... La verdad es que él no entendía gran cosa de *papelotes*★ .... A cada paso se le confundía más en la cabeza toda aquella *papelería*★ ... malditos *papelorios* indescifrables ....

(PARDO BAZÁN, *Los Pazos de Ulloa*, pp. 55, 57, 61, 62)

... [on all sides] there were more papers, more bundles of documents, yellowish, aged, worm-eaten, crumpled and torn; .... The fact is he didn't know a great deal about old papers ....

[1] See *bodorrio*, under *-orrio*.

[2] Sometimes written *holgorio*, but always pronounced *jolgorio*.
Cf. *juerga* and *jarana* — similar sense.

[3] In colloquial speech always pejorative or jocular in tone, but, when used in a literary or especially in a religious context, quite the contrary, e.g. *lavatorio de pies* = bathing of feet (Gospels).

[4] Cf. *papelajo(s), papeleo, papelería, papelote(s), papelucho(s)* — similar sense. See also under *-ajo*.

[5] Much more common are: *trámites y gestiones* = formalities; *rodeos y ambages* = beating about the bush.

[6] Cf. *antigualla* — similar sense. See under *-alla*.
Cf. *carcamal* — similar sense (person only).

At every step all that mass of papers became increasingly confused in his mind ... cursed, indecipherable, wretched old papers....

En la penumbra de aquel lugar casi subterráneo, en el hacinamiento de *vejestorios* retirados por inservibles y entregados a las ratas, la pata de una mesa parecía un brazo momificado....

(PARDO BAZÁN, *Los Pazos de Ulloa*, p. 292)

In the half-light of that almost underground place, amid the stacks of old junk which had been discarded as useless and given up to the rats, a table-leg looked like a mummified arm....

[Two further examples illustrating different uses of the word:

— ¿Dónde han comprado ustedes este *vejestorio*? — dijo don Alvaro — ¡Demonio, qué penco!

(BAROJA, *La Dama Errante*, p. 244)

"Where did you buy this old wreck?" asked Don Alvaro. "Good Lord, what a nag!"

— ... vivió en la miseria hasta que se casó con aquel pelele, con aquel *vejestorio*, con aquel maldito usurero....

(VALERA, *Pepita Jiménez*, p. 128)

"... she lived in poverty until she married that dummy, that old fossil, that damned money-lender...."]

### 14. -ORRIO

*-orrio* NOUN — *MASCULINE*
*(Pejorative — diminutive)*

| | |
|---|---|
| *aldeorrio*[1] <br> *villorrio* | = wretched little village, tin-pot little place. |
| *bodorrio*[2] | = second-rate or tin-pot wedding, apology for a wedding. |
| †*cantorrio* | = second-rate or tin-pot song, apology for a song. |

[1] The form *aldeorro* also exists. More common than any of these, however, are *aldehuela* and *aldeúcha*. See under *-ucha*, and see also *poblacho*, under *-acho*.

[2] Little used, as is also *bodijo*. See *casorio*, under *-orio*.

... era taller de zapatería, y los *golpazos*★ que los zapateros daban a la suela, unidos a sus *cantorrios*, hacían una algazara de mil demonios.

(PÉREZ GALDÓS, *Fortunata y Jacinta*, I, p. 257)

... it was a shoe-mending workshop, and the hefty thumps the cobblers were giving the shoe-soles, together with their apologies for singing, made an unholy din.

## 15. -ORRO, -ORRA

*-orro (A) NOUN — MASCULINE*
*(Pejorative)*

| | |
|---|---|
| *abejorro* | = bumble-bee; person who drones on interminably, droner. |
| *beatorro*[1] | = insufferably sanctimonious person, revoltingly goody-goody type. |
| *ceporro*[2] | = useless old vine-stock; hefty, squat person; fat or chubby child; fat, slow-witted child. |
| *chistorro* | = coarse joke. |
| *quintorro*[3] | = wretched or thick recruit, slow-witted national serviceman. |
| *tintorro* | = poorish, heavy or crude red wine. |
| *vascorro*[4] | = coarse, oafish Basque. |
| †*ventorro*[5] | = miserable inn. |
| *viejorro* | = unpleasant or unattractive old man. |

---

[1] Cf. *beatón* — same sense.

[2] When used to refer to a person this word is often given an affectionate tone which diminishes or even cancels its pejorative effect; this is especially so in the case of children: *un ceporro = un niño hermosote* = a fine chubby child.

[3] Cf. *militarote*. See under *-ote*.

[4] Cf. *vascote*. See under *-ote*.

Cf. use with Christian names, e.g. *el Peporro ese* = that oafish fellow Joe. (Cf. feminine form *Peporra*.)

[5] Cf. *ventorrillo* = wretched, poky little inn.

*-orro* EXAMPLE FROM LITERATURE
(GROUP A)

... siguieron adelante, hasta detenerse en un *ventorro* .... Era la venta una *casuca*★ baja, de tejado terrero, colocada en lugar solitario y triste.

(BAROJA, *La Dama Errante*, pp. 166, 167)

... they went on until they came to a mean inn, where they stopped .... The inn was a wretched, low building, with an earth roof, situated in a lonely, depressing spot.

*-orro (B)* ADJECTIVE
*(Pejorative)*

| | |
|---|---|
| *anchorro*[1] | = over-wide, excessively broad. |
| *bastorro* | = really or awfully coarse or rough. |
| *blandorro*[2] | = over-soft, soggy, pappy. |
| †*caldorro*[3] | |
| *calentorro* | } = over-hot, unpleasantly warm, tepid. |
| *gordorro*[4] | = over-fat, obese. |

*-orro* EXAMPLE FROM LITERATURE
(GROUP B)

Uno de ellos continuaba tumbado a la sombra de la *furgoneta*★. El otro venía hacia el restaurante con las dos chicas, que se habían puesto unas *chaquetillas*★ cortas sobre los bañadores ....

[1] Cf. *anchote* — similar sense. See under *-ote*.
Also *anchón,* but less common.
[2] Cf. *blanducho* — similar sense. See under *-ucho*.
Also *blandón,* but less common.
[3] *caldorro* is a not very common adjective formed on *caldo* (< L. *calidu*); *calentorro* (< *caliente*) is far more frequently found.
Cf. *calentucho* — similar sense. See under *-ucho* (special note).
Also *calentón.* See under *-ón*.
[4] Cf. *gordote* — similar sense. See under *-ote*.
Also *gordón,* but less common.
Also *gordoncho.*

Pidieron café y una botella de coca-cola.

— Mejor luego — dijo una de ellas — Hasta que se la llevemos se va a poner *caldorra*.

(GARCÍA HORTELANO, *Tormenta de Verano*, p. 115)

One of them was still lying in the shade of the estate-car. The other was coming towards the restaurant with the two girls, who had put on short jackets over their bathing-costumes . . ..

They ordered coffee and a bottle of Coca-cola.

"Better leave that till later", said one of the girls. "It's going to get hideously warm before we take it to him."


*-orra NOUN — FEMININE*
*(Pejorative — augmentative)*

| | |
|---|---|
| *faltorra* | = atrocious or really bad mistake, real whopper, regular howler. |
| *manchorra*[1] | = dirty great stain, revolting stain. |
| *natorra* | = horrible thick cream; thick scum, sickly scum. |
| *pintorra* | = real tart, revolting whore. |
| †*tiorra*[2] | = horrible or disgusting creature, bitch. |
| †*vidorra*[3] | = great life, good-time existence; life of ease and plenty. |


*-orra EXAMPLES FROM LITERATURE*

— . . . Suéltame, *tiorra* pastelera, o de una mordida te arranco media cara.

(PÉREZ GALDÓS, *Fortunata y Jacinta*, III, p. 255)

". . . Let me go, you meddling bitch, or I'll bite away half your face."

---

[1] Cf. *manchurrón* — similar sense.

[2] Cf. *tiona* and *tiota* — similar sense.

[3] *Darse (pegarse) una (la) vidorra* = to have a jolly good time, to live it up.

Despite its apparently favourable tone in some contexts, this word nearly always implies excess or over-indulgence.

[Cf. *tiona* in the same work:

— Dile a esa *tiona* que si quiere correr los pañuelos que los corra ella, y que si no, que los deje.

(Ibid., p. 197)

"Tell the besom that if she wants to hawk the handkerchiefs, she can hawk them herself, and if she doesn't, she can leave them."]

PILAR. — (A Silverio) ¿Es el gordo?
SILVERIO. — Sí . . ..
MANOLA. — (A Silverio) ¿Cuánto me toca con seis pesetas?
SILVERIO. — Cuarenta y cinco mil.
TOMASA. — ¡Y a mí setenta y cinco mil del ala! ¡Diez *pesetazas*★ con doña Balbina! . . . *Menuda*★ *vidorra* nos vamos a dar todos ahora.

(BUERO VALLEJO, Hoy es Fiesta, pp. 184, 185, 187)

PILAR. — (To Silverio) Is it the big prize?
SILVERIO. — Yes, it is . . ..
MANOLA. — (To Silverio) How much do I get on six pesetas?
SILVERIO. — Forty-five thousand.
TOMASA. — And I get a cool seventy-five thousand! Ten whole juicy pesetas with Doña Balbina! . . . A regular whale of a time we're all going to have now.

16. -UCO, -UCA

*-uco* (A) NOUN — MASCULINE
(*Pejorative and diminutive*)

| | |
|---|---|
| *frailuco* | = wretched little friar. |
| *ventanuco* | = poky little window. |

*-uco* (B) NOUN — MASCULINE
(*Specialized sense*)

| | |
|---|---|
| *almendruco* | = green almond, almond not yet ripe. |
| (< almendra | = almond) |
| *hayuco* | = beech-mast. |
| (< haya | = beech-tree) |

*-uca NOUN — FEMININE*
*(Pejorative and diminutive)*

| †*casuca* | = mean little house. |
| *iglesuca* | = mean or wretched little church. |
| †*mujeruca* | = wretched little woman. |

*-uca* EXAMPLES FROM LITERATURE

La plaza del mercado en Pilares está formada por un ruedo de *casucas* corcovadas, caducas, seniles.

(PÉREZ DE AYALA, Tigre Juan, p. 13)

The market square in Pilares is made up of a ring of hump-backed, decrepit, senile, mean little houses.

Una *mujeruca* dormitaba en una de las sillas.... Tenía un pelo sucio, gris y pobre, que producía una patética sensación de derrota.

(POMBO ANGULO, Hospital General, p. 260)

A wretched little woman was dozing in one of the chairs.... Her hair was dirty, grey and scanty and gave a moving impression of defeat.

17. -UCHO, -UCHA

*-ucho (A) NOUN — MASCULINE*
*(Pejorative and, in some cases, diminutive)*

| *animalucho*[1] ⎫ | = wreck of an animal, wretched creature, beastly |
| *bichucho* ⎬ | insect. |
| †*artistucho*[2] | = wretched artist, two-penny ha'penny artist fellow. |
| *avionzucho*[3] | = wretched 'plane, old crock of a 'plane. |

---

[1] See *animalejo*, under *-ejo*.

[2] Cf. *artistejo* — similar sense.

Cf. *artistilla* (m.). For the not dissimilar but considerably milder pejorative force attached to *-illo, -illa* see appropriate sections.

[3] Cf. *avioncejo* — similar sense.

Cf. *avioncillo*. See note to *artistucho*.

Cf. *avioneta*. See under *-eta*.

| | | |
|---|---|---|
| *bichucho*[1] | = | beastly creature, wretched insect. |
| *calducho* | = | poor, weak or watery broth. |
| *caminucho*[2] | = | wretched lane, path or track. |
| *cientificucho*[3] | = | tenth-rate scholar; wretched scientist. |
| *cinucho* | = | poky little cinema, dump of a cinema, flea-pit. |
| †*cuartucho*[4] | = | wretched or poky little room. |
| *dependientucho*[5] | = | twopenny ha'penny shop assistant. |
| *fonducho* | = | wretched inn, dump of an inn. |
| *lapizucho*[6] | = | miserable pencil, rotten old pencil. |
| *medicucho*[7] | = | tenth-rate doctor. |
| †*papelucho(s)*[8] | = | wretched bit of old paper, trash; gutter press, rag. |
| *pelucho(s)*[9] | = | wretched hair, rotten or ugly hair. |
| †*periodicucho*[10] | = | tenth-rate newspaper, rag. |
| †*perrucho* | = | wretched dog, mongrel hound, pooch. |
| *politicucho*[11] | = | tenth-rate politician. |
| *pueblucho*[12] | = | tin-pot little village, dump of a village. |
| *teatrucho*[13] | = | tin-pot little theatre, miserable little theatre. |

[1] See *animalucho*, above.
[2] Cf. *caminejo* — similar sense.
  Cf. *caminillo*. See note to *artistucho*.
[3] Cf. *cientifiquillo*. See note to *artistucho*.
  Cf. *cientificón, cientificote*. See under *-ote*.
[4] Cf. *cuartejo* — similar sense.
[5] Cf. *horterilla* (m.) (Madrid) — similar sense.
[6] Cf. *lapicejo* — similar sense.
  Cf. *lapicillo*. See note to *artistucho*.
[7] Cf. *medicastro* (uncommon) — same sense.
  Cf. *mediquillo*. See note to *artistucho*.
[8] See *papelajo(s)*, under *-ajo*.
[9] Cf. *pelillo(s)*. See note to *artistucho*.
[10] Cf. *periodiquillo*. See note to *artistucho*.
[11] Cf. *politicastro* (uncommon) — same sense.
  Cf. *politiquillo*. See note to *artistucho*.
[12] See *poblacho*, under *-acho*.
[13] Cf. *teatrillo*. See note to *artistucho*.

| | | |
|---|---|---|
| *terminucho*[1] | = | wretched, crude or vulgar expression. |
| *vestiducho*[2] | = | miserable dress, rotten old dress. |

## -ucho EXAMPLES FROM LITERATURE
## (GROUP A)

— Usted dijo que ... se quemó los labios, y que el *artistucho* ese se los quemó también ... .. Con los besos de pasión, ¿no?

(PASO, *Los Pobrecitos*, p. 220)

"You said that ... you burnt your lips and that that two-penny ha'penny artist fellow burnt his too ... .. With your passionate kisses, eh?"

La casa era grande, con esos pasillos y recovecos un poco misteriosos de las construcciones antiguas.

Para llegar al nuevo cuarto de Andrés había que subir unas escaleras, lo que le dejaba completamente independiente.

El *cuartucho* tenía un aspecto de celda ... ..

(BAROJA, *El Arbol de la Ciencia*, p. 455)

The house was large, with those somewhat mysterious corridors and twists and turns that you get in old buildings.

To reach Andrew's new room it was necessary to go up some stairs, and this gave him complete privacy.

The poky little room looked like a cell ... ..

... había *periodicuchos* en donde unos políticos se insultaban y se calumniaba a otros ... ..

(BAROJA, *La Dama Errante*, p. 95)

... there were rags in which some politicians insulted one another and others were slandered ... ..

---

[1] Cf. *terminacho* (uncommon) — same sense.
  Cf. *palabreja*, *palabrota*. See under *-eja*, *-ota*.
[2] Cf. *vestidejo* — similar sense.
  Cf. *vestidillo*. See note to *artistucho*.

[Cf. this quotation in which *papeluchos* is used, exceptionally, with the same sense:

— No quiero que esos *papeluchos* carlistas digan que nos hemos ensañado con una mujer.

(PALACIO VALDÉS, *Marta y María*, p. 161)

"I don't want those Carlist rags to say that we have behaved savagely to a woman."]

... saltaba ladrando de alegría junto a sus faldas el feo *perrucho* que pasaba la noche fuera de la barraca ....

(BLASCO IBÁÑEZ, *La Barraca*, p. 61)

... the ugly (mongrel) hound that spent the night outside the hut used to jump round her skirts barking joyfully ....


*-ucho (B) NOUN — MASCULINE*
*(Specialized diminutive sense)*

| | |
|---|---|
| †*aguilucho* | = eaglet, young eagle (lit. and fig.). |
| (< águila | = eagle) |
| *serrucho* | = hand-saw, small saw. |
| (< sierra | = saw) |


*-ucho EXAMPLE FROM LITERATURE*
(GROUP B)

— Cuando voy a la Bolsa todos los *aguiluchos* de por allí me miran como a una *palomita*★, mas cuando van a darme un *picotazo*★ en el cuello se dan cuenta de que llevo un collar de "fierro".

(Words of JUSTO DE GOÑI quoted by PÉREZ
FERRERO in *Vida de Pío Baroja*, p. 219)

"When I go to the Stock Exchange all the young eagles thereabouts look at me as if I were a delicate young dove, but when they are about to give me a (savage) peck on the neck they realize that I'm wearing an 'iron' collar."

| | | |
|---|---|---|
| *blancucho*[1] | = | whitish, unpleasantly white, pallid. |
| *blanducho*[2] | = | softish, unpleasantly soft, over-soft, pappy, soggy. |
| *calentucho*[3] <br> *templaducho* | } = | tepid. |
| *debilucho*[4] <br> *delicaducho* <br> *endeblucho* <br> *flojucho* | } = | weakish, a bit weak, rather weak or delicate. |
| †*delgaducho*[5] <br> *flacucho* | } = | scraggy, scrawny, really skinny. |
| *delicaducho*[6] | = | rather delicate or weak in health. |
| *endeblucho*[7] | = | weakish. |

[1] Cf. *blancuzco* — same sense.
Cf. *blancote* — similar sense. See under *-ote*.
See *paliducho*, below.

[2] Cf. *blanduzco* (less common), *blandujo* (rare) — same sense.
Cf. *blandorro* — similar sense. See under *-orro*.
Cf. *suavón* — similar sense. See under *-ón*.

[3] Cf. *calentorro, calentón*. See under *-orro, -ón*.
*Calentucho* and *templaducho* are exact equivalents of the English "tepid" in its usual pejorative sense. The two words are not, however, identical in their use, which is illustrated by the following examples. A Spaniard who wants a glass of ice-cold water on a hot summer day, but gets it tepid, may well exclaim: *¡qué calentucha está esta agua !* (i.e. tepid, warmish, when it is required cold); bath water, if not hot enough, is liable to be condemned as *templaducha* (i.e. tepid, coolish, when required hot).
Cf. *calentito* and *templadito. El agua está calentita* = the water's nice and hot; *el agua está templadita* = the water's (just) nice and warm or (just) pleasantly warm. See under *-ito*.

[4] Cf. *debilillo, delicadillo, endeblillo, flojillo* — similar sense.
These words are often close in shade of meaning to *enfermucho* and *malucho*. See below.
Substantival use is common, e.g. *es un debilucho* = he's a weakling; *son unos flojuchos* = they're a lot of softies.

[5] See *embadanudo*, under *-udo*.

[6] See *debilucho*, above.

[7] See *debilucho*, above.

| | | |
|---|---|---|
| enfermucho[1] ⎫ | = | a bit ill, off-colour or off-song, rather groggy |
| malucho ⎭ | | or under the weather. |
| estropeaducho[2] | = | a bit spoilt or the worse for wear, rather messed-up, in rather a bad way. |
| †feúcho[3] | = | uglyish, on the ugly side, plain. |
| finucho[4] | = | thinnish, excessively thin, flimsy, trashy. |
| †flacucho[5] | = | scraggy. |
| flojucho[6] | = | weakish. |
| †larguirucho[7] | = | lanky, gawky. |
| malucho[8] | = | a bit off-song. |
| pachucho[9] | = | over-ripe, very soft, mushy (fruit); off-colour (people). |
| †paliducho[10] | = | pallid, pale and wan, unpleasantly pale. |
| templaducho[11] | = | tepid. |

## -ucho EXAMPLES FROM LITERATURE
## (GROUP C)

... yo era una niña cetrina y *delgaducha*, de esas a quienes las visitas nunca alaban por lindas . . ..

(LAFORET, Nada, p. 222)

[1] Cf. *enfermito, malito* = poorly. See under -*ito*.

Cf. *malillo*. See under -*illo*.

*Pachucho* is also used sometimes to refer to a person, with the sense "off-colour". See below.

[2] Cf. *estropeadillo, estropeadejo, estropeadete* — similar sense.

[3] Cf. *feíllo* — similar sense. Also *feuchillo*.

Cf. *feúco* (uncommon) — similar sense.

Cf. *feón, feote*. See under -*ón*, -*ote*.

[4] Cf. *finillo* — similar sense.

Cf. *finito* = nice and thin, pleasantly thin or slender.

[5] See *delgaducho*, above.

[6] See *debilucho*, above.

[7] Cf. *altote, desgalichadote*. See under -*ote*.

[8] See *enfermucho*, above.

[9] See *enfermucho*, above.

[10] See *blancucho*, above.

[11] See *calentucho*, above.

... I was one of those sallow, scraggy little girls that visitors [to the house] never praise for their prettiness.

— ¿Qué puedo yo ocultar a esta mona golosa? ... *¡ Curiosona,\* fisgona,\* feúcha !* ¿Tú quieres saber? Pues te lo voy a contar....
(PÉREZ GALDÓS, *Fortunata y Jacinta*, I, p. 108)

"What can I hide from this avid creature? ... Nosy, prying, ugly monkey! You want to know? Well, I'm going to tell you ...."

Mi madre quería que ... me casara. Me tenía destinada la hija de un propietario de Lúzaro, más vieja que yo, *feúcha, flacucha* y mística.
(BAROJA, *Las Inquietudes de Shanti Andía*, p. 131)

My mother wanted ... me to get married. She had in mind for me the daughter of a Lúzaro property owner, a female older than I, [decidedly] on the ugly side, scrawny and mystical.

— ¡Vaya unos santos más mal hechos y unas santas más *larguiruchas* y sin forma humana!
(PARDO BAZÁN, *Los Pazos de Ulloa*, p. 141)

"What clumsily fashioned saints! And as for the female figures, what spindly and gangling, shapeless and unnatural-looking creatures!"

El profesor de Literatura era un padre *paliducho*, sonriente y amable....
(ZUNZUNEGUI, *¡ Ay, Estos Hijos !*, p. 76)

The Literature master was a pallid, smiling, genial priest....

---

*-ucha NOUN — FEMININE*
*(Pejorative and, in some cases, diminutive)*

| | |
|---|---|
| *aldeúcha*[1] | = wretched little village, miserable little place. |
| *callejucha*[2] | = wretched or narrow little lane or alley. |

[1] See *poblacho,* under *-acho.*
[2] See *calleja,* under *-eja.*

| | |
|---|---|
| †*casucha*[1] | = miserable little house, poky little place; hovel. |
| *clasezucha* | = rotten class or lesson; miserable bit of tutoring work. |
| †*coplucha*[2] | = rotten song or verse, wretched ditty. |
| *cosucha*[3] | = wretched thing or object, rotten old thing, bit of old rubbish, trash. |
| *florezucha*[4] | = wretched or miserable flower, rotten old flower, apology for a flower. |
| *frasezucha*[5] | = wretched phrase or sentence. |
| *novelucha*[6] | = tenth-rate novel, rotten novel. |
| †*paparrucha*[7] | = drivel, tripe, humbug. |
| †*tabernucha*[8] | = poky little pub, dump of a pub. |
| *tascucha* | = wretched or poky little eating-house or pub, dump. |
| *telucha*[9] | = tenth-rate cloth, rotten cloth. |
| *tenducha*[10] | = wretched little shop, mean little establishment. |
| †*ventanucha* | = poky little window. |

## -ucha EXAMPLES FROM LITERATURE

... Y empiezan a aparecer barriadas inmensas, monótonas, de *casuchas* bajas, feas, iguales, todas grises y negras ....

(BAROJA, *La Ciudad de la Niebla*, p. 73)

[1] Cf. *casuca* — similar sense.
 Cf. *choza* = hovel.
[2] Cf. *copleja* — similar sense.
 Cf. *coplilla*. See note to *artistucho*.
[3] Cf. *coseja* — similar sense.
 Cf. *cosilla*. See note to *artistucho*.
[4] Cf. *florecilla*. See note to *artistucho*.
[5] Cf. *frasecilla*. See note to *artistucho*.
[6] Cf. *novelón*. See under *-ón*.
 Cf. *novelilla*. See note to *artistucho*.
[7] From *papa(s)* = pap, soft food. Note double suffix *(papa + arra + ucha )*.
[8] Cf. *tabernucho* — same sense and equally common.
[9] Cf. *telilla*. See note to *artistucho*.
[10] Cf. *tenducho* — same sense and equally common.

... And there begin to come into view vast, monotonous suburbs of ugly, low, wretched little houses, all the same, all grey and black ....

— ¿Qué es eso? ¿Canta aquel demonio? ... Aquélla se cree que está todavía en la posada de su pueblo .... En casa de un sacerdote no se deben cantar *copluchas*.

(ALVAREZ QUINTERO, *Puebla de las Mujeres*, pp. 12, 13)

"What's that? Is that infernal creature singing? ... She imagines she's still at the inn in her village .... Common ditties should not be sung in a priest's house."

Todos esos otros sistemas metafísicos y éticos, como el anarquismo, le parecían vueltas a concepciones pedantescas y a *paparruchas* semejantes al Krausismo.

(BAROJA, *La Dama Errante*, p. 79)

He considered all those other metaphysical and ethical systems, like anarchism, to be a throwback to pedantic conceptions and drivel of the Krausist type.

Había por todo el barrio *tabernuchas* como cuevas, negras, obscuras, cuyos cristales, empañados por el polvo y el humo, no permitían ver el interior.

(BAROJA, *La Ciudad de la Niebla*, p. 165)

All over the district there were dark, gloomy, poky little pubs, like caves, the windows of which, obscured with dust and smoke, did not enable one to see inside.

Las chicas no eran malas, pero eran *jovenzuelas*,* y ni Cristo Padre podía evitar los atisbos ... por la *ventanucha* que daba al *callejón** de San Cristóbal. Empezaban a entrar en la casa *cartitas*,* y a desarrollarse esas *intrigüelas** inocentes que son juegos de amor.

(PÉREZ GALDÓS, *Fortunata y Jacinta*, I, p. 62, 63)

They weren't bad girls, but they were young creatures, and there wasn't a power on earth that could prevent their spying ... out of the poky little window looking onto St. Christopher's Lane.

Little notes started to come into the house, and those innocent, petty little intrigues, which are part of the love-game, began to spring up.

## 18. -UJO, -UJA

*-ujo (A) NOUN — MASCULINE*
*(Pejorative and diminutive)*

| | | |
|---|---|---|
| *granujo*[1] | = | nasty or wretched little spot or pimple. |
| *ramujo(s)*[2] | = | wretched little branch(es), dead branch(es), dead wood, brushwood. |
| †*tapujo(s)* | = | under-cover or under-hand behaviour, dealings or goings-on, jiggery-pokery. |

*-ujo (A) EXAMPLE FROM LITERATURE*

— ¡Todo eso da asco! ¡Y verte a ti terciando en tales *tapujos* me avergüenza y me duele en el alma!
— ¡Carolinita*, te·obcecas y me apesadumbras con apreciaciones injustas! *¡ Tapujos !* ¡Francamente, empleas un vocabulario! ... *¡ Tapujos !*
— Jerónimo, las obligaciones de tu sangre te vedan esas tercerías.
(VALLE-INCLÁN, *La Corte de los Milagros*, p. 177)

"The whole thing is disgusting! And to see you taking part in jiggery-pokery of this sort makes me ashamed and grieves my heart."
"Caroline, my darling, you refuse to see reason and you distress me with unfair judgments! Jiggery-pokery! Really, you do use some expressions! ... Jiggery-pokery indeed!"
"Jeremy, the duties of one of your birth prohibit you from such connivance."

[1] Cf. the more common *granillo*.
[2] Also found in feminine. See below.

## -ujo (B) ADJECTIVE
*(Pejorative and/or diminutive)*

blandujo[1]   = unpleasantly soft, soggy, pappy.

chiquitujo[2]  
pequeñujo   } = miserably or wretchedly small or tichy.

estrechujo[3]   = miserably or wretchedly narrow, cramped or confined.

mamujo[4]   = suckling, just able to suck.

## -uja NOUN — FEMININE
*(Pejorative and/or diminutive)*

granuja[5]   = loose or odd grape; (fruit) pip.

ramuja(s)   = wretched little branch(es), dead branch(es), dead wood, brushwood.

### .9. -UTE

## -ute NOUN — MASCULINE
*(Pejorative)*

†franchute[6]   = Frenchy, Froggy.

### -ute EXAMPLE FROM LITERATURE

TRANSEÚNTE. — Y hasta dicen que corre sus *aventurillas*★ . . ..
ALFONSO. — ¡Je! ¿Ah, sí?
T. — Pero, ahora, sentará la cabeza. Dicen que se casa.

---

[1] Also in combination with -ón: *blandujón.*
Cf. the more common *blanducho.*
[2] Cf. *chiquitajo, pequeñajo* — similar sense.
[3] Cf. *estrechuelo* — similar sense.
[4] Also in combination with -ón: *mamujón.*
[5] Widely used as a masculine noun meaning "rascal, rogue, scoundrel".
[6] Cf. *gabacho* — same sense.

A. — ¡No me diga!

T. — ¡Sí, hombre, sí! Con la Princesa Mercedes de Orléans; una hija de aquel mal bicho de Montpensier.

A. — Pues no había oído nada. ¿Y a usted, qué le parece esa boda?

T. — Pues, mire usted, la verdad; a mí muy bien, aunque la novia sea hija de ese *franchute* ambicioso. Dicen que la muchacha es preciosa.

> (LUCA DE TENA, *¿Dónde vas, Alfonso XII?*, p. 171)

PASSER-BY. — And they even say that he has his little escapades . . ..

ALFONSO. — Really! Do they?

P. — But now he'll settle down. It's said he's going to get married.

A. — You don't say so!

P. — I do indeed, my dear fellow! To Princess Mercedes of Orleans; one of the daughters of that dirty blighter Montpensier.

A. — Well, this is the first I've heard of it. And what do you think of the match?

P. — Well, look here, to be quite honest, I think it's fine, even though his fiancée is a daughter of that self-seeking Frenchy. They say she's a lovely girl.

## 20. -UZA

*-uza* NOUN — *FEMININE*
*(Pejorative)*

†*gentuza*[1]     = rabble, scum, gentry (fig.).

[1] Cf. *gentualla* (uncommon), *canalla, chusma* — similar sense.
  Cf. *gentezuela* = petty scum.
  Cf. *gentecilla* = petty riff-raff.
  The order *gentuza, gentezuela, gentecilla* represents a descending scale of pejorative severity. *Gentecita* (iron.) is also used pejoratively.
    Cf. the following allied expressions:
  *populacho, vulgacho* = common herd, great unwashed, dregs, rabble.
  *morralla* = small fry, rag-tag and bob-tail.

Otras veces era la *gentuza* de la ría la que se aprovechaba de su estado para robarlos y luego hacía desaparecer al robado tirándolo al agua . . ..

(Zunzunegui, *¡ Ay, Estos Hijos !*, p. 113)

On other occasions it was the estuary scum who took advantage of their condition to rob them and then get rid of the victims' bodies by pitching them into the river . . ..

# Alphabetical List of Authors, Works and Editions

(For Illustrative Examples)

ALARCÓN, PEDRO ANTONIO DE. *El Escándalo*. Victoriano Suárez, 43rd ed., Madrid, 1960.
*El Sombrero de Tres Picos*. Victoriano Suárez, 34th ed., Madrid, 1958.
ALDECOA, IGNACIO. *La Despedida* in *Caballo de Pica*. Taurus, Madrid, 1961.
ALVAREZ QUINTERO, SERAFÍN Y JOAQUÍN. *El Genio Alegre*. Espasa-Calpe, Austral, 7th ed., Madrid, 1956.
*Puebla de las Mujeres*. Idem.
AZORÍN (MARTÍNEZ RUIZ, JOSÉ). *Lecturas Españolas*. Nelson, Edinburgh, 1959.

BAROJA, PÍO. *Camino de Perfección*. Las Américas Publishing Co., New York, 1952.
*El Arbol de la Ciencia* in *Obras Completas II*. Biblioteca Nueva, Madrid, 1947.
*La Ciudad de la Niebla*. Nelson, Edinburgh, 1951.
*La Dama Errante*. Nelson, Edinburgh, 1961.
*Las Inquietudes de Shanti Andía*. Biblioteca Nueva, Madrid, 1946.
*Paradox, Rey*. Espasa-Calpe, Austral, 3rd ed., Madrid, 1960.
*Zalacaín el Aventurero*. Losada, 4th ed., Buenos Aires, 1961.
BENAVENTE, JACINTO. *Cartas de Mujeres (Dos Comedias)*. Aguilar, Crisol, 5th ed., Madrid, 1955.
*La Malquerida*. Espasa-Calpe, Austral, 8th ed., Madrid, 1957.
*La Noche del Sábado*. Idem.

BLASCO IBÁÑEZ, VICENTE. *Entre Naranjos.* Planeta, Barcelona, 1955.
*Flor de Mayo.* Planeta, Barcelona, 1958.
*La Barraca.* Espasa-Calpe, Austral, 5th ed., Buenos Aires, 1952.
*Sangre y Arena.* Planeta, Barcelona, 1958.
BRAVO-VILLASANTE, CARMEN. *Vida y Obra de Emilia Pardo Bazán.*
Revista de Occidente, Madrid, 1962.
BUERO VALLEJO, ANTONIO, *En la Ardiente Oscuridad* in *Teatro.* Losada,
Buenos Aires, 1959.
*Hoy es Fiesta* in *Teatro.* Losada, Buenos Aires, 1959.
*Un Soñador para un Pueblo* in *Teatro Español 1958—59.* Aguilar,
Madrid, 1960.

CALVO-SOTELO, JOAQUÍN. *La Muralla.* Sociedad General de Autores,
12th ed., Madrid, 1955.
*Una Muchachita de Valladolid* in *Teatro Español 1956—57.* Aguilar,
Madrid, 1958.
CELA, CAMILO JOSÉ. *Judíos, Moros y Cristianos.* Destino, Barcelona,
1956.
*Recuerdo de don Pío Baroja.* Andrea, Mexico City, 1958.
*Viaje a la Alcarria.* Destino, Barcelona, 1954.

DELIBES, MIGUEL. *El Camino.* Harrap, London, 1963.

EGUIAGARAY, FRANCISCO. *Historia Contemporánea de España.* AULA,
Madrid, 1964.

FERNÁNDEZ ALMAGRO, MELCHOR. *Vida y Literatura de Valle-Inclán.*
Editora Nacional, Madrid, 1943.
FERNÁNDEZ FLÓREZ, WENCESLAO. *El Bosque Animado.* Planeta,
Barcelona, 1957.
FRANCÉS, JOSÉ. *Revelación* in *Cuentos de Autores Contemporáneos.*
Harrap, London, 1948.

GARCÍA HORTELANO, JUAN. *Tormenta de Verano.* Seix Barral, Barce-
lona, 1962.
GARCÍA LORCA, FEDERICO. *Impresiones (Granada)* in *Obras Completas.*
Aguilar, 3rd ed., Madrid, 1957.

GIMÉNEZ-ARNÁU, JOSÉ ANTONIO. *El Canto del Gallo*. Destino, Barcelona, 1954.

GIRONELLA, JOSÉ MARÍA. *Un Millón de Muertos*. Planeta, Barcelona, 1961.

GONZÁLEZ-CASTELL, RAFAEL. *Brindis* in *Mil Mejores Poesías de la Lengua Castellana*. Ediciones Ibéricas, 19th ed., Madrid, 1958.

GOYTISOLO, JUAN. *Campos de Níjar*. Seix Barral, 2nd ed., Barcelona, 1961.

*Fin de Fiesta*. Seix Barral, Barcelona, 1962.

*La Isla*. Seix Barral, Barcelona, 1961.

GUTIÉRREZ-SOLANA, JOSÉ. *Florencio Cornejo*. Francisco Beltrán, Madrid, 1926.

JIMÉNEZ, JUAN RAMÓN. *Platero y yo*. Losada, 12th ed., Buenos Aires, 1952.

LAFORET, CARMEN. *Nada*. Destino, 9th ed., Barcelona, 1952.

LAÍN ENTRALGO, PEDRO. *La Generación del Noventa y Ocho*. Espasa-Calpe, Austral, 4th ed., Madrid, 1959.

LUCA DE TENA, JUAN IGNACIO. *¿Dónde vas, Alfonso XII?* in *Teatro Español 1956—57*. Aguilar, Madrid, 1958.

MAEZTU, RAMIRO DE. *Don Quijote, Don Juan y La Celestina*. Espasa-Calpe, Austral, 5th ed., Buenos Aires, 1945.

MARAÑÓN, GREGORIO. *Vida e Historia*. Espasa-Calpe, Austral, 6th ed., Madrid, 1953.

MENÉNDEZ PIDAL, RAMÓN. *El Cid Campeador*. Espasa-Calpe, Austral, 3rd ed., Madrid, 1955.

MIHURA, MIGUEL. *Maribel y la Extraña Familia* in *Teatro Español 1959—60*. Aguilar, Madrid, 1961.

MIRÓ, GABRIEL. *Libro de Sigüenza*. Losada, Buenos Aires, 1953.

NEVILLE, EDGAR. *La Familia Mínguez*. Lauro, Barcelona.

ORTEGA Y GASSET, JOSÉ. *Introducción a un Don Juan* in *Teoría de Andalucía y Otros Ensayos*. Revista de Occidente, 3rd ed., Madrid, 1952.

Palacio Valdés, Armando. *José*. Fax, 2nd ed., Madrid, 1959.
*La Hermana San Sulpicio*. Nelson, Edinburgh, 1949.
*Marta y María*. Fax, 2nd ed., Madrid, 1957.
Pardo Bazán, Emilia. *La Sirena Negra* in *Obras Completas II*. Aguilar, Madrid, 1947.
*Los Pazos de Ulloa*. Aguilar, Crisol, 3rd ed., Madrid, 1959.
*Mujer* in *Obras Completas II*. Aguilar, Madrid, 1947.
Paso, Alfonso. *Los Pobrecitos* in *Teatro Español 1956—57*. Aguilar, Madrid, 1958.
Pereda, José María. *Peñas Arriba* in *Obras Completas XVII*. Aguilar, 4th ed., Madrid, 1957.
Pérez de Ayala, Ramón. *El Anticristo* in *Bajo el Signo de Artemisa*. Emecé, Buenos Aires, 1943.
*Belarmino y Apolonio*. Losada, 3rd ed., Buenos Aires, 1956.
*Tigre Juan y el Curandero de su Honra*. AHR, Barcelona, 1957.
Pérez Ferrero, Miguel. *Vida de Pío Baroja*. Destino, Barcelona, 1960.
Pérez Galdós, Benito. *Doña Perfecta*. Hernando, Madrid, 1961.
*Fortunata y Jacinta*. Hernando, Madrid, Vol. I, 1958; Vol. II, 1959; Vols. III and IV, 1952.
*La de Bringas*. Hernando, Madrid, 1952.
*Misericordia*. Nelson, Edinburgh, 1951.
*Torquemada en la Hoguera*. Aguilar, Crisol, 2nd ed., Madrid, 1962.
Pérez Lugín, Alejandro. *La Casa de la Troya*. Galí, 67th ed., Santiago de Compostela, 1957.
Pombo Angulo, Manuel. *Hospital General*. Destino, 4th ed., Barcelona, 1951.

Rivas, Josefina. *Tengo una Hermana Solterona* in *Cuentistas Españolas Contemporáneas*. Aguilar, Crisol, Madrid, 1946.

Sainz de Robles, Federico Carlos. *Cuerpo y Alma de Madrid* in *Costumbristas Españoles II*. Aguilar, Madrid, 1951.
*El Madrid de 1761 a 1861* in *El Madrid de Cuatro Siglos*. Publicaciones Españolas, Madrid, 1961.
Sampedro, José Luis. *Congreso en Estocolmo*. Aguilar, 3rd ed., Madrid, 1962.

Sánchez Ferlosio, Rafael. *El Jarama.* Destino, 5th ed., Barcelona, 1961.

Sánchez-Silva, José María. *Marcelino, Pan y Vino.* Cigüeña, 9th ed., Madrid, 1955.

Serrano Suñer, Ramón. *Entre Hendaya y Gibraltar.* Publicaciones Españolas, 8th ed., Madrid, 1947.

Sordo, Enrique. In *Baroja y su Mundo, I.* Arion, Madrid, 1961.

Torrente Ballester, Gonzalo. In *Baroja y su Mundo, I.* Arion, Madrid, 1961.

Unamuno, Miguel de. *Andanzas y Visiones Españolas.* Espasa-Calpe, Austral, 7th ed., Madrid, 1959.
*Mi Religión y Otros Ensayos Breves.* Espasa-Calpe, Austral, Buenos Aires, 1942.
*Paz en la Guerra.* Espasa-Calpe, Austral, 6th ed., Madrid, 1960.

Valera, Juan. *Juanita la Larga.* Nelson, Edinburgh, 1949.
*Pepita Jiménez.* Espasa-Calpe, Clásicos Castellanos, Madrid, 1958.

Valle-Inclán, Ramón María del. *Baza de Espadas.* Espasa-Calpe, Austral, Madrid, 1961.
*La Corte de los Milagros.* Plenitud, Madrid. 1954.
*Sonata de Primavera, Sonata de Estío.* Espasa-Calpe, Austral, 3rd ed., Buenos Aires, 1949.
*¡Viva mi Dueño!* Espasa-Calpe, Austral, Madrid, 1961.

Zunzunegui, Juan Antonio de. *¡Ay, Estos Hijos!* Aguilar, Madrid, 1951.

# *Short Bibliography*

GIVEN here are works referred to in the introduction to this book and also a selection of other works which may be of assistance to readers who wish to deepen their knowledge of the Spanish suffixes or of allied aspects of the language. Those who desire fuller information will find the *Manual de filología hispánica* by Gerhard Rohlfs and the *Bibliografía de la lingüística española* by Homero Serís of particular help.

ALEMANY BOLUFER, J. *Tratado de la derivación y composición de las palabras en la lengua castellana.* BAE, Madrid, 1917–19.

ALONSO, A. *Para la lingüística de nuestro diminutivo.* Nosotros, Buenos Aires, 1930.

*Noción, emoción, acción y fantasía en los diminutivos* in *Estudios lingüísticos : temas españoles.* Madrid, 1954.

ALONSO, A. and HENRÍQUEZ UREÑA, P. *Gramática castellana.* Buenos Aires, 1950.

ALONSO, M. *Ciencia del lenguaje y arte del estilo.* Madrid, 1960.
*Enciclopedia del idioma.* Madrid, 1958.

AMUNÁTEGUI REYES, M. L. *Una lección sobre diminutivos.* AUCh, Santiago de Chile, 1904.

BAILLY, C. *Linguistique générale et linguistique française.* Berne, 1950.

BEINHAUER, W. *El español coloquial.* Madrid, 1963. (Translation by F. Huarte Morton.)

BELLO, A. and CUERVO, R. J. *Gramática de la lengua castellana.* Buenos Aires, 1954.

BOURCIEZ, E. *Éléments de linguistique romane.* Paris, 1956.

BRAUE, A. *Beiträge zur Satzgestaltung der spanischen Umgangssprache.* Hamburg, 1931.

CASARES, J. *Diccionario ideológico de la lengua española*. Barcelona. 1959.
*Introducción a la lexicografía moderna*. Madrid, 1950.
*Novedades en el diccionario académico*. Madrid, 1963.

CELA, C. J. *Diccionario secreto*. Madrid, 1968.

CISNEROS, L. J. *Los diminutivos en español*. Mercurio Peruano, Lima, 1956.

CLAVERÍA, C. *Estudios sobre los gitanismos del español*. Madrid, 1951.

COROMINAS, J. *Diccionario crítico etimológico de la lengua castellana*. Madrid, 1954–7.

COSTE, J. and REDONDO, A. *Syntaxe de l'espagnol moderne*. Paris, 1965.

CRIADO DE VAL. M. *Fisonomía del idioma español*. Madrid, 1954.

CUERVO, R. J. *Sobre los usos del sufijo -o en castellano* in *Obras*, Bogotá, 1954.

DVOŘÁK, J. *Deminutiva v jazycich románskych. I Vulgární latina a Španělština*. LGRPh, Leipzig, 1936.

FERNÁNDEZ RAMÍREZ, S. *Gramática española*. Madrid, 1950.

FLÓREZ, L. *Diminutivos in Lengua española*. Bogotá, 1953.

GARCÍA DE DIEGO, V. *Diccionario etimológico español*. Madrid, 1954.
*Gramática histórica española*. Madrid, 1951.

GILI GAYA, S. *Vox, Diccionario general ilustrado de la lengua española*. Barcelona, 1953.

GIMENO CASALDUERO, J. *Sentido del diminutivo en la poesía moderna española*. Murcia, 1953.

GIMENO CASALDUERO, J. and MUÑOZ CORTÉS, M. *Notas sobre el diminutivo en García Lorca*. Archivum, Oviedo, 1954.

GONZÁLEZ OLLÉ, F. *Los sufijos diminutivos en castellano medieval*. Madrid, 1962.

GRANDGENT, C. H. *Introducción al latín vulgar*. Madrid, 1952. (Translation and notes by Fr. de B. Moll.)

HANSSEN, F. *Gramática histórica de la lengua castellana*. Buenos Aires, 1945.

HARMER, L. C. and NORTON, F. J. *A Manual of Modern Spanish*. London, 1949.

HASSELROT, B. *Études sur la formation diminutive dans les langues romanes*. Uppsala, 1957.

JORDAN, J. and ORR, J. *An Introduction to Romance Linguistics*. London, 1937.

KANY, C. E. *American-Spanish Semantics*. Berkeley, 1960.

LAPESA, R. *Historia de la lengua española*. Madrid, 1951.

LASLEY, M. M. *Nominal Suffixes in Old Spanish* (Columbia University Thesis).

LATORRE, F. *Diminutivos, despectivos y aumentativos en el siglo XVII*. AFA, Saragossa, 1956–7.

LÓPEZ ESTRADA, F. *Notas del habla de Madrid* in *Cuadernos de literatura contemporánea*. Madrid, 1943.

MALKIEL, Y. *The Hispanic Suffix -(i)ego. A Morphological and Lexical Study based on Historical and Dialectical Sources*. Berkeley, 1951.
*The Two Sources of the Hispanic Suffix -azo, -aço*. Language, Philadelphia, 1959.

MARTÍNEZ AMADOR, E. M. *Diccionario gramatical*. Barcelona, 1954.

MENÉNDEZ PIDAL, R. *Manual de gramática histórica española*. Madrid, 1944.
*Orígenes del español*. Madrid, 1926.

MEYER-LÜBKE, M. *Introducción a la lingüística románica*. Madrid, 1926. (Translation by A. Castro.)
*Romanisches etymologisches Wörterbuch*. Heidelberg, 1935.

MOLINER, M. *Diccionario de uso del español*. Madrid, 1966.

PETERSEN, W. *Suffixes, Determinatives and Words*. Language, Philadelphia, 1928.

RAMSEY, M. M. and SPAULDING, R. K. *A Textbook of Modern Spanish*. New York, 1965.

RANSON, H. M. *Diminutivos, aumentativos, despectivos*. Hispania, 1954.

REAL ACADEMIA ESPAÑOLA. *Diccionario de la lengua española*. Madrid, 1956.
*Gramática de la lengua española*. Madrid, 1931.

RESTREPO, F. *El alma de las palabras*. Bogotá, 1939.

ROHLFS, G. *Das spanische Suffix -arrón und Verwandtes*. ASNS, 1943.

SELVA, J. B. *Crecimiento del habla; acción de los sufijos*. RUBA, Buenos Aires, 1916.
*Los sufijos en el crecimiento del habla*. BAAL, Buenos Aires, 1945.
*Disquisiciones etimológicas. Sufijos olvidados*. La Lectura, Madrid, 1920.

287

SPITZER, L. and GAMILLSCHEG, E. *Beiträge zur romanischen Wortbildungslehre*. Geneva, 1921.

*Das Suffix -one im Romanischen*. Geneva, 1921.

TISCORNIA, E. F. *La lengua de Martín Fierro*. Buenos Aires, 1930.

UNAMUNO, M. DE. *Contribuciones a la etimología castellana ; el sufijo -rrio, a, -rro, a*. RFE, Madrid, 1920.

WAGNER, M. L. *Grammatikalisation der Suffixfunktion in den iberoromanischen Sprachen*. ASNSL, 1924.

*Zum spanisch-portugiesischen Suffix -al*. VKR, Hamburg, 1930; *-apo*. ZRPh, Halle, 1943; *-azo*. ZRPh, Halle, 1944.

WALSH, D. D. *Spanish Diminutives*. Hispania, 1944.

WANDRUSZKA, M. *Romanische und germanische quantifizierend-qualifizierende Suffixe*. ASNSL, 1966.

WARTBURG, W. V. *Problemas y métodos de la lingüística*. Madrid, 1957. (Translation by D. Alonso and E. Lorenzo.)

WEST, A. *The Spanish Suffix -udo*. PMLA, Baltimore, 1948.

# Appendix. Additional Suffixes of Pejorative Bias

# CONTENTS

# FOREWORD

In this Appendix are given nine suffixes which, although not exclusively or even, in all cases, predominantly pejorative in use, nevertheless have a marked tendency either in themselves to convey a derogatory impression or to be added to root-words the sense of which is already derogatory.

It will be seen that these suffixes thus have a close affinity to a large number of those listed in the main body of the volume, and not only indeed on the pejorative plane but also because of the strong colloquial and jocular elements variously to be found among them and the link here and there with augmentatives and diminutives.

The first suffix of the nine, *-ada*, happens to be a particularly good example of this in that, by its blend of the pejorative with a certain augmentative tendency, often involving an idea of action, it offers many instances of more or less exact correspondence with *-ón* and *-azo*, as in the following pairs: *bofetada/bofetón, morrada/morrón, cuartelada/cuartelazo, tizonada/tizonazo.*

Not dissimilar correspondences are frequently to be observed in the group formed by *-ada* and the other two noun suffixes now listed, i.e. *-eo* and *-ería*: *cursilada/cursilería, chulada/chulería, mangoneo/mangonería, palabreo/palabrería*.

In the case of the adjectival forms *-esco* and *-il*, in which there is a particular tendency for the jocular to mingle with the pejorative, the same type of parallelism is in evidence: *abogadesco/abogadil, estudiantesco/estudiantil, ratonesco/ratonil*.

The last four suffixes — *-ero, -izo, -izante, -oide* — may also be considered as comprising a group in so far that, to a greater or lesser degree, an idea of propensity or proneness is common to them all. Outstanding here is the similarity between *-izante* and *-oide* and the affinity of these two with the diminutive-pejorative *-illo*, testified to by such trios as: *comunistizante/comunistoide/comunistilla, intelectualizante/intelectualoide/intelectualillo, liberalizante/liberaloide/liberalillo*.

The list of nine suffixes now presented does not exhaust all possibilities in the pejorative sphere; there are yet others which, although not to the same degree, command consideration. One such is *-ez*: *altivez* = haughtiness, arrogance; *aridez* = aridity, aridness, dryness; *arisquez, esquivez* = distrustful standoffishness, wary unsociability; *candidez* = ingenuousness, simple-mindedness; *cretinez, estupidez, idiotez, insensatez, memez, sandez* = stupidity, damn fool thing to do or say; *dejadez* = laziness, propensity to put things off or let things go; *delgadez, escualidez* = thinness, skinniness, scrawniness, scragginess; *doblez* = deceit, secretiveness; *embriaguez* = drunkenness, intoxication; *escasez* = scarcity, shortage; *estrechez* = narrowness; tightness; shortage of money;[1] *fofez* = softness, sponginess, flabbiness; *frigidez* = frigidity, coldness; *insulsez* = insipidness, tastelessness; flatness, dullness; *languidez* = languidness; *morbidez* = sensuousness; *ordinariez* = commonness, vulgarity, common or vulgar thing to do or say; *paletez* = hickishness, country bumpkinishness, cloddish thing to do, say or wear; *pequeñez* = smallness; pettiness, triviality; *pesadez, plumbez* = heaviness; sluggishness; tediousness, bore; *rigidez* = rigidity, stiffness; *rustiquez* = rusticity, cloddishness; *testarudez* = pigheadedness,

---

[1] E.g. *no quiero tener que andarme con estrecheces* = I don't want to be short of cash, I don't want to have to mess about penny-pinching.

stubbornness; *tirantez* = tenseness, tension, strain; *vejez* = old age; old stuff, old thing; *verdez, verderulez* = blueness, risqué quality.

Another suffix in which the pejorative strain can be discerned is -*ario*, akin both etymologically and semantically to -*ero*: *atrabiliario* = atrabilious, black-humoured, evil-tempered; *convulsionario* = of up-heaval and chaos; *formulario* = purely formal, done purely as a matter of form, bound by set procedures and red-tape, going strictly by the book; *gregario* = (of the) herd, following the herd, sheep-like, easily-led, unthinking; *incendiario* = incendiary, arsonist, fire-bug; *parasitario* = parasitic, of parasites and drones; *patibulario* = of the gallows, having the look of a gallows bird, sinister; *perdulario* = rake, good-for-nothing; *presidiario* = convict; *prostibulario*[1] = brothel, of brothels; *protestatario* = of protest and complaint; *rutinario* = set in a rut, done through force of habit, dull, humdrum, uninspiring; *sanguinario* = blood-thirsty, savagely cruel; *tabernario*[1] = of taverns or pubs; low, coarse, vulgar.

Further cases, in which the pejorative element occurs to a more or less sporadic degree, are -*aje*, -*ata*, -*ato*, -*iego*, and, in a few jocular formations, -*itis*, -*ología* and -*óptero*: *brebaje* = concoction, ghastly brew; *caudillaje* = military leadership, government by military dictatorship; *chantaje* = blackmail; *espionaje* = espionage, spying; *libertinaje* = libertinage, profligacy; *sabotaje* = sabotage; *visaje* = grimace;[2] *bravata(s)* = bravado; *caminata, paseata, viajata* = long trek, plod, slog or haul, hell of a walk or trip; *perorata* = tedious, long-winded rigmarole, speech or address that is a pain-in-the-neck;[3] *cegato* = weak-eyed, feeble-sighted; *novato* = novice, green-horn; *pacato* = weak- or feeble-spirited, meek and mild to a fault; *timorato* = timorous, pusillanimous;[4] *aldeaniego* = village, typical of village life; mean, petty, narrow; *mujeriego* = (over-)fond of women, wenching or womanizing; *nocherniego* = (over-)fond of night or night-time, (too much) given to staying up late; *rebañego* — senses as

---

[1] Cf. *carcelario* = (of the) jail-house; low, coarse, vulgar. Note like figurative sense in each case.

[2] Most such forms in -*aje* are gallicisms.

[3] Many words in -*ata* are italianisms. There is a close relation between this suffix and -*ada*.

[4] Cf. *temeroso de Dios* = God-fearing.

for *gregario*, above; *mieditis* = condition of being scared, funk; *tonteritis* = condition of stupidity, addle-headedness; *tronitis* = condition of being hard-up or broke;[1] *gandulología* = science of loafing about, art of idleness; *mundología* = science of how to get on in the world, art of wordly wisdom; *chupóptero* = blood-sucker, sponger, parasite.

And, finally, there are a number of minor suffixes of pejorative or pejorative-jocular tenor which, although they are comparatively uncommon, do nevertheless occur in the odd word of fairly general interest, and which, for this reason and because they are closely akin to others among those originally listed, are worthy at least of brief mention. In this category are -*aina*, -*arro*, -*arra*, -*asco*, -*asca*, -*ijo*, -*ija*, -*is*, -*ongo*, -*onte*, -*ungo*, -*usco*, as in: *sosaina* = terribly dull, unamusing individual; *tontaina* = foolishly blundering, muddle-headed or tactless (individual); *pequeñarro* = tichy, wretchedly or pitifully small; *uñarra* = hideous or revolting (great) finger- or toe-nail; *peñasco* = rough or jagged rock or bounder; *rubiasco* = (individual) with an uninspiring or uninviting fair complexion or ginger-mop; *hojarasca* = dead leaves; dead wood, rubbish; *amasijo, revoltijo* = medley, jumble, hodgepodge; muddle, mess; *enredijo* = tangle, muddle; *escondrijo* = hidey-hole, hide-out; *baratija* = cheap little article, small object of little value, trifle; *sabandija* = insect, vermin; *perdis* = rake, good-for-nothing; *finolis* = lah-de-dah or terribly fussy (individual); *locatis* = hare-brained (individual); nut case; *malongo* = baddy; *clerizonte* = down-at-heel, bum or blasted priest; *polizonte* = cop, copper, rozzer, flat-foot; *chatungo* = pug-nose, ugly mug; *pedrusco* = rough stone, jagged lump or chunk of rock.

Although the availability and use in English of suffixes of the type under consideration in this book are extremely limited, there are, nevertheless, in this pejorative field, at least two which enjoy vigorous life, i.e. -ist and -ism, this giving rise to a large number of exact correspondences: *anarquista, anarquismo*/anarchist, anarchism; *egoísta, egoísmo*/egoist, egoism (also, selfish, selfishness); *materialista, materialismo*/materialist, materialism, etc., and to yet others in which, though the root-word differs, the suffix remains common: *gam-*

---

[1] Cf. *estar tronado* = to be broke.

*berrismo* = hooliganism, rowdyism; *patrioterismo* = jingoism; *pistolerismo* = gangsterism (also, gun-fighting, gang warfare).[1] Even here, however, it transpires that Spanish goes far beyond the bounds observed by English, as will be made abundantly clear by the forms now to be detailed. First, in *-ista*: *bromista* = joker, practical joke merchant; *carterista* = pick-pocket; *cuentista* = yarn-spinner, tall story merchant; *gorrista, sablista* = sponger, cadger; *juerguista* = merry-maker, reveller, one who goes on the randan, one who lives it up; *macarronista* = macaroni merchant, Eye-tie, Wop; *ordenancista* = martinet; *pancista* = one who does his best to keep on the right side of everybody or sits on the fence, one who runs with the hare and the hounds; *partidista* = individual who shows party spirit or bias; *petardista* = trickster, swindler; *preciosista* = writer in the *précieux* style; *prestamista* = money-lender; *trapisondista* = schemer, mischief-maker; *ultrancista* = die-hard[2]. Second, in *-ismo*, which, for example, in addition to *autoritarismo*, paralleled by "authoritarianism", offers such allied terms as *caudillismo* = government by military dictatorship, *dirigismo* = state planning or control, *caciquismo* = system of political bossing, *pucherismo* = cooking or rigging of elections, and *partidismo* = partisanship, party spirit, bias; in addition to *provincianismo* = provincialism, *aldeanismo* = village meanness, pettiness and narrow-mindedness, *cerrilismo* = boorishness, hickishness and narrowness of outlook, and *paletismo* = country bumpkin manner or attitude; in addition to *favoritismo* = favouritism, and *nepotismo* = nepotism, *amiguismo* and *personalismo*, words of like sense. Many such clusters of related terms, going far beyond the limits of English *-ism*, can be quoted: *belicismo* = war-mongering, *chulismo* = bellicoseness, pugnaciousness, attitude and behaviour of those who like to throw their weight about, *matonismo* = attitude and behaviour of the bully and roughneck, *machismo* and *machotismo*

---

[1] In a few cases Spanish uses a shorter root-form than English, e.g. *cinismo/*cynicism; *erotismo/*eroticism; *fanatismo/*fanaticism. (Cf. *escepticismo/*scepticism.) Other words, such as *autoritarismo* and *sectarismo*, formed logically on *autoritario* and *sectario*, also show a morphological difference from their English counterparts: authoritarianism, sectarianism.

[2] Among the latest formations is *volantista* = road-hog, speed-merchant.

= attitude and behaviour of the he-man or tough-guy type, glorification of the male, *señoritismo* = attitude and behaviour of the upper-class male element, upper-class parasite or drone existence; *divismo* = deification or glorification of artists, stars or show people, *hinchismo* = rabid support for football clubs or teams; *dramatismo, efectismo* = dramatic quality or effect, striving after or quest for effect, *histrionismo* = histrionics, play-acting, playing to the gallery; *enfermismo* = morbidness, morbid or obsessive attitude, *histerismo* = hysteria, hysterics, hysterical attitude or behaviour, *nerviosismo* = nervousness, jitteriness, state of nerviness or jitters, *raquitismo* = rickets, rickety or shaky state; *hermetismo* = extreme closeness, secretiveness, or reserve, closed-in and totally uncommunicative attitude, *mutismo* = extreme taciturnity or silence, totally uncommunicative attitude; *latifundismo* = system of division of land into large or vast estates, *minifundismo* = system of division of land into small or tiny estates or into small-holdings. And, finally, a few odd examples taken in isolation: *abogadismo* = legalistic scheming or interference; *atrevismo* = daring or insolent attitude or behaviour; *bandolerismo* = banditry; *chabolismo* = phenomenon or proliferation of shanty building or of living in huts, shanty, Nissen-hut or pre-fab existence, living in shanty towns; *indiferentismo* = (systematic or habitual) indifference, apathy or lack of interest; *practicismo* = excessively practical or hard-headed attitude or nature. Among the latest formations are: *dedismo* = system of random selection (cf. *elegir a dedo*); *enchufismo* = jobs for the boys; *follonismo* = chaotic lack of organization; *tipismo* = colourful, superficial aspects (of a country, etc.).

I. -ADO

*-ada NOUN — FEMININE*

*alcaldada*[1] ⎫ = the kind of thing to be expected from a mayor or
*principada* ⎭      prince; high-handed behaviour or action.

*alemanada*[2] = (typical) piece of German behaviour, stuff or

---

[1] Cf. *generalada* and *militarada*, below.

[2] Cf., below, a whole series of similar terms: *americanada, andaluzada, catalanada, escocesada, españolada, francesada, gallegada, gitanada, inglesada, mejicanada, polacada, portuguesada, suecada*, a list which, at least in theory, could be extended to include every race, nationality and regional identity.

|  |  |
|---|---|
| | rubbish, (just) the sort of thing to be expected from a German or (the) Germans. |
| †*americanada*[1] | — senses for "American(s)" similar to those given under *alemanada*. |
| *andada*[2] | = well-worn track or path; former bad habit, old trick. |
| *andaluzada*[3] | — senses for "Andalusian(s)" similar to those given under *alemanada*. |
| *andanada*[4] | = broadside; hefty blast. |
| *animalada*[5] ⎫<br>†*burrada* ⎭ | = piece of assing or fooling about; piece of stupidity, nonsense or drivel, lot of tripe; bloomer, blunder, howler, clumsy or oafish thing to do or say; terribly coarse or crude thing to do or say; frightful, shocking or beastly thing to do or say. |
| *baladronada* ⎫<br>*fanfarronada* ⎭ | = piece of boasting, bragging or showing off. |
| *barrabasada*[6] | = ghastly piece of clumsiness, fearful blunder, dreadful mess; filthy trick. |
| *barriada*[7] | = large or sprawling quarter or district, outer district, suburb. |

[1] Can refer to South, Central or North America.

[2] The literal sense is of uncommon occurrence. Both literal and figurative uses usually involve the plural, as in the phrase *volver a las andadas* = to get up to one's old tricks again. Cf. *desandar lo andado* = *volver sobre sus pasos* = to retrace one's steps.

[3] Sometimes used with the specific sense of "piece of showing-off or exaggeration".

[4] Used especially in the phrase *soltarle a alguien una andanada* = to let someone have it good and hard, give someone a good dressing down.

[5] Cf., below, a whole series of allied terms: *besugada*, etc.

[6] Lit. act (worthy) of Barabbas.

[7] Closely linked with this word are the term *afueras* and *extrarradio* = suburbs. Cf. *suburbio(s)* = slum(s).

| | |
|---|---|
| besugada[1] | |
| bobada | |
| gansada | = silly, foolish or muttish thing to do or say, thing |
| primada | typical of a simpleton, naïve individual or nit-wit. |
| simplada | |
| tontada | |
| bobada | — vide *besugada*, above. |
| bocanada | = puff; blast; mouthful; rush. |
| bofetada[2] | = slap. |
| boqueada[3] | = last gasp. |
| bufonada[4] | = (piece of) buffoonery or clowning, buffoonish or |
| †payasada | clownish thing to do or say. |
| burrada[5] | — vide *animalada*, above. |
| cabezonada | — vide *cabezonería*, under -ería. |
| cabronada[6] | |
| canallada | |
| charranada | |
| judiada | = filthy, foul or rotten trick. |
| perrada | |
| putada | |
| señoritada | |

[1] In the case of *besugada* (< *besugo* = sea-bream), a rather more graphic possible translation would be "thing typical of or to be expected from a poor fish"; in the case of *gansada* (< *ganso* = goose, gander), "thing typical of or to be expected from a silly goose". [2] Cf. *bofetón*, under -ón.

[3] Used mainly in the phrase *estar dando las boqueadas* = to be at one's last gasp, be on one's beam ends, have just about had it. [4] Cf. *fantochada*, below.

[5] Used also with a sense similar to that which frequently attaches to terms such as *atrocidad*, *barbaridad* and *bestialidad*, i.e. hell of a lot, terrific amount, as in *se ha zampado una burrada de pan* = he's polished off a shocking amount of bread.

[6] The literal sense of these words is as follows: act of a cuckold or bastard; act of a cur or tyke; act of a rogue or knave; act of a Jew; act of a (dirty) dog or (dirty) hound; act of a whore; act of a young, upper-class parasite.

With *perrada* cf. *perrería*, under -ería.

Cf. the less colourful and rather less virulent *mala jugada*, *mala pasada*, *trastada* = dirty trick. Another similarly less forceful word of like meaning is *faena*: *hacerle a alguien una faena* = to play a dirty trick on someone. Also worthy of note is the allied expression *hacerle a alguien un flaco servicio* = to do someone a scant favour.

| | | |
|---|---|---|
| †*calaverada*[1] | = | (piece of) behaviour typical of or to be expected from a rake; crazy, wild or mad-cap escapade. |
| *camada*[2] | = | brood, litter; crowd, gang, mob. |
| †*canallada* | — | vide *cabronada*, above. |
| *carcajada* <br> *risotada* } | = | guffaw, bellow of laughter, uproarious outburst of laughter. |
| †*carlistada*[3] | = | (typical) piece of Carlist behaviour, stuff or rubbish, (just) the sort of thing to be expected from a Carlist or (the) Carlists; Carlist war, do or business. |
| *catalanada* | — | senses for "Catalan(s)" similar to those given under *alemanada*. |
| *cencerrada* | = | charivari, tin-pan serenade. |
| *cerdada*[4] <br> *cochinada* <br> *gorrinada* <br> *guarrada* <br> *marranada* } | = | (just) the sort of thing to be expected from a pig or swine; dirty, filthy or disgusting thing to do or say. |
| *cochada*[5] | = | (piece of) showing off or throwing one's weight about in a car, (piece of) flamboyant or aggressive driving. |
| *cochinada* | — | vide *cerdada*, above. |
| †*corazonada*[6] | = | hunch, inkling; foreboding. |

[1] Cf. *escapada*, below.

[2] Cf. *ventregada* — similar first sense, but less common. *ser de la misma camada* = to be of the same brood, come of the same stock; to belong to the same crowd or mob.

Cf. *ser de la misma calaña* or *ralea*, *ser del mismo jaez* = to be of the same ilk.
For another term of allied meaning cf. *hornada*, below.

[3] The phrases *primera carlistada* and *segunda carlistada* are frequently used as variants of the formal *primera guerra carlista* and *segunda guerra carlista*.

Cf. *francesada*, below.

[4] Cf. the parallel forms *cerdería, cochinería, gorrinería, guarrería, marranería*, of similar sense.

[5] Used mainly in the phrase *dar* or *pegar cochadas* = *chulear en* or *con un* or *el coche* = to show off or throw one's weight about in a or one's car.

[6] Cf. the more formal *presentimiento, intuición* = presentiment, premonition, intuition.

| | |
|---|---|
| *cornada* | = horn-goad or goading, horn-thrust, gore, goring, gore-wound. |
| *cuartelada*[1] | = barrack mutiny, military uprising, revolt or coup. |
| *cursilada* | — vide *cursilería*, under *-ería*. |
| *charranada* | — vide *cabronada*, above. |
| *chiquillada* | = kid's or kids' trick or prank; piece of childishness. |
| *chulada* | — vide *chulería*, under *-ería*. |
| *churretada* | = streamy, runny mess; dirty smear. |
| *chuscada* | = wise-crack. |
| *escapada*[2] | = quick dash; quick trip; quick visit. |
| *escocesada* | — senses for "Scottish, Scotch or Scot(s)" similar to those given under *alemanada*. |
| *espantada* | = shying away; sheering off, clearing out. |
| †*españolada* | — senses for "Spanish or Spaniard(s)" similar to those given under *alemanada*. |
| *espolada*[3] | = dig, prick or thrust with a spur; swig, one-for-the-road. |
| *fanfarronada*[4] | — vide *baladronada*, above. |
| *fantochada*[5] | = piece of clownish tom-foolery or conceited assing about; mob of clownish individuals. |
| *flamencada* | — vide *chulería*, under *-ería*. |
| †*francesada*[6] | = (typical) piece of French behaviour, stuff, rubbish or nonsense, (just) the sort of thing to be expected from a Frenchman, Frenchmen or the French; French war, do or business. |
| †*gallegada* | — senses for "Galician(s)" similar to those given under *alemanada*. |

[1] Cf., below, *generalada*, *militarada* and *sargentada*.

Cf. *Vicalvarada* = *pronunciamiento* of Vicálvaro (1854). See also *cuartelazo*, under *-azo* and *intentona*, under *-ona*.

[2] For "escapade" cf. *calaverada*, above, and *tenoriada*, below.

[3] Cf. *latigazo*, under *-azo*.

[4] Cf. the parallel form *fanfarronería*, of similar sense.

[5] Cf., below, *mamarrachada* and *payasada*.

[6] The phrase *la francesada* is frequently used as a variant of the formal *la guerra de la Independencia*, known in English as the Peninsular War.

Cf. *carlistada*, above.

| | |
|---|---|
| *gamberrada*[1] | = piece of hooliganism or rowdyism, the sort of thing to be expected from a hooligan, larrikin or rowdy; mob of hooligans, larrikins or rowdies. |
| *gansada* | — vide *besugada*, above. |
| *generalada*[2] | = (typical) piece of general-like or soldier-style behaviour, stuff, rubbish or nonsense, (just) the sort of thing to be expected from a general or soldier or from generals or soldiers; high-handed action; general's or generals' revolt, coup or pronunciamiento. |
| *gitanada* | — senses for "gipsy or gipsies" similar to those given under *alemanada*. |
| *gorrinada* | — vide *cerdada*, above. |
| *gozada* | = thrill, kick. |
| *granujada* | = piece of rascality or roguery; mischievous or impish trick. |
| *guarrada* | — vide *cerdada*, above. |
| *hinchada*[3] | = (just) the sort of thing to be expected from a football or sports fan, supporter, enthusiast or fanatic, or from a mob of football or sports fans, supporters, enthusiasts or fanatics; (typical) piece of cup-tie rowdyism; body, crowd or mob of football or sports fans, supporters, enthusiasts or fanatics. |
| *hornada*[4] | = batch, bake, lot (of bread, bricks, etc.); batch, group, year. |
| *horterada* | = (just) the sort of thing to be expected from or likely to find favour with a low-class or cheap shop assistant. |

[1] Cf. *hinchada*, below.

[2] Cf. *cuartelada*, above.

[3] The root word is *hincha* (masc. & fem.) = football fan, etc.
The last sense given is that most commonly found.
Cf. *gamberrada*, above.

[4] Commonly used as a popular variant of the formal *promoción*, in such phrases as *él y yo somos de la misma hornada; los dos sacamos el título en 1954* = he and I belong to the same batch of graduates; we both got our degree in 1954. Only on occasion vaguely pejorative.

| | | |
|---|---|---|
| *indiada*[1] | = | body, crowd or mob of Indians. |
| *inglesada* | — | senses for "English, Englishman or Englishmen" similar to those given under *alemanada*. |
| *inocentada*[2] | = | (just) the sort of thing to be expected from a simple-minded, artless or guileless individual; ingenuous blunder; April Fool-type practical joke. |
| *jaimitada*[3] | = | tactless blunder, piece of assinine stupidity. |
| *javierada*[4] | = | St. Xavier's trek or do. |
| *judiada* | — | vide *cabronada*, above. |
| *jugada*[5] | = | move, stroke, throw (in games); move, stroke, deal (on the Stock Exchange, etc.). |
| †*llamarada*[6] | = | flare-out or -up, flaring out or up, flash, blaze, blaze-up; outburst. |
| *machada*[7] | = | piece of (real) he-man or tough-guy behaviour, he-man exploit; piece of damn-fool truculence; piece of ham-fisted, nitwittish or mindless stupidity; drove of he-goats. |

---

[1] This word does not appear to be used in what would be the logical sense of "(typical) piece of Indian behaviour, etc.". Cf., in the case of *hinchada*, the predominance of the "body, crowd or mob" sense.

[2] In the last sense given the word is used particularly in connexion with the Spanish equivalent of April Fools' Day — *El día de los Inocentes* (28th December).

Cf. *jaimitada* and *novatada*, below. Cf. *bromazo*, under -*azo*.

[3] Formed on *Jaimito* — i.e. little or young James, Jimmy—the epitome of the "little terror" type.

[4] An annual pilgrimage and celebration held in Navarre in honour of St. Francis Xavier.

Cf. *sanjuanada* = St. John's do, festivities and picnicking on the Feast of St. John.

Cf. *sanmartinada* = St. Martin's do or time, celebration of the Feast of St. Martin, associated with the slaughter of swine for food.

Cf. *sanmiguelada* = St. Michael's do or time, celebration of the Feast of St. Michael, Michaelmastide.

[5] For *mala jugada* see note to *cabronada*, above.

[6] Frequently close in sense to *fogonazo* and *chispazo*. See under -*azo*.

[7] Frequently close in sense to *chulada*, *chulería*. See under -*ería*.

For last sense given cf. *torada*, *vacada* = herd or drove of bulls, cows, cattle.

| †*mamarrachada* | = | piece of clownish or grotesque stupidity; collection or mob of clownish or grotesque individuals or figures; daub. |
| †*manotada*[1] | = | swipe with the hand, hefty slap. |
| *marranada* | = | vide *cerdada*, above. |
| *meada* | = | piss, pissing; piss stain. |
| *mejicanada* | — | senses for "Mexican(s)" similar to those given under *alemanada*. |
| *militarada* | — | sense for "military, the military, one of the (thick-headed) military or soldier(s)" similar to those given under *generalada*. |
| *millarada*[2] | = | (roughly a) thousand; terrific amount, fortune. |
| †*millonada*[3] | = | (roughly a) million; hell of a lot of money, mint of money, fortune, packet. |
| *monada* | = | piece of monkey-play, monkey trick; cute or delightful little thing or trick; pretty little thing or creature; (iron.) fine thing, nice thing, fine state of affairs, nice way to carry on. |
| *morrada*[4] | = | header, cropper, head-on or face-first crash or smash. |
| †*novatada*[5] | = | rag, practical joke or prank (played on a new boy, newcomer or novice); novice's or beginner's blunder. |
| *paletada* | = | (typical) piece of country-bumpkin or provincial behaviour, (just) the sort of thing to be expected from a yokel or hick, or from someone from the provinces. |
| *palmada* | = | slap; clap. |

---

[1] Cf. *manotazo*, under *-azo*.

[2] Cf. *millonada*, below.

[3] Cf. *dineral*, etc., under *-al*.

[4] Cf. *morrón* — similar sense.

For illustration of use see *rasponazo*, under *-azo* (Examples from Literature).

[5] Worthy of note is the phrase *pagar la novatada*, as in *hay que pagar la novatada* = one usually puts one's foot in it the first time, there's often a blunder or hitch the first time, things rarely go smoothly the first time.

| | |
|---|---|
| *panzada* ⎫ *tripada* ⎭ | = bellyful. |
| *parrafada* | = talk, chat, chin-wag; long rigmarole. |
| †*pasada*[1] | = passing; stroke. |
| *patada*[2] | = kick. |
| *patochada*[3] | = clumsy or gauche thing to do or say; piece of blundering tactlessness or thoughtless stupidity. |
| †*payasada* | — vide *bufonada*, above. |
| *perogrullada* | = truism. |
| *perrada* | — vide *cabronada*, above. |
| *pijada*[4] | = piece of bloody nonsense or stupidity. |
| *polacada*[5] | — senses for "Polish, Pole(s)" similar to those given under *alemanada*. |
| *porrada*[6] | = clout or swipe with a truncheon or bludgeon; hell of a lot. |
| *portuguesada*[7] | — senses for "Portuguese" similar to those given under *alemanada*. |
| *primada*[8] | — vide *besugada*, above. |
| *principada* | — vide *alcaldada*, above. |
| *punzada* | = prick, sting; pang; stabbing or shooting pain. |
| *puñalada* | = stab. |
| *putada* | — vide *cabronada*, above. |
| *quijotada* | = piece of quixotic foolishness. |

[1] For *mala pasada*, see note to *cabronada*, above.

[2] E.g. *echar a patadas* = to kick out.

[3] Closely akin to *patosería* and the less common *patarronería* (vide under -*ería*), all deriving from the basic *pata* as used in the phrase *meter la pata* = to put one's foot in it, blunder.

Worthy of note in this connexion are the phrases *salida de pie de banco* = stupidly tactless or out-of-place remark; *salida de tono* = rude remark, remark in bad taste.

[4] Extremely vulgar.

[5] Sometimes used with the specific sense of "dirty or filthy trick".

[6] Used especially in the phrase *una porrada de dinero* = a hell of a lot of money. Cf. *burrada*, above.

[7] Sometimes used with the specific sense of "wild boasting or exaggeration".

[8] Worthy of note in connexion with this word is the phrase *hacer el primo* = to get taken for a fool, be taken in, be taken for a ride.

| | |
|---|---|
| *quintada*[1] | = (just) the sort of thing to be expected from a raw recruit; beginner's blunder. |
| *repipada* | = piece of childish affectation or precociousness. |
| *riada* | = flood, spate; rush. |
| *risotada* | — vide *carcajada*, above. |
| †*salvajada*[2] | = piece of savagery, savage brutality or savage cruelty; appalling, frightful or ghastly thing to do or say. |
| *sanjuanada* | — vide *javierada*, above (note). |
| *sanmartinada* | — vide *javierada*, above (note). |
| *sanmiguelada* | — vide *javierada*, above (note). |
| *sargentada* | — senses for "sergeant(s) or thick-headed sergeant(s)" similar to those given under *generalada*. |
| *señorada*[3] | = fine, grand or lavish gesture; sweeping or flamboyant gesture. |
| *señoritada* | = (just) the sort of thing to be expected from a young upper-class drone, parasite or fop, or from the mindless young upper-class set; filthy trick. |
| *simplada* | — vide *besugada*, above. |
| *suecada* | — senses for "Swedish, Swede(s)" similar to those given under *alemanada*. |
| *talonada*[4] | = kick with the heels; (pl.) trapsing, tramping. |
| *tarascada* | = shrewish thing to do or say; bite. |
| *televisionada* | = typical piece of television stuff or rubbish. |
| †*tenoriada* | = (typical) piece of Don Juan Tenorio-type behaviour, piece of Don Juan stuff, Don Juan act or escapade, (just) the sort of thing to be expected from a Don Juan. |

[1] Coincides very closely in usage with the much more common *novatada* (second sense), above.

[2] Cf. *animalada*, *burrada*, above.

[3] Cf. *señoritada*, below.

[4] E.g. *hemos dado muchas talonadas por estas calles* = we've trapsed or tramped about or around these streets a great deal.

Cf. *talonazo* — similar sense, but less common.

Cf. *taconazo*, under *-azo*.

| | |
|---|---|
| *tizonada*[1] | = swipe with a firebrand. |
| *tontada* | — vide *besugada*, above. |
| *torada* | — vide *machada*, above (note). |
| *trastada* | — vide *cabronada*, above (note). |
| *tripada* | — vide *panzada*, above. |
| *vacada* | — vide *machada*, above (note). |
| *vejada*[2] | = sudden growing old, sudden going down hill. |
| *zancada* | = long gangling stride. |
| *zarpada*[3] | = clawing slash, gash, rent, or slash of claw, paw or talon. |

## *-ada EXAMPLES FROM LITERATURE*

Este país de *Tirano Banderas* es imaginario, pero nos hace pensar sobre todo en Méjico, el Méjico aún vibrante de sacudidas revolucionarias . . .. El lenguaje artificial, compuesto de americanismos de todas partes . . .. Valle, con recuerdos de todo lo visto, oído, imaginado, hace, pues, una *americanada* que no difiere mucho de las *españoladas* del romanticismo francés.

(MONTESINOS, *Modernismo, Esperpentismo*
in *Homenaje a Valle-Inclán*, p. 161)

This country we see in *Tirano Banderas* is fictional, but it reminds us particularly of Mexico, a Mexico still quivering from the shock of revolution . . .. The made-up language, put together with Spanish-Americanisms from all over . . .. Valle Inclán, with recollections of everything he had seen, heard or imagined, thus wrote a piece of typically South American[4] stuff, not greatly different from the pieces of typically Spanish stuff churned out by the French Romantics.

[1] Cf. *tizonazo* — similar sense.
These words are used especially in the phrase *las tizonadas* or *los tizonazos del infierno* = hell-fire.
[2] E.g. *de la noche a la mañana dio* or *pegó una gran vejada* = he got terrifically older overnight, just like that.
Cf. *bajón*, under *-ón*.
[3] Cf. *zarpazo* — similar sense.
[4] Used in its broadest and loosest English sense.

. . . un cuento espeluznante y horroroso, titulado "No lo invento", de un naturalismo feroz y nauseabundo que trata de un sepulturero profanador de cadáveres . . .. Es una *burrada*, es una *salvajada* del naturalismo . . ..

(BRAVO-VILLASANTE, *Vida y Obra de Emilia Pardo Bazán*, p. 187)

. . . a hair-raising and ghastly story, entitled "I haven't made it up", savage and sickening in its naturalism, about a grave-digger who defiles dead bodies . . . It is a shocking, indeed an appalling tale in the naturalist manner . . ..

Ella siempre estaba oyendo hablar de las *calaveradas* de Martín.

(BAROJA, *Zalacaín el Aventurero*, p. 26)

She was always hearing about Martin's wild escapades.

. . . liar el equipaje cuando me diera la gana y volverme a Madrid por el camino más corto . . . me parecía una *canallada* que podía costar la vida al bondadoso octogenario.

(PEREDA, *Peñas Arriba*, p. 72)

. . . to pack up my bags when I felt like it and go off back to Madrid by the shortest route . . . seemed to me a rotten thing to do and one which might cause the death of the kindly old octogenarian.

Veintidós años más tarde, durante la primera *carlistada*, fue el propio cura Merino quien incendió Roa.

(CELA, *Judíos, Moros y Cristianos*, p. 66)

Twenty-two years later, during the first Carlist "do", it was the priest Merino himself who set fire to Roa.

Pero en medio de su inmensa tarea, no cesaba de tener *corazonadas* pesimistas . . .. Y este presentimiento, por ser de cosa mala, vino a cumplirse al cabo . . ..

(PÉREZ GALDÓS, *Fortunata y Jacinta*, I, p. 102)

But in the midst of her vast task she continually had gloomy forebodings . . .. And this presentiment, because it was of something unpleasant, eventually turned into hard fact.

Para aquellos rudos montañeses . . . toda construcción de parecida traza es debida a los moros . . . o a *la francesada*.

(PEREDA, *Peñas Arriba*, p. 30)

For those rough mountain-dwellers . . . any building of similar appearance is the work of the Moors . . . or a result of "that business with the Frenchies".

— Que se le quite, grandísimo gallego.[1]
— ¡Vuelta con la *gallegada*! — dije para mí, cada vez más inquieto.

(PALACIO VALDÉS, *La Hermana San Sulpicio*, p. 156)

"You can get that idea out of your head, you great Galician."[1]
"There she is harping on again about his being a Galician," I said to myself, feeling more and more uneasy.

Riego y Narváez, por ejemplo, son, como pensadores, ¡la verdad!, un par de desventuras; pero son, como seres vivos, dos altas *llamaradas* de esfuerzo.

(ORTEGA Y GASSET, *Vieja y Nueva Política*, p. 32)

Riego and Narváez, for example, are, as thinkers—let us make no bones about it!—a couple of duds; but, as living human beings, they are two towering pillars of blazing energy.

. . . me sonreí pensando que mi imaginación me jugaba *malas pasadas* en las primeras impresiones.

(LAFORET, *Nada*, p. 25)

---

[1] Galician, native of Galicia. The word is sometimes used as a term of abuse by Spaniards from other regions.

... I smiled, thinking that my imagination was playing nasty tricks on me in my first impressions.

— Si la Gloriosa[1] no se hubiera quedado en su camino, ya se hubiera visto lo que era España.
Y poco después, la voz del hijo, que gritaba burlonamente:
— ¡La Gloriosa! ¡Valiente *mamarrachada*!
(BAROJA, *El Arbol de la Ciencia*, p. 454)

"If the Glorious Revolution[1] had not stopped in its tracks, we should have seen by now just what stuff Spain was made of."
And shortly after, the voice of the son shouting in a jeering tone:
"The Glorious Revolution! A fine piece of grotesque clowning!"

— Puerca, fantasmona, mamarracho. — gritó doña Lupe, destruyendo con *manotada* furibunda todos aquellos perfiles . . ..
(PÉREZ GALDÓS, *Fortunata y Jacinta*, II, p. 101)

"You filthy creature, conceited show-off, grotesque object," shouted Doña Lupe, destroying all that frippery with a furious swipe of her hand.

En mis tiempos de chico, hablaba de minerales y de filones de hierro un señor que se llamaba don Juan Beracochea ... y decía que los alrededores de Izarte valían una *millonada*.
(BAROJA, *Las Inquietudes de Shanti Andía*, p. 135)

When I was a lad a gentleman called Don Juan Beracochea used to talk about ore and seams of iron ... and he used to say that the area round Izarte was worth a fortune.

... Allá, en Segovia, el pobre alumno, víctima quizá de los rigores de la cruel *novatada* . . ..
(PARDO BAZÁN, *Los Pazos de Ulloa*, p. 137)

[1] The Revolution of 1868, also known as *la Septembrina*.

. . . away in Segovia the poor [Military Academy] cadet, a victim perhaps of the harsh, cruel ragging that is given to new arrivals . . . .

. . . tocábale a él poner los juegos de chasco y pantomima, hacer las *payasadas* . . ..

(ALARCÓN, *El Sombrero de Tres Picos*, p. 20)

. . . it fell to him to arrange the games of tricks and mime, to do the clowning . . ..

Aquí [en Fuerteventura] no hay campo para Don Juan Tenorio. Aquí no hay más Tenorio que los camellos en esta época del celo . . .. Aquí no se comprenden *tenoriadas* . . .. Bajo este clima prospera la humanidad; pero una humanidad recatada y resignada, enjuta y sobria, una humanidad muy poco teatral. Y es que el clima no es teatral.

(UNAMUNO, *Paisajes del Alma*, p. 66)

Here [on Fuerteventura] there is no scope for Don Juans. The only Don Juans here are the camels in this the mating-season . . .. One cannot conceive of an escapade in the Don Juan manner here . . . the human race thrives in this climate; but it is a withdrawing and resigned, a spare and frugal human race, a human race that is notably undramatic. And the whole point is that the climate is undramatic.

## 2. -EO

*-eo*[1] *NOUN — MASCULINE*

| | |
|---|---|
| *abucheo*[2] | = booing, cat-calling, giving the bird by booing. |
| *bailoteo*[3] | = dancing, hopping, jigging or jiving (about). |

[1] It is noteworthy, in regard to *-eo*, that even technical or semi-technical terms such as *ceceo*, *seseo* and *tuteo* tend to be of pejorative tenor, the implication in the case of these three being, more often than not, one of defect or of over-familiarity.

[2] Cf. *pateo* and *siseo*, below.

[3] The corresponding verb is *bailotear*, a pejorative-frequentative formation on *bailar*. Cf., below, other similar formations in *-oteo*: *charloteo*, *parloteo* (*charlotear/charlar*, *parlotear/parlar*); *fregoteo* (*fregotear/fregar*); *fumeteo* (*fumetear/fumar*); *lagrimoteo* (*lagrimotear/lagrimar*); *tiroteo* (*tirotear/tirar*).

| | | |
|---|---|---|
| *balbuceo*[1] | = | babble, babbling; stammer, stammering. |
| *bamboleo*[2] | = | swaying, heaving. |
| †*besuqueo*[3] | = | sloppy kissing, slobbering. |
| *bombardeo* | = | bombardment, shelling; bombing. |
| *cabreo* | = | (damned) rattiness or ratty mood, filthy or foul temper or mood. |
| *cacareo*[4] | = | cackling, crowing; boasting, bragging, vaunting. |
| *cachondeo*[5] *choteo* *pitorreo* | = | (boisterous) ribbing or taking the mickey; damn-fool larking about, mucking or arsing about. |
| *cañoneo* | = | gun-fire, artillery fire, exchange of fire. |
| *contoneo*[6] | = | strutting, swaggering. |
| *copeo*[7] | = | drinking, boozing. |
| *coqueteo*[8] *flirteo* | = | coquetry, flirting. |
| *cotilleo*[9] *chismorreo* | = | gossiping, tittle-tattling, scandal-mongering. |
| *cuchicheo* | = | whispering, talking under one's breath. |
| †*charloteo* *parloteo* | = | chatter, prattle, gabble, empty or idle talk. |

[1] Cf. *tartamudeo*, below.

[2] Cf. *tambaleo*, below.

[3] The corresponding verb is *besuquear*, a pejorative-frequentative formation on *besar*.

[4] In connexion with the last English equivalent given, note the translation of the adjectivally used past participle of the verb *cacarear* in phrases such as *la tan cacareada campaña de desarme* = the much-vaunted disarmament campaign.

[5] These words are decidedly vulgar. Note the phrase *tomar a cachondeo* (*choteo, pitorreo*) = to treat as a damn fine or bloody good joke (i.e. vulgar equivalent of such less crude expressions as *tomar* or *echar a broma* or *a guasa* = to treat as a joke, treat facetiously or flippantly). Similarly the verbs *cachondearse* (*de*), *chotearse* (*de*), *pitorrearse* (*de*) = (boisterously) to rib or take the mickey (out of), are the vulgar equivalent of more neutral expressions of the *burlarse* (*de*) type.

[6] Cf. *meneo*, below.

[7] Cf. *tasqueo*, below.

[8] Cf. *chicoleo, devaneo, escarceo, mariposeo* and *tonteo*, below.

[9] Other allied expressions are *chismería, chismografía, habladuría(s), habilla(s), murmuración.*

| | |
|---|---|
| *chicoleo* | = going out with or running around with boys, gadding or gallivanting about with boys, dating, fooling about with boys. |
| *chismorreo* | — vide *cotilleo*, above. |
| *chisporroteo*[1] | = sparking, crackling, sputtering, spluttering. |
| *chorreo* | = spouting, gushing, stream; dripping, trickle; (never-ending) drain (on one's resources), stream (of money). |
| *choteo* | = vide *cachondeo*, above. |
| †*devaneo* | = craziness; frittering away of time; flirtation, (bit of an) affair. |
| *escarceo* | = swirling (of water); cavorting. |
| *expedienteo*[2] | = (never-ending) passing to and fro of files; paper-work; (fig.) red-tape. |
| *faroleo* | = bluffing, blustering; showing off. |
| *flirteo* | — vide *coqueteo*, above. |
| *forcejeo* | = struggle, tussle. |
| *fregoteo* | = splashing, sploshing, sloshing about in the sink or on the floors, washing-up or scrubbing of a ham-fisted or any-old-how type. |
| *fulaneo*[3] | = tarting, messing about like a tart or with tarts, whoring, womanizing. |
| *fumeteo* | = (continual) puffing away at cigarettes or fags, smoking like a chimney. |
| *jaleo* | = boisterous or rowdy clapping and shouting; din, uproar; rumpus, to-do; bother, trouble, mix-up. |
| *lagrimoteo* | = blubbery weeping, blubbering. |
| *mangoneo* | — vide *mangonería*, under -*ería*. |
| *manteo* | = tossing in a blanket. |
| *mareo* | = sickness, sea-sickness, travel-sickness; dizziness; crazy whirl. |
| *mariposeo* | = flitting from one infatuation to another or from one thing to another. |

[1] Note specific double pejorative suffix element -*orr*, -*ot*.
[2] Cf. *papeleo*, below.
[3] Cf. *pendoneo*, below.

| | |
|---|---|
| *martilleo* | = hammering, thumping. |
| *meneo*[1] | = wagging, swaying, wriggling, jiggling; going-over, working-over; shake-up. |
| *palabreo* | — vide *palabrería*, under *-ería*. |
| *papeleo*[2] | = paper-work; form-filling; red-tape; bumph. |
| *parloteo* | — vide *charloteo*, above. |
| *pataleo*[3] | = waving about of feet or legs; kicking up a fuss, rumpus or shindy; grumbling, grousing. |
| *pateo*[4] | = stamping, banging or thumping with the feet; giving the bird with stamping. |
| *peloteo* | = pitching or tossing back and forth of a ball; passing the buck. |
| *pendoneo*[5] | = gadding or gallivanting about like a tart. |
| *pitorreo* | — vide *cachondeo*, above. |
| *politiqueo* | — vide *politiquería*, under *-ería*. |
| *pordioseo* | — vide *pordiosería*, under *-ería*. |
| †*pregunteo* | = questioning, repeated questions. |
| *recochineo*[6] | = gloating enjoyment or pleasure, gloating bloody-mindedness, damned nastiness or bitchiness. |
| *regateo* | = haggling, bargaining; arguing the toss. |
| *regodeo* | = revelling or wallowing delight, enjoyment or pleasure; gloating. |

[1] E.g. *le pegaron un meneo de miedo* = they gave him the devil of a going-over; *hay que pegarle un meneo a este cuarto* = we've got to give this room a shake-up (i.e. re-arrange, tidy and clean it up).

[2] Cf. *papelería, papelajo(s), papelorio(s), papelote(s)*. See under *-ajo*.
Cf. *expedienteo*, above.
The somewhat archaic term *balduque* (< Bois-le-Duc, name of a tape-manufacturing town in the Low Countries) has the literal sense of "red tape".

[3] Much used contemporarily in the phrase *el derecho al pataleo* = the right to grumble, entitlement to a grouse (especially in things political).

[4] Cf. *abucheo*, above.

[5] Cf. *fulaneo*, above.

[6] A vulgar word. For somewhat similar sense and register cf. *puñetería*, under *-ería. regodeo*, given below, although in some respects akin in sense, is considerably less crude in tone.

| | |
|---|---|
| *rodeo*[1] | = going round, long way round, detour; beating about the bush, hedging. |
| *saqueo* | = sacking, pillaging, plundering, looting. |
| *secreteo* | = whispering together, talking together in undertones, under-tone exchange of confidences. |
| *sermoneo* | = sermonizing, preaching, lecturing. |
| *siseo*[2] | = hissing; giving the bird by hissing. |
| *sopeteo* | = sopping, dunking. |
| *tableteo*[3] | = rattle, rattling; clatter, clattering; tap, tapping. |
| *tambaleo* | = violent, swaying, wobbling, reeling, staggering, tottering. |
| *tartamudeo* | = stammer, stammering, stutter, stuttering. |
| *tasqueo*[4] | = going round from one pub or eating-house to another, pub-crawling. |
| *tiroteo* | = (wild) shooting or firing, (wild) exchange of shots or fire, sniping, blazing away. |
| *titubeo* | = wavering, hesitation. |
| *tonteo* | = fooling about, tom-foolery; flirting. |
| *toreo*[5] | = bullfighting; leading a dance, giving the run-around. |
| *trapicheo*[6] | = messing or shifting about, scheming, jiggery-pokery. |
| *traqueteo* | = rattle, rattling, clatter, clattering; jolting, jerking. |
| †*visiteo* | = (never-ending) paying of visits or calling on people; (tedious) round of one 'at-home' after another. |
| *zarandeo* | = shake-up, shaking up. |

---

[1] Especially common in the expressions *andarse con rodeos* = to beat about the bush, and *sin rodeos ni ambages* = without beating about the bush.

[2] Cf. *abucheo*, above.

[3] Cf. *traqueteo*, below.

[4] < *tasca* = pub, eating-house.

[5] For similar colloquial pejorative sense cf. use of the word *marcha* in the phrase *dar la marcha a*, to lead a (merry) dance, give the run-around to.

[6] For somewhat similar sense cf. the term *tejemaneje*. Cf. also *politiqueo*, *politiquería*.

... dadas las despedidas, con sus lágrimas y *besuqueos* correspondientes, marido y mujer se fueron a la estación.

(PÉREZ GALDÓS, Fortunata y Jacinta, I, p. 103)

... after everyone had said goodbye, with the concomitant weeping and sloppy kissing, husband and wife went off to the station.

... los árboles hicieron lo posible ... para ahogar entre sus hojas el *charloteo* de los huéspedes alados ....

(FERNÁNDEZ FLÓREZ, El Bosque Animado, p. 17)

... the trees did everything possible ... to stifle the chattering of their winged guests in their leaves ....

El motivo de la ruina fue la mala conducta de la esposa de Nicolás Rubín, mujer desarreglada y escandalosa, que ... dio mucho que hablar por sus *devaneos* y trapisondas.

(PÉREZ GALDÓS, Fortunata y Jacinta, II, p. 7)

The reason for the collapse was the disgraceful behaviour of Nicholas Rubin's wife, an improvident and shocking woman who ... gave rise to a great deal of talk because of her flirtatious carryings-on and mischievous scheming.

— ¿No sabes a qué función es la que vais?
— ¡Ay, padre! ¿Qué me pregunta tanto? A cualquier cine iremos, ¿qué más dará? ¿Cómo quiere que lo sepa desde ahora? — cambió el tono — No, si de algo me viene usted como queriendo enterarse, con tanto *pregunteo*.

(SÁNCHEZ FERLOSIO, El Jarama, p. 116)

"Don't you know what programme you're going to see?"
"Oh, father! Why do you question me so much? We'll be going to any cinema that's to hand. What difference does it make? How do

you expect me to know now?" Then she altered her tone of voice. "But you've been trying to find something out from me with all this questioning. You're after something."

La monotonía de su labor, el *visiteo* de siempre para comprar o vender, y el teléfono, con sus consabidos avisos y peticiones *negocieriles*,\* acabaron llenándole de un desplacer hondo.

(ZUNZUNEGUI, *¡Ay, Estos Hijos!* p. 152)

The monotony of his work, the same old round of calls time after time for buying or selling, and the telephone, with its only too familiar business messages and requests, eventually filled him with a profound loathing.

### 3. -ERÍA

*-ería NOUN — FEMININE*

†*alcahuetería* = pimping, procuring, acting as go-between.
†*aldeanería*[1] = village narrowness, narrow-mindedness, meanness or pettiness; mob of villagers.

[1] It will be observed that the quotation given to illustrate this word is taken from Unamuno, a writer in whose work one finds a particularly marked and ubiquitous tendency to use pejorative terms in *-ería*, not a few of them coined by Don Miguel himself—in this, as in other matters, rarely diffident. Two further examples: ... la psicología es una especie de combinación de la fisiología y la sociología, ya que la conciencia humana es un producto de la acción de la sociedad humana sobre el organismo animal humano. Y basta de *filosoferías*. (i.e. And that will be enough of philosophical hair-splitting.) (*De Vuelta* in *Obras Completas X*, p. 104); ... las peor escritas de nuestras publicaciones periódicas son las de matiz reaccionario .... Transpiran una insoportable *pedantería*, una infecunda afectación de pureza, un necio cuidado en la elección de vocablos. Son las que más aborrecen del galicismo, las que más descienden a *cuestioncillas de propiedad de lenguaje, a gramatiquerías y tiquismiquis lingüísticos* ... (i.e. pedantry ... petty issues of correctness of language, grammatical hair-splitting and linguistic fiddle-faddle ....)(*La Prensa y el Lenguaje* in *Obras Completas VI*, pp. 468, 469). In the case of these words, as in that of many others in *-ería*, and indeed in Spanish generally, a plural idea is usually conveyed by a grammatical plural, e.g. *¡nada de blandenguerías!* = [let's have] no soft stuff! (i.e. no manifestations of a soft attitude). In this connexion it is noteworthy that a singular is often best rendered by the formula "piece of", e.g. *una aldeanería* = a piece of village narrow-mindedness.

| | |
|---|---|
| *bellaquería* | — vide *granujería*, below. |
| *blandenguería*[1] | = softness, soft talk or behaviour, soft stuff, feebleness, over-indulgence. |
| *bribonería* | — vide *granujería*, below. |
| *brujería* } *hechicería* | = witchcraft, black magic, spell-casting. |
| *cabezonería*[2] | = pig-headedness, stubbornness or self-willedness. |
| *cicatería*[3] *roñería* *roñosería* *tacañería* | = stinginess, tight-fistedness. |
| *comadrería*[4] | = gossip, tittle-tattle; mob of gossiping women. |
| *correría(s)*[5] | = gallivanting about, gadding about. |
| † *cursilería*[6] | = silly or foolish affectation or snobbery, fatuous |

[1] Cf. *blandura* — similar sense.

[2] Cf. *cabezonada* — similar sense.

Other terms of like sense and tone are *terquedad, testarudez* and *tozudez*. Cf. the more formal *obstinación* = obstinacy.

[3] Cf. *roñosidad* — similar sense and tone.

Cf. the less colloquial *mezquindad* = meanness.

[4] Cf. *chismería*, below.

[5] In this sense, almost exclusively used in plural. The singular form does not have the same popular and pejorative tone and usually means "trip, excursion" or "raid, foray".

Cf. *andanza(s)* — similar sense.

[6] In connexion with this difficult word it is of interest to note the following comments of Ortega y Gasset (*Intimidades* in *El Espectador VII*, p. 169):

"Si se quiere penetrar en los secretos de un país conviene fijarse en las palabras de su idioma que no se pueden traducir, sobre todo cuando significan modos de ser. La razón es perogrullesca. Si falta el equivalente en el lenguaje de otros pueblos es que en ellos la realidad significada no existe o existe insólitamente. En cambio, la existencia de un vocablo intraducible revela que cierta clase de hechos forma en aquella sociedad compacta masa y se impone a la mente exigiendo una denominación. Así, la palabra española *cursi* no puede verterse en ninguna de otro idioma. El hecho que enuncia es — en rigor, fue — exclusivamente español. Si se analizase, lupa en mano, el significado de *cursi* se vería en él concentrada toda la historia española de 1850 a 1900. La *cursilería* como endemia sólo puede producirse en un pueblo anormalmente pobre que se ve obligado a vivir en la atmósfera del siglo XIX europeo, en plena democracia y capitalismo. La *cursilería* es una misma cosa con la carencia de una

putting it on, fatuous pretentiousness; vulgar ostentation, ostentatious bad taste; foolish or sloppy sentimentality; silly nonsense or rubbish, corny stuff, romantic guff; mob of affected, fatuous people.

†chabacanería[1] = commonness, vulgarity, bad taste; mob of common people.

chapucería = bungle, botch, mess, slipshod work.

†chinchorrería[2] = nagging or keeping on (at someone); needling, digging or getting on (at someone).

†chinería = Chinese or Chinese-type stuff; mob of Chinese or Chinks.

chiquillería[3] = mob of children, kids or brats.

chismería[4] = gossip.

chulería[5] ⎫
flamenquería ⎭ = obstreperous, bellicose or pugnacious behaviour or talk, truculence, swaggering aggressiveness, aggressive throwing or chucking one's weight

---

fuerte burguesía, fuerte moral y económicamente. Ahora bien, esa ausencia es el factor decisivo de la historia de España en la última centuria."

This is the famous phenomenon otherwise variously known as *el querer y no poder, el querer sin poder, el quiero y no puedo*. However, contemporary usage lends to *cursilería* a semantic range far beyond this basic original sense.

Cf. *cursilada* — similar sense.

[1] Cf. *ordinariez* — similar sense.

Cf. *vulgaridad, adocenamiento* = commonplaceness, ordinariness, humdrumness, humdrum nature.

Cf. *ramplonería*, below.

[2] Cf. *puñetería*, below.

[3] Cf. *chiquillada*, under -*ada*.

Cf. *pequeñería*, below.

Common in the south of Spain is the variant *chiquillerío*, as are others, such as *palabrerío* for *palabrería* and *pobrerío* for *pobrería* (see below). Similar doublets exist within Standard Castilian, e.g. *griterío/gritería, vocerío/vocería* (see below). In a few instances only the masculine form is found, as in *forasterío* = crowd or mob of strangers or visitors, *mujerío* = crowd or mob of females.

[4] Cf. *chismorreo*, under -*eo*.

[5] Cf. *chulada, flamencada* — similar sense.

Cf. *matonería*, below.

318

about, "do-you-want-a-fight?" or "for-two-pins-
I'd-knock-your-block-off" attitude.

*filosofería*[1]    = philosophical hair-splitting or fiddle-faddle.

*flamenquería*    — vide *chulería*, above.

*gandulería*  
*holgazanería*    }= loafing (around), idling (about).

*gazmoñería*[2]  
*mojigatería*    } = prudery, prudishness, Grundyism.  
*ñoñería*

*gitanería*    = gypsy behaviour, slyness or wheedling; typical gypsy stuff; shambles; mob of gypsies.

*gramatiquería*[3]    = grammatical hair-splitting or fiddle-faddle.

*granujería*[4]  
*pillería*    }= rascally piece of mischief, mischievous lark or ploy; mob of rascals, blighters or urchins.

*gritería*[5]    = shouting, outcry, uproar.

*grosería*    = coarseness; rudeness.

*hechicería*    — vide *brujería*, above.

*holgazanería*    — vide *gandulería*, above.

*ladronería*[6]    = stealing, pinching.

*majadería*    = damned foolishness or foolery, stupidity.

*mangonería*[7]    = interfering, meddling, having a finger in the pie or in every pie, sticking one's nose or oar in; bossing or running the show.

*marinería*    = mob of sailors or ratings.

*matonería*[8]    = bullying; aggressive throwing one's weight about.

*melindrería*  
*remilgosería*    }= mincing fastidiousness, finickiness or fussiness; squeamishness.

[1] See note to *aldeanería*, above.

[2] Cf. the more academic *pudibundez*.

[3] See note to *aldeanería*, above. Cf. *gramaticalismo* and *filologiquería*.

[4] Cf., above and below, the following terms of similar meaning but rather archaic tone: *bellaquería*, *bribonería*, *truhanería*, *tunantería* = rascality, roguery.

[5] See note to *chiquillería*, above.

[6] Cf. *latrocinio* = theft, thieving, i.e. same sense but more academic register.

[7] Cf. *mangoneo* — similar sense.

[8] Cf. *chulería*, above.

| | |
|---|---|
| *milagrería* | = so-called or would-be miracles or wonders, miracle mummery; fantastic tales. |
| †*mistiquería* | = mystical or sanctimonious blah, religious mumbo-jumbo. |
| *mojigatería* | — vide *gazmoñería*, above. |
| *nadería*[1] | = thing of no account, mere trifle. |
| *ñoñería* | — vide *gazmoñería*, above. |
| *novelería*[2] | = new things or fads; craze for anything new or different, craze for the latest novelty; rubbish read in trashy·novels; craze for trashy novels. |
| †*palabrería*[3] | = empty or idle words or talk, just so much talk or hot air, drivel, twaddle, verbiage. |
| *patanería* ⎫<br>*zoquetería* ⎭ | = cloddishness, boorishness, churlishness, behaviour of a country bumpkin, yokel or hick; mob of clods. |
| *patosería*[4] | = clumsiness, ham-fistedness; gaucheness; tactlessness. |
| *patriotería* | = unbridled or fanatical patriotic sentiment, travesty of patriotism, jingoism. |
| *pelmacería* | = tediousness; bore, pain-in-the-neck, drag. |
| *pequeñería* | = mere trifle; mob of children, kids or brats. |
| *perrería* | = dirty or filthy trick; pack of dogs; mob of scum. |
| *pillería* | — vide *granujería*, above. |
| †*pobretería*[5] | = poverty-stricken condition; mere pittance; mob of beggars. |
| †*politiquería*[6] | = political jobbery, scheming or jiggery-pokery; meddling or dabbling in politics; political talk or chatter. |

[1] Another similar term is *fruslería*.
  Cf. *pequeñería*, below.
[2] Another term of similar meaning (first two senses) is *esnobismo*.
[3] Cf. *palabreo* — similar sense.
  Cf. *verborrea* — similar sense.
[4] Cf. *torpeza* — similar sense, but more academic register.
[5] Cf. *miseria* — similar senses (one and two), but more academic register.
[6] Cf. *politiqueo* — similar senses (one and two).

| | |
|---|---|
| *pordiosería*[1] | = begging; cadging. |
| †*porquería*[2] | = filth, filthy object, rubbish or muck, revolting or disgusting stuff or mess; trash. |
| *puñetería*[3] | = damned awkwardness, cantankerousness, cussedness, or nastiness, bloody-mindedness, bitchiness. |
| *putería* | = whoring; whore-house set-up. |
| *ramplonería*[4] | = coarse or bad taste mediocrity or banality, dull, dreary, vapid, shallow or uninspiring mediocrity or banality, stodgy or trite humdrumness. |
| *remilgosería* | — vide *melindrería*, above. |
| *romantiquería* | = sloppy romanticism, romantic nonsense, drivel or guff. |
| *roñería* *roñosería* | — vide *cicatería*, above. |
| *santurronería* | = sanctimoniousness. |

[1] Cf. *pordioseo* — similar sense.

[2] Similar terms are *cerdez* and *asquerosidad*.

[3] Cf. *chinchorrería*, above.

[4] A difficult word the sense of which, although partaking to some extent of that of *chabacanería* = commonness, vulgarity, bad taste, is nevertheless much more akin to that of *vulgaridad* = commonplaceness, ordinariness, and of *trivilidad* = triteness, hackneyed nature or expression. Some light is thrown on the term by the following quotations from Unamuno: Las grandes ciudades son fundamentalmente *democráticas*, y debo confesar que siento un invencible recelo platónico hacia las democracias. La cultura se difunde y esparce en las grandes ciudades, pero *se ramploniza*. Las gentes dejan la lectura sosegada del libro por asistir al teatro, esta escuela de *vulgaridad*. Sienten la necesidad de estar juntos; les azuza el instinto *rebañego*; tienen que verse unos a otros (i.e. democratic, plebeian ... becomes coarse, dreary and mediocre ... commonplace ordinariness ... herd, of the common herd, sheep-like, unthinking.) (*Por Tierras de Portugal y de España*, p. 101); ... cuando oigáis hablar de pesimismo y optimismo, advertid que es la *ramplona frivolidad*, que es la *frívola ramplonería* que os está cercando para devoraros el alma. Eso de pesimismo y optimismo es el lenguaje de la más *hojarascosa tontería*. ... La tontería no es más que *superficialidad* ... la tontería no es más que *frases hechas, lugares comunes* (i.e. coarse, stick-in-the-mud mindlessness ... mindless, vapid mediocrity ... empty-headed stupidity ... shallowness ... set phrases or clichés, banalities.) (*Paisajes del Alma*, p. 71.)

Another word to which *ramplonería* is in some respects akin is *plebeyez*.

| | | |
|---|---|---|
| *sensiblería*[1] | = | sloppy or maudlin sentimentality, sentimental nonsense, drivel or guff. |
| *sinvergüencería* | = | shameless or bare-faced behaviour, barefaced impudence. |
| *sosería*[2] | = | insipidness, vapidness, flatness, dullness. |
| *tacañería* | — | vide *cicatería*, above. |
| *tontería*[3] | = | foolishness, stupidity; nonsense, drivel, rubbish, rot, tripe. |
| *tragonería* | = | hogging, stuffing food. |
| *trapacería* | = | tricking, hoodwinking, diddling, taking for a ride. |
| *truhanería* | — | vide *granujería*, above. |
| *tunantería* | — | vide *granujería*, above. |
| *vocería*[4] | = | yelling, clamour, uproar. |
| *zoquetería* | — | vide *patanería*, above. |

### -ería EXAMPLES FROM LITERATURE

Por muchas ínfulas que se dé el que Góngora llamó Don Dinero, la verdad es que no pasa de ser un alcahuete. De éxito universal, eso sí, el más solicitado de todos los tiempos, no hay duda. Pero celestino, al fin y al cabo, continuo trajinero que no se da punto de reposo, yendo de las manos de los viejos verdes a las de las doncellitas, del deseo a lo deseado, del hombre a la cosa. A esto, si no me engaño, es a lo que llaman los economistas circulación monetaria. ¡Pura *alcahuetería*!

(SALINAS, *Ensayos de Literatura Hispánica*, p. 84)

However cocky he who was called by Góngora Master Moneybags may get, the fact remains that he reaches no higher status than that of common pimp. A universally successful one, it's true, undoubtedly the most sought after in every period. But, when all is

---

[1] Cf. *sentimentalismo* — similar sense, but more academic register.

[2] Note variant *sosez* and parallel term *insulsez*. Another similar expression, used mainly in Andalusia, is *esaborería* (cf. *esaborío* for *desaborido*).

[3] Cf. *tontada*, under -ada.

[4] See note to *chiquillería*, above.

said and done, a common go-between, a constant, never-resting
bustler, passing from the hands of "dirty old men" to those of young
maidens, from desire to that which is desired, from man to object.
This, unless I am mistaken, is what is called by economists monetary
circulation. It is sheer, unadulterated pimpery!

— En la aldea — decía — se entontece, se embrutece y se empobrece
uno. Y añadía:
— Civilización es lo contrario de ruralización; ¡aldeanerías no!,
que no hice que fueras al Colegio para que te pudras luego aquí,
entre estos zafios patanes.

. . .

— Conque, ¿tu hermano Lázaro — me decía Don Manuel — se
empeña en que leas? Pues lee, hija mía . . . . Vale más que leas que no
el que te alimentes de chismes y comadrerías del pueblo.

(UNAMUNO, San Manuel Bueno, pp. 38–39)

"In a village," he would say, "you become stupid, besotted and
spiritually impoverished."
And he would add: "Civilization is the opposite of ruralization;
I won't have village meanness, pettiness and narrowness; I didn't
see that you went to secondary school for you to rot away afterwards here, among these uncouth clods."

. . .

"So," said Don Manuel, "your brother Lazarus insists on your doing
some reading? Why, then, my dear child, do some reading . . . . It's
better for you to read than to feed on the village gossip and tittle-
tattle."

. . . todo en el mundo era despreciable, excepto los teatros . . . . La
astronomía, la química, la filosofía, . . . cursilerías propias para ser
cultivadas por los hombres inferiores . . . .

(PALACIO VALDÉS, La Hermana San Sulpicio, p. 10)

. . . everything in the world was contemptible, except theatres . . . .
Astronomy, chemistry, philosophy, . . . affected, pretentious blah,
suitable for the attention of the second-rate . . ..

. . . nunca se desnaturalizan para hacerse más bellas, delicadas y
decentes, sino para estropearse y percudirse al contacto de la ordinariez y la *chabacanería*.

(ALARCÓN, *El Sombrero de Tres Picos*, p. 25)

. . . they never lose their original form to become more beautiful,
refined and decorous, but to be spoilt and sullied by contact with
commonness and vulgarity.

Dirigía la casa despóticamente con una mezcla de *chinchorrería* y de
abandono, de despotismo y de arbitrariedad, que a Andrés le sacaba
de quicio.

(BAROJA, *El Arbol de la Ciencia*, p. 451)

He ruled the household despotically, with a mixture of needling
and neglect, despotism and arbitrariness which drove Andrew wild.

Los chinos . . . decidieron desembarcar . . .. Salían de la bodega en
grupos de treinta, con su hatillo, entraban en la ballenera, y los
llevábamos hasta un arenal de la playa, y cuando había una braza de
fondo o algo menos, echábamos toda la *chinería* al agua.

(BAROJA, *Las Inquietudes de Shanti Andía*, p. 213)

The Chinese . . . decided to go ashore . . .. They left the hold in
groups of thirty, with their little bundles of possessions, and got into
the long boat one group at a time, and we took them to a stretch of
sand on the beach, and each time, when there was a fathom or rather
less of water, we chucked all the mob of Chinks into the sea.

324

Podría suceder muy bien que, cuando todo iba como una seda, saliese con ciertas *mistiquerías* propias de su oficio, sacando el Cristo de debajo de la sotana y alborotando la casa.

(PÉREZ GALDÓS, *Fortunata y Jacinta*, II, p. 153)


It could very well happen that, now everything was going smoothly, he would come out with a load of mystical, sanctimonious blah, the sort of thing you might expect from one of his calling; that he would trot out Religion with a capital R from under his cassock and set the household in a turmoil.


CARLOS. — . . . tu influencia es destructora. Si no te vas, esta casa se hundirá. ¡Pero antes que eso ocurra, tú te habrás ido!
IGNACIO. — *Palabrería*. No pienso marcharme, naturalmente . . ..
CARLOS. — Es el interés del Centro el que me mueve a hablarte.
IGNACIO. — Más *palabrería*. ¡Qué aficionado eres a los tópicos!

(BUERO VALLEJO, *En la Ardiente Oscuridad*, p. 51)


CARLOS. — . . . yours is a destructive influence. Unless you leave, the Centre is going to fold up. But before that happens, you'll have gone!
IGNACIO. — That's a lot of hot air. Of course I've no intention of leaving . . ..
CARLOS. — I'm driven to speak to you for the good of the Centre.
IGNACIO. — More hot air. How keen you are on clichés!


— . . . me ha dicho que aquí todo es *pobretería* . . . que la gran mayoría de los que pasan por ricos y calaveras, no son más que unos cursis . . ..

(PERÉZ GALDÓS, *La de Bringas*, p. 253)


" . . . he's told me that everything here is in a poverty-stricken state . . . that the great majority of those who pass for wealthy men and mad-caps are just putting it on . . ..

[Another example of this word, used in a different sense:

... y despidiéndose al fin de la *pobretería* con un sermoncillo gangoso ... se metío en la iglesia.

(PÉREZ GALDÓS, Misericordia, p. 24)

... and finally taking his leave of the mob of beggars with a brief little homily delivered in a twangy tone of voice ... he slipped into the church.]

Sus irrisorias *politiquerías* locales, su lid contra los caciques adversarios, [todo esto] tiene para él la grandeza de la lucha de Borgia por la conquista de Italia.

(SORDO, Baroja y su Mundo, p. 151)

His ludicrous dabbling in local politics, his fight against the opposing political bosses, [all this] is for him something as grand as Borgia's struggle for the conquest of Italy.

[Another example.

— Te ... ruego que te abstengas de minarme el terreno con tus *politiquerías*. ¡En eso no te metas!

(BUERO VALLEJO, Un Soñador para un Pueblo, p. 220)

"I beg you to refrain from undermining my position with your scheming in politics. Do not interfere in such matters!"]

— Es una película escandalosa. Se pasan mil metros besuqueándose . . .. Yo, con esas *porquerías*, soy inflexible. Vamos a hacer una protesta oficial . . ..

(CALVO-SOTELO, La Muralla, p. 104)

"It's a scandalous picture. They spend a thousand yards [of film] slobbering over each other . . .. With that sort of revolting stuff I am quite uncompromising. We are going to make an official protest . . .."

## *-esco* ADJECTIVE

| | | |
|---|---|---|
| *abogadesco* | — vide *abogadil*, under *-il*. | |

| | |
|---|---|
| †*andantesco*[1] ⎫<br>*caballeresco* ⎪<br>*hidalguesco* ⎬<br>*quijotesco* ⎭ | = of or typical of a knight-errant, knights-errant or knight-errantry; knight-errant-like; of or typical of a nobleman; foolishly or ludicrously noble or gallant; that is or was an apology for or travesty of a knight-errant or nobleman; quixotic, out of touch with reality. |
| *bandoleresco* | = of or typical of bandits or brigands; bandit-like, brigand-style; that is an apology for or travesty of a bandit or brigand. |
| *bradominesco*[2] ⎫<br>†*donjuanesco* ⎬<br>†*tenoriesco* ⎭ | = of or typical of the Marqués de Bradomín; Don Juan- or Tenorio-like, Don Juanish, Tenorioish, to be expected of a Don Juan or Tenorio; philandering, outrageous; wild, flamboyant. |

---

[1] Cf. *caballeril*, under *-il*.

Cf. *sanchesco, sanchopancesco*, below.

In connexion with these forms it is interesting to note that Pedro Salinas, when he refers, in an essay on Don Quixote, to the matter of Sancho Panza and the *pollinos*, uses a form in *-esco* in order to highlight the ludicrous inappropriateness of the subject of asses to the particular situation in question— the delivery of a grand missive of love to Dulcinea: El asunto *pollinesco* se halla en el opuesto polo del amoroso, y nadie se atrevería a pensar que pueden tener punto de contacto. Nadie, menos Cervantes. Porque él quiere precisamente eso, y para eso escribe la novela: para jugar con fuegos, para acercar Dulcineas a borricos y encontrarse con los lampos insólitos que brotan de tales tangencias. (*Ensayos de Literatura Hispánica*, pp. 118–119.)

[2] It is significant that when the Marqués de Bradomín is in question the adjectival form invariably chosen to refer to his creator is *valleinclanesco*, and that Zorrilla's Don Juan, described by Ortega as *un mascarón de proa, un figurón de feria, pródigo en ademanes chulescos y petulantes*, should be referred to as *el Don Juan zorrillesco*.

For similar forms referring to literary characters in some respects akin to Don Juan, see *cyranesco* and *tartarinesco*, below.

| | |
|---|---|
| *brujesco*[1] <br> *hechiceresco* | — vide *brujeril*, *hechiceril*, under *-il*. |
| *bufonesco*[2] | = of or typical of a buffoon or buffoons, or of a clown or clowns; buffoon-like, clownish. |
| *burlesco*[3] | = burlesque, comic; mocking, jibing. |
| *caballeresco* | — vide *andantesco*, above. |
| *cabronesco*[4] | = of or typical of a rotten or filthy swine or bugger; beastly, foul. |
| *canallesco* | = of or typical of scum or of a cad, rotter or heel; caddish; rotten, sunk in filth. |
| *cancilleresco*[5] | = terribly or absurdly ceremonious, excruciatingly or ridiculously formal, painfully or ludicrously courteous. |

[1] In connexion with these words it is interesting to observe how the subject of witchcraft has triggered off, in the passage that follows, the use of a whole series of forms in *-esco*:

... [Pardo Bazán] escribe una novela corta, muy curiosa, de maleficios y *hechicerías*.★ Se titula "Belcebú" y trata de un caso de embrujamiento y de prácticas *brujeriles*★ ... la Pardo es en todo precursora, incluso en el esperpentismo *valleinclanesco*, hecho de esguinces y de *caricaturescas* muecas .... La veta *quevedesca* ... : "... una sombra *grotesca* avanzó penosamente: era una vieja apoyada en dos muletas ... pronto la hoguera sanjuanera crepitó. Entonces se vio una cosa ridícula y espantable: los vestiglos se desnudaron a prisa de sus andrajos, y, cogiéndose de las manos, parodiaron, en ronda empecatada y *bufonesca*, el ancestral baile aldeano ... un cuadro del Bosco, una comedia satánica, juego de bufones *sardescos* que quieren distraer el aburrimiento del diablo ...." ... se agitan gentecillas *grotescas* y monstruosos engendros. Ella, que es tan aficionada al Carnaval, describe con pincel *solanesco* ... la comitiva desastrada .... (Bravo-Villasante, *Vida y Obra de Emilia Pardo Bazán*, p. 283.)

[2] Cf. *chaplinesco* and *fantochesco*, below.

[3] Cf. *caricaturesco* and *sainetesco*, below.

[4] A highly vulgar expression. Cf. the somewhat similar, though far less coarse, *canallesco*, below.

[5] Cf. *versallesco*, below.

For other terms to a greater or lesser degree akin cf. *caballeresco*, above, and *dieciochesco* and *madrigalesco*, below.

Cf. the much less colourful expressions *ceremonioso etiquetero, formalista*, *formulista, formulario* and *protocolario*.

| | | |
|---|---|---|
| *caricaturesco* | = | of or typical of caricature; caricaturish, caricature-like; that is or was a parody, travesty or distortion. |
| †*carnavalesco*[1] | = | of or typical of Carnaval; carnival-like; ridiculous and outlandish, comic-opera-ish, Gilbert and Sullivanish. |
| *celestinesco*[2] | = | of or typical of Celestina, or of a Celestina, or of a go-between or go-betweens; Celestina-like; bawdy. |
| *cervantesco*[3] | = | of or typical of Cervantes; Cervantes-like; far-fetched, fantastic. |
| *cristianesco*[4] | = | of or typical of a Christian or Christians; Christian-like; to be expected from a Christian or Christians. |
| †*cuartelesco*[5] | = | of or typical of the barrack-room; barrack-room-like; coarse; severe. |
| †*curialesco*[6] | = | of or to do with the courts or law; legalistic. |
| †*cyranesco* | = | of or typical of Cyrano de Bergerac or of a Cyrano de Bergerac type; Cyrano de Bergerac-like; swashbuckling and flamboyant. |
| *chalanesco*[7] | = | of or typical of a horse-dealer; artful, crafty, sly. |
| *chaplinesco* | = | of or typical of Charlie Chaplin; Charlie Chaplin-like; clownish, slap-stick, hammy. |
| *charlatanesco* | = | of or typical of a charlatan, quack, humbug or loud-mouth. |

[1] Frequently more or less synonymous with such terms as *estrafalario, estrambótico, extravagante.*

Cf. *sainetesco,* below.

[2] Cf. *chulesco* and *fulanesco,* below.

[3] Cf. the neutral forms *cervantino* and *çervántico.*

[4] Cf. the neutral *cristiano.*

[5] Similar in semantic content is the form *cuartelero.*

[6] Cf. *abogadesco,* above.

[7] For figurative sense cf. *sacristanesco,* below.

| | |
|---|---|
| *chinesco*[1] | = Chinese-looking; Chinese-like, Chinese-style; mock-Chinese; enigmatic. |
| *chulesco*[2] | = of or typical of a pimp; pimp-like; bragging, bullying, bellicose, pugnacious, truculent, given to throwing one's weight about, looking for fights. |
| *churrigueresco* | = Churrigueresque; excessively ornate, terribly over-done. |
| *dantesco*[3] | = of or typical of Dante; Dante-like; inferno-ish, hell-like; grotesque, nightmarish, grim. |
| *diablesco*[4] | = of or typical of the Devil; devilish; impish, hobgoblin-like, gremlin-like, mischievous. |
| †*dieciochesco*[5] | = of or typical of the eighteenth century; eighteenth-centuryish; old-worldly, genteel and gracious, minuet-like, minuettish; belonging to the past, outmoded. |
| †*donjuanesco* | — vide *bradominesco*, above. |
| *dueñesco*[6] | = duenna-like; matronly. |
| *estudiantesco* | — vide *estudiantil*, under -*il*. |

[1] Cf. the literal and neutral *chino*.

Cf. *tudesco* and *turquesco*, below.

[2] A variant of *chulo*.

Cf. *matonesco*, below.

Somewhat surprisingly, the terms *belicoso* and *pugnaz* are considerably more academic in register and limited in use than the English "bellicose" and "pugnacious".

A term similar in sense to *chulesco*, but considerably more refined in tone is *petulante* = arrogant, truculent. For Spanish *truculento*, see *granguiñolesco*, below.

[3] For other words of sense to a greater or lesser extent allied with that of *dantesco*, see *goyesco*, *quevedesco*, *solanesco*, *valleinclanesco*, *zolesco*, *granguiñolesco*, *grotesco*, and *pesadillesco*.

[4] The literal sense attaches rather to *diabólico*.

[5] Cf. *cancilleresco*, above, and *versallesco*, below.

It is worthy of note that the allied term *decimonónico* is much used with a figurative sense similar to the last-given here, and frequently equates with the pejoratively tinged "Victorian" in English.

[6] Cf. *matronil*, under -*il*.

It is interesting to observe that Cervantes speaks of *caterva dueñesca* (*Quijote*, II, chap. XLVIII) in much the same tone as that attaching to John Knox's *Monstrous Regiment of Women*.

| | |
|---|---|
| *fantochesco*[1] | = of or typical of a puppet; puppet-like; clownish. |
| *folletinesco*[2] | = melodramatic, penny-dreadfulish. |
| *frailesco*[3] | = of or typical of a friar or monk; monkish; priestlike, clerical. |
| *fulanesco* | = of or typical of a whore or whores; whorish, tartish; bawdy. |
| *fulleresco*[4] | = of or typical of a card-sharper or sharpers, or of a trickster or tricksters, or of a crook or crooks; crooked. |
| *funambulesco* | = of or typical of a tight-rope walker or tight-rope walkers; fantastic, crazy, wild. |
| †*gatesco*[5] | = of or typical of a cat or cats; cat-like. |
| *gauchesco* | = of or typical of the Gaucho; Gaucho-like, Gaucho-style; cowboy-fashion. |
| *gauguinesco* | = of or typical of Gauguin; Gauguin-like, Gauguin-style; unconventional; exotic. |
| *gigantesco*[6] | = giant-like; gigantic, colossal, huge, outsize. |
| *gitanesco*[7] | = of or typical of a gypsy or gypsies; dirty, messy; chaotic, in a state of shambles, higgledy-piggledy, any-old-how. |

[1] Cf. *guiñolesco*, below.

[2] Cf. *granguiñolesco*, below.

[3] See *antifrailesco*, under Examples from Literature.

[4] Cf. *hampesco*, *picaresco* and *truhanesco*, below.

[5] The quotations given under Examples from Literature provide a good illustration of the fact that, despite the strong general tendency, a form in -*esco* may not necessarily or always be pejorative in implication, and that even the jocular element may, on occasion, be tenuous. It is interesting in this connexion to draw a contrast between, on the one hand, *gatesco*—usually but not invariably pejorative or jocular—with, on the other, *gatuno* and *felino*—almost always but, again, not unexceptionally neutral.

[6] *gigantesco* has a strong tendency to imply, beyond the basic concept "of tremendous size", the specifically pejorative concept "of excessive size". It is significant that in the phrase *a pasos agigantados* = with huge strides, or at a terrific pace, where the implication is one of magnificent strides or superb pace, the -*esco* form is not used.

An interesting variant for *gigantesco*, where food is involved, is *pantagruélico*, i.e. gargantuan.

[7] Cf. the neutral *gitano*.

| | |
|---|---|
| *goyesco* | = of or typical of Goya; Goyaesque, Goya-like; grotesque, nightmarish. |
| *gramaticalesco* | = of or typical of grammatical hair-splitting or fiddle-faddle. |
| †*granguiñolesco*[1] | = blood-and-thunderish, Frankenstein-like, Boris Karloff-style, horror-style, gruesome, ghoulish, grisly. |
| *grotesco*[2] | = grotesque. |
| *guiñolesco* | = of or typical of Guignol, or of Punch and Judy, Punch and Judyish. |
| *hampesco*[3] | = of or typical of the underworld; of rogues, crooks and vagabonds. |
| *hechiceresco* | — vide *brujesco*, above. |
| *hidalguesco* | — vide *andantesco*, above. |
| *hospitalesco* | = of or typical of a hospital or hospitals; hospital-like. |
| *juglaresco* | = of or typical of a minstrel or of strolling players. |
| *ladronesco* | = of or typical of a thief or thieves; thievish. |
| *liberalesco*[4] | = flamboyantly or outrageously liberal. |
| *libresco* | = book, of books; bookish; book-wormish; unreal, divorced from reality. |
| *madrigalesco* | = of madrigals, madrigalian; madrigal-like; genteel, mincing, lah-de-dah. |
| *marinesco* | = of or typical of a sailor or sailors; sailor-like. |
| †*matonesco*[5] | = of or typical of a bully or bullies; to be expected from a bully or tough. |

[1] Cf. the much less colourful but semantically akin *melodramático, truculento, terrorífico, horripilante, espeluznante.*

Cf. *guiñolesco*, below.

[2] Etymologically the sense is "grotto-, cave- or cavern-like".

[3] Cf. *picaresco* and *truhanesco*, below.

[4] Cf. the neutral *liberal.*

[5] For illustration of use see under *gusanil* in Section -*il* (Examples from Literature).

| †*matrimoñesco*[1] | = of or typical of matrimony, marriage, married life or married people; matrimonial; to do with dreary domesticity. |
|---|---|
| *medievalesco*[2] | = of or typical of the Middle Ages, Mediaeval; Mediaevalish, Mediaeval-like, Mediaeval-style; ancient, antiquated. |
| *minifaldesco*[3] | = of or typical of the mini-skirt; mini-skirted; swinging, switched-on. |
| *momiesco* | = of or typical of mummies; mummy-like; death-like, deathly-looking. |
| †*niagaresco* | = of or typical of Niagara; Niagara-like; torrential. |
| *notariesco*[4] | = of or typical of a notary or notaries; legalistic. |
| *novelesco*[5] | = of or typical of the novel or novels; novelish, novel-like; fantastic, far-fetched, unreal, divorced from reality. |
| *oficinesco*[6] | = of or typical of offices; office-like; routine, dull, dreary. |
| *oropelesco*[7] | = of or typical of tinsel; tinselly; flashy; tawdry, trashy. |
| *pasquinesco* | = of or typical of a lampoon or lampoons; lampoon-ish; satirical. |
| *pedantesco*[8] | = ludicrously or trivially pedantic. |
| *perogrullesco*[9] | = platitudinous. |
| *pesadillesco* | = nightmarish. |

[1] Cf. the neutral *matrimonial*.

[2] Cf. the neutral *medieval*.

[3] E.g. *el ambiente novedoso del minifaldesco Londres de hoy* = the trendy atmosphere of present-day swinging London.

Also *minifaldero*.

[4] Cf. *abogadesco*, above.

[5] Cf. *libresco*, above, and *romancesco*, below.

[6] Cf. *rutinesco*, below.

[7] For other words expressing concepts closely akin to those contained in *oropelesco* cf. *llamativo*, *chillón* = gaudy, flashy, showy, and *de relumbrón* = dazzling, glaring, flashy, showy, tawdry.

[8] Cf. the basic *pedante*, which equates, simply, with "pedantic".

[9] Cf. the closely allied concepts conveyed by *trivial*, *trillado* = trite, hackneyed.

| | |
|---|---|
| *picaresco* ⎫<br>*rufianesco* ⎬<br>*truhanesco* ⎭ | = picaresque, roguish, scoundrelly, of knaves, cheats and crooks. |
| *pintoresco*[1] | = picturesque; colourful; fanciful, crazy, wild. |
| *piratesco* | = of or typical of a pirate or pirates; piratish, pirate-like; looking ludicrously pirate-like, looking like an apology for or travesty of a pirate. |
| †*porcelanesco* | = of or typical of porcelain or china; porcelain- or china-like; delicate, fragile. |
| *principesco* | = princely; extremely lavish, sumptuous or magnificent; excessively lavish, sumptuous or magnificent. |
| *pulpesco*[2] | = of or typical of the octopus; octopus-like. |
| *quevedesco*[3] | = of or typical of Quevedo; Quevedo-like; grotesque, nightmarish; satirical. |
| *quijotesco* | — vide *andantesco*, above. |
| *ratonesco* | — vide *ratonil*, under -*il*. |
| *robinsonesco* | = of or typical of Robinson Crusoe; Robinson Crusoe-like; solitary. |
| *romancesco* | = novel-like, romantic; unreal, divorced from reality. |
| *rufianesco* | — vide *picaresco*, above. |
| *rutinesco*[4] | = of or typical of routine; slave to routine, in a rut; humdrum, dull. |
| *sacristanesco* | = of or typical of a sacristan or sacristans; sly, devious; hypocritical and sanctimonious. |
| *sainetesco* | = of or typical of a farce or farces; farcical, burlesque comic-opera-ish. |

[1] For expressions in some wise akin cf. *carnavelesco* and *funambulesco*, above.

[2] E.g. *Madrid se va volviendo pulpesco: cada vez extiende más allá sus tentaculares barriadas* = Madrid is taking on the characteristics of an octopus, spreading its tentacle-like outer suburbs ever further afield.

[3] Cf. the neutral *quevediano*. See note to *valleinclanesco*, below.

Referring to the highly exaggerated and impressionistic nature of the word *bermejazo*, in Quevedo's sonnet *A Apolo siguiendo a Dafne*, Dámaso Alonso has spoken in lectures of *lo quevedesco de la desinencia*, adding *hace pensar en Goya* (cf. *goyesco*, above).

[4] Cf. the rather more neutral *rutinario*.

†*sanchesco*[1] ⎱=of or typical of Sancho, Sancho Panza; terribly
†*sanchopancesco* ⎰ or hopelessly down-to-earth, practically-minded
with a vengeance.

*sardanapolesco*[2] = Sardanapalian; pleasure-loving, voluptuous, sensual.

*sardesco* = of or typical of a Sardinian, Sardinians or Sardinia; intractable, unmanageable, mischievous; fidgety, never still; sardonic.

†*simiesco* = of or typical of a monkey or monkeys; monkeyish, monkey-like.

*solanesco* = of or typical of Gutiérrez Solana; sombre, nightmarish.

*soldadesco* = of or typical of a soldier or soldiers; to be expected from the licentious soldiery; of the barrack-room.

*tartarinesco*[3] = of or typical of Tartarin de Tarascon; typically Mediterranean or Latin; flamboyant, wild; fanciful, full of crazy notions.

†*tenoriesco* — vide *bradominesco*, above.

*tobosesco*[4] = of or typical of El Toboso; El Toboso-like; typical of a wretched little village, dump or hole; ghastly.

*torremolinesco* = of or typical of Torremolinos; Costa del Sol-style; fast, flashy, brash, get-away-style.

*tudesco*[5] = of or typical of a German or (the) Germans; German- or Prussian-style.

*turquesco*[6] = of or typical of a Turk or (the) Turks; Turkish-style.

---

[1] The second form given tends to be more specifically pejorative than the first, as is evidenced by the examples quoted.

[2] Not in very common use. Other similar terms of more frequent occurrence are: *hedonista*, *hedonístico*, *sibarita*, *sibarítico*. Another closely allied adjective is *asiático*, at least as used in the phrase *lujo asiático*.

[3] Semantically, a mixture of *fanfarrón* and *fantasioso*.

[4] Cf. the more neutral *toboseño*.

[5] Cf. the neutral *alemán*, *germánico*.

[6] Cf. the neutral *turco*.

*unamunesco*[1]  = of or typical of Unamuno; Unamuno-like, Unamuno-style; overdone, far-fetched, crazy; self-obsessed.

*valleinclanesco*[2] = of or typical of Valle-Inclán; far-fetched, crazy, wild; grotesque, nightmarish.

[1] Cf. the neutral *unamuniano*. See note to *valleinclanesco*, below.

[2] It is noteworthy that certain authors, because of the nature of their subject-matter or because of characteristics of temperament which come through in their style, are especially prone either themselves to make lavish use of forms in *-esco* or to attract the use of such forms in commentaries on their work by other writers. The literary gyrations of Valle-Inclán make of this author an outstanding example of the phenomenon in question. Thus, in any writing on Valle one constantly comes across expressions such as *esguinces y contorsiones valleinclanescos, extravagancias valleinclanescas, furibundeces valleinclanescas*, in which the form in *-esco* is instinctively chosen in preference to the neutral *valleinclaniano*. In an article by Carlos Seco Serrano entitled *Valle-Inclán y la España Oficial* one finds in rapid succession the following phrases: . . . las desconcertantes imágenes *solanescas* de los esperpentos . . . la exquisitez *bradominesca* . . . la ironía *caricaturesca* de su pluma . . . una crítica que se cebará en la Corte isabelina, a través de una deformación *guiñolesca* . . . la maligna intención que envuelve esta comedia *burlesca* . . . el *pintoresco* trasunto de Isabel II con que se inicia *La corte de los milagros*: "La majestad de Isabel II, pomposa, frondosa, bombona . . ." . . . una antología *caricaturesca* de la oratoria castrense o política reducida a la inconsistencia de los tópicos patrioteros . . . el nihilismo de Valle se formula en su *pintoresca* frase: "En el siglo XIX la historia de España la pudo escribir don Carlos; en el siglo XX la está escribiendo Lenin." (*Homenaje*, pp. 212–221.)

For other forms constantly to be found in reference to Valle see *brujesco*, *donjuanesco*, *fantochesco* and *grotesco*, above.

Another author in connexion with whom and in whose work the suffix *-esco* makes especially frequent appearance is Unamuno. The latter's irrepressible passion for jocular word-play and for the linguistically out-of-the-way, on the one hand, and his propensity to the vehement, the satirical and the grotesque, on the other, lead automatically in many contexts to a predominance of *unamunesco* over *unamuniano*, paralleling that of *valleinclanesco* and *quevedesco* over *valleinclaniano* and *quevediano*. An example of Unamuno in chidingly jocular mood: Parmentier hizo más obra y más duradera trayéndonos las patatas, que Napoleón revolviendo a Europa, y hasta más espiritual, porque ¿qué no influirá la alimentación *patatesca* en el espíritu? (*A Angel Ganivet* in *Obras Completas IV*, p. 989.) And again a more or less jocular pleasure taken in the linguistically out-of-the-way: . . . al otro extremo del parquecito, otro monumento *parquesco*. Un soldado francés y otro de los Estados Unidos de la América del

| | |
|---|---|
| *versallesco* | = of or typical of Versailles; highly genteel, gracious to a fault, of extreme, old-worldly courtesy. |
| *villanesco* | = of or typical of a peasant; boorish, cloddish; base. |
| *zolesco* | = of or typical of Emile Zola; sombre, grim. |

### -esco EXAMPLES FROM LITERATURE

. . . este hombre hubiera sido en los siglos medios caballero andante o cruzado; pero le tocó nacer en estos tiempos descoloridos y prosaicos, y sus arremetidas *andantescas* le resultan muy a menudo *qu ijotadas*★. . ..

(PEREDA, *Peñas Arriba*, p. 169)

. . . in the Middle Ages this chap would have been a knight-errant or a crusader, but it fell to his lot to be born in these dull, prosaic

---

Norte — ¿cómo le llamaremos? ¿Estadounidense? ¿Norteamericano? ¿Yanqui? — se dan las manos . . .. (*Paisajes del Alma*, p. 88.) And, finally, an -esco form repeated time after time, with every drop of pejorative implication squeezed from it in the service of vehement criticism and bitter satire: ¿Y es que lo que se suele llamar revolución, sarta de motines y de pesadas bromas legislativas y ejecutivas, no es también algo *carnavalesco*? . . . De su carroza hacen como que tiran dos leones antropomórficos distraídos, como si se rieran desdeñosamente y con una mueca *carnavalesca* . . .. Y luego todas esas nuevas termiteras de traza babilónica o neoyorquina, esos edificios *carnavalescos* que se retuercen en contorsiones barrocas o se estiran en tiesuras cúbicas . . .. En aquel estadillo *carnavalesco* que fue lo de las quemas aquellas, hubo quien sintió toda la tontería — peor que barbarie — del acto. (*Paisajes del Alma*, pp. 168–171.)

Not unexpectedly, the cynical, ironic and acid Baroja likewise has frequent recourse to such forms, as evidenced by the following series: . . . Montecristo, Artagnán, el príncipe Rodolfo, todos estos héroes de la mitología *folletinesca* . . . el primo Benedicto, tipo *caricaturesco* de la novela *Un capitán de quince años* . . .. El primo Benedicto no dejaba de ser un guasón . . .. En uno de los altos de la marcha, volviéndose a María, ingenuamente, le dijo: — Esto es bastante *tartarinesco*, ¿verdad? . . . Todos esos otros sistemas metafísicos y éticos, como el anarquismo, le parecían vueltas a concepciones *pedantescas* y a paparruchas semejantes al Krausismo . . . de noche, las calles, las tabernas y los colmados estaban llenos; se veían chulos y chulas con espíritu *chulesco* . . .. Desde Londres enviaron a Madrid una información *folletinesca* de lo más absurdo posible. (*La Dama Errante*, pp. 22, 51, 52, 79, 95, 146.)

times, and more often than not his gallant, knight-errantly sallies
back-fire on him in Don Quixote fashion . . ..

Y si la confianza es mucho mayor, entonces os lee también,
sonriendo con ironía, una sátira terriblemente *antifrailesca* . . .
(AZORÍN, *La Ruta de Don Quijote*, p. 61)

And if there exists a considerably greater degree of friendly
informality, then, smiling the while sarcastically, he will read a
bitterly anticlerical satire to you in addition . . ..

Entre los jefes había muchos extranjeros con flamantes uniformes
austríacos, italianos y franceses, un tanto *carnavalescos.*
(BAROJA, *Zalacaín el Aventurero*, p. 99)

Among the commanding officers there were a large number of
foreigners in spick-and-span, somewhat comic-opera-ish Austrian,
Italian and French uniforms.

Bajaron las recogidas al refectorio, a tomar el chocolate con re-
banada de pan. Animación mundana reinaba en el frugal desayuno, y
aunque las monjas se esforzaban por mantener un orden *cuartelesco,*
no lo podían conseguir.
(PÉREZ GALDÓS, *Fortunata y Jacinta*, II, p. 289)

The inmates came down to the refectory to have a cup of chocolate
and a slice of bread. There was an atmosphere of worldly liveliness at
the meagre breakfast, and although the nuns did their best to maintain a military barrack-type discipline, they failed to do so.

Y luego, cuando ha hablado durante un largo rato, contándome
otra vez todo el intrincado enredijo de la escritura, de los testigos,
del notario, se levanta; . . . entra otra vez . . . y pone, al fin, en mis
manos el abultado cartapacio . . . mis ojos pasan sobre los negros
trazos. Y yo no leo, no me doy cuenta de lo que esta prosa *curialesca*
expresa . . ..
(AZORÍN, *La Ruta de Don Quijote*, p. 23)

And then, when she had been talking for a long while, recounting to me once more the whole involved tangle of the title-deed, the witnesses, the notary, and so on, she got up; . . . she came in again . . . and finally placed the bulky folder in my hands . . . my eyes moved over the black strokes. But I wasn't reading anything, I wasn't taking in any of the meaning conveyed by the legalistic prose before me . . ..

En cada autor francés se le figuraba a Hurtado ver un señor *cyranesco*, tomando actitudes gallardas y hablando con voz nasal . . . todos los italianos le parecían barítonos de zarzuela.

(BAROJA, El Arbol de la Ciencia, p. 50)

In every French author Hurtado imagined he could see a Cyrano de Bergerac-type gentleman striking grand postures and talking through his nose . . . all the Italians he thought of as comic-opera baritones.

Valle-Inclán cede al hechizo de la "tradición erótica y galante del Renacimiento florentino", y no prescinde de algún que otro tópico *dieciochesco*.

(FERNÁNDEZ ALMAGRO, Vida y Literatura de Valle-Inclán, p. 60)

Valle-Inclán yielded to the bewitching spell of the "erotic, gallant tradition of the Florentine Renaissance", and did not forbear to throw in the odd eighteenth-century-style cliché for good measure.

Viéndola a tal extremo temerosa, yo sentía halagado mi orgullo *donjuanesco* . . .. Tenía la petulancia de los veinte años.

(VALLE-INCLÁN, Sonata de Primavera, p. 54)

To see her in such straits of fearfulness was flattering to my pride as a Don Juan . . .. I was possessed of the arrogance typical of a twenty-year-old.

Luisito, . . . comparando la fisonomía de las tres con la del micho que en el comedor estaba, . . . halló perfecta semejanza entre ellas . . .. No siguió adelante en sus *gatescas* presunciones . . ..

(Pérez Galdós, *Miau*, pp. 11, 12)

Luisito, . . . comparing the faces of the three women with that of the pussy in the dining-room, . . . found a perfect likeness between them . . .. He did not go any further with his conjectures on the subject of cats . . ..

[Another example from Galdós:

Todas las crías de la hermosa *menina* de doña Paca se conservaban, al menos mientras les duraba el donaire de la infancia *gatesca*.

(Pérez Galdós, *Fortunata y Jacinta*, IV, p. 179)

All the offspring of Doña Paca's superb "Princess" used to be kept, at least as long as they retained the charm of kittenhood.]

Gustó mucho *La cabeza del Bautista* a la actriz Mimí Aguglia, muy inclinada, por las predilecciones *granguiñolescas* de su repertorio, a la truculencia de esta "novela macabra" . . ..

(Fernández Almagro, *Vida y Literatura de Valle-Inclán*, p. 227)

The actress Mimi Aguglia, strongly inclined, because of the marked ghoulishness of her repertoire, to the blood-and-thunder style of this "macabre novel", found *La cabeza del Bautista* much to her liking.

El quid estaba en colocar bien a las siete chicas, pues mientras esta tremenda campaña *matrimoñesca* no fuera coronada por un éxito brillante, en la casa no podía haber grandes ahorros.

(Pérez Galdós, *Fortunata y Jacinta*, I, p. 60)

The crux of the matter lay in getting the seven girls decently situated, for, until such time as this formidable campaign in the field of matrimony were carried to a victorious conclusion, there could be no great saving in the household.

Los discursos *niagarescos* de Castelar . . ..
(BRAVO-VILLASANTE, *Vida y Obra de Emilia Pardo Bazán*, p. 179)

Castelar's torrential speeches . . ..

Por su talle delicado y su figura y cara *porcelanescas*, revelaba ser una de esas hermosuras a quienes la Naturaleza concede poco tiempo de esplendor . . ..
(PÉREZ GALDÓS, *Fortunata y Jacinta*, I, p. 100)

In the daintiness of her waist and the porcelain-like delicacy of her figure and features, she showed that she was one of those beauties to whom Nature grants but a brief span of glory . . ..

Pero eso sería entrarse por los recovecos de la psicología *sanchesca*, quizá más retorcidos de lo que aparenta.
(SALINAS, *Ensayos de Literatura Hispánica*, p. 124)

But that would be to delve into the twists and turns of the Sancho Panza psychology—possibly more subtly involved than might appear.

El jugador . . . suele ser un hombre pobre de imaginación. Y es pobreza de imaginación, es achatamiento mental, es plétora de sentido común, y del más común, es decir, del más *sanchopancesco*, lo que arrastra a jugar a estas gentes.
(UNAMUNO, *Por Tierras de Portugal y de España*, p. 140)

The gambler . . . is generally a man of weak imagination. And it is weakness of imagination, dull flatness of mind, it is glut of common sense, the commonest sense, i.e. the most utterly down-to-earth kind, that drags these people into gambling.

[Another example:

... estos mílites *sanchopancescos* que llevan escrito en sus sables pretendidamente heroicos el "¡Viva mi dueño?" de las cachicuernas de los matones de burdel.

(G. DE NORA, *La Novela Española Contemporánea*, I, p. 95)

... these inglorious specimens of the military, whose would-be heroic swords bear the inscription "Long live my master!", typical of the horn-handled knives used by whore-house toughs.]

A cada instante sonaba una exclamación de espanto viendo salir incólume, con agilidad *simiesca*, de entre las ruedas de un carruaje, algún chicuelo ... ..

(BLASCO IBÁÑEZ, *Sangre y Arena*, p. 24)

Every other moment one could hear an exclamation of horror as some urchin was seen to emerge unscathed, with monkey-like agility, from between the wheels of a carriage ... ..

Cacarean las gallinas, y un gallo, farsantón y petulante, con sus ojos redondos como botones de metal, y su cresta y su barba de carnosidad roja, se pasea con ademanes *tenoriescos*.

(BAROJA, *Camino de Perfección*, p. 177)

The hens are clucking, and a cock, arrogantly over-acting his part, his round eyes like brass buttons, with his fleshy red crest and wattle, struts up and down in the truculent fashion of a Don Juan.

## 5. -IL

*-il ADJECTIVE*

| | |
|---|---|
| *abogadil*[1] | = lawyer, of, to do with or typical of a lawyer or lawyers; lawyer-like; legalistic. |
| *aceitunil*[2] | = olive, to do with olives; sickly olive, sallow. |

[1] Cf. *abogadesco*, under *-esco*.
[2] Cf. with the pejorative tendency of this form the neutral tone of *aceitunado* = olive in colour or complexion.

342

| | |
|---|---|
| †*barberil* | = barber, of, to do with or typical of a barber or barbers. |
| *borreguil*[1] | = lamb or sheep, of or to do with lambs or sheep; lamb- or sheep-like; having the instinct of the common herd, easily led. |
| *brujeril* } <br> †*hechiceril* } | = of or to do with witchcraft, sorcery, spells or black magic. |
| *caballeril*[2] | = of knights or chivalry; foolishly or ridiculously knightly or chivalric. |
| †*caciquil* | = of, to do with or typical of a (contemptible) political boss or bosses; tyrannical. |
| *cencerril* | = of or to do with a charivari or tin-pan serenade, or with charivaris or tin-pan serenades. |
| *cerril*[3] | = wild, unbroken; uncouth, crude; narrow, inward-looking. |
| *cleopatril* | = of or to do with Cleopatra; Cleopatra-like; siren-like, sultry. |
| *cocineril*[4] | = of or to do with cooks, cooking or kitchens; typical of a cook or cooks; low, menial. |
| \* *cocheril*[5] | = of, to do with or typical of a carriage- or coach-driver or drivers; coarse. |

[1] Neutral adjectives referring to lambs and sheep are *corderino*, *ovejuno* and *lanar*. Other forms which, like *borreguil*, tend to be markedly pejorative in tone are *gregario* and *rebañego*.

Cf. *caballeresco*, under *-esco*.

[2] Cf. *caballeroso* = chivalrous, gentlemanly.

[3] Literally the word means "of or from the hills", being formed on *cerro*. Cf. *montaraz* < *monte*. The sense of "narrow, inward-looking", which sometimes attaches to *cerril*, has probably arisen in part at least because of a false association in the minds of speakers with *cerrado* = shut-in, closed-in. The frequency of such expressions as *cerrado de mollera* = thick-headed, dim-witted, and *acento cerrado* = heavy local accent, would tend to foster this semantic cross.

[4] In pejorative-jocular mood a speaker might well refer to *arte cocineril* where in a neutral context he would use *arte culinario*.

[5] E.g. *lenguaje cocheril*.

Cf. *choferil*, below.

| | |
|---|---|
| *condesil* | = of, to do with or typical of a count or counts; affected, lah-de-dah. |
| *conejil*[1] | = rabbit, of or to do with a rabbit or rabbits; rabbit-like; timorous, diffident. |
| †*cortijil* | = farm, country estate, of or to do with a farm or farms, country estate or estates; country, rustic, boorish, typical of bumpkins, clods, hicks or yokels. |
| *choferil* | = of, to do with or typical of drivers or chauffeurs; coarse. |
| *doncellil* | = of, to do with or typical of a maiden or maidens, or of a lady's maid or ladies' maids; maidenly, virgin-like; mincing, simpering, lah-de-dah. |
| *entremesil*[2] | = of, to do with or typical of a short farce or short farces; light, trivial, insubstantial. |
| *escuderil*[3] | = of, to do with or typical of a squire or page; subservient. |
| *esproncedil*[4] | = of, to do with or typical of Espronceda; Lord Byronish; desperately or hopelessly romantic. |
| *estafetil* | = of, to do with or typical of a sub-post-office or sub-post-offices; slow, inefficient. |
| *estudiantil*[5] | = student, of, to do with or typical of a student or students; boisterous, rowdy. |
| *fabril*[6] | = factory, of or to do with a factory or factories; manufacturing, industrial. |
| *febril*[7] | = fever, of or to do with fever; feverish. |

[1] Cf. the neutral *conejuno*.

[2] E.g. *comicidad entremesil* = trivial humour, insubstantial wittiness.

[3] Cf. *sanchesco, sanchopancesco*, under *-esco*.

[4] For parallel cases, see *valleinclanesco*, etc., under *-esco*.

[5] E.g. *protestas, disturbios estudiantiles*.

[6] More or less synonymous with *industrial*, both in the neutral and the pejorative senses.

[7] Often similar in tone to adjectives such as *calenturiento* and *tropical*, e.g. in the phrase *imaginación febril*.

| †*femenil*[1] ⎫ *mujeril* ⎭ | = woman, of, to do with or typical of a woman or women; woman-like, womanly, womanish. |
|---|---|
| *fregonil*[2] | = kitchen-maid, of, to do with or typical of a kitchen-maid or kitchen-maids. |
| *gusanil* | = worm, of, to do with or typical of a worm or worms; worm-like, wormish; cowardly. |
| †*hechiceril*[3] | — vide *brujeril*, above. |
| *horteril*[4] | = of or typical of a cheap or two-penny ha'penny shop-assistant or shop-assistants; common, riff-raffish, low-class. |
| *infantil*[5] | = childhood, of, to do with or typical of childhood; childish, infantile. |
| †*ingenieril* | = engineer, engineering, of, to do with or typical of engineering, an engineer or engineers; engineer-like; (merely) technical or mechanical. |
| *juvenil* | = youth, of, to do with or typical of youth; youthful; immature. |
| †*labradoril* | = peasant, of, to do with or typical of a peasant, peasant-woman, countryman, countrywoman, farmer, farmwoman; peasant-like. |
| *libreril*[6] | = book, of, to do with or typical of a bookseller or booksellers or the book-trade. |
| †*matronil*[7] | = matronly, heavy and dignified, portly. |

---

[1] Cf. the neutral *femenino*.

Although *femenil* and *mujeril* are, as often as not, identical in purport and register, there is, however, a tendency for *mujeril* to be slightly more pejorative in tone and to occur rather more frequently in phrases such as *¿qué se podrá esperar de semejante tropa mujeril?* = what can be expected or hoped for from a mob of females like this or like that?

[2] Cf. *tatil*, below.

[3] Cf. *hechiceresco*, under *-esco*.

[4] < *hortera*. This word, associated especially with Madrid, invariably implies disparagement. Cf. the neutral *dependiente* (*de tienda*). For second sense cf. *mediopelesco* ( < [*de*] *medio pelo*).

[5] Cf. *juvenil*, *mocil*, *moceril*, *muchachil*, *muchacheril*, *pueril*, below.

[6] Cf. *libresco*, under *-esco*.

[7] Cf. the literal and neutral *matronal* = of or to do with a matron or matrons.

| | |
|---|---|
| *mensil*[1] | = of the month; of the menses. |
| *mesetil* | = meseta, of, to do with or typical of the meseta, plateau or table-land, or of plateaus or table-lands; flat, monotonous and barren. |
| *mesonil*[2] | = inn, of, to do with or typical of inns; foul, ghastly. |
| *mocil*<br>*moceril*<br>*muchachil*<br>*muchacheril* | = of, to do with or typical of a lad or young fellow, or of lads or young fellows; youthful; boyish; wild. |
| *monjil* | = nun, of, to do with or typical of a nun or nuns; nunnish, nun-like; prudish, prim and proper. |
| *muchachil*<br>*muchacheril* | — vide *mocil*, above. |
| *mujeril* | — vide *femenil*, above. |
| †*negocieril*[3] | = business, of, to do with or typical of business; keen on or astute at business scheming, highly commercial, throat-cutting, soulless. |
| *ogril* | = ogre, of, to do with or typical of an ogre or bogeyman, or of ogres or bogeymen; ogre-like, ogreish. |
| *patatil*[4]<br>*patateril* | = potato, of, to do with or typical of the potato or of the potato trade or of people in the potato trade; keen on potatoes, a devil for the spuds. |
| *peonil* | = of, to do with or typical of a labourer or labourers; lowly, menial. |
| *pueril* | = puerile, boyish, childish. |

---

[1] E.g. *el mal mensil* = the female period.

[2] Cf. *venteril*, below.

[3] For the root form *negociero*, see under *-ero*.

For illustration of use of *negocieril* see under *visiteo* in Section *-eo* (Examples from Literature).

[4] The last sense given attaches in colloquial usage to the root form *patatero*. See under *-ero*.

| | |
|---|---|
| *ratonil*[1] | = mouse, of, to do with or typical of a mouse or mice; mouse-like, mousish, mousy; tinny (of music). |
| *reporteril* | = reporter, of, to do with or typical of a reporter or reporters, or of the newspaper reporting game; reporter-like, reporterish. |
| *señoril*[2] | = lordly, of, to do with or typical of (one of) the (bloated) aristocracy or gentry; very grand. |
| †*señoritil* | = of, to do with or typical of a lordling, young blood, playboy or parasite, to be expected from the mindless young aristocracy. |
| *servil* | = of, to do with or typical of a serf or servant, or of serfs or servants; servile, obsequious, cringing. |
| *solteril* | = bachelor, of, to do with or typical of a bachelor or bachelors. |
| *tatil*[3] | = of, to do with or typical of a maid-servant or maid-servants, to be expected from a maid or maids. |
| †*toreril*[4] | = bull-fighting, bull-fight, of, to do with or typical of a bull-fighter or bull-fighters or of the bull-fight game. |
| *venteril* | = of or typical of inns or inn-keepers; ghastly, rotten. |
| †*zapateril*[5] | = shoe, of, to do with or typical of a shoemaker or shoemakers, of a cobbler or cobblers, or of the shoe-trade. |

[1] Cf. *ratonesco*, under *-esco*.

There is a form *ratonero* which is more neutral in tone. It is, however, that most commonly used to convey the sense of "tinny" in connexion with music.

[2] Cf. *señorial* = lordly, stately, noble; magnificent, superb.

[3] The root form *tata*, hypochoristic in origin, is a colloquial and rather derogatory term, similar in tone to *chacha* (< [mu]chacha).

[4, 5] In connexion with these words and with the quotations given under Examples from Literature see note to *gatesco*, the purport of which is largely applicable to them.

347

. . . alentada por la *barberil* elocuencia y *liberalesca*★ conducta de su esposo, se había hecho una gran política, y . . . era muy entusiasta de Riego y de Quiroga.

(PÉREZ GALDÓS, *La Fontana de Oro*, p. 18)

. . . spurred on by her husband's soap-box oratory and flamboyantly liberal conduct, she had become a great one for politics, and . . . was a strong enthusiast of Riego and Quiroga.

— Luisito, procura correr las órdenes para que cese la persecución de mi administrador Segismundo Olmedilla. Está siendo víctima de una venganza *caciquil*.

(VALLE-INCLÁN, *La Corte de los Milagros*, p. 291)

"Luisito, do your best to spread instructions that there must be an end to the victimization of my estate-steward Segismundo Olmedilla. He is being hounded because of a vendetta on the part of a contemptible political boss."

El gremio *cocheril* exhibía allí también sus más característicos individuos.

(PÉREZ GALDÓS, *La Fontana de Oro*, p. 14)

There too the carriage-driving fraternity's most colourful characters could be seen on show.

La tropa *cortijil*, morena, sudada de soles labradores, extasiaba la bárbara risa, tensa y suspensa en las voces dramáticas del preso.

. . .

Trotaba el preso, *zarandil*[1] sobre los bastes del rucio . . ..

(VALLE-INCLÁN, *La Corte de los Milagros*, pp. 244, 246)

The mob of swarthy, boorish estate-workers, with the sweat of their farm-labour in the hot sun upon them, went into ever greater

---

[1] In other instances Valle uses *zarandero*. The form in *-il* adds to the basic concept of "swaying", a pejorative implication rendered here by "floppily".

raptures of pitiless laughter, as they hung tensely on the prisoner's dramatic cries.

. . .

The prisoner jogged along, swaying floppily on the gray's saddle pads . . ..

¡El momento supremo iba a llegar! El héroe marchaba hacia ella para estrujarla con *varonil*[1] apasionamiento . . .. Pasaron atropelladamente por su pensamiento todos los convencionalismos *femeniles*, los reparos tradicionales . . ..

(BLASCO IBÁÑEZ, Sangre y Arena, p. 109)

The supreme moment was at hand! The hero was striding towards her to crush her in his passionate, manly embrace . . .. All the considerations of womanly conventionality, all the time-honoured qualms rushed helter-skelter through her mind . . ..

. . . Su verdadero mundo, el que corresponde a la plena actualidad, es enormemente complejo, preciso y exigente. Pero tiene miedo — el hombre medio es hoy muy débil, a despecho de sus gesticaciones *matonescas*★ — tiene miedo a abrirse a ese mundo verdadero, que exigiría mucho de él, y prefiere falsificar su vada reteniéndola hermética en el capullo *gusanil* de su mundo ficticio y simplicísimo.

(ORTEGA Y GASSET, Misión de la Universidad, p. 63)

. . . his real world, the world answering to the fully contemporary situation, is tremendously complex, precise and demanding. But he is frightened—the average man to-day is very weak, despite his bullying gesticulations—he is frightened to lay himself open to that real world, which would demand a great deal of him, and he prefers to falsify his life by keeping it hermetically sealed inside the cowardly worm's cocoon of his ridiculously over-simplified, sham world.

Era, añade el libelo, once el número de estas monjas que rodeaban la impúdica escena, para recordar, porque así lo manda el rito *hechiceril*, a los apóstoles sin Judas.

(MARAÑÓN, El Conde-Duque de Olivares, p. 145)

[1] An example of a form in *-il* which is generally favourable in tone.

The lampoon adds that the nuns standing round the obscene happening were eleven in number, to recall, in accordance with the injunctions of black-magic rite, the Apostles without Judas.

La materia, el elemento real donde y con el cual el hombre puede llegar a ser de hecho lo que en proyecto es, es el mundo. Este le ofrece la posibilidad de existir y, a la par, grandes dificultades para ello. En tal disposición de los términos, la vida aparece constituida como un problema casi *ingenieril*: aprovechar las facilidades que el mundo ofrece para vencer las dificultades que se openen a la realización de nuestro programa.

(ORTEGA Y GASSET, *Meditación de la Técnica*, pp. 59, 60)

The matter, the real element in which and with which man has the possibility of becoming in actual fact what he is potentially, is the world. The world gives him the chance to exist, and, at the same time, places very considerable difficulties in the way of his achieving his aim. Looked at in this light life is seen in the form of a problem that is almost purely mechanical—a question of making use of the facilities offered by the world to overcome the difficulties obstructing the carrying through of our programme.

. . . por magia del lenguaje, Don Quijote, al escribir a Aldonza cual si fuese soberana señora, saca a la moza de su condición *labradoril* y la sitúa en las alturas de la hermosura y la principalidad.

(SALINAS, *Ensayos de Literatura Hispánica*, p. 122)

. . . by the magic of language Don Quixote, in writing to Aldonza as if she were a fine lady, raises the wench from her lowly peasant condition and places her upon the heights of loveliness and grandness.

— Me gusta bailar contigo porque me llevas muy bien.
La voz tenía una intimidad insinuante. Adolfito, advertido, estrechó el talle *matronil* de la Señora:
— Vuestra Majestad me honra en extremo.

(VALLE-INCLÁN, *La Corte de los Milagros*, p. 36)

"I like dancing with you because you hold me very well."
There was a suggestive intimacy in her voice. Apprised of this fact,
Adolfito grasped the Lady's portly waist more tightly:
"Your Majesty does me exceeding honour."

. . . era mucho . . . lo que me hacía gozar su carácter resuelto,
desenfadado, tan poco *monjil*, que verdaderamente en ocasiones
asombraba.

(PALACIO VALDÉS, *La Hermana San Sulpicio*, p. 43)

. . . her determined, uninhibited character was a great source of
enjoyment to me—there was so little about her of the primness and
properness that one would expect from a nun that at times it was
really quite astonishing.

. . . unos cuantos hermanos a la deriva, huérfanos de madre, bajo
la autoridad, entre displicente y despótica, de un padre *señoritil*,
irresponsable, desalmado y ególatra.

(G. DE NORA, *La Novela Española Contemporánea*, I, p. 170)

. . . several motherless brothers and sisters, adrift in life, under the
half-supercilious, half-despotic authority of an irresponsible, heartless
and self-loving father—a typical product of the upper-class, para-
sitical, play-boy school.

El espada, sintiéndose locuaz, hablaba de graciosos incidentes de la
vida *toreril* . . ..

(BLASCO IBÁÑEZ, *Sangre y Arena*, p. 106)

The matador, feeling in garrulous mood, talked about amusing
incidents in the lives of people in the bull-fight game.

. . . la duquesa de Alba . . . no se ponía cada par de zapatos más que
un solo día. Igual fausto *zapateril* exhibió . . . la emperatriz Eugenia . . ..

(MARAÑÓN, *Vida e Historia*, p. 158)

... the Duchess of Alba ... wore each pair of shoes for one day only. The Empress Eugénie ... displayed like lavishness in the matter of footwear.

## 6. -ERO

*-ero ADJECTIVE*[1]

| | |
|---|---|
| *alcoholero*[2] | = (very) keen on alcohol, (over-)fond of alcohol. |
| *arrabalero*[3] *barriobajero* | = slum, of or to do with a slum or (the) slums; low, vulgar. |
| *cafetero* | = (very) keen on coffee, (over-)fond of coffee. |
| *callejero* | = street, of or to do with (the) streets; (very) keen on going out, (over-)fond of gadding about. |
| *carero* | = dear, expensive, (much) given to charging high prices or profiteering. |
| †*casamentero* | = (very) keen on getting people married off, (over-)fond of match-making. |
| *cochero* | = (very or over-) keen on or fond of cars, car-crazy, car-mad. |
| *congresero* | = (very) keen on attending conferences, (over-)fond of conferences, (very or over-) conference-minded. |
| *convenienciero* | = (much) given to doing only what suits one or to doing things only if and when it suits one, (excessively) guided by considerations of self-interest. |
| *corralero* | = barn-yard or back-yard, of or to do with the barn-yard or back-yard; ill-bred, common, vulgar. |
| *cuartelero*[4] | = barrack or barrack-room, of or to do with barracks or the barrack-room; coarse, crude, rough. |

[1] Many of these forms are also used substantivally.
[2] Cf. especially *cafetero*, *patatero* and *tomatero*, below.
[3] E.g. *lenguaje arrabalero*, *barriobajero* = slum or vulgar language or talk. Cf. *corralero* and *cuartelero*, below.
[4] Cf. *cuartelesco*, under *-esco*.

| | | |
|---|---|---|
| *cumplimentero*[1] = | (very or over-) addicted to courtesy, formality and ceremony, excessively courteous, formal and ceremonious. |
| *chapucero*[2] = | (much) given to botching, bungling or doing things any-old-how, slap-dash. |
| *dominguero*[3] = | Sunday, of Sunday or Sundays; holiday, of holidays; festive, noisy and common. |
| †*electorero*[4] = | (much) given to, engaged in or concerned with rigging, fixing or cooking elections. |
| *escasero*[5] = | (much) given to doling out in dribs and drabs, cheese-paring, mingy, stingy. |
| *etiquetero* = | (much) given to being a stickler for etiquette or to standing on ceremony, (very or over-) addicted to formality. |
| *faldero* = | of the skirt, of skirts; (very or over-) keen on women; of the lap, of laps; (very or over-) keen on fuss, fussy. |
| *familiero* = | (very or over-) keen on or fond of contact with one's family or relatives. |
| *farolero*[6] = | (much) given to bluffing, blustering or yarn-spinning. |
| *friolero* = | (very or over-) sensitive to cold. |

[1] Cf. *etiquetero*, below, and *cancilleresco*, under *-esco*.

[2] Cf. *chafallón* — similar sense, but less common.

[3] For the figurative sense attaching to this word one must bear in mind the characteristics of the Continental Sunday. These latter explain the fact that a phrase such as *ambiente dominguero* conveys a meaning similar to that of English expressions of the type "fun-fair or bank-holiday atmosphere", *dominguero* thus frequently coming close to synonymity with *populachero*, below.

Cf. the academic register and neutral sense of *dominical*, as in *misa dominical* = Sunday mass.

[4] In connexion with this word see *pucherazo*, under *-azo*.

[5] Cf. such allied terms as *agarrado*, *mezquino*, *miserable* and *tacaño*.

[6] Cf. *farolón*, under *-ón*.

| | |
|---|---|
| *garbancero*[1] | = (very or over-) keen on or fond of chick-peas; stodgy, dull, uninspiring. |
| †*iglesiero*[2] | = (very or over-) keen on or fond of church-going, always going to church, always in or around the church; Bible-punching. |
| *iaranero*[3] | = (very or over-) fond of merry-making or rowdy jollification. |
| *justiciero* | = (very or over-) zealous in the cause of justice, (much) given to being a stickler for the letter of the law; justice-dealing. |
| *lastimero*[4] | = (much) given to whining or griping, plaintive, piteous. |
| *negociero* | = (very or over-) keen on or fond of business dealing or scheming, (much) given to tough, cut-throat dealing or hard bargaining. |
| *niñero* | = (very or over-) keen on children. |
| *novelero* | = (very or over-) keen on new things or fads, or on the latest novelty, craze or fashion; (very or over-) keen on novels or trashy literature. |
| *patatero*[5] | = potato, of potatoes; (very or over-) keen on potatoes. |
| *patriotero* | = blusteringly and aggressively patriotic, jingoistic. |
| *pelotillero*[6] | = toadying, fawning, creepish. |
| *pendenciero*[7] | = (much) given to looking for quarrels, fights or trouble, quick to pick a quarrel or fight, bellicose, pugnacious. |

[1] As an illustration of the figurative sense it is interesting to note that, because of the everyday, humdrum nature of many of the subjects treated by him, Galdós was termed by Valle-Inclán *el garbancero*.

[2] Cf. *beatón* and *santurrón*, under *-ón*.

[3] Cf. the allied term *juerguista*.

[4] Cf. *lastimoso* = pitiful, lamentable.

[5] E.g. *es un patatero de miedo* = he's a real devil for the spuds.

*Militar patatero* = *militar de cuchara* = officer or N.C.O. who has come up from the ranks.

[6] Cf. *adulón*, under *-ón*.

[7] Cf. the allied term *chulo*.

| | | |
|---|---|---|
| †*politiquero* | = | (much) given to political jobbery, scheming or jiggery-pokery; (very or over-) keen on meddling or dabbling in politics; (very or over-) fond of talking politics or of laying down the law on politics. |
| *populachero* | = | of the common people, rabble or mob; vulgar, rowdy and garish; fun-fairish, bank-holidayish; rabble-rousing. |
| *postinero*[1] | = | posh, ritzy, flash. |
| *puñetero* | = | damned awkward, cantankerous, cussed or nasty, bloody-minded, bitchy. |
| *putañero*[2] *putero* } | = | (much) given to wenching or whoring. |
| *sensiblero* | = | (much) given to sentimentality or mawkishness. |
| *taquillero*[3] | = | box-office, of box-offices; good box-office, money-spinning, that packs the masses in. |
| *teatrero* | = | (very or over-) keen on or fond of the theatre, always going to the theatre; theatre-going. |
| *tesonero*[4] | = | (much) given to sticking at it, tenacious, dogged; obstinate, stubborn. |
| *testimoniero* *testimoñero* } | = | (much) given to bearing false witness or to calumny; hypocritical. |
| *tomatero* | = | tomato, of tomato or tomatoes; (very or over-) keen on tomatoes. |
| *topiquero*[5] | = | (very or over-) keen on clichés or set phrases. |
| *traicionero*[6] | = | treacherous, (dangerously) deceptive. |

[1] Cf. *de postín* — similar sense.

[2] Cf. *mujeriego* = (very or over-) keen on or fond of women, womanizing.

[3] Used mainly with the words *película* and *obra* (*de teatro*).

[4] Cf. *tesonudo* — similar sense. It is interesting to observe that the root-word *tesón* is not used with pejorative implication, being equivalent to such English terms as "tenacity, perseverance, stickability", while *tesonero* may or may not be pejorative—"tenacious, dogged", or "obstinate, stubborn"—and *tesonería* is invariably pejorative—stubbornness, pigheadedness.

[5] Formed on the noun *tópico*.

[6] Almost always used figuratively, in such phrases as *de carácter traicionero, aguas traicioneras, una curva traicionera*. For the literal sense "treacherous, traitorous, who betrays or commits treachery", the form *traidor* is that invariably chosen.

| | | |
|---|---|---|
| *trastero* | = | of or to do with lumber, junk or jumble. |
| *visitero* | = | (very or over-) keen on visiting or social calls. |
| *vocinglero*[1] | = | loud-mouthed; bawling, blaring. |
| *zaragatero* | = | boisterous, rowdy. |

## *-ero* EXAMPLES FROM LITERATURE

. . . aquel hidalgo de cepa vieja sentía a la vez gana ardentísima de casar a las chiquillas y un orgullo de raza tan exaltado, . . . que no sólo le vedaba descender a ningún ardid de los usuales en padres *casamenteros*, sino que le imponía suma rigidez y escrúpulo en la elección de sus relaciones y en la manera de educar a sus hijas . . ..

(PARDO BAZÁN, *Los Pazos de Ulloa*, pp. 131, 132)

. . . that member of a minor noble family of long standing was subject at one and the same time to the most ardent desire to get his young daughters married and to so extreme a form of pride in his stock . . . that not only did it preclude his descending to any of the tricks commonly used by parents set on match-making, but it indeed imposed upon him the utmost strictness and fastidiousness in his choice of connexions and in the manner of his daughters' upbringing.

La etapa un poco bohemia de Baroja no se limitó exclusivamente al campo de lo literario, sino que se extendió a la política . . . gustó de observar a jefes y caciques, y contemplar a lo vivo la burda trama de mítines y combinaciones *electoreras* . . . aventuras entre manipuladores y desarticuladores del gran tinglado nacional . . . divertíale refrescarse de su tarea de novelista, y de escritor de artículos, con el espectáculo de *politiqueros* y politiquillos, y oírles criticarse las pifias que constantemente cometían en sus delirios oratorios.

(PÉREZ FERRERO, *Vida de Pío Baroja*, pp. 138–140)

---

[1] Cf. the highly colloquial allied substantive form *voceras* = loud-mouthed braggart or blusterer. (Also frequently written *boceras*, because of the possibility of the double etymology *voz/boca*.)

The more or less Bohemian stage that Baroja went through was not confined exclusively to the sphere of literature but extended into that of politics . . . he enjoyed observing party leaders and political bosses, and watching the crude pattern of rallies and election-rigging arrangements . . . adventures among people engaged in manipulating the country's grand political set-up, or in putting it out of joint . . . he found it amusing to seek a change from his work as a novelist and writer of articles in the spectacle offered by political schemers and petty little second-raters; he got fun out of listening to them criticize one another for the howlers they made all the time in their flights of ranting oratory.

. . . para Aracil, sus cuñadas y primos, por parte de su mujer, eran miserables, gente ruin, *iglesiera*, de mal corazón y de sentimientos viles.

(BAROJA, *La Dama Errante*, p. 27)

. . . as far as Aracil was concerned his sisters-in-law and cousins on his wife's side were mean, low people, Bible-punching churchgoers with base feelings and no heart.

### 7. -IZO

*-izo* ADJECTIVE[1]

| | |
|---|---|
| *ablandadizo*[2] | = easily softened, persuaded or brought round. |
| *acomodadizo*[3] | = easily persuaded to agree, ready to agree to anything, a bit too ready to give way. |
| †*advenedizo*[4] | = newly arrived, only recently arrived, upstart, parvenu. |

[1] Many forms in *-izo* are also used substantivally.

[2] It will be noted that the majority of words listed in this section represent a past participle + *izo*. The exceptions are *castizo* < *casta* + *izo*; *enfermizo* < *enfermo* + *izo*; *rollizo* < *rollo* + *izo*.

[3] Cf. *acomodaticio* = (over-)accommodating, (over-)obliging, i.e. similar sense but more academic register.

[4] Cf. the academic and technical *adventicio* = adventitious. *advenedizo* derives from an Old Spanish form.

| | | |
|---|---|---|
| *ahogadizo* | = | easily choked, stifled or drowned; that makes one choke, hard to swallow; that sinks easily, heavier than water. |
| *alborotadizo* | = | easily excited, stirred up or set astir; ready to riot at the slightest provocation. |
| *alcanzadizo* | = | easily reached or attainable. |
| *anegadizo* | = | easily flooded, (very) liable or prone to flooding. |
| *antojadizo*[1] | = | (much) given to whims and fancies, always taking a fancy to this, that or the other. |
| †*asustadizo*[2] <br> †*espantadizo* | = | easily frightened or frightened away, easily scared or scared away, shying or shying away at the slightest provocation; jittery, jumpy. |
| *castizo*[3] | = | pure, pure-bred; essentially, really, thoroughly or |

[1] Cf. *caprichoso* = capricious, fickle, i.e. similar sense, but considerably more academic tone.

[2] A similar word of like meaning is *asombradizo*. It is, however, little used.

Another more or less synonymous form is *asustón*, of particular interest in so far that it might well be expected-to have not a passive but an active meaning —"(much) given to frightening or scaring". Cf. *deprimentón* = easily depressed, (much) given to depression; *deslumbrón* = easily dazzled or taken in; *preocupón* = easily worried, (much) given to worry. In this connexion it is interesting to note, conversely, the active role commonly played by many past participle forms used as adjectives, e.g. *aburrido* = boring; *cansado* = tiring; *divertido* = amusing.

[3] E.g. *inglés castizo* = thoroughly or typically English; *una obra española castiza* = a work in the true Spanish tradition; *una frase española castiza* = an essentially Spanish expression or a highly idiomatic Spanish expression.

The following words of Unamuno help to clinch this basic sense:

*Castizo deriva de casta, así como casta del adjetivo casto, puro. Se aplica de ordinario el vocablo casta a las razas o variedades puras de especies animales . . ..*

*Se usa lo más a menudo el calificativo de castizo para designar a la lengua y al estilo. Decir en España que un escritor es castizo es dar a entender que se le cree más español que a otros.* (*En Torno al Casticismo*, p. 13)

The pejorative implication which frequently attaches to the term derives largely from the fact that, in the opinion of many, the qualities which may be considered as most typically Spanish are those associated with the common people. Thus we find that in many cases *castizo* is practically synonymous with such terms as *populachero*, *chabacano*, *ordinario* and *chulo*.

*continued on next page*

> typically X, having the essence or true spirit of X, truly typical of X, X in the true sense; (highly) idiomatic; typical of the lower orders or common people.

*contentadizo·* = easily pleased or satisfied, undemanding.

†*descontentadizo*[1]= hard to please or satisfy, never pleased or satisfied, always discontented or dissatisfied; fussy, finicky.

*enamoradizo* = quick to fall in love, always falling in and out of love, prone to infatuation, susceptible.

†*encontradizo*[2] ⎫
*topadizo* ⎭ = easy to meet, find or bump into, always being met, found or bumped into, bobbing up constantly.

---

Beyond this, however, there is to be found a more subtly pejorative use of the word, in which it is taken as referring to what the speaker or writer considers to be objectionable aspects of Spanish history, life and society as a whole. This can be clearly seen in the following words of Ortega y Gasset:

. . . todo grande estilo encierra un fulgor de mediodía y es serenidad vertida sobre las borrascas.

Esto ha solido faltar en nuestras producciones castizas. Nos encontramos ante ellas como ante la vida. ¡ He aquí su grande virtud ! — se dice. ¡ He aquí su gravo defecto ! — respondo yo. Para vida, para espontaneidad, para dolores y tinieblas me basta con los míos, con los que ruedan por mis venas; me basto yo con mi carne y mis huesos y la gota de fuego sin llama de mi conciencia puesta sobre mi carne y sobre mis huesos. Ahora necesito claridad, necesito sobre mi vida un amanecer. Y estas obras castizas son meramente una ampliación de mi carne y de mis huesos y un horrible incendio que repite el de mi ánimo. Son como yo, y yo voy buscando algo que sea más que yo — más seguro que yo . . ..

Tradición castiza no puede significar, en su mejor sentido, otra cosa que lugar de apoyo para las vacilaciones individuales — una tierra firme para el espíritu. Esto es lo que no podrá nunca ser nuestra cultura si no afirma y organiza su sensualismo en el cultivo de la meditación.

(*Meditaciones del Quijote*, pp. 74, 75)

[1] Cf. such words as *exigente* = exacting, demanding, *escrupuloso* = scrupulous, fastidious, and *meticuloso* = meticulous, i.e. similar sense, but more academic register.

[2] Used mainly in the expression *hacerse el encontradizo* = to pretend to meet or bump into someone by chance or accidentally, arrange to meet or bump into someone pretending that it is by chance.

Cf., below, *hacerse el invitadizo*, *hacerse el olvidadizo*, and *hacerse el perdidizo*.

359

| †*enfermizo*[1] | = sickly, ailing; unhealthy, being an obsession or "thing". |
| *enojadizo*[2] | = easily angered, quick to anger, quick-tempered; irritable, peevish. |
| †*escurridizo*[3] | = slippery; prone or quick to dodge or shirk things or issues, always dodging or shirking something, hard to pin down. |
| †*espantadizo* | — vide *asustadizo*, above. |
| *huidizo* | = prone or quick to flee, dodge or shy away; unsociable; shifty. |
| *invitadizo*[4] | = (always) ready or prepared to be invited or treated, or to be stood a drink or drinks. |
| *manchadizo*[5] | = easily stained or soiled, prone to get stained, soiled or dirty. |
| *olvidadizo*[6] | = prone or inclined to forget things, always forgetting something, forgetful. |

[1] Cf., for first sense, *enfermucho*, under -*ucho*.

Cf., for second sense, *malsano*, *morboso* = unhealthy, morbid, i.e. similar meaning, but more academic register.

Often the most exact register equivalent of *enfermizo* is "thing", as in *se le ha convertido en una cosa enfermiza* = it has become a thing with him, he has developed a thing about it, he has a thing about it.

[2] Cf. *irritable* = of a choleric disposition, i.e. similar sense, but more academic register.

[3] Cf. *resbaladizo*, *huidizo*, and *perdidizo*, below.

Cf. *esquivo*, *huraño*, *zahareño* = shying or dodging away, unsociable, stand-offish.

[4] Used mainly in the expression *hacerse el invitadizo* = to arrange things so that one gets invited or treated, fix things so that one gets stood a drink or drinks.

[5] Sometimes used with the same sense is the phrase *poco sufrido*, which, however, tends more commonly to be applied to persons, with the meaning "lacking in patience, not inclined to suffer fools gladly".

[6] Worthy of note is the phrase *hacerse el olvidadizo* = to pretend to have forgotten, pretend not to remember.

The basic *olvidado* is frequently used in much the same way, with the sense "forgetful" or "oblivious". Cf. *desmemoriado* = having lost one's memory; having a poor memory, forgetful.

| | |
|---|---|
| *pegadizo*[1] | = sticky; catching; catchy; not easy to shake off or get rid of. |
| *perdidizo*[2] | = prone or tending to get lost, easily lost, easy to lose; prone to lose, (always) losing; prone to sneak away or skive off. |
| *quebradizo*[3] | = easily broken or cracked, brittle, crumbly. |
| †*resbaladizo* | = slippery. |
| *rollizo*[4] | = chubby, portly. |
| *topadizo* | = vide *encontradizo*, above. |

## *-izo* EXAMPLES FROM LITERATURE

— Los gobernantes de esta hora no solemos tener abuelos linajudos. Somos unos *advenedizos* que saben trabajar . . ..

      (BUERO VALLEJO, *Un Soñador para un Pueblo*, p. 231)

"We who are running the country at the moment don't usually have a long line of noble forebears behind us. We are a pack of upstarts who [happen to] know the meaning of work . . .."

El llevar en su bolsillo su fortuna le hacía ser más *asustadizo* que una liebre.

      (BAROJA, *Zalacaín el Aventurero*, p. 112)

Carrying his worldly wealth in his pocket made him more jumpy than a hare.

---

[1] Cf. *pegajoso* — often synonymous with *pegadizo* in first and last senses given.

[2] Used mainly in the following expressions: *hacer perdidiza una cosa* = to lose something on purpose, get something out of the way or out of sight, get rid of something (cf. *hacer desaparecer* — similar sense); *hacerse perdidizo* = to lose on purpose (at a game); *hacerse el perdidizo* = to sneak away, make oneself scarce.

    Cf. *perdidoso* — senses similar to the first two given for *perdidizo*.

[3] Cf. *frágil* — similar sense, but academic register.

[4] Cf. *regordete*, under *-ete*.

[Cf. similar use of *espantadizo*:

Julián pertenecía a la falange de los pacatos, que tienen la virtud *espantadiza* . . ..

(PARDO BAZÁN, Los Pazos de Ulloa, p. 47)

Julian belonged to the company of the meek and mild poor in spirit, those whose virtue is easily startled . . ..]

. . . Gallardo, escrupuloso y *descontentadizo* en el arreglo de su persona . . ..

(BLASCO IBÁÑEZ, Sangre y Arena, p. 21)

. . . Gallardo—fastidious and fussy about his personal appearance . . ..

. . . espié sus pasos, y, cuando la vi en el patio, salí de mi cuarto . . . y me hice el *encontradizo*.

(PALACIO VALDÉS, La Hermana San Sulpicio, p. 110)

. . . I watched her movements, and, when I saw her in the courtyard, I came out of my room . . . and bumped into her as if by chance.

Fue Ena . . . quien me hizo . . . desprenderme de mis morbosidades *enfermizas* . . ..  (LAFORET, *Nada*, p. 249)

It was Ena . . . who made me . . . shake off my unhealthy, morbid preoccupations . . ..

. . . en su facha, maneras y conducta, era evasivo, *resbaladizo*, *escurridizo*, seductor . . ..

(PÉREZ DE AYALA, Tigre Juan, p. 161)

. . . in the look of the chap, in his way of doing things and general behaviour he was evasive and hard to pin down—a slippery customer of wheedling, superficial charm . . ..

362

*-izante ADJECTIVE*[1]

†*anarquizante*[2] = favouring or tending towards anarchy, having anarchic tendencies or leanings, prone to be anarchic, tinged or tainted with anarchy, anarchistic, pro-anarchic, pro-anarchy.

*arcaizante* — senses for "(the) archaic, things archaic or archaism" similar to those given under *anarquizante*.

*centralizante* — senses for "centralism or centralist" similar to those given under *anarquizante*.

*comunistizante*[3]— senses for "communism or communist" similar to those given under *anarquizante*.

*cristianizante* — senses for "Christianity or Christian" similar to those given under *anarquizante*.

†*europeizante* — senses for "things European, Europeanism, Europe or European" similar to those given under *anarquizante*.

*extranjerizante*— senses for "things foreign, foreign influence, foreign ideas or foreign" similar to those given under *anarquizante*.

†*fascistizante* — senses for "fascism or fascist" similar to those given under *anarquizante*.

†*hebraizante* — senses for "things Hebrew, Hebraism, Hebrew, or Judaic" similar to those given under *anarquizante*.

*islamizante* — senses for "Islam or Islamic" similar to those given under *anarquizante*.

*italianizante* — senses for "things Italian, Italianism or Italian" similar to those given under *anarquizante*; Italianate.

*judaizante* — senses for "things Jewish, Judaism, Jewish or Judaic" similar to those given under *anarquizante*.

*latinizante* — senses for "things Latin, Latinism, Latinization or Latin" similar to those given under *anarquizante*.

---

[1] Many forms in *-izante* are also used substantivally.
[2] Cf. *anarcoide*, under *-oide*.          [3] Cf. *comunistoide*, under *-oide*.

| | |
|---|---|
| *modernizante* | — senses for "(the) modern, things modern or modernism" similar to those given under *anarquizante*. |
| *simpatizante* | = sympathizing; (subst.) sympathizer, fellow traveller. |
| *sodomizante* | — senses for "sodomy, sodomitic or homosexual" similar to those given under *anarquizante*. |
| *sovietizante* | — senses for "(the) Soviet or things Soviet" similar to those given under *anarquizante*. |
| *teorizante*[1] | — senses for "(the) theoretical, theorizing or (vain) theory" similar to those given under *anarquizante*. |

## *-izante EXAMPLES FROM LITERATURE*

La escisión ... entre la facción *anarquizante* de Bakunin y la socialista ortodoxa, que sigue aceptando la jefatura de Marx, se traduce, en España, en un predominio, al principio absoluto, de la orientación anarquista ...; los únicos *europeizantes*, valga el calificativo, en el mosaico de fuerzas políticas de la España finisecular, fueron las minorías socialista y anarquista.

(GRANJEL, *Panorama de la Generación del 98*, pp. 21, 24)

The split ... between Bakunin's pro-anarchy faction and the orthodox socialist faction, which still accepted the leadership of Marx, led, in the case of Spain, to the predominance—in the early stages the total predominance—of those of the anarchist persuasion ...; the only pro-Europe elements—if I may use this term— among the motley array of political groups in Spain at the end of the nineteenth century were the socialist and anarchist minorities.

... las vicisitudes de la guerra hicieron que la Falange siguiera una peripecia contradictoria y vacilante, llegando en algunos momentos ... a estructurarse casi como un partido fascista ...; la desgraciada etapa *fascistizante* hizo salir de sus filas a un núcleo importante de intelectuales españoles ....

(EGUIAGARAY, *Historia Contemporánea de España*, p. 173)

[1] Cf. the neutral *teórico* = theoretical. Cf. also the noun forms *teorizante* = theorizer; *teórico* = theoretician.

... the varying fortunes of the war caused the Phalange to follow a contradictory and vacillating course, so much so that on one or two occasions it actually came near to being organized on the lines of a fascist party ...; the regrettable fascist-tinged stage resulted in a considerable body of Spanish intellectuals leaving the movement's ranks.

... en Belmonte, vio la luz fray Luis de León, el del legendario "decíamos ayer" — siempre decimos lo que ayer dijimos —, que, libre ya de la Inquisición, que le husmeó *hebraizante*, y acaso marrano, cantó la descansada vida del que huye el mundanal ruido ...

(UNAMUNO, Paisajes del Alma, p. 108)

... it was in Belmonte that Fray Luis de León came into the world, the Fray Luis of the legendary "as we were saying yesterday" — we always say what we said yesterday—the Fray Luis who, free at last from the Inquisition, which had scented in him one tainted with Judaism and perhaps actually a Yid, sang of the peaceful life of the man who flees far from the madding crowd . . ..

## 9. -OIDE

*-oide*[1] *ADJECTIVE*[2]

| | |
|---|---|
| †*anarcoide*[3] ⎫<br>*anarquistoide* ⎭ | = anarchic or anarchistic in form, having anarchic or anarchistic traits or tendencies; having pretensions to being an anarchist; tainted or tinged with anarchy. |
| *comunistoide*[4] | — senses for "communist, communistic or communism" similar to those given under *anarcoide*. |
| †*divinoide* | = divine or sacred in form or attributes; god-like. |

[1] Spanish shares with English many scientific terms in *-oide*, such as *antropoide/*anthropoid; *elefantoide/*elephantoid; *negroide/*negroid. Words belonging to this category are not given here.

[2] Many forms in *-oide* are also used substantively.

[3] Cf. *anarquizante*, under *-izante*.

[4] Cf. *comunistizante*, under *-izante*.

| †*feminoide* | = feminine or female in form or shape; having feminine or female traits or tendencies; tinged with femininity. |
| †*feudaloide* | = feudal or feudalistic in form; having feudal or feudalistic traits or tendencies; tainted or tinged with feudalism. |
| †*imbeciloide* | = having half-wit or damn-fool traits or tendencies; half-wit-like. |
| *intelectualoide*[1] | — senses for "intellectual or intellectualism" similar to those given under *anarcoide*. |
| *liberaloide*[2] | — senses for "liberal or liberalism" similar to those given under *anarcoide*. |
| *maricoide* | — senses for "homosexual or homosexuality" similar to those given under *feminoide*. |
| *monarquistoide*[3] | — senses for "monarchist, royalist, monarchism or royalism" similar to those given under *anarcoide*. |
| *sinvergonzoide* | = having a tendency to be a bounder or shameless devil, having rascally traits. |
| *socialistoide*[4] | — senses for "socialist, socialistic or socialism" similar to those given under *anarcoide*. |
| *viriloide*[5] | — senses for "masculine, male or masculinity" similar to those given under *feminoide*. |

## -oide EXAMPLES FROM LITERATURE

— Seguimos pensando que . . . sólo un señorito *anarcoide* es capaz de confundir con el pueblo a un matón *electorero*★ . . ..

(LUIS LANDÍNEZ, *Baroja y su Mundo*, p. 119)

[1] Cf. *intelectualizante* — similar sense.

[2] Cf. *liberalizante* — similar sense.

[3] It is curious to note that the usual Spanish for monarchist or royalist is *monárquico*, the form *monarquista*, in theory at least, being non-existent. In contradiction to this, *monarquistoide* is common, while *monarquicoide* is, at best, rare—a situation probably to be explained by the analogy of such frequently used forms as *comunistoide* and *socialistoide*.

[4] Cf. *socialistizante* — similar sense.

[5] Cf. *hombruno* = mannish.

"We still think that . . . only a young man belonging to the privileged classes yet having pretensions to be an anarchist is capable of equating an election-rigging tough with the ordinary people . . .."

. . . el fuego era para él [el hombre primitivo] un poder *divinoide* del mundo y le suscitaba emociones religiosas.
(ORTEGA Y GASSET, *Meditación de la Técnica*, p. 85)

. . . for him [primitive man] fire was a force of this world which yet had god-like qualities and gave rise in him to feelings of a religious nature.

Era una estampa amanerada y relamida la del Señor: ojos dulces de tarjeta escarchada y una barba caprina, rizosa y negreante. Resultaba un Dios blando y *feminoide*. Desde luego, no era . . . el Dios airado que con látigo en mano arrojara a los mercaderes del templo.
(ZUNZUNEGUI, *¡Ay, Estos Hijos!*, p. 74)

The picture of Our Lord was a mannered, terribly neat and tidy one; the eyes were the gentle sort you see on postcards sprinkled with glitter-dust, and the face had a curly, blackish, goat-like beard. The impression was of a soft, rather effeminate God. It certainly wasn't . . . the infuriated God who, whip in hand, drove the traders from the Temple.

. . . Valle-Inclán, para hacer patente su desagrado, unas veces se acercaba a las corrientes revolucionarias, otras a la violencia *feudaloide* de los camisas negras italianos . . ..
(SENDER, *Valle-Inclán y la Dificultad de la Tragedia*, p. 82)

. . . in order to make his displeasure manifest Valle-Inclán would by turns draw near to the currents of revolution, on the one hand, or to the violence of the Italian Black Shirts, with its tinge of feudalism, on the other.

367

— El Fascio? El Fascio no es una partida de la porra, como generalmente creen en España los radical-*imbeciloides* . . ..

(VALLE-INCLÁN, quoted by Fernández Almagro
in *Vida y Literatura de Valle-Inclán*, p. 274)

"The *Fascisti*? The *Fascisti* are not a mob of bludgeon-wielding toughs, as the half-wit-type radicals in Spain usually imagine . . .."

# LIST OF ADDITIONAL WORKS
# QUOTED IN APPENDIX

AZORÍN. *La Ruta de Don Quijote*. Manchester U.P., Manchester, 1966.

G. DE NORA, E. *La Novela Española Contemporánea I*. Gredos, Madrid, 1958.

GRANJEL, L. *Panorama de la Generación del 98*. Guadarrama, Madrid, 1959.

MARAÑÓN, G. *El Conde-Duque de Olivares*. Espasa-Calpe, Austral, 9th ed., Madrid, 1956.

MONTESINOS, J. F. *Modernismo, Esperpentismo* in *Homenaje a Valle-Inclán*. Revista de Occidente, Madrid, Nov.–Dec. 1966.

ORTEGA Y GASSET, J. *Intimidades* in *El Espectador VII*. Revista de Occidente, Arquero, Madrid, 1964.

*Meditación de la Técnica*. Revista de Occidente, Arquero, Madrid, 1968.

*Meditaciones del Quijote*. Revista de Occidente, Arquero, Madrid, 1963.

*Misión de la Universidad*. Revista de Occidente, Arquero, Madrid, 1965.

*Vieja y Nueva Política*. Revista de Occidente, Arquero, Madrid, 1963.

PÉREZ GALDÓS, B. *La Fontana de Oro* in *Obras Completas IV*. Aguilar, Madrid, 1964.

*Miau*. Espasa-Calpe, Austral, Buenos Aires, 1951.

SALINAS, P. *Ensayos de Literatura Hispánica*. Aguilar, Madrid, 1967.

SECO SERRANO, C. *Valle-Inclán y la España Oficial* in *Homenaje a Valle-Inclán*. Revista de Occidente, Madrid, Nov.–Dec. 1966.

SENDER, R. *Valle-Inclán y la Dificultad de la Tragedia*. Gredos, Madrid, 1965.

UNAMUNO, M. DE. *A Angel Ganivet* in *Obras Completas IV*. Afrodisio Aguado, Madrid, 1958.

*De Vuelta* in *Obras Completas X*. Afrodisio Aguado, Madrid, 1958.

*En Torno al Casticismo*. Espasa-Calpe, Austral, 4th ed., Madrid, 1957.

*La Prensa y el Lenguaje* in *Obras Completas VI*. Afrodisio Aguado, Madrid, 1958.

*Paisajes del Alma*. Revista de Occidente, Madrid, 1965.

*Por Tierras de Portugal y de España*. Anaya, Salamanca, 1964.

*San Manuel Bueno*. Espasa-Calpe, Austral, 5th ed., Madrid, 1963.

# Index

Variant and allied forms, synonyms and cross-references are given passim in the notes. Forms illustrated in Examples from Literature sections are marked in the alphabetical lists with the symbol†